CATALOGUING

CATALOGUING

BY

JOHN HORNER

B.A., F.L.A., A.L.A.A.

Senior Lecturer, College of Librarianship, Wales

LONDON
ASSOCIATION OF ASSISTANT LIBRARIANS
1970

First Published 1970
Reprinted 1980
SBN: 900092 04 1

© JOHN HORNER, 1970

Printed in Great Britain by Galliard (Printers) Ltd Great Yarmouth

TO

EFF

AND

THE KIDS

(who know)

ACKNOWLEDGEMENTS

ACKNOWLEDGEMENT is made to the following for the reproduction of copyright material:

Penguin Books Ltd., for the extract from Caesar's *Conquest of Gaul*; trans. by S. A. Handford; Sun Books of Melbourne, for the extract from *Trooper to the southern cross*; The Library Association, for extracts from the Lionel McColvin festschrift, the *Seminar on the Anglo-American cataloguing rules*, and extracts from other publications; National Lending Library for Science and Technology, for a sample of KWIC indexing; the H. W. Wilson Co., for samples of catalogue cards and extracts from *Sears list of subject headings*; The Library of Congress, for a sample entry from the *National union catalog*, sample catalogue cards, and an organisation chart; The University of Wales Press, for the song reproduced in illus. no. 7; The Council and Editor of the British National Bibliography, for samples of catalogue cards, an extract from the *British catalogue of music*, and for an example of MARC printout; The British Film Institute for an extract from the *British national film catalogue*; Aslib, for an extract from *Aslib film cataloguing rules*; The Trustees of the British Museum, for an extract from the *General catalogue of printed books*, and Readex Microprint Ltd., for an extract from the 'Compact Edition' of the *General catalogue*; Remington Rand Ltd., Rotadex Systems Ltd., W. J. Plumbe, Esq., and the *Library Association Record*, for illustrations of catalogues; The Long Playing Record Library Ltd., Record Specialities Ltd., The Controller of Her Majesty's Stationery Office, The Governors of the College of Librarianship Wales, and The Catalog Card Corporation of America, for sample catalogue cards; Guardian Newspapers Ltd., and The District Bank for illus. no. 20; Librarians of Institutes and Schools of Education, for the extract from the *Union list of periodicals in institute of education libraries*; the publishers of *RILM abstracts*, for a sample of computer produced abstracts; the Librarians of The University of Warwick and The University of Bradford (formerly Bradford Institute of Technology), for extracts from their library guides; The American Library Association, for extracts from *Library resources and technical services*; P. R. Lewis, Esq., as copyright owner of the flow-charts in illus. nos. 26 and 27, reproduced from *Catalogue and Index*.

I am indebted to my colleagues in the College of Librarianship Wales, who read and commented on parts of this book, particularly to David Batty.

Especial gratitude is due to Michael Ramsden, President of the AAL for 1969, for working through almost all of the work in rough manuscript, word by word; and for his continual encouragement, which kept me at it in the small hours, when most of it was written. I began the work at his suggestion, and if anybody deserves recognition for perseverance and advice, it is he.

Messrs Joel Downing, Richard Coward and Derek Austin read most of the BNB parts, and I much appreciate the time and trouble to which they went, when they were busy themselves.

Thanks are due to Mrs Lona Jones and to Mrs Sylvia Ramsden for helping out with typing at short notice.

Mr Alan White, Publications Officer of the AAL, must also be thanked, and publicised, for his patience and advice during the technical production. His name does not usually appear prominently enough (or at all) in AAL publications, bearing in mind what he puts into them.

My most heartfelt appreciation goes to my wife for her professional advice, editing and typing, from the inception of the book. And to our children for their temporary semi-orphanhood. This sort of acknowledgement appears so often in what is just another book, that perhaps Mr White will allow me to emphasise it with some of his rare *italics*.

Acknowledgement is due to the hundreds of students of cataloguing, in Australia and Britain, who have made me think about cataloguing. Their interest and enthusiasm have persuaded me that it is a topic worth thinking about.

JOHN HORNER

Erw Goch Farmhouse
Waun Fawr
Aberystwyth
Wales

LIST OF CONTENTS

LIST OF ILLUSTRATIONS

SECTION I

CHAPTER I

Introduction

We are in the middle of a revolution in cataloguing which started after the Second World War.

The newcomer to librarianship in the 1970's may take for granted many practices and events which were either only dreamed of, or not even imagined, twenty years ago.

Americans had long become used to the contribution made to national cataloguing by the Library of Congress, but the *British national bibliography*—a unique and highly influential service in Britain and in other countries did not start until 1950. Since then, we have become accustomed to the idea of national central cataloguing agencies which send out ready-made catalogue cards covering British and American books, and certain other library materials.

During this time, however, American librarians in particular had it brought home to them that their library needs went far beyond the Anglo-American world. Therefore, the major American research libraries embarked upon a voluntary scheme of cooperation to acquire other works needed for American research. Eventually, the U.S. Government started financing the acquisition of all such printed materials, wherever they were produced in the world. With this came a scheme for ensuring that catalogue entries for them were made available. A convenient way of acquiring catalogue entries was to tap any existing national central cataloguing systems in the countries concerned. Thus was born the idea of a vital part of the present revolution: international central cataloguing. Already we take it for granted that catalogue entries made out in London are now printed on cards in Washington. Nation may have been speaking unto nation in other ways, but the achievement of this simple ideal—but complicated practice—of shared cataloguing did not come until the 1960's.

Mechanisation is no innovation in itself, but, since 1950, the whole mechanically developed world has turned increasingly to computers to try to help solve its problems. Computers have helped men to land on the moon, so why should they not become part of libraries' cataloguing apparatus? During the 1960's, computer-printed catalogues became increasingly common. But towards the end of the decade, computers were being developed as catalogues and indexes in themselves, and even conceived as substitutes for the very stocks of libraries in some cases.

However, decisions have to be made about the actual words and classification numbers through which books and other materials are approached and described. These are intellectual decisions—which at present at least must be made by humans. How to enter a book under its author or title, or under its subject, may sound simple, but simple solutions to all problems have not been easy to come by. With the oft-cited information explosion of post-war years, these problems have multiplied many-fold, but with them a demand for increased speed as well as accuracy and detail. So there has emerged an increasingly scientific and consistent approach to subject cataloguing and indexing. Alongside this, there has come too another aspect of the revolution—in author and title cataloguing, part of the result of which has been the publication of a new international cataloguing code which is still being tested in libraries throughout the English-speaking world.

It is not surprising that these new intellectual processes are being integrated with machine methods. So the contents of some at least of the new computer tapes are being compiled according to the new code.

However, revolutions inevitably bring unsettlement and the need for re-adjustment, and some people do not re-adjust easily. One manifestation of the change which touches on all librarians is that new terms have been coined or adopted to deal with the new library science technology. In this book, a particular effort is made to avoid jargon, and to explain new ideas in conventional language: each 'new' word has been carefully considered and either rejected or explained. For this reason, the book is longer than it otherwise might have been. But it is hoped that what is said here will be comprehensible to any literate interested person. At present, there is a degree of alienation between some information retrieval specialists and the rest of the profession. Not only is this not necessary: it is wrong. Cataloguing in all its senses is basic to librarianship.

CHAPTER 2

The Need for Catalogues

Certain definitions must be learnt, and understood. The very terms 'catalogue' and 'index' have become confused. 'Indexing' is now used by some library science research workers to embrace all that has been meant in the past by the three terms classification, cataloguing, and indexing. In this work it is used in its more conventional limited sense. Nevertheless, many of the objects of catalogues, and methods used in them, are similar to those not only of indexes but also of bibliographies. So the word 'catalogue' may apply to bibliographies and indexes. Its basic definition, as used here, is given later in this chapter.

In general, cataloguing is concerned with identifying works, which are then used for the information contained in them. This is part of the practice of bibliography, and the two activities of: (*a*) Reference, information, and readers' advisory work; and (*b*) Cataloguing, classification, and indexing, not only meet but overlap, so that it is hard to distinguish between them. This is as it should be. There is a growing need for 'generalists' who ignore the different fields and view library science as a whole.

At this point, the term 'documents' must be introduced as being common to all branches of library practice. It is used, along with terms like 'works' and 'library materials', as embracing all types and forms of records in which information is stored. And by 'information' we mean not only short items of fact as obtained from, say, a directory, but also long 'through-reading' (or 'through-viewing' or 'through-listening') items as an ordinary novel, film, or gramophone record. So 'document' may embrace monographic books, periodicals and other serials, technical reports, trade catalogues, moving films, film strips, slides, sound recordings, and all the results of documentary reproduction whether full-size or microform. As it happens, special applications of principles may be used with some of these special materials. Nevertheless, the basic principles often apply to them as well as to the commonplace 'book'—usually a monographic work—and they must be taken as inferred throughout.

Next: it is not only cataloguers and indexers who need to know about the intricacies of catalogues and indexes. Anybody who uses them should really know almost as much about their objects as their compilers, e.g. what 'author' really means, which types of title entries are used if any, how the subject approach works. The user must know what types of entry the catalogue actually includes, and which it specifically excludes. This may be where other records of information take over, e.g. published indexes to periodicals. The public lending library assistant must know if the fiction catalogue includes information on sequels; if it does not, he must expect to use the published work *Sequels*—and in turn to know its limitations. All readers' advisory and reference staff must know how up to date the catalogue is, and where to look for records of documents received by the library but not yet entered in the catalogue. This in turn may take staff back to an 'In progress' or 'Works received' file, kept in the Catalogue Department, and so the assistant may need to know something of the administration of this department. Finally, if such staff find what they consider to be a lack in a catalogue, they must make this known. They can then be told if, or how, the deficiency will be met. Conversely, cataloguers themselves must be in intimate contact with the problems of the readers' service staff: the best way for a cataloguer to find out if a catalogue works is to use it himself for readers' enquiries, i.e. with real human beings who state (or mis-state) their needs.

There are two basic purposes of libraries: the conservation and the exploitation of library materials. Cataloguing, as a technical process, is concerned with both of these. It can help where the two conflict, by obviating the handling of unwanted materials, as well as ensuring that the wanted items are found and used. Materials are selected; they come into the library; they are classified and catalogued among other processes; they are stored; finally, when the information in them is needed, they are retrieved. So all library practice employs what is often called information storage and retrieval, despite the fact that the term has come to have a more limited application: that of organising knowledge in libraries in depth. The same principles apply throughout, but the more restricted meaning of 'isar' entails developing certain techniques to a greater, or deeper, degree of complexity than, say, telling a reader the order in which he should read the Hornblower novels. However, it must be emphasised that there is no firm dividing-line between the meanings of macrothought and microthought, as S. R. Ranganathan has called them. If one does insist on specifying a difference, one could say that macrothought is mainly concerned with whole, ordinary 'books', but microthought is mainly concerned with periodical articles. But there still are quite a few books whose subjects are more minute than many periodical articles. The Library of Congress, for instance, has a short one about African tribes who stand on one leg.

BASIC DEFINITIONS

Conventionally, a library's catalogue is the record of the stock of whole bibliographic items of the library. It should be, within defined limits, (*a*) a complete record and (*b*) a record arranged in a useful order, or, more usually, in several useful orders, or with several approaches, i.e. each document being represented under several different headings. Some library catalogues also record certain parts of some of the items in their stocks. An example in a public library might be individual records for the plays in collections or anthologies. An example in a special library might be the individual papers of the published proceedings of conferences and seminars.

No library should try to maintain a complete service from its own stock alone, so it needs to know whether required documents are in the stock of other libraries. Therefore, union catalogues are needed to record, preferably in one sequence, the stocks of several libraries.

Before one library applies to another for a document, or before it orders one for its own stock, it usually—despite one interesting American experiment with computers—needs to check that the details of the required document are full and accurate. So it needs bibliographies: published lists of works. Bibliographies vary in their arrangement, but it is particularly useful if they are in the same order as the library's catalogue. Just as the librarian needs to know the limitations of his own catalogue, so also must he know the limitations of any bibliography: whether it lists works in print at a particular time; works published during a particular period; works published in a particular country; its subject limitations; and the forms of materials covered, e.g. whether it includes maps or not. A bibliography, then, has its own limitations, but usually it is not confined to the stock of one library or group of libraries: this is the essential difference between a bibliography and a catalogue. But unfortunately the terms are not always used consistently, e.g. the *British catalogue of music* is misnamed, since it is in fact a list of works published in Britain during a particular period, i.e. it is a bibliography, although documents listed in it happen to have gone into the British Museum. Also, Her Majesty's Stationery Office's 'catalogues' are in fact bibliographies.

Before a library tries to borrow a document, it must make sure that the document is not in its own stock, perhaps in the form of an article in a periodical. So it will buy published indexes, or compile its own: usually works which analyse the contents of larger bibliographical units. The library may subscribe to the *British technology index*, which records by subject the contents of articles of many British periodicals, and certain other materials, giving details of title, author and length of the article, the title of the containing periodical and the appropriate issue.

At this stage, it may be necessary to check in the library's catalogue of periodicals, to see if the required periodical is in stock. If it is not, a union catalogue of periodicals will probably be consulted to find which library does stock it.

The word 'index' may apply also to very abbreviated entries in a library's catalogue recording whole bibliographic units, just as the published *Fiction index* gives brief entries of authors and titles of fiction under alphabetical-subject headings, e.g. a library may have a title index simply naming the author and classification or shelf location of works. Sequences of analytical entries, i.e. entries for parts of whole bibliographical units, will also be known as an index, especially if they are filed in a separate sequence from the main catalogue. 'Index' is also applied to the part of a classified catalogue which names subjects, in alphabetical order, and gives the class numbers at which these subjects may be sought in the classified sequence of the catalogue or on the shelves: in this case it is a subject index.

It should be appreciated by now that libraries' catalogues, union catalogues, and published bibliographies and indexes, are all dovetailed in use to ensure easy identification and location of given documents, however incomplete the information given may be.

THE BASIC CATALOGUE

A library's catalogue records the library's stock. Each record consists basically of three essential parts:

 (*a*) the Heading under which it is filed, or arranged, in the catalogue;

(b) the Description which identifies the document and shows the user whether the document will satisfy his needs; and

(c) the Location of the document on the shelves or in the files of the library—usually a class mark or shelf mark or number—in older times sometimes known as a press mark, sets of shelves being called presses.

In some instances, (c) may be virtually the same as (a): i.e. in a classified file of entries.

Each document is usually recorded at several different points in the catalogue to cater for a variety of approaches, usually (a) Author, and collaborators such as editors, translators and illustrators; (b) Title; and (c) Subject. The entry at one of these approaches is known as the main entry because: (a) if there is any variation in quantity of detail in various entries, this will be the fullest; and (b) this entry includes also tracings, i.e. a note of headings at which other entries for the document are made, their basic purpose being to ensure control of all entries for a work, e.g. to maintain accuracy of records when a document is withdrawn, relocated, etc.

However, where unit entries (usually unit cards) are used, all entries in the catalogue give the same amount of information about a document. In this case, the main entry becomes less significant. But it is still important, because:

(a) The choice of the main entry decides in turn the term by which a document is sub-arranged at a class number.

(b) If the number of entries in a catalogue must be limited—a fairly common situation in practice—the main entry must be the one most likely to be looked for. This applies particularly to the entry filed under the author heading.

(c) The main entry heading is that used for selective reading lists and bibliographies, e.g. new additions lists and lists compiled for individual requests.

In short, the main entry, author and/or shelf classification decisions can be of considerable importance in the use made of a library.

DETAIL IN CATALOGUE ENTRIES

This detail will be examined through the medium of the unit entry (previously defined). A copy of this unit entry will be filed into the catalogue at every point at which it is estimated that it will be useful. The heading is typed or is ready-printed at the top of the copy of the card used for the approach being catered for—author, title, and so on. Here we are concerned with the author heading and the description.

Most of the information used in compiling the catalogue entry for the average book is taken from the title page, including its verso, or back. Other information required is taken from elsewhere in the book, and occasionally from sources of information other than the book, e.g. when the author's name is needed for the cataloguing of a work published anonymously, or when the date of publication is not given. This raw material from which an entry is compiled is exemplified in the facsimiles on pages 11, 12 and 13.

The data, from the book or external source, is selected, re-arranged and presented in a form and order according to conventions as embodied in the catalogue code used, and according to the instructions laid down by the individual library—a form of 'house-style' or code of practice. If cards are usually bought from a central cataloguing agency, there may be differences between its cards and those produced by the library for documents not covered by the agency's service.

A short summary of the principles of descriptive cataloguing is given in *Anglo-American cataloguing rules, British text*, 1967, p. 159. It will be assumed that the reader has access to this code—AACR—throughout the use of this book.

The layout and content of an average unit entry may be as follows, the punctuation being given according to AACR, Appendix V, p. 295-6:

HEADING　　　　　　　　　　　　　　　　　　　　[usually author]
　　[Uniform title, if necessary]
　　Transcription of title as on title page; sub-title, by Author if different from form used in heading. Edition statement. Place of publication: Name of publisher, Date of publication.
　　Number of pages, Number of plates; Description of illustrations. Size. (series statement)
　　　　　　　　　　　　　　　　　　　　　　　CLASS NUMBER

　　Notes, supplementing the information given elsewhere in the entry, and, if necessary, including full or selective contents list.

　　Tracings of added entries.　　　　　　　　[in some cases]

CAESAR
THE CONQUEST
OF GAUL

A NEW TRANSLATION BY

S. A. HANDFORD

PENGUIN BOOKS

1. Most of the information required for cataloguing most books is taken from the first few pages, especially the title page. The resulting unit entry is shown on page 14.

1 (*a*). Title page.

Penguin Books Ltd, Harmondsworth, Middlesex
U.S.A.: Penguin Books Inc., 3300 Clipper Mill Road, Baltimore 11, Md
AUSTRALIA: Penguin Books Pty Ltd, 762 Whitehorse Road,
Mitcham, Victoria

—

This translation first published 1951
Reprinted 1953, 1956, 1958

Made and printed in Great Britain
by Richard Clay & Company, Ltd,
Bungay, Suffolk

1 (*b*). Back (verso) of title page.

THE PENGUIN CLASSICS

EDITED BY E. V. RIEU

L21

1 (*c*). Half-title page.

CONTENTS

1 (*d*). Contents list.

An actual unit entry might be as follows:

> CAESAR, Caius Julius
> [De bello Gallico]
> The conquest of Gaul; a new translation by S. A. Handford.
> Harmondsworth, Middlesex: Penguin, 1951 (1958 reprint).
> 283 p.; map. 18 cm. (Penguin classics, ed. by E. V. Rieu)
>
> 936
> Includes introduction on Rome, Gaul, the Roman Army, and
> Caesar; with notes and glossary.
> HANDFORD, S. A.   GAUL: History   CONQUEST of Gaul

(The method of recording tracings varies a great deal in practice, and according to whether a classified or dictionary catalogue is used. Also, many libraries put the class number at the extreme top left or top right of the entry.)

A copy of this unit entry is filed under each of the headings given in the tracings, the added entry heading being typed, or ready-printed-in, above the heading given in the unit entry. In a classified catalogue, the main entry is automatically filed under the class number, with an author entry under the unit entry heading. Also, in a classified catalogue, the subject tracing will refer to the subject index entry, not a unit entry, details of which are explained later.

The detail given is 'full' or 'standard' cataloguing practice. It is likely that many libraries will give less information than is shown. Also, each library or central cataloguing agency works out its own layout: indentation, position of class number and of tracings, and so on.

The information about the parts of an entry which follows is mainly explanatory; criticism is incorporated in the later chapter on Limited cataloguing.

Heading. This may be:

(a) a personal author; or
(b) a corporate author; or
(c) a title:

all as prescribed by a code, e.g. AACR, and the library's interpretation or adaptation of it. Examples of personal and corporate author headings are given in subsequent chapters on codes. A periodical entered under title would have some such heading as:

> SCIENTIFIC Australian   Vol. 1-   1964-

this being an 'open' entry with spaces left for 'closing' it if or when the periodical ceases publication or if the library stops taking it.

Uniform title. This is not always needed, and some libraries do not use it anyway. Its purpose is to ensure that various editions, translations, etc., of a work are filed together, whatever the title page wording may be. Details of sample uniform titles and their value may be found in AACR chapter 4. They show that the use of uniform titles can considerably and usefully broaden the 'bibliographic unit' (a term explained and exemplified in more detail in later chapters). A disadvantage is that possibly a catalogue could become overloaded with author-title references from title page form of title to the author-uniform title form used in the catalogue, and that readers will become irritated by them. One of the objects of a catalogue given by C. A. Cutter is 'to assist in the choice of a book as to its edition (bibliographically)'. The uniform title will help to fulfil this object conveniently and systematically. Another Cutter object for which the uniform title may be useful is to 'show what the library has by a given author', since the uniform title may more readily enable the user to gauge the full range of an author's works in a systematic way. This applies particularly in the entries filed directly under author of course, and in what order they are arranged under author.

Title transcript. Basically this is in the form as given on the title page, so it helps in identifying a specific form, translation, etc., of the work. It is followed by any sub-title or alternative title as given on the title page. These may help identify a specific form of the work, and— probably more important—they may help explain the subject, approach, and intellectual level of the work. This helps achieve Cutter's object 'to assist in the choice of a book as to its character . . .'. Codes, including AACR, usually allow the insertion of short explanatory statements in brackets where necessary to obviate notes which might appear out of place later in the entry, e.g. Four quartets [poems].

Author statement, including statement of any collaborators (translators, editors, illustrators, etc.) if required in the entry. AACR allows omission of the function, or designation, of the name used for heading; so if this practice is followed, and if the heading 'author' is in fact an editor of, say, a collection, this fact is brought out by repeating, e.g. 'selected and arranged by . . .'. The pros and cons of using designations should be considered.

Edition statement. This of course is vital in selecting the exact edition required. If one expects it to show a user how much revision has taken place, a disadvantage is that the wording given by the publisher is used, and this information may possibly be misleading: some publishers dub a mere reprint 'nth edition'. In such a case a correction has to be given in the form of a note later in the entry—as long as the cataloguer is sure of his facts.

Imprint: comprising Place(s) of publication; Name of publisher(s); Date of publication. AACR allows considerable manipulation of title page data, e.g. transposing author's name from 'head of title' to following title, yet it has perpetuated the traditional order and contents of the imprint. However, it does allow a far shorter expression of place and publisher than previous twentieth-century codes. But one must be wary of over-abbreviation: one library journal in 1969 carried adjacent reviews of two Bingley publications, but one was published by Clive Bingley and the other by Anne Bingley. AACR allows both date of edition and date of reprint in hand to be given here, e.g. 1960 (1962 reprint), rather than making the cataloguer put the less useful reprint date here, and a correcting date in the notes where it is probably less likely to be reached by the user as quickly. This practice was initiated by some libraries long before it was codified. All of the imprint may help to identify the required work, e.g. if two works have identical or similar titles, while the date may reinforce the edition statement. Place of publication in the past has often given some idea of national slant in a work, but that is less likely today with repeat and simultaneous publication of an identical work in different countries, e.g. some Bingley librarianship books, aimed primarily at a British public, have been published in Australia by Cheshires with no indication, as reproduced in standard catalogue entries, that they originated in Britain.

Collation: comprising number, and sequences, of pages, and (AACR) number of plates; Details of types of illustrations; Spine height in centimetres. In multi-volume works, number of volumes is given instead of, or in addition to, number of pages. The intention of this information is to describe concisely the physical nature of the work. This in turn may lead one to a knowledge of how much information there is in it and how the information is enhanced graphically. The student should go through AACR Rule 143 and come to his own conclusions as to the value of the information, bearing in mind various types of library.

Series statement (series 'note' in codes before AACR). Certain series come to be well known, and the physical and intellectual characteristics of such series can be applied to an individual work in evaluating it for a particular purpose. A handy application of the series statement in AACR is its use for Command paper numbers and similar official publications, e.g. (Cmnd. 644). As with other details, the series statement can help differentiate between similarly or identically titled works. Also, the series statement is essential for a clerical assistant to make a heading for a series added entry, if required, because the series tracing may consist only of (series) or even just Sr.

Class number. This has been included at this point because the idea is that one reads the essential information about the document and then arrives at the statement of its shelf location. However, to make the number more obvious, and assuming that many catalogue users do not need to go through all of the entry to the point shown, an alternative place is at the top left corner of the entry, whether or not it is the filing medium for that particular copy of the entry. The class number should include clear prefixes as necessary to indicate sequence, e.g. Q for quarto sequence, P for pamphlet sequence, and even PQ for pamphlet quarto sequence. There is one library which uses E for elephant folio sequence—the unacquainted reader may well be startled to be told 'it's with the elephants, down at the end'. In a classified catalogue this (shelving) number will be a different number from that under which an added class entry is filed, and the difference must be made clear to users. Some sample layouts are given later in this chapter.

Notes, etc. This part of the entry, strangely, is not included in the traditional 'body of the entry' in AACR (R. 130). Notes are used for two Cutter objects: 'To assist in the choice of a book: as to its edition (bibliographically) [sometimes]; and as to its character'. It is the cataloguer's chance to show his individuality, in choice of terms and style, especially conciseness, and particularly in what in the past has been annotations, as included under AACR's 'Nature, scope, language or literary form of the work' (R. 145C8). The basic purpose of the notes is to give information not available elsewhere in the entry. Even tracings could be covered by this statement, as long as they are accessible and comprehensible enough: some subject heading tracings in a dictionary catalogue and some subject index tracings in a classified catalogue can obviate subject annotations. Since notes amplify other parts of the entry, AACR recommends that where relevant they should be given in the order of the parts of the entry. A note on the imprint might be 'Also published from Colombo by Ceylon Government Press'. Notes can make or mar the value of the catalogue—rendering it comprehensible to readers who otherwise are put off by the cryptic cataloguer's cyphers in the collation, whose value is open to doubt even when it is fully understood. It might well be better to sport a few more letters and put in a more understandable form in the notes of, say, 'geneal. table (on lining paper)' than keep it buried in its shortened form in the collation. A particularly valuable part of the notes is that which allows explanation of the relation between the work being catalogued and another work. So, Aldous Huxley's non-fiction work *Brave new world revisited* could have a note on its connection with his fiction work *Brave new world*: this note would be particularly useful in the classified file of the classified catalogue, where the work would not be entered immediately after *Brave new world*. A further useful type of note is that which explains how the library's own copy is different from the perfect copy envisaged in, say, AACR. It may explain that it is an imperfect copy, or even a grangerised copy—i.e. uniquely enhanced by additional, often illustrative, material, as in the case of one copy of Hasted's *History of Kent* in Kent County Library Headquarters.

Notes can include partial or complete Contents of works. These can range from a brief note indicating the presence of a bibliography to a complete copy of the contents list—particularly necessary in omnibus volumes, the individual parts of which may also be available as separate bibliographic units, and symposia or collections of conference papers where there is often a range of topics and authors.

ADDED ENTRIES

Using copies of the unit entry as a basis, added entries can quite easily be made by merely adding at the top of the entry the heading for the added entry, and filing each in the appropriate place. Libraries vary in the number which they have time and space or estimated need to manage, and it must be admitted that some codes go to inordinate lengths to cater for some imagined need. A catalogue in a computer store has less inconvenience and expense in this extension of its service once it has been established, although the 'tags' needed to gain access to the variety of approaches, e.g. language in which written or year in which published, all take up valuable storage space and cause extra inconvenience in both programming and putting information into the computer store. In manual catalogues, some or all of the following may be considered:

1. Collaborators, etc.: 'author-type' entries, joint authors not chosen for main entries, and editors, translators and illustrators, especially if on title page and worthy of transcription in entry. Also, possible headings in a pseudonymous work other than that chosen for main entry.

2. Other outstanding names, especially on title pages, e.g. person honoured in a festchrift.

3. Series title, if this is likely to be useful, e.g. as in AACR R.33N.

4. Titles, especially distinctive ones and most especially ones beginning with a distinctive word. Title added entry should particularly be used when narrowly rejected as main entry heading, even when not very distinctive. Titles which are identical with the form used in the subject approach to the same work, whether alphabetical-subject or subject index, can usually be safely omitted.

5. Analyticals, especially for works which:

(*a*) may in addition be stocked, or exist, or were originally published, as whole bibliographical units in their own right; and

(*b*) are also contained in other collections, e.g. the individual works in an omnibus volume. A pro indication is when they have been mentioned in the unit entry.

Subject entries in the dictionary catalogue. Strictly these are added entries, the main entry traditionally, as it happens, being regarded as that under the author or author-equivalent. In the 'conventional' dictionary catalogue it is quite common to find two or more subject entries: whether one of these is more 'main' than the others is immaterial, since the document will be filed by one class or shelf number. Subject entries can also be in the form of analyticals, when part of a work is entered separately because it is sufficiently distinct from, and would be, if independent, far enough shelved from, the parent or containing work.

Added entries may be made selectively: just because one part of a contents list needs its own entry according to the needs of a library, this

does not mean that all other parts need it. The same applies to names
(collaborators, etc.) mentioned elsewhere in the entry. An added entry
should be invoked only when its heading has been included in the unit
entry. Added subject entries in the classified catalogue may also be
needed; how they may be dealt with is described below.

These approaches meet Cutter's other objects, which may be summed
up as:

(*a*) specific document requests under author, or title, or subject; and

(*b*) range of books by an author, or on a subject, or in a literature.

The exact wording is given in his *Rules for a dictionary catalog*, 4th
ed., 1904, p. 12, and in QUIGG, 2nd ed., 1968, p. 9, full details of which
are given at the start of Section II, following this chapter.

CONSTRUCTION OF ADDED ENTRIES

The main decisions are:

(*a*) Layout: type of indentation.

(*b*) At what point to cut off a long title.

(*c*) A possible shortage of space if an author-title, especially an
analytical, added entry is used with a unit entry. This could be
cured by bringing author and title on to one line, e.g.

VAN DRUTEN, John: I am a camera *in*

FAMOUS PLAYS OF 1954   [heading of unit entry]

[etc. etc.]

One final problem in construction and layout is that of added class
entries in a classified file. Using our unit entry in its original form, one
would simply have:

994   [as added entry heading]

then Unit entry, culminating in

942 [as shown previously]

If it were felt that this method were too indefinite, one might have:

994→942

or   994

(942)

or better still:

994 *shelved at* 942.

At least one library has used

994+942

but this could possibly be confused with the *Universal decimal classification*, while it also seems to make the number following the + less important than that preceding it.

Some further comments on layouts of cards in general are given in Chapter 25, on Physical forms of catalogues.

REFERENCES

However carefully a cataloguer selects the heading under which he enters a work, there may always be someone who looks under another heading. To ensure that such a user is redirected to the chosen entry point in a catalogue, references, usually *see* references, are used.

Perhaps the most common type of reference is that from an unused form of a personal author's name to that which is used, i.e. under which his works are entered: a heading away from which one is redirected by a *see* reference is never used as a heading.

e.g.   1. (different name) THIBAULT, Jacques Anatole
    see
    FRANCE, Anatole

or Thibault, etc.: i.e. in lowercase; if 'non-distinctive' typography is employed for an 'unused' heading, readers will get accustomed to not finding entries under it: it gives an impression of lack of importance.

e.g.   2. (entry under different element)
    MARE, Walter de la
    see
    DE LA MARE, Walter

Although codes prescribe it, one doubts if it is worth having references when the two forms file very near each other, and especially when the unused form is likely to be unpopular; e.g. 3: the following reference seems unnecessary:

HOMERUS
see
HOMER

Similar references can also be used from one form or construction of a corporate author's name to another.

e.g.   GREAT BRITAIN. *National Coal Board*
    see
    NATIONAL COAL BOARD

Sometimes general (or 'blanket'), or in this case explanatory, references can be made for the sake of economy.

> e.g.   MINISTRY . . .
>
> For executive departments of governments *see* name of country with the name of the department as subdivision, e.g. GREAT BRITAIN. *Department of Education and Science*
>
> There would be a similar reference under DEPARTMENT . . .

See references can be used from unused to used forms of titles.

> e.g.   HOLY BIBLE
>> *see*
>> BIBLE

A slightly more complex form is the explanatory *see also* type of reference between (both ways) two forms of an author's name, if the library decides to use both forms of name.

> e.g.   STEWART, J. I. M.
>> For works of this author written under his pseudonym
>> *see*
>> INNES, Michael

> also   INNES, Michael
>> For works by this author written under his real name
>> *see*
>> STEWART, J. I. M.

A briefer, but less satisfactory form would be:

> STEWART, J. I. M.
> *see also*
> INNES, Michael

> and vice versa.

References should only very rarely, if ever, be used in a unit entry catalogue for documents as differentiated from headings, e.g. one should not find OPERATION PAX *see* INNES, Michael. Note that BNB is not a unit entry bibliography and so it would use, e.g. HAMLET *see* SHAKESPEARE, William. One exception in general use is for uniform titles, as in the Bible example. Similar references could be in the form of author-title references. Another might be to obviate multiple repetition of entries when a great number of editions and other forms of a standard writer's works are stocked. This could be in the BNB form used above, although this would not be self-explanatory. A more explanatory form is AACR's

> HAMLET
> SHAKESPEARE, William
> Editions of this work will be found under the author's name.

One other possibly acceptable form might be between certain independent but related documents

> e.g. HANNAH, Walter
> Darkness visible. [etc. etc.: usual unit entry]
> For a reply to this work *see* VINDEX. Light invisible.

with a similar reference the other way also.

Other versions and applications of references will be found in AACR, chapter 5.

A variety of purposes is served by subject references in subject catalogues. These are explained at length in Section III, on the Subject approach.

FINDING LIST VERSUS BIBLIOGRAPHIC CATALOGUE

Occasionally one still comes across the discussion about:

(*a*) whether a library's catalogue is a finding list; or
(*b*) whether it is what is known as a bibliographic catalogue.

There are two aspects to this:

(*a*) length of entries, and
(*b*) breadth of bibliographic unit.

The argument runs that if a catalogue is intended as a finding list, it will have short, direct entries which are

(*a*) easy to find,
(*b*) used to identify the required work quickly, and then
(*c*) used to locate it on the shelves.

The finding list type of catalogue assumes that the chief use made of it is as a finding and locating list for a specific document which an enquirer has in mind, and whose title page or title page transcript he has probably remembered: the document's connection with any other work, perhaps even another edition of the same work, is irrelevant.

On the other hand, the bibliographic catalogue would have to ensure that the catalogue brought together entries for all materials related bibliographically, e.g.:

(a) all editions, versions, translations and excerpts of one book of the Bible, but also in the required proximity to the next more related book; or

(b) the complete run of a periodical from its inception to the present, and irrespective of changes of title.

This form of catalogue would also give a detailed description of each document, so that the enquirer could visualise fully what it was like as a physical article, as well as what its contents were, and what its relation was with other works by author, textual treatment, physical characteristics, and so on.

Feeling at the moment runs generally in favour of the finding list type of catalogue, although in fact many catalogues try to satisfy both needs to some extent at least. In some instances of detail and collocation, there is no firm dividing line between the two. AACR itself manifests a compromise between the two objectives.

SECTION II

CATALOGUE CODES

Catalogue Codes

This section is concerned mainly with author and title entry, and only to a lesser extent with description, a critical approach to which is given in Chapter 22, on Limited cataloguing. To obviate repetitious footnotes, works cited are listed here with the abbreviations used when they are cited in the text. Codes and directly relevant readings are given first in chronological order, followed by a second sequence of readings in alphabetical order. Further readings may be found in QUIGG, chapters 2, 3 and 4.

Codes and readings cited

BRITISH MUSEUM. Rules for compiling the catalogue of printed books, maps and music in the British Museum. rev. ed. London: B.M., 1936.

BM

The PRUSSIAN instructions: rules for the alphabetical catalogues of the Prussian libraries; translated from the 2nd ed. by Andrew Osborn. Ann Arbor, 1938.   PI

CUTTER, CHARLES A. Rules for a dictionary catalog. 4th ed. rewritten. Washington: Government Printing Office, 1904 (various reprints by Library Association, London).   CUTTER

(1st ed. 1876; 2nd ed. 1889; 3rd ed. 1891.)

LIBRARY ASSOCIATION. Cataloguing rules: author and title entries; compiled by committees of the Library Association and of the American Library Association. English ed. London: L.A., 1908 (various reprints). [Anglo-American code.]   AA 1908

AMERICAN LIBRARY ASSOCIATION. *Catalog Code Revision Committee.* A.L.A. catalog rules, preliminary American 2nd ed. Chicago: A.L.A., 1941.   ALA 1941

AMERICAN LIBRARY ASSOCIATION. *Division of Cataloging and Classification.* A.L.A. cataloging rules for author and title entries. 2nd ed. Chicago: A.L.A., 1949. [A.L.A. code.]   ALA 1949

LIBRARY OF CONGRESS. *Descriptive Cataloging Division.* Rules for de-

scriptive cataloging in the Library of Congress (adopted by the American
Library Association). Washington: L.C., 1949.   LCRDC
VATICAN. *Library*. Rules for the catalog of printed books; translated
from the 2nd Italian ed. . . . Chicago: A.L.A., 1948.   VATICAN
OSBORN, ANDREW D. The crisis in cataloging. *in* Library quarterly,
vol. 11, no. 4, Oct. 1941, p. 393-411; *and in* Library assistant, vol. 35,
no. 4, Apr. 1942, p. 54-62 and vol. 35, no. 5, May 1942, p. 69-75.
                                                                 OSBORN
LUBETZKY, SEYMOUR. Cataloging rules and principles: a critique of the
A.L.A. Rules for entry, and a proposed design for their revision.
Washington: L.C., 1953.   LUBETZKY
LUBETZKY, SEYMOUR. Code of cataloging rules: author and title entry;
an unfinished draft. . .; with an explanatory commentary by Paul
Dunkin. [Chicago]: A.L.A., 1960.   CCR 1960
DUNKIN, PAUL. Cutter redivivus: American catalog code revision. *in*
Libri, vol. 11, 1961, p. 181-189.
INTERNATIONAL CONFERENCE ON CATALOGUING PRINCIPLES, *Paris,
9th-18th October 1961.* [Report.] 1963.

Statement of principles . . . annotated edition with commentary and
examples; by A. H. Chaplin assisted by Dorothy Anderson. . . . Pro-
visional ed. Sevenoaks, Kent, England: International Federation of
Library Associations, 1966.   ICCP
ANGLO-AMERICAN CATALOGUING RULES, British text. London: L.A.,
1967.   AACR
North American text. Chicago: A.L.A., 1967.

Other readings
BRITISH NATIONAL BIBLIOGRAPHY. Issue dated 27th Dec. 1967, p.
2-3: B.N.B. and the Revised Anglo-American cataloguing rules, 1967.
[A statement of BNB's interpretation of AACR.] Summarised *in* Catalogue
and index, no. 9, Jan. 1968, p. 4-5.
GORMAN, MICHAEL. A study of the rules for entry and heading in the
Anglo-American cataloguing rules, 1967 (British text). London: L.A.,
1968. SBN 85365 011 X.
JOLLEY, L. The principles of cataloguing. London: Crosby Lockwood,
1960 (1961 reprint). [Predates AACR; still valuable as a critical work.]
LIBRARY resources and technical services, v. 10, no. 4, Fall, 1966:

p. 421-436: Field, F. B. The new Catalog code: the general principles and the major changes. [Assumes North American text.]

p. 437-444: Rosenthal, J. A. The administrative implications of the new Rules.

p. 444-449: Sanner, M. A program for a public library's adapting to the new Code.

NEEDHAM, C. D. Organizing knowledge in libraries . . . London: Deutsch, 1964. [Predates AACR, includes summaries of rules up to LUBETZKY.]

NEW rules for an old game; ed. by Thelma E. Allen and Daryl Ann Dickman: proceedings of a workshop on the 1967 Anglo-American cataloguing code. [North American text.] London: Bingley, 1968. SBN 85157 049 6. First published 1967 by University of British Columbia.

NORRIS, DOROTHY MAY. A history of cataloguing and cataloguing methods . . . London: Grafton, 1939. [Especially Chapter X: The British Museum catalogues.]

OLDING, R. K. Readings in library cataloguing; ed. and intr. by R. K. Olding. London: Crosby Lockwood, 1966. First published by Cheshire, Melbourne, 1966.   OLDING

QUIGG, PATRICK. Theory of cataloguing: an examination guidebook. 2nd ed. rev. London: Bingley, 1968. SBN 85157 061 5. [2nd ed. includes AACR; includes summaries of code rules.]   QUIGG

SEMINAR ON THE ANGLO-AMERICAN CATALOGUING RULES (1967), *University of Nottingham, 1968.*

Seminar on the Anglo-American Cataloguing Rules (1967): proceedings . . .; edited by J. C. Downing and N. F. Sharp. London: L.A., 1969. SBN 85365 271 6. [Includes comprehensive bibliography, by A. G. Curwen.]

STROUT, RUTH FRENCH. Toward a better cataloging code . . . ed. by Ruth French Strout. Originally published *in* Library quarterly, 26, Oct. 1956, p. 251-366. Published separately by University of Chicago. Graduate Library School. [p. 137-159: chart correlating AACR rule numbers with relevant rules in ALA 1949. p. 161-165: selective bibliography chronologically arranged from 1953 to 1966.]

VERONA, EVA. Literary unit versus bibliographical unit. *in* Libri, vol. 9, no. 2, 1959, p. 79-104.

CHAPTER 3

The Need for Catalogue Codes

Basically, codes are compiled in an attempt to ensure that in turn a catalogue will be compiled to be as efficient as possible in whatever approaches and details its users require. Though this appears to beg the question, it is not a bad idea occasionally to get right back to root principles, as Osborn, Lubetzky and others have had need to remind us.

The word consistency almost always crops up when the 'why' of code compilation is discussed.

The most obvious need for consistency is that a cataloguer should not unwittingly enter one document written by an author under one form of heading, and then later enter another document by the same author under another heading. We say 'unwittingly' because the author 'unit' may occasionally be split deliberately. For example, it may be decided to enter the Alice books under CARROLL, Lewis, but to enter *Notes by an Oxford Chiel* and *Euclid and his modern rivals* under DODGSON, Charles Lutwidge, even though all of these works came from the same brain. Usually, then, a 'bibliographic unit' of a single author is established and adhered to. It has been said that without a code 'there might be inconsistencies in the same author—the Institution of Electrical Engineers, for example, being entered under Institution of Electrical Engineers on one occasion, and under an inverted form on another' (NEEDHAM, p. 23). A code is not needed to solve such a simple problem. Surely, any cataloguing system worth its salt will ensure the checking of authors' names in its existing catalogue, or author authority file, to obviate such superficial examples of inconsistency. However, a slightly more subtle form of inconsistency would arise if, say, the Institution of Electrical Engineers were entered directly, i.e. as normally spoken, while the Institute of Chartered Accountants were entered under an inverted form, e.g. ACCOUNTANTS, INSTITUTE OF CHARTERED, or some other permutation. A code could help by stating perhaps that names of corporate authors (e.g. organisations) should be entered directly. It should also give examples to demonstrate its rules—preferably carefully chosen ones to cover as many variants as are likely to be encountered in practice. However, the code may find it necessary to make exceptions in the interest of common sense: one regrets the inferred sacredness of syntactical or grammatical consistency in some writings, and it is suggested here that consistency of purpose is more important than merely consistency of syntax. Examples of the difference occur frequently throughout this work, but here is one typical example: AACR would enter the Library of the University of London as UNIVERSITY OF LONDON. *Library*, but that of Oxford University as BODLEIAN LIBRARY, even though the parent body is entered as UNIVERSITY OF OXFORD. The consistency lies in the fact that all these institutions are entered as directly and briefly as possible provided they can be clearly identified. Therefore, one has consistency of purpose but lack of uniformity in the construction of headings for the same categories of bodies, i.e. university libraries.

Nevertheless, it would be hoped that any libraries following the same code would finish up with an author's being entered in a uniform way in all their catalogues: such an achievement would make for economy in time and patience on the part of both library staffs and readers who use more than one library.

Other—probably more important—advantages arise from uniformity:

1. A system of central cataloguing (defined in Chapter 27) is more likely to become viable and worth its while.

2. Much time is saved in the compilation of union catalogues.

3. Much use of catalogues takes place in conjunction with bibliographies—either general, or special with restricted coverage. Uniformity of headings and description between them and library catalogues can obviously lead to improved efficiency.

4. Librarians and users of libraries also check catalogues for records of works listed in reviewing sources, dealers' check-lists, students' recommended reading lists, and so on. Again, uniformity of treatment for all of these—though rarely achieved in fact—could save time and prevent mistakes.

5. If codes did not exist, cataloguers would have to work from scratch with every work they catalogued, from choice of author heading to the use of punctuation. Probably this would produce more inconsistent catalogues overall than would even the poorest code, and with greater loss of time as well. Precedents would have to be remembered, sought, checked and thought about in an effort to arrive at a coherently efficient record of a library's stock. As it is, even with some codes, e.g. AA 1908,

many types of work are not catered for, and a similar procedure has to be gone through. Further, since most past codes have contained inconsistencies themselves, differing solutions might be reached depending on which cases were used as precedents. In short, the best codes quickly present the cataloguer with ready-made efficient decisions. How this is effected will be discussed later.

Codes may possibly include rules for all or some of the following:

1. Author and/or title main entry headings: both choice and form of headings.

2. Author and/or title added entry headings: both choice and form of headings.

3. Author and/or title references: both choice and form.

4. What items to include in the description, their order, and the method by which given.

5. Presentation: punctuation, capitalisation, italicisation, and, possibly, recommended layouts for all types of entries and references.

6. Transliteration into the 'home' alphabet (i.e. roman in most countries) from other alphabets.

7. Choice and construction of subject headings and references, or subject index entries.

8. Filing rules.

9. Limited cataloguing for various needs.

10. Lists of definitions.

11. Lists of abbreviations, showing where and how they are used.

It is emphasised that no single code includes all these contents, and some librarians may doubt whether any single code should do so.

Most of the codes dealt with in this work concentrate mainly on items 1, 2, 3, 4, and 5. Most of the criticism of codes revolves around the choice and form of author and title headings, since they decide if a searcher shall even begin to find what he is looking for. Further, there is a growing doubt about the value of detail in the description, and of a consequent exasperation with codes which are finicky about such detail. It is becoming increasingly accepted that entries from different sources, with consequent differences in quantity and type of detail, can be interfiled if economy results, attention being paid mainly or only to the headings under which the entries are filed.

The subject rules in codes, in the few occasions where they exist, will be discussed in Section III, on Subject work.

COMPILATION OF CODES

Most past codes have been, as the word 'code' implies, a consolidation and reconciliation of existing practices. But academically one is entitled to criticise a code retrospectively, using principles which the original codifiers did not necessarily think of but which in fact have been evolved from an analysis of past codifications.

Modern classification theory sees what—to a certain extent retrospectively—may be called two schools of thought and practice: (a) the Enumerative, in which all likely needs are listed ready for the copying; and (b) the Synthetic, in which elements of subjects (isolates) are listed, with instructions on the order in which to combine them to produce the class marks required for any subject dealt with in the document.

Similarly, modern cataloguing theory sees—again to an extent retrospectively—two schools of thought: (a) the 'Case' code, which enumerates all types of documents likely to be encountered, with rules for how to enter and describe them; and (b) the 'Conditions' code, which, first, identifies underlying author and title characteristics in documents, irrespective of the 'case' or category to which they belong; and second, outlines general rules on how to deal with them. It is important that the student of today shall thoroughly understand what is meant here—if only because AACR, the current code for English-speaking countries, is more of a 'conditions' code than a 'case' one. And this is the code which will be more and more used in the very near future.

EXPLANATION OF 'CASES' AND 'CONDITIONS'

Librarians are accustomed to categorising books according to their subjects and the form in which they are presented. In making catalogue rules it was to be expected then that librarians should make rules for the different forms of works, using terms to which they were already accustomed. Hence rules were worked out for, say, encyclopaedias, dictionaries, periodicals, directories, and even some actual works themselves when there existed a variety of editions, translations, etc., e.g. the Bible. These are nowadays known as 'cases'. However, it so happens that with some of the cases mentioned here all the relevant examples of works in those cases receive main entry under title, while often examples in the other cases also go under title. Therefore, the condition common to these works is title entry. An exception, such as Thomas Landau's *Encyclopaedia of librarianship*, belongs to another, very broad, condition, that of single personal authorship. The fact that it is in the form of an encyclopaedia is not as relevant to the cataloguer as the fact that LANDAU features very prominently on the title page as the one person most responsible for the intellectual content of the work.

Peter and Linda Murray's *Dictionary of art and artists* belongs to the 'case' dictionaries. But it is also an example of shared authorship. Another dictionary, *Dictionary of science* by E. B. Uvarov and D. R. Chapman, has its third edition revised by Alan Isaacs. As well as belonging to the case dictionaries, it is also an example of the condition mixed authorship. Fuller details of these conditions are given in Chapter 4.

There are fewer conditions of authorship than there are cases of forms of works, and it is therefore economical to compile codes using conditions rather than cases. If conditions are identified, described and exemplified clearly enough, it should be possible to finish up with a code which should cover most or all of the works which a cataloguer is required to deal with. To compile a code which enumerates all the cases concerned would take up a far greater space—and there would always be the fear that some cases might be overlooked. So, there would be a risk of inconsistency, because probably the code would not have been based on sound principles, and because different cataloguers might use different cases as precedents for new cases as they arose.

On the other hand, before a 'principles' or 'conditions' code can be applied intelligently it must by understood coherently, in the way that facets cannot be used in a synthetic classification scheme without an overall knowledge of the scheme's layout and an understanding of the 'fundamental categories' used in it. Some cases do belong completely or almost completely to a condition, e.g. a concordance is always a dependent work because it necessarily is a manipulation and re-arrangement of all or part of another author's works. Therefore, a 'conditions' code—at least, in the present transition period—requires (*a*) under each rule for a condition a list of common cases wholly embraced by that condition; (*b*) index entries for cases naming the rule(s) of which the cases are examples; (*c*) liberal explanatory cross references between rules. A great disadvantage of AACR is its unaccountable deficiencies in these respects.

A further disadvantage, apparently, is that codes cannot be wholly principle-based. Certain cases are so common and complex, e.g. Bible, that the codifiers find it convenient to lapse into 'legalistic' case study. Perhaps this happens too much in AACR. A further contributing factor is that perhaps librarians as a whole are too conservative to plunge wholly into a new method, and the few cases enumerated in AACR help form a bridge between the old and the new styles of code compilation. Conditions in principles codes should either be mutually exclusive, or, if they overlap, they must be consistent both with each other and with the underlying philosophy (or basic principle) of the code as a whole.

A principles code must not be expected to be over-generalised, otherwise it becomes meaningless. For example, one can imagine an author/title headings code which contained only two rules: (i) Enter a work under the single named author or corporate body chiefly responsible for its intellectual content, except: (ii) A work of 'diffuse authorship' is to be entered under its title. Apply this shortest-ever code to a set of complex documents, and see how many cause trouble. Get a colleague to apply it to the same documents, and see how many divergencies emerge in your resulting headings. More practically, the shortest author/title heading code is Lubetzky's CCR, of 1960. While one may not necessarily agree with all its rules, one would recommend it as a short easily understood code which deals with most conditions likely to be encountered. It is unfortunate that Lubetzky's clear conciseness has become muddied and over-embellished in AACR.

A vital factor for codifiers is the type of catalogue which may be required. The objects of catalogues have already been discussed in Chapter 2, and one of these is whether the catalogue is to be a specific-work finding list or whether it is a so-called 'bibliographic' list, incorporating detailed descriptions of the works and editions recorded and illustrating, perhaps minutely, their relationships with each other. In addition one must consider whether the catalogue is to be used primarily by people who have received some training in how to use a catalogue (whether staff or library users) or by people who know or care little about catalogues (usually library users, but sometimes staff).

Something which must be understood by users is the 'bibliographic unit', or 'unit of collocation' of a catalogue, i.e. how many works shall be entered at one point in the catalogue.

A personal author—a human being with one brain—may be a single unit, all of whose works are recorded at the same point in the author catalogue (but within certain limits—few catalogues would include entries for every contribution by the author to periodicals and encyclopaedias). Sometimes, a personal author will be regarded as an 'author unit' in one capacity, while works written in another capacity will be entered under a name—probably a pseudonym—associated with that other type of work. These will appear at a separate point in the catalogue, as already mentioned in the CARROLL/DODGSON example on page 30.

The 'unit' of corporate authorship is harder to define. Some catalogues have all central government publications, for example, recorded together at one point, under the name of the country, with subdivisions and sub-subdivisions and so on as required. Another may regard as the unit one government executive department, e.g. DEPARTMENT OF EDUCATION AND SCIENCE. Yet another may accept as a unit the works issued by a particular department under a certain name, e.g. MINISTRY OF EDUCATION. Yet again, a catalogue may be required to collocate entries for only certain sub-departments, or even of individual committees, e.g. SECONDARY SCHOOLS EXAMINATIONS COUNCIL. The same principle may be applied to the treatment of actual works. One catalogue may be expected to have the broadest possible 'bibliographic unit' for a given work, so as to include at the same place all versions, translations, changes in literary form, excerpts, etc., plus all commentaries and works *on* the work, plus works about the author. All these would go under the same heading, with subdivisions and sub-subdivisions as required. At the other extreme, the bibliographic unit may be solely the physical copy in hand at one time. One of the broadest bibliographic units existing in a present-day catalogue is PERIODICAL PUBLICATIONS in the BM's *Catalogue of printed books*. Perhaps one of the narrowest is the *Lord's prayer*, allowed for in AACR, Rule 109E1; another might be a noteworthy literary translation which the *Prussian instructions* has put under the translator.

If at all possible, a code should take into account the classification scheme, shelf arrangement and subject approach to be used with it, and whether all materials of a library are to be recorded in one comprehensive catalogue or if some different types of materials are to have their own separate catalogues. If for example, the Bible is classified from complete editions to individual books and even small excerpts, all arranged systematically, with this arrangement also reproduced in a classified subject catalogue, then there may be more value in letting the author catalogue treat physically separate parts of the Bible as individual units, thereby obviating the need for many added author-type entries. Again, if a classification scheme specifies exactly a poet, sav Milton, then there is no point in repeating all entries for his works in both the classified file and the author catalogue under his name: better to let the author catalogue cater for editor and similar approaches. The subject index will provide the basic key to the class mark for the Bible and Milton, for example. Further, if separate catalogues are maintained for the various physical forms of stock, e.g. gramophone records, it is pointless to have 'Phonodisc' or similar in a prominent place on each entry, even though it may be prescribed in the code.

But it is probably unrealistic to expect a code to produce ready-made answers to all these problems, so we come to the next consideration: the practical application of codes.

PRACTICAL APPLICATION OF CODES

No single code can stand on its own as the sole authority in the cataloguing of works for a library's stock. In the first place, no modern code includes rules for all the cataloguing decisions which must be made. Local decisions will also have to be made concerning layouts of entries and references, for example.

Apart from omissions, even the most rigid code will require interpretation and will result in genuine differences of opinion: not to be confused with misinterpretation through poor professional education. AA 1908 has American alternatives, while many codes fall back on criteria like 'decidedly better known' or 'most commonly used in reference sources'. AACR includes some alternatives—decisions must be made over these.

So the working copies of a code in a library will almost certainly need to be annotated to clarify ambiguities, to indicate choices of alternatives, and to instruct what to do in case of doubt between various choices not covered by the code itself, e.g. 'If in doubt prefer later' for choice of headings in a certain condition or case, and 'If in doubt, leave it out' (or 'put it in') for title added entries.

General instructions on the use of the library's choice of code or codes may be included in the Staff instruction manual.

Authority files should be maintained for all forms of headings, showing how a particular author is entered, and what references, if any, are implemented in each case. Authority cards may occasionally need scope notes, explaining perhaps when an author's real name and when a pseudonym is used, if the library uses the divided 'author unit'.

Authority files for names of people, corporate bodies, places, etc., should be used in subject as well as in author/title cataloguing; in fact there is something to be said for interfiling an author/title authority file with the subject authority file—if it is used as an adjunct to a list of subject headings or a thesaurus. Or the author/title authority file may be interfiled into the library's union catalogue if this is readily accessible to the cataloguers.

In general, it might be said that a code will help ensure overall consistency in the 'sense' or 'conditions' meaning, while the library's locally compiled aids ensure consistency at individual headings or bibliographic units, and in entries themselves.

CHAPTER 4

Author and Title Approach

The types of problems dealt with here are arranged mainly according to modern conditions (either LUBETZKY or ICCP), with variations to incorporate what are here called 'diffuse authorship' and 'concealed authorship'.

Systematic summaries of main codes' decisions are not given, as they are readily available in the second edition of QUIGG and other works; although the later section of this work on 'special' materials does include summaries as they are not easily available in detail elsewhere.

Examples are given in the codes, and these must be examined: access to AACR at least is assumed throughout. Other examples may be found in CHAPLIN'S annotated edition of the ICCP principles.

A revolution in author/title cataloguing was started in the 1950's. It is still going on, and all that is said is subject to criticism—including the personal opinions in this chapter.

The problems are discussed under the following headings:

1. Personal names: (*a*) Form.
                        (*b*) Change.
2. Multiple authorship: (*a*) Shared authorship.
                        (*b*) Mixed authorship.
                        (*c*) Related/dependent works.
3. Concealed authorship: (*a*) Pseudonymous.
                        (*b*) Anonymous.
4. Title entry, including Uniform titles (see also other items, especially 6).
5. Corporate authorship: (*a*) Form.
                        (*b*) Change.
                        (*c*) Subordinate/related bodies.
6. Corporate authorship versus Personal authorship versus Title.

In some instances these categories overlap each other. The factors mentioned in each category may apply to:

(*a*) codifiers;

(*b*) chief cataloguers in interpreting codes, e.g. when compiling staff instructions; and

(*c*) practising cataloguers in day-to-day decisions.

The basic problem is to work out general rules which give satisfactory results in all individual cases. An underlying conflict throughout is 'intellectual responsibility' versus a 'sought label'. Serious problems arise in perhaps only 10 to 20 per cent of a library's intake; the simple decisions are taken for granted here.

1 (*a*) Personal: Form

Factors to be taken into account in choice, which sometimes overlap:

(1) The person's own preference if known.

(2) How he has been known in the past.

(3) How he is known at present.

(4) Factors contributing to items 1, 2 and 3 are how he is generally cited in: (*a*) his own books; (*b*) authoritative reference works; and (*c*) authoritative bibliographies and catalogues.

(5) Vernacular versus Anglicised form

e.g.   PLINIUS SECUNDUS, Gaius or PLINY THE ELDER.

(6) Transliteration: rigid formulae versus accepted Anglicised form

e.g.   TCHAIKOVSKY or CHAIKOVSKY, and

TCHEKOV or CHEKOV, also

HOMERUS or HOMER.

(7) Surname versus forename, e.g. some mediaeval names.

(8) Multi-word surnames, i.e. (*a*) compound names; (*b*) prefixed names—with prepositions and/or articles and various combinations of these, or with attributive prefixes. A simple but rigid rule would choose for all cases either the whole name or the final component as entry term. A simple permissive rule would add to the above, say, 'unless cited differently in his works'. AACR devotes some six pages to practices for various national usages, and a whole monograph has been compiled on the subject: CHAPLIN, A. H. *Names of persons: national usages for entry in catalogues*. IFLA/FIAB, 1967.

A suggested simple permissive rule is: Enter under first part except when decidedly more frequently cited by another form

e.g.   BEETHOVEN, Ludwig van, not VAN BEETHOVEN, Ludwig.

(9) Persons with same name; Fullness of name. These are dealt with jointly because it is suggested that a name as used should be of minimum

length short of confusing with another similar name, e.g. ELIOT, T. S., cannot be confused with ELIOT, George: neither needs dates. Consider how much of the following is needed to recognise and identify the person (ALA 1949):

SULAIMAN I, *the Magnificent, Sultan of the Turks,* 1494-1566.

Does AACR (p. 87-88) need to fill half a page with 'Indonesian honorific words'? Does it matter if a cataloguer makes an occasional howler with a foreign name, even in these days of international cooperation, including cataloguing? In fact, when international ('shared') cataloguing is fully developed, presumably the whole world will draw on Indonesia's own decisions.

1 *(b)* Personal: Changed

This problem is strictly a manifestation of 1 *(a)*, since it is about how one person is entered. It is not concerned with concealment of a name, or with sobriquets or nicknames.

The basic conflict is between:

    (1) Earliest.
    (2) Latest.
    (3) Best known.

ALA 1949 seemed to assume that 2 and 3 were usually the same· However, examples may be found in which earliest is best known and others in which latest is best known.

How to decide on 'best known' takes into account 'most-used', and this in turn depends on many of the factors given in 1 *(a)*. 'Best known' is undoubtedly the most 'sought', but it may take time to determine. However clearly the types of evidence are named, e.g. title pages or authoritative reference works, the evidence itself may be conflicting, especially between libraries' stocks, and especially if an author is still writing.

2. Multiple authorship

This condition can apply to personal and corporate authorship, either each or both in the same work. It was accepted by ICCP (Principle 10): 'When two or more authors have shared in the creation of a work'—but it was splintered in AACR into the three sub-conditions mentioned here (though it was mentioned in passing without definition in Rule 4).

Of these, AACR defines and exemplifies (a) Shared authorship, which includes joint authorship and composite authorship (defined in Appendix I Glossary of AACR). However, 'Works produced under editorial direction' (Rule 4) are in a limbo between 'Shared authorship' (Rule 3) and 'Works with authorship of mixed character' (Rule 7-18): a 'centred heading' (in Dewey Decimal Classification terminology) would have been useful preceding Rule 3. As it is there is some possibility of confusion between (a) 'Shared', and (b) 'Mixed'—which nominally infers 'different kinds of functions' (AACR p. 21). A clearer distinction between (a) and (b) might have been that (a) covers verbal, but (b) covers non-verbal, sharing or mixing, even though this may be an artificial distinction. As it is, the two conditions might well have been made one condition, with cases enumerated if necessary.

Choice of main entry seems to oscillate between:

(a) The author most intellectually responsible.

(b) The author most prominently named on title page.

(c) Title: as an Occam's razor to cut the Gordian knot when (a) and (b) become too confused, e.g. up to three authors results in entry under first-named, or most significant typographically. But four or more contributors often results in title entry (ICCP and AACR)—except that editor may be given the main entry heading if 'primarily responsible for the existence of the work' (AACR).

It is suggested that Osborn's plea for the cataloguers' own judgement should apply. If a work is manifestly of 'diffuse authorship'—i.e. if there is doubt about who receives main entry decision—then entry should be under title. There is no evidence that title has gone out of favour as the most popular approach to works of diffuse authorship. And one queries whether cataloguers must put academic justice before direct usefulness in a catalogue. Further, ICCP decided that the first function of a catalogue was to identify specific documents.

This latter object is not confined necessarily to title citation: PALMER AND WELLS' *Fundamentals of library classification* is usually cited by the phrase-personal-author label, and conceivably could be entered as such. The same applies to gramophone records by SIMON AND GARFUNKEL.

(c) Related and/or Dependent works constitute the third sub-condition. In AACR main entry decision is decided by title pages and established titles, i.e. potentially artificial devices. Entry under the original work is decided by a dependent title; entry under later is decided by an independent title. The distinction, therefore, is decided by title pages, not necessarily corresponding with real intellectual responsibility.

It is suggested here that the whole category is artificial especially since AACR (Rule 19; and Glossary) does not attempt a definition, but merely exemplifies—a criticism often made of earlier codes, e.g. the types of related works named under Rule 19 do not include thematic catalogues. So the condition seems to fall into two main sub-categories: (*a*) Supplements and similar, belonging intellectually to Shared authorship; and (*b*) Concordances and similar, which are a manifestation of author versus subject entry, e.g. CRUDEN versus BIBLE for his *Concordance*.

Some general conclusions on the various manifestations of multiple authorship are:

1. True multiple-authorship cases can belong to one basic category.
2. In cases of diffuse authorship entry should be under title.
3. Some cases of dependent/related works are not relevant to an author/title code.

Summary of criteria in deciding on main entry heading in works of multiple authorship:

(*a*) Detail of specification possible in the classification scheme used (expanded on later in this work in Chapter 24, on Filing; also touched upon in Chapter 3, p. 36 and 37).

(*b*) Number of added entries allowed in the library concerned. If none is allowed, a preference is suggested for original author to prevent more distantly related versions becoming virtually lost in the catalogue. An alternative, even if unorthodox, approach may be effected via the subject or form entries.

(*c*) Title page: size and position of rival names, with explanatory phrases, e.g. 'freely adapted by' is weaker than the simple 'by'.

(*d*) In the case of commentaries, expositions, critical notes, and similar works: the proportion of the total work devoted to commentary, the position of the commentary on the page, and the type-size of the commentary.

(*e*) Precedent in the library involved: admittedly a pragmatic criterion.

(*f*) The cataloguer's intuitive judgement derived from experience with documents and contact with users of the library: rather controversial to the theoretician, perhaps, but a criterion which may prove to be the deciding factor in practice.

3. Concealed authorship

It is suggested that this should be a single condition in which the author wishes to conceal his real name, unlike:

(a) Spurious or doubtful authors (e.g. ALA 1949, Rule 31);
(b) Sobriquets—there is no evidence that El Greco was trying to conceal his real name;
(c) Works of diffuse authorship, like periodicals and newspapers; and
(d) Works whose authorship has become overlaid by time, as in 'anonymous classics' (ALA 1949 term), and possibly part of the diffuse authorship condition.

Further, we should distinguish between:

(a) standard works, like *Tom Brown's schooldays*, by An Old Boy—now commonly known to be Thomas Hughes, or *The life and strange surprising adventures of Robinson Crusoe, told by himself*—now commonly looked for under DEFOE; and
(b) present-day works like the confessions of a murderer by one 'Zeno' in a Sunday newspaper, or westerns by F. C. Robertson who also writes under the name Robert Crane.

Pseudonymous and anonymous works are not always easy to differentiate, as can be seen by reading the ALA 1949 definitions, Rules 30 and 32. To say the least, these are entertaining.

A relevant factor in concealed authorship is the breadth of the bibliographic unit. It may be important for the research worker to have *Predictions for the year 1708* by one Isaac Bickerstaff Esquire entered under Jonathan Swift, and to have the early works by Boz under Charles Dickens. But it is less vital as yet if *How to run a bassoon factory* is entered under Mark Spade and not its real author, Nigel Balchin. Libraries which bought *Trooper to the Southern Cross* when it first came out in 1934—at the time apparently a non-fiction work by an Australian soldier called Leslie Parker—and which later bought the reprint published in 1966, scarcely have any alternative but to recatalogue under the author's real name as a work of fiction: see the facsimile on page 45.

3 (a) Pseudonymous works: basic problems

(a) Whether a cataloguer should acknowledge that a pseudonym has been used.
(b) It is not always obvious that a pseudonym has been used.

Trooper to
the Southern Cross

ANGELA THIRKELL
'Leslie Parker'

SUN BOOKS
Melbourne

2 (i). A straightforward example of pseudonymous authorship.

(*c*) Whether a cataloguer should try to identify the real name of the author.

Potentially relevant are the types of pseudonym:

(*a*) Real-sounding names, e.g. Nevil Shute (Nevil Shute Norway).

(*b*) Artificial but viable names, e.g. Stendhal.

(*c*) Verbal, but possibly not viable names, e.g. 'by the author of . . .'.

(*d*) Unreal and not viable, because not conveniently spoken or filed, e.g. asterisks.

3 (*b*) Anonymous works

Such works are published with no author's name on the title page, etc., or with such 'weak' labels as to be not worth considering as used headings.

The main problem is whether it is worth trying to discover the real name, and why. One can still be guided by AACR Rules 1 and 2, but set a limit of time, or number of sources consulted. The title is a ready label not to be lightly cast aside. A catalogue entry for a present-day work is not necessarily compiled once and for all: recataloguing in the future, when conditions change and new needs emerge, should be a normal, not an exceptional, matter in the few instances of works which are first issued anonymously.

4. Title entry

This was a Principle at ICCP, but it is not used as a condition in ACCR. In fact, it is a solution to a variety of conditions and cases.

Three aspects should be borne in mind throughout:

(*a*) Title as main entry.

(*b*) Use of uniform titles, in (i) Main entry; and

    (ii) Description as demonstrated in Chapter 2 of this work.

(*c*) Title as added entry.

Title main entry should be considered for works of:

(*a*) Unknown authorship when it is likely that authorship will never be discovered: ALA 1949 'anonymous classics' like the *Bible* and *Arabian nights* are typical examples. Arising from ICCP, an *International list of uniform headings for anonymous classics* was issued, and it may be assumed therefore that standard works named in this are to be given title main entry indefinitely.

(*b*) Uncertain authorship, where there is doubt about who actually wrote a work, and in cases where evidence is uncertain. Much time should not be used by the ordinary cataloguer in sifting evidence which skilled historical bibliographers have already worked over a great deal.

(*c*) Unrecognised authorship, where authorship is fairly certain, but the works are commonly cited by title. An example is the *Koran*, apparently conceived by Mohammed and told to Zaid-ibn-Thabit, but usually thought of by title; and also the *American declaration of independence*, literally 'by Thomas Jefferson [and others]'. This category includes works issued by unnamed groups of people, given an artificially-constructed form of corporate authorship by ALA 1949, e.g. LONDON. *Women*; BOSTON. *Citizens*—cases of librarians being blinded by their own (library) science?

(*d*) Diffuse authorship, in which either: (*a*) many authors are named or known; or (*b*) authors are very insignificantly cited on title pages, etc., with the result that works are very commonly cited by titles. It could also include cases where there is an unresolvable conflict between, say, an editor and a well-known title of a work: the Oxford books of verse are examples—the titles being less likely to change than the editors. Between them, these instances could include examples like personal author of a report versus corporate body sponsoring the report. A further obvious example is that of many periodicals and other serials.

In general, it is suggested here—contrary to most code rulings—that title main entry could be used in all cases where: (*a*) intellectual responsibility is not clearly defined; and (*b*) title is more likely to be cited, especially when editors, contributors, etc., change from edition to edition.

Many cases of the past might be covered by this condition, e.g. certain encyclopaedias, dictionaries, directories, and similar frequently revised and reprinted quick-reference works.

ICCP covered such contingencies with phrases like 'known primarily or conventionally by title', and even 'formal or conventional titles indicating the nature of the material', although the latter is not an excuse for 'substitute-subject' entry. Perhaps a future edition of AACR will interpret ICCP more literally—and sensibly?

More than one title

Works may be known by more than one title, either in English, or in their vernacular form. A decision may have to be made between the earliest, vernacular, form, and a later, English, form or several later English forms. An example is given in Chapter 2: Caesar's *De bello Gallico*, or *Gallic War*, or *Conquest of Gaul*.

Anonymous classics are even more of a problem because their main entry is under title.

A further complication is that of excerpts: whether the main heading, under an author (or composer, say) is arranged directly by excerpt title or indirectly via 'parent' title.

The vital factor is that of bibliographic unit: the conception of the work as a whole versus the document in hand. From AACR has crystallised the concept of the uniform title: an attempt to collocate all editions, translations, and parts, of a work, although strangely certain versions are entered under later author.

Changed titles, e.g. of periodicals. An important innovation, reflecting Lubetzky and in turn Cutter, is that periodicals with changed titles should be entered 'consecutively', i.e. 'a periodical which changes its name is to be entered under each name' (CUTTER, Rule 145, p. 62), there being explanatory references to and from other titles. Other solutions, in addition to (*a*) consecutive entry, are (*b*) earliest, (*c*) latest, (*d*) best-known forms. (*a*) narrows the bibliographic unit, but may well be the most useful form for most purposes, except for, perhaps, union catalogues of periodicals when used for checking complete holdings.

5. Corporate authorship

Background to what Lubetzky calls 'the corporate complex' is given in LUBETZKY (excerpted in OLDING), and in GORMAN. JOLLEY, although pre-dating AACR, is still controversial, and CUTTER, as always, provides interesting havering. A concise summary of code decisions is given in QUIGG, 2nd ed., p. 41-44.

Despite the past antidote of PI, which refrained from recognising corporate authorship, ICCP recognised the need for corporate authorship —but in moderation.

The term itself is defined in AACR only in passing (p. 10), but the footnote includes the important characteristics: 'identified by a name', and acting 'as an entity'. The British text gets away from the past artificial categorising of institutions and societies, and in general advocates simple direct entry under name of organisation.

5 (a) Form of name

Possible conflict may arise between the following:

1. Official, legal name. But it is suggested that this may be discounted if never used in publications.

2. The form used in publications. But two or more forms may be used, especially if the organisation is an international one, with its name in several languages, or even a national one with its name in, say, two languages (e.g. AACR, Rule 64: examples).

3. That used in reference sources, sometimes the same as 2.

4. A colloquial, often abbreviated, form.

In the past, there has been differentiation in codes between direct entry and some manipulated form, the manipulated form often being under place as in past so-called institutions. Although AACR British text has come out in favour of direct entry, it should be acknowledged that place name often supplies a significant entry word.

Organisations are often colloquially referred to by initials in various forms: acronyms, elided syllables (Unesco, Euratom), etc. AACR could conceivably have gone further, even to the point of entering organisations under plain initials, e.g. A.A. for Automobile Association—though it is acknowledged that this could be confused with Alcoholics Anonymous. Despite occasional potential confusion, it is suggested here that AACR could have 'colloquialised' and abbreviated more.

5 (b) Change of name

This condition is often associated with a change of function, and so it must be respected. However, one must beware of being forced into extensive studies of a body's history and functions before feeling able to catalogue it. We have accepted by now that the catalogue is not a directory of organisations.

Choice is between:

(a) Earliest
(b) Latest   } with relevant *see* references.
(c) Best known
(d) 'Consecutive' entry, with explanatory *see also* references.

Discussion of these choices is rather similar to other parallel conditions, e.g. change of title of periodicals.

Consecutive entry results in narrower bibliographic units, as with consecutive entry of titles and as in some instances of direct entry.

This is in line with the current trend towards what might be called specific as opposed to collocative entry, and is the AACR ruling.

5 (c) Subordinate and Related bodies
Theoretically, two factors influence a choice:

- (a) The independence or dependence of name.
- (b) The degree to which the functions of the parent and the subordinate bodies are interwoven.

It is suggested that ready identification should be the primary object, so (a) is the more important. In any case, it often happens that (a) and (b) do coincide.

This condition reflects form of name. One gets BODLEIAN LIBRARY, but UNIVERSITY OF CAMBRIDGE. *Library*. Some critics may complain that this is inconsistent: it is, grammatically. Does this matter? AACR thinks not, because its consistency is that of directness, as explained in Chapter 3, and we have decided that a catalogue is not a directory. Still, a fair objection is that the form of entry—direct or indirect—may help a reader decide on the authority or purpose of a document. In the few instances where the cataloguer considers clarification necessary, a note could be included in the entry.

Finally, certain form sub-headings are perpetuated in AACR—it is suggested here that these are form and not author as claimed by GORMAN (p. 6-7). An example is:

GREAT BRITAIN. *Laws, statutes, etc.*

In contrast, individual bills are given accurate author entry, even if wastefully indirect, e.g.:

GREAT BRITAIN. *Parliament. House of Commons*

Why not simply HOUSE OF COMMONS, especially in Britain? Bodies common to more than one country, e.g. HOUSE OF REPRESENTATIVES, could be qualified by country (Australia; U.S., etc.) as in the LABOUR PARTY example in AACR Rule 65B:

LABOUR PARTY
LABOUR PARTY (*New Zealand*)

As might be expected, there is a case for direct title entry rather than indirect pseudo-author entry, e.g.

BUILDING code for the City of Richmond, Virginia
rather than, in effect, alphabetical-classed entry under

RICHMOND. *Ordinances, local laws, etc.*

AACR's form headings are commented upon further in Chapter 7 of this
work.

6. Corporate authorship versus Personal authorship versus Title (the crunch?)

Corporate versus Personal authorship is a game played ever since BM
started to formalise corporate entry. The rules were stretched to
breaking point by ALA 1949 which conceded corporate entry to any
group of people with or without a group name. A compromise was
attempted by ICCP, which allowed title entry for certain cases, which are
included in this book under the 'diffuse authorship' condition. Unfortunately, even the British text of AACR allows corporate entry for many
works better known by title.

It is suggested that the surface of the whole problem is only scratched
by such cited cases as routine reports by an official employed by a
body, as differentiated from non-routine reports by a person not
normally employed by a body. AACR incorporates a further turn of the
'legalistic' screw by making the cataloguer decide if a report embodies
'the results of scholarly investigation . . .', etc. (Rule 17A1). Evidently
the principle of intellectual responsibility applies here with a vengeance.
However, Rule 17A2 allows a form of quasi-subject entry (in an author
code) for routine works about an organisation, as in BM. Sometimes,
though, AACR seems to favour personal authorship entry, e.g. Rule 17B.

After all this, one might be excused for wondering if the theoretical
principle of 'intellectual responsibility' is worth pursuing so far.

The simple truth is:

(a) intellectual responsibility was abandoned by ICCP, and is
repeatedly queried by practical reference workers and thoughtful
cataloguers; hence
(b) the main use of catalogues is for finding individual works, whose
chief distinguishing feature is often title—and possibly even in
certain cases a title not appearing on the title page; as is usually
the case with the various reports cited below.

This contradiction between: (a) intellectual responsibility; (b) collocated corporate authorship; and (c) a handy sought label is brought to a head by a type of publication which has become increasingly common since a work known as the *Beveridge report* came out in Britain in 1942. Its official title was *Social insurance and allied services* (Cmd. 6404), and its legal author was the Interdepartmental Committee on Social Insurance and Allied Services. It is possible to conjure up several headings under which this document might be entered in a catalogue:

(a) GREAT BRITAIN. *Interdepartmental Committee on Social Insurance and Allied Services*; or
(b) INTERDEPARTMENTAL COMMITTEE ON SOCIAL INSURANCE AND ALLIED SERVICES (*Great Britain*); or
(c) BEVERIDGE, William Henry, *Baron Beveridge of Tuggal*; or
(d) BEVERIDGE REPORT.

Whatever the title page may say, there is little doubt that the work is commonly referred to as the Beveridge report—because of the name of the Chairman of the reporting committee—just as works of similar types of origin are known as the *Kenyon report, McColvin report, Maud report,* and so on, even *before* they are published nowadays. It seems pedantic to insist on giving such works complex and indirect corporate authorship entry under GREAT BRITAIN; or even CARNEGIE UNITED KINGDOM TRUST? Especially in the increasing number of cases where reports are government-sponsored, it seems futile to load catalogues with headings according to the formula: COUNTRY. *Department. Committee.*

Those people who seek a report under its sponsoring government department, committee, etc., can usually be answered through the use of official bibliographies, while those remembering the subject-nature or name of the committee (e.g. on public libraries) can often be satisfied via the subject catalogue, even if indirectly. Perhaps the time is coming for this extra-complicated knot to be cut by simple, and even 'colloquial', title entry: i.e. a commonly cited title which possibly does not even appear on the title page.

A summary is given here of the main examples of possible title entry, mentioned under various previous problems:

(a) Works of multiple authorship in which several authors are named on the title page, insignificantly compared with the title. Such works would be regarded as of diffuse authorship.

(*b*) Modern works with no author or only an insignificant pseudonym on the title page.

(*c*) Works with many revised editions, especially when they have come to be commonly cited by title, e.g. *Fiction index* and *Sequels*.

(*d*) Many anthologies such as the Oxford books of verse, because they are often cited by title, and because editors sometimes change.

(*e*) Children's and other much changed versions of 'anonymous classics'.

(*f*) Most periodicals and other serials.

(*g*) Works of corporate authorship which are of diffuse or complex authorship, including those commonly cited by 'colloquial' titles.

A basic guiding principle—and assuming that no added entries or references are allowed—should always be 'Is this the most likely heading to be sought?' If the answer is NO, then the rules should be changed. Catalogue rules are made for users, and not to vindicate codifiers.

A revealing study of the case for title entry is: 'Authors versus title: a comparative survey of the accuracy of the information which the user brings to the library catalogue', by F. H. Ayres [and others]: *Journal of documentation* v. 24 no. 4, Dec. 1968, p. 266-272. The article cites other articles supporting the pro-title case. Basically, it shows that 90·4 per cent of titles were cited correctly compared with 74·7 per cent authors in a large scientific special library.

CHAPTER 5

Codes: Nineteenth Century

British Museum; Prussian Instructions

Chapters 5, 6 and 7 attempt to outline the general principles of the main codes and to try to fit them into an historical evolution. Detail on each code is not given, since this is available in existing works such as QUIGG, NEEDHAM, and GORMAN (for AACR), and such works should be used in conjunction with this one. The codes themselves should be referred to as source material and to check examples.

The codes dealt with here should be considered, for three basic reasons:

(*a*) Some have been used in the compilation of bibliographies and bibliographic catalogues, which are likely to remain in use in libraries, e.g. BM: The British Museum's own printed catalogues, not only of printed books, but also of other materials such as music; AA 1908: Many libraries' own catalogues, and BNB up to 1967; ALA 1949: Most American bibliographies and catalogues. It must also be remembered that central cataloguing agencies are very unlikely to revise systematically their back stocks of cards, or stencils, etc., from which cards are reproduced.

(*b*) An academic comparative study of other periods' codes contributes to one's profound understanding of cataloguing problems. Today's students and practising librarians are tomorrow's code compilers and revisers.

(*c*) They can be just plain interesting, and can provide hours of at least harmless, and possibly even useful, entertainment.

BRITISH MUSEUM CODE

The nineteenth century saw a growth in the British Museum's enforcement of its copyright deposit rights or privileges with a rapid expansion of its stock. The period also was one of great industrial and commercial expansion, with a consequent growth of bureaucracy, hence of government publications such as the famous 'Blue books' on factory conditions. Education was compulsory from around 1870, and at this time came the founding of the popular press, while the first socialised popular libraries in Britain were consolidated. All of this—from the cataloguer's point of view—meant rapidly increasing library stocks and the increased need to retrieve items from them quickly and accurately to satisfy demands for data of all sorts: Karl Marx was not the only thinker and world-changer to rely largely on the British Museum for his research materials.

This century was also the last one of closed access, making the need for catalogues of stocks all the more necessary. The single-unit record (e.g. the catalogue card) had not yet become popular in libraries, and in any case readers often wanted to refer to catalogues in places other than in the relevant libraries. Hence the conventionally printed catalogue, with occasional supplements but fairly infrequent revised editions— hence in turn a reluctance to change catalogue entries, especially their filing headings—once they had become established.

By the nineteenth century, the alphabetical author catalogue was the most common form, though with various rudimentary attempts at subject approach added to it or occasionally incorporated into it. It has to be remembered that subject catalogues as such of BM stock were not started upon until the 1880's, while the published BM Code dates from 1841.

Our purpose here is to deal with the printed code upon which the BM's nineteenth-century catalogue of printed books was based. This code was, and is still, used for compiling the mammoth 1,000-volume guard-book form catalogue in the circular Reading Room, and it is from this that the current 300-volume printed and bound form of the catalogue of printed books has been made by a special photo-litho-offset technique: this accounts for the occasional short manuscript alterations and additions to be found in it. A 'mini' form of the cata-logue has been produced by reducing each large folio-size page to one quarter of a quarto size page: at present (1969) this, the Compact Edition, is the only complete form of the catalogue in print. The catalogue is nominally an author catalogue, but with various forms of title and form entry incorporated into its alphabetical sequence. Each work has one main entry, quite short compared with the 'standard' fullness recommended in more recent codes. Other approaches to certain documents are in the form of what might be called 'added-references'—shorter than added unit entries but longer than heading-to-heading *see* references. Judging by other libraries' printed catalogues, e.g. Glasgow Public Libraries', this structure seems to have had considerable influence in the days of the conventionally printed catalogue. More information on the BM catalogue is given in Chapter 25, on Physical forms of catalogues.

The code includes rules for headings, references and description; it deals mostly with printed books and serials but has short supplementary sections on printed maps and music.

Usually, information from which catalogue entries are derived is obtained from the book being catalogued at the time: the bibliographic unit is usually the work in hand, and external sources are not used. However, other forms of the bibliographic unit concerned are often connected with the item in hand by 'added-references'.

The title page is usually used as a basis for the main heading, so if no author's name appears on the title page of one edition of a work but it does appear on another, the two editions may be entered in different parts of the catalogue. There are a few exceptions to this—a play by Shakespeare being an example in the code. Therefore the 'author unit' is not necessarily comprehensive, and if an author has produced several works anonymously, the main entries for these will be scattered.

However, a work will be entered under an author if he is named on the title page even though the work is only 'attributed' to him (R. 21).

In general, one might conclude that the 'intellectual responsibility' principle is not taken much into account, but rather a convenient 'sought label' is used for many books.

The 'sought label' principle tends to favour personal names, e.g. a festschrift is entered under the person in whose honour the work is compiled (see facsimiles on pages 57 and 58), while the rule for anonymous works illustrates a very distinctive order of priorities for selecting a sought term (R. 18) i.e.:

1. Person
    e.g. JOHN, *the Baptist*, Saint.—Order of St John of Jerusalem in England. The origin and development of the St John Ambulance Association. [Note that this work is not given corporate entry.]

2. Group
    e.g. GERMANS. L'Occupation de Templeure par les Allemands.

3. Place or, similar
    e.g. SCOTLAND.—Church of Scotland.—*Elders.*
    and BOUNTY, H.M.S.

4. Other proper name
    e.g. PEEL [for an anonymous letter to Sir Robert Peel].

LIBRARIES FOR THE PEOPLE

INTERNATIONAL STUDIES
IN LIBRARIANSHIP

In honour of

LIONEL R. McCOLVIN, C.B.E., F.L.A.

Edited by

Robert F. Vollans

THE LIBRARY ASSOCIATION
1968

2 (ii). A classic example of 'sought label' versus 'intellectual responsibility'.
2 (ii) (*a*). Title page.

To

LIONEL ROY McCOLVIN

from

ALL HIS COLLEAGUES

with gratitude for

50 YEARS OF DEVOTED AND

DISTINGUISHED SERVICE TO

THE PUBLIC LIBRARY MOVEMENT

Published by
THE LIBRARY ASSOCIATION

on his
Seventy-Second Birthday

30th November, 1968

2 (ii) (*b*). Page facing title page.

5. First noun
   e.g. BOOK.—A first book of algebra. [Note that, unlike other anonymous works' entries, this is not a substitute-subject entry.]
6. First word of title, if no noun in title
   e.g. JUST. Just as I am. [Apparently mere pronouns do not count.]

Apart from the peculiarities of this rule, others also show preferences for outstanding proper names, e.g. Place for libraries and museums. This was probably the unwitting start of the societies-institutions syndrome which lasted up to ALA 1949.

Place as a basis for government publications will be touched on again later.

Again, country place-names are used for entry word for national societies, and town place-names for local societies.

Indirect entry, often under place, for the purpose of collocation—establishing a broad bibliographic or author unit—as mentioned above, had its most important and influential manifestation through the establishment of the corporate author concept. Such author headings are constructed (i.e. formalised) and reach alphabetical-classing proportions. This is most apparent in the hierarchical chains produced in the entry of government publications.

e.g. ENGLAND—Army—Infantry—*Royal Warwickshire Regiment* The Antelope. A monthly journal.

But place-names are also used for non-government or semi-government institutions.

e.g. ENGLAND—*Church of England.*
PARIS—*Bibliothèque Nationale.* [Compare with the use of 'Germans' for 'Allemands' above.]
CANTERBURY—*Cathedral Church.*

Place-names are also brought to the front, as a filing medium, in inverted headings, e.g. VERSAILLES, Treaty of.

Place-names, however, are not always used consistently, e.g. some 'official' institutions go under name of country or state, but national libraries and museums go under town.

One type of collocation which is rather out of time with the general treatment of monographic works, i.e. the limited bibliographic unit, is that anonymous 'replies' to other works are entered under the heading of the original.

A further important type of collocation is the extensive use of form terms as entry words.

e.g. Congresses [international only, others under place].
    Dictionary [but occasionally 'dictionaire' if that is the form used in the title].
    Encyclopaedias, even for a work whose title begins with a proper name, e.g. *Cassell's Modern encyclopaedia*, and even for an anonymous work, e.g. *The first part of a dictionary of chemistry*.

Other form headings include Ephemerides; Directories; Catalogues; Liturgies; and Hymnals.

But the most striking—and possibly hardest to use in bibliographical searching—is the omnibus heading Periodical publications. Second-cited term is place of publication; only third comes the title, and that is the earliest form (reflecting the conventionally printed form of catalogue).

So a typical example might be:

PERIODICAL PUBLICATIONS.—London. The Quarterly review.

However, only some periodicals receive this treatment; those issued by societies are entered under the headings appropriate to the societies, often with country or place-name as entry word.

Language

BM normally uses the vernacular for names in other languages. However, it stipulates English form for ancient Greek (HOMER, not HOMEROS); place-names are usually given in English, a practice followed by all significant codes since. But, unaccountably, it occasionally gives an English translation of an allegedly sought word in the title selected for entry word.

e.g. I. FRENCH CEREMONIAL. Project du nouveau cérémonial français.
    2. the 'Allemandes'/'Germans' example quoted above.

This practice inclines one to the belief that some form of haphazard and unconscious subject approach is intended in the entering of these anonymous works.

To run the risk of summing up this Code:

1. The principle of corporate authorship was established but left a little ragged and over-indirect in heading structure.

2. There is no consistent policy of what is regarded as the 'bibliographic unit'.

3. There is an extensive and often confusing use of form heading.

4. Some curious entry words result from the apparent attempt to bring to the fore a sought term for the entry of anonymous works.

5. In changes of name, etc., the earliest form is preferred.

6. Since BM is the first code of its type, and because of the BM's policy of issuing printed catalogues, it is probably true to say that the BM Code has had a considerable influence—sometimes useful, but sometimes 'how not to do it'.

It should be emphasised, in conclusion, that the staff of the British Museum itself are the first to acknowledge that the Code is now out-dated.

PRUSSIAN INSTRUCTIONS

This code is dealt with out of its strict chronological place to prevent its coming between CUTTER and AA 1908: CUTTER influenced AA 1908 and later codes a great deal directly, and it seems justifiable to include it in the twentieth century even though the first three editions came out in the nineteenth.

The need for a German code was appreciated when a *Prussian union catalogue* was initiated in the 1890's—some thirty years after the unification of Germany and about forty years before similar union catalogues were started in Britain. The catalogue began publication in 1931, and in 1936 it became the *German union catalogue*. The code was issued in a preliminary edition in 1899, with a basic edition in 1908. It was not available in English until 1938, when the Australian librarian Dr Osborn translated it and added a long and lucid Introduction to it. Most of the examples of the present author's account of PI are derived, with thanks, from Osborn's Introduction. Although not very influential in English-speaking countries, PI did influence cataloguing in Sweden, Norway, and Denmark, and in Holland, Hungary, and Switzerland. This should be borne in mind when we come later to the international renunciation of one of PI's chief features: its non-acknowledgement of corporate entry.

However, some indication of the waning of influence of PI had been noted before that, e.g. in H. R. Kleineberger's 'Some current projects of catalogue code revision': *Library Association Record*, vol. 57, no. 9, Sept. 1955, p. 341-344. In 1938, German public libraries adopted a more 'mechanical' form of direct title entry. Since the Second World War, a new code for public libraries in the German People's Republic has been compiled: referred to in *Der Bibliothekar* vol. 5, 1951, p. 605-621.

The basic PI, like BM, has fairly short entries, and a few 'added-references' are used for alternative approaches to some documents. In addition, PI is one of the few codes to include specific instructions for various degrees of limited cataloguing. Filing instructions are also included.

The bibliographic unit is usually very limited, partly because of the use of the 'real title', explained below, and partly because, for example, a work such as Cowper's translation of Homer's *Odyssey* would receive its main entry under COWPER, not the original author.

An idea of the way PI operates is illustrated by the following brief summaries of its treatment of four major categories: Corporate works; Anonymous works; Pseudonymous works; and Periodicals.

The most outstanding feature of PI is that it does not recognise the concept of corporate authorship. Works which the English-speaking world would regard as those of corporate authorship are treated either (*a*) as of personal authorship, e.g. entered under editor or the personal element of a firm's name; or (*b*) as anonymous works, as explained below.

Anonymous works. External sources are used to establish the authors of works published anonymously. To this extent, PI tends to collocate the works of an author, i.e. to broaden its bibliographic unit, to a greater degree than BM. If no author is ascertainable, the work is entered according to rather curious rules, which are unique to PI and probably more complex than BM's treatment of anonymous works. A 'real title' is worked out by selecting and possibly re-arranging certain key words from the title page title. Thus, *Revised statutes of the United States* has the real title *Statutes revised United-States*. This becomes the filing heading, and the body of the entry will then include a transcription of the title page as in English-language code cataloguing. Selection of words for the real title and the order in which they appear—so vital to the location of works in a catalogue—do not seem to English thinkers to have any recognisable system, which at least BM has for its entry words for anonymous works, however bizarre the system may seem.

For example, the British Museum's *General catalogue of printed books* receives the real title *Catalogue general books* but the *Short title catalogue of books printed in England* has for its real title *Short-title-catalogue books England*.

So, these two works do not have their entries collocated, e.g. by the choice of 'catalogue' as an entry word for both, yet both have something in common. On the other hand, there does not seem to be any rule for systematically selecting the entry word. Thus, both 'soughtness' and collocation seem to be defeated.

Pseudonymous works are treated rather similarly as by BM. If the pseudonym has become established through usage, entry is under that. But in case of doubt the real name of the author is preferred.

Periodicals are always treated as anonymous works, even if an editor is named. The principle here is approximately the same as in other codes, except that other codes allow corporate entry in varying degrees depending on either apparent intellectual responsibility or sought names in titles. The earliest form of title is used as a basis for the real title, corresponding in principle to BM, and presumably for the same reason—that both codes were designed for use with a printed catalogue.

The rules used here to exemplify PI make it appear more unorthodox, to English-speakers, than in fact it is: many other rules are similar to those in other codes, which is why they are not dwelt on here.

Dr Osborn makes three criticisms of PI in the Introduction to his translation:

(a) Rules are too complicated.
(b) Too few references are allowed. (It has to be remembered that the degrees of limited cataloguing prescribed in PI are mandatory.)
(c) Too many titles do not lend themselves readily to the prescribed formulae.

However, (a) may well be applied to almost all other codes, while (b) is a failing in many libraries' catalogues, irrespective of which codes they use. The main complaint against PI seems to be—even to German thinkers, apparently—the unsatisfactory treatment of corporate and anonymous works. However, ICCP in 1961 adopted principles which if implemented will take care of this complaint.

PI has been important for two very good reasons:

(a) It facilitated the compilation of a pioneering national union catalogue.
(b) It has ventilated alternative methods of entering anonymous works and works of 'diffuse authorship' and has therefore served a useful academic and practical purpose. It has made us think.

CHAPTER 6

Codes: Twentieth Century

*Cutter 4th Edition; Anglo-American 1908; American Library Association
1949; Library of Congress Rules for Descriptive Cataloging; Vatican*

CUTTER

CUTTER provides one of the most thought-provoking sets of source
material—the other being Lubetzky. Only the 4th edition is easily
available, but his evolving thoughts are described in LUBETZKY, excerpted in OLDING, and these should be read. If Hamlet is the story of a
man who could not make up his mind, then Cutter was the cataloguer's
Hamlet. But with the essential difference that there has been a resolving
sequel in the form of Lubetzky.

In discussion here, CUTTER means the fourth edition, 1904.

CUTTER is probably the most comprehensive code, apart from
VATICAN. Its overall arrangement is logical. It includes rules for the form
and entry of personal authors, corporate authors, and titles; main entries,
added entries, and references; description; subject and form; limited
cataloguing and filing; definitions; and certain special materials:
manuscripts, music, maps, and atlases, and even an acknowledgement
of paintings, drawings, and statues as 'bibliographic' units. The rules
are accompanied by a great deal of lively discussion, much of it still very
relevant today.

CUTTER's influence is evident in AA 1908, especially the American
alternatives, and this influence was carried further in ALA 1949. Despite
Lubetzky's originality of thought, CUTTER probably influenced his
CCR 1960 more than any other single code.

Here we are mainly concerned with CUTTER's rules for author and
title entry; the rules for subject entry and reference will be discussed in
Section III, on the Subject approach.

Perhaps the most basic guiding principle of CUTTER is the convenience
of the user—that the cataloguer should follow public usage and not
shape it. Because of this, it is no wonder that we shall find Coates
disagreeing so often with CUTTER when we reach subject cataloguing.
CUTTER assumes that the catalogue is there for the public, and not only

for the librarian—something to do with democracy perhaps, the first edition having come out during the centenary of American Independence. Such a principle militates directly against that of the rigid rule, and it is in the (comparatively few) cases of conflict between these two principles that much of the discussion has centred in the past. There seems to be some feeling against CUTTER in Britain, perhaps because the British tended to stick to the rigidity of AA 1908 over a period of about sixty (glorious?) years, while the Americans have always tended more towards permissiveness in author entry—witness CUTTER itself, the American alternatives in AA 1908, ALA 1949, and finally Lubetzky's CCR. Ironically, however, it is in AACR that the British, and not the North American, text has more followed public usage—perhaps a reflection of 'swinging' British attitudes in the 1960's?

CUTTER further analyses, discusses and then consolidates corporate authorship. One interesting result is that laws, etc., are entered under their authors, i.e. legislative bodies, and do not receive form entry as in other codes. As in its subject rules, there is some indecision over the position, if any, which place should occupy in the heading, with the result that many cases and even individual bodies are given their own rules. The downward path towards the distinction between societies and institutions is started on, to reach its depth of casuistic rationalisation in ALA 1949. This could be regarded as one of CUTTER's bad influences, but he was actually teetering on the edge of the type of solution produced by AACR British Text, i.e. normal direct entry. But in other instances of corporate authorship, CUTTER advocates inverted entry: a ruse to bring out terms which he thought would be more sought, e.g. CHRISTIAN ENDEAVOUR, YOUNG PEOPLE'S SOCIETY OF. Here we reach the point of unashamed quasi-subject entry—and in a code for a dictionary catalogue too.

Change of name of corporate authors, although dealt with rather casually and by precedent (R. 93 Conventions, etc.), established the 'best known form' formula, which Lubetzky revived in his CCR 1960 and which manifests itself in a variety of conditions and contexts in AACR.

However, under Periodicals (R. 133), changes of name may, if desired, be treated by the now well-known 'consecutive' entry with connecting references, although CUTTER's first preference was for earliest form.

Latitude is allowed also in the treatment of other changes of name, cited cases being married women and noblemen, although in cases of doubt, positive guidance is given—contradictively, earliest for married women and latest for noblemen!

CUTTER's treatment of pseudonymous works also makes interesting reading. He allowed entry under pseudonym, including merely initials, in cases of established usage, but in case of doubt the decision is for the real name, the reason being that, as time goes by, the real name becomes better known. Some doubt over this assumption is demonstrated in ALA 1949, which prophesied wrongly (to date anyway) by entering Mark Twain under CLEMENS.

CUTTER's bibliographic unit is broader than that of either BM or PI. Anonymous works are entered under their authors when these are known, and, if one likes, even in cases of attributed authorship. Other works receive first word entry (not an article), which Panizzi wanted decades before, but he was over-ruled by the Trustees of the British Museum. This was the first time that such a direct form of entry was unequivocally chosen in one of the main codes. CUTTER, like BM, established what we now call uniform titles for 'anonymous classics' (ALA 1949 term), e.g. BIBLE, including the collocation of excerpts and translations under the title of the whole work. He gave the KORAN title entry (the sought form) also, but it is characteristic of his perception and respect for academic accuracy that he included a reference to it from Mohammed.

CUTTER's first word entry is applied to periodicals (compare BM's cumbersome form entry), and he shows a working towards a Lubetzky-type condition by realising that they may be regarded as anonymous works. His breadth of bibliographic unit (presumably the most sought form) is further enhanced by his rule that selections from periodicals also go under the title of the periodical. Here he does not practise uniform title entry, but uses an inverted form, e.g. PUNCH, A BOWL OF. However, periodicals which change their titles receive consecutive entry, with a second preference for collocation under first title.

It is hoped that enough has been said here to demonstrate CUTTER's importance. Recognition of his influence on Lubetzky has not yet been acknowledged fully. This interesting aspect of code development may be pursued by reading the article by Paul DUNKIN cited on page 28.

AA 1908

Although sometimes referred to as 'international', this code was in fact bilateral in its compilation. Nevertheless, it became the most standard code for English-speaking countries until ALA 1949 supplanted it in most of them, other than Britain. Despite the publication of AACR in 1967, it is still of practical value because many of its rules for choice of heading were used in BNB from 1950 to 1967. It is of value in academic study as being: (*a*) among the more rigid, i.e. less permissive, codes; and (*b*) an example of a 'case' code, but with the disadvantage of enumerating comparatively few cases. For this reason, use of it requires consistent skill in applying precedents and analogies between cases named and those not named but encountered in practice. The value of some of the examples included is doubtful since quite a few are rather rare, old or foreign-language works.

It deals with choice and form of personal and corporate author and title main entry headings, added entries, references, and description, including some Library of Congress supplementary rules. It incorporates a list of definitions, although there are some noteworthy omissions, e.g. of societies and institutions as categories of corporate authorship; also it has a list of abbreviations stating where they may be used; and several transliteration alphabets. A final rather unusual feature among the codes studied here is a supplement of sample entries and layouts.

The overall arrangement is reasonably satisfactory, remembering that it is a 'case' code, e.g. all rules for corporate authorship are in the same section. But the fact that it is a case code means that some rules dealing with the same or similar conditions are separated, e.g. Rule 2 deals with joint author entry, but Rule 126 includes composite works (in the section on Title entry) although nowadays we should include both in the condition of Shared authorship.

In many of its rules the Code aims at academically correct headings, and those which are most closely associated with true intellectual responsibility, e.g. pseudonyms are not allowed, whether or not they are well known, the only obvious exception being when the real name cannot be discovered. A similar rule applies to works issued anonymously. Again, even in cases of 'diffuse authorship', the tendency is to prefer some form of author entry rather than 'cleaner' title entry, e.g. cyclopaedias and dictionaries go under name of editor, unless 'decidedly' better known by their titles.

Another characteristic is a preference for earliest forms, e.g. of names of married women and noblemen; and of titles of periodicals. This practice seems to be an unconscious hang-over from previous codes intended for printed catalogues, although elsewhere in the code, card-form is assumed.

The bibliographical unit is broad, on the whole, as already exemplified by the collocation of main entries of all works by an author, whatever the title pages say, also by the collocation of a translation or other version of an anonymous work with the original, e.g. Bible, and by the tendency to prefer the original author as main entry for works which have been extensively revised. This 'author unit' is sometimes carried to inaccurate limits, e.g. a concordance to an author's work is entered under the author concordanced, and thematic catalogues are entered under the composer concerned—in effect alphabetical-subject entry in an author/title code.

However, academic accuracy re-asserts itself with librettos, which are entered under librettist; and maps, which are entered under cartographers: a more sought (but technically inaccurate) choice in the former would have been the relevant composer, and in the latter, some form of subject or place entry.

Inevitably, there are many exceptions to these generalisations, since the code was compiled piecemeal and not according to basic 'conditions'. The few American exceptions normally relate to important principles, e.g. the ALA rule for concordances specifies entry under compiler, although, strangely, no parallel exception is made for thematic catalogues. In instances of changes of name, the ALA tends to prefer latest, e.g. in the general rule (Rule 40), and in the case of married women (Rule 41), and—but less decidedly—in the case of 'princes of the blood' (Rule 32). The ALA also decided for the latest form of a periodical whose title is changed (Rule 121). A footnote to the rule for pseudonyms (Rule 38) mentions the Library of Congress practice of using well-known pseudonyms as headings, and it also allows use of a pseudonym when it represents two or more joint authors; however, not even the ALA endorsed this daring modernity.

Corporate authorship is dealt with under the now-infamous categories of government publications, societies, institutions (establishments), and miscellaneous.

Government publications are entered more directly than in BM—intermediate stages in hierarchies may normally be omitted. Intellectual responsibility gives way to form headings for laws, etc., unlike CUTTER. A concessionary *see* reference is made from the true corporate author, e.g. U.S. *Congress* in the case of laws, but not for other form headings, e.g. constitutions, treaties, and charters. This technical inaccuracy of form instead of corporate author entry has remained, even in Lubetzky's CCR, but in this case perhaps because he unconsciously catered for a dictionary catalogue, thus obviating multiple entry.

Societies are entered under name, but a footnoted and traditionally ignored alternative allows entry of societies with localities in their names under the locality. There are various exceptions and variations, one being that guilds (though societies) are entered under name of city, yet political parties are entered under their name direct.

Institutions are entered under place. But one vital exception is that if the body's name begins with a 'proper noun or adjective' it goes under its name. The only examples given are of institutions in Britain or the U.S. There follow two suggested modifications: (*a*) to extend this rule to all institutions with distinctive names; or (*b*) to confine the rule to Britain and the U.S. Cataloguing history thus hung poised on a razor edge—but it fell the wrong way and in ALA 1949 the second modification was crystallised. And so the many exceptions, qualifications and rationalisations piled up; e.g. state schools go under name of place, but private British and American schools are entered under name 'when this begins with a proper noun or adjective'. Now, sixty years after, we can guess that the underlying reason for such rules was that British and American 'proper nouns and adjectives' were distinctive to people whose mother tongue was English. But it took a Lubetzky, when talking of similar rules in ALA 1949 which extended the rules to include the British Empire, to point out the absurdity of hingeing cataloguing rules to the political fortunes of the British Empire. Cutter's misbegotten quasi-corporate author of the 'BOSTON. *Citizens*' type was perpetuated in AA 1908 and on into ALA 1949.

BM had its zenith in the form of its rule of precedence for entry of anonymous works. AA 1908's equivalent is the rule for Exploring expeditions (Rule 111) which reaches Heinz-length proportions in the varieties of headings available and takes up one page of the total of 61 pages devoted to actual rules. This is probably one of the prime examples of the 'minor cases' explosion—societies and institutions being the prime example of a major case. But this book's prize for the most useless rule goes to Rule 3: Dissertations, which, including two supplementary Library of Congress rules, takes up three pages.

BNB's use of AA 1908 is dealt with in Section V, on Centralisation of cataloguing services.

ALA 1949

During the three years before the Second World War, the British and Americans had started preparations for a revised AA code, but the British then became preoccupied with a rather larger international event, with the result that the revision emerged as an ALA draft in 1941; it covered, like AA 1908, both author/title headings and description.

The rules for author/title entry were further revised and embellished and published in 1949. The description part was not continued with, and was replaced by a separate work: LCRDC 1949. This pair, known to the initiated as the Red Rules and the Green Rules, thus became the basic combined code for most of the English-speaking world; a few British libraries adopted or partly adopted them, some using them as a sort of long stop on the occasions when AA 1908 failed. In fact, AA 1908 and ALA 1949 could be used in conjunction with each other, without too much conflict, especially in libraries which had evolved towards the ALA alternatives in AA 1908.

There are two good reasons for knowing ALA 1949:

1. It is applied in the Library of Congress printed catalogues, which are widely used all over the world, but especially in English-speaking countries. It is also largely applied in many trade and specialised bibliographies and other printed catalogues and lists of American origin, as well as bibliographies and catalogues from other parts of the English-speaking world, including Canada, Australia, and in some cases South Africa.

In fact, AACR North American Text is only gradually being introduced into Library of Congress cataloguing, and in any case it is far more like ALA 1949 than is the British Text.

2. It is the ultimate in 'case' codes, being the immediate object of Lubetzky's critical attention. Therefore, to understand fully the new 'conditions' approach one needs to know exactly what Lubetzky was demolishing.

It assumes the unit card, which is probably the best way of making added entries. Students justifiably have been confused by the two types of reference encountered in previous codes, namely the heading-to-heading reference and the work-to-work reference.

However, it tends to assume a dictionary catalogue: when added subject entries are needed, these are assumed to be under alphabetical-subject headings. Generally, this need not inconvenience the classified cataloguer, though in a few instances the structure of a corporate author's headings may violate the principles of the subject index to a classified catalogue if it is constructed according to chain procedure. In such cases, it is suggested that the chain procedure rather than the author heading construction should give way.

Unlike AA 1908, it does not include description.

Compared with AA 1908 it identifies and gives rules for many more cases. Some of these are quite likely to be actually used, e.g. works whose intellectual responsibility is a spirit, Rule 11, Mediumistic writings—in fact this rule manifests prejudice since it puts such works under medium as main entry. Other cases are less likely to be in hot demand, e.g. U.S. volunteer fire companies, and the Basilion Monastery at Mt. Sinai.

The form of personal author headings is more complicated than in AA 1908, since dates of birth and death are mandatory. Also, where there is a choice between a popular form of a classical writer and an academically correct form, the latter usually triumphs. So, we still have monstrosities like HOMERUS, not HOMER (Rule 58), and ARISTOTELES, not ARISTOTLE (Rule 31). But perhaps the ultimate is reached in Rule 31:

THEOTOCOPULI, Dominico, *called* El Greco, d. 1614

the only saving grace being a reference from El Greco.

ALA 1949 gives more definitions and specifications than AA 1908. In fact, those on anonymous and pseudonymous works define, extend and exemplify these cases to the point that it becomes increasingly difficult to distinguish between them; e.g. a work by 'The Prig' is pseudonymous (Rule 30), while one by 'A lover of justice' is anonymous (Rule 32). But it may be unfair to generalise overmuch on the strength of such examples, for these rules cover several quite well-known categories excluded from AA 1908, despite their presence in BM and CUTTER, e.g. initials on their own, and obviously artificial but pronounceable names like ACUTUS.

There is a considerable increase in the number of corporate authorship rules, yet the term itself is still not adequately defined, as opposed to exemplified, either in the rules themselves or in the Glossary. The four main categories of corporate authorship of AA 1908 are perpetuated. Societies and Institutions are defined, but the definitions are really retrospective rationalisations of the existing rules for the two artificial categories, that is, that societies may be entered under name because they need not be in a particular place, while institutions must be entered under place because they have plant and buildings requiring a particular location. As in AA 1908, but even more so, the categories are sub-categorised, exemplified and excepted to the point of confusion—because, of course, the wrong characteristics are used to establish the categories—as already shown—and then attempts made to sub-catego-rise: until one finishes up with individual named buildings having rules of their own.

However, many of the rules are potentially more useful—to a careful cataloguer—than in AA 1908, because often the cataloguer is allowed to use his own judgement. But then there is the disadvantage of lack of explanation on how conditions arise, including how names appear on title pages, while there is rarely any advice on what criteria to use in exercising judgement. For these reasons, examples sometimes appear to contradict the rules, e.g. a pseudonym may be used as entry term if it 'has become fixed in literary history' (Rule 30), though earlier in the same rule Mark Twain is entered under CLEMENS, Samuel Langhorne; yet probably 'Mark Twain' has become fixed in literary history.

Both the overall and the rule-by-rule arrangement is much better than in AA 1908, e.g. 'Works of doubtful or unknown authorship' includes juxtaposed rules for Pseudonymous works, Spurious works and works of doubtful authorship, Anonymous works (general), and Anonymous classics. This group includes some cases which a 'con-ditions' code would place elsewhere, e.g. Adaptations of anonymous classics comes under 'Works of authorship of mixed character' in AACR along with other versions, revisions, etc. But, to judge ALA 1949 according to its own lights, the arrangement is very helpful. Again, rules for Works of joint authorship, Composite works and Collections and Serials are juxtaposed, and coincide for the most part with the contents of AACR's 'Works of shared authorship', 'Works produced under editorial direction', 'Collections', and 'Serials'. In fact, AACR is not foolproof, since, for example, one might regard Serials as being produced under editorial direction. However, AACR's introduction to its rules does clarify its meanings—to those who have the patience to read them, which they must or they cannot use the code properly.

This useful juxtaposition more readily reveals inconsistencies, e.g. that works of joint authorship are entered under 'the first-named on the title page', while composite works are entered under the author chiefly responsible.

Almost always, ALA 1949 prefers latest forms of names, titles, etc., but, characteristically, with a let-out if some other form is likely to be 'better known' or more established. One of the few exceptions is the case of the anonymous multi-volumed monographic work whose title varies in successive volumes, in which case the preferred rule is earliest form of title: but even so there is an escape clause for cases where the later title is 'decidedly better known'.

The bibliographic unit is broad, a characteristic normally associated with research or other academic libraries. So, an author is always a complete unit, whether earlier, later or best known. This accounts for the 'Alice' books being entered under DODGSON. Also, conventional titles are devised to provide a single entry point for versions, renderings, translation, excerpts, etc., for most complex anonymous works: Rule 33, Anonymous classics. Unlike CUTTER, ALA 1949 does not usually practise inversion to bring a significant word to the front, e.g. CHANSON DE ROLAND, not ROLAND, CHANSON DE. But, ARTHUR, *King* is used, perhaps because the person concerned is not always referred to as 'King' and there is great doubt about whether he was king anyway. Confusingly, the bibliographic unit does not cover complete cycles, except as an alternative.

ALA 1949 respects the 'intellectual responsibility' principle with reminders in relevant rules that added subject entries are also necessary. Examples are the rules for concordances, thematic catalogues, and maps and atlases.

The code includes rules for punctuation and style (but not examples of possible layouts of complete entries); a list of abbreviations; transliteration alphabets with particular emphasis on the system of the Soviet period; and a glossary, as already mentioned. The index is effective and satisfyingly comprehensive; but sometimes one remembers rules by examples given in the code, and an index of these would not have been a luxury.

As a 'case' code, one would conclude that it is quite comprehensive and satisfactory in use—far more so than AA 1908. The old order must change, but one cannot suppress a sneaking feeling of sympathy for the cataloguers who have come to know ALA 1949 practically cover to cover over decades and who now find themselves presented with not only a new code to learn, but also with a new dogma to accompany it.

LCRDC 1949

This code on description was intended as a companion to ALA 1949. It derived from a preliminary edition of 1947, but with the inclusion of parts of the draft code ALA 1941 and of parts of the Music Library Association's preliminary version of a *Code for cataloging music* of 1941.

The introduction to the work carefully defines descriptive cataloguing as ' . . . to apply not only to the description of an item but also to the choice and determination of the form of the headings' (p. 1). Nevertheless, as has been stated, ALA 1949 was used for the heading element, in conjunction with LCRDC. Since then, however, in Britain at least, the description part of an entry has usually been taken as covering only the parts of the entry other than the author (or title) heading. In this book, 'description' is used in the latter sense.

The introduction goes on to give an outline history of LC cataloguing rules from CUTTER'S first edition of 1876 to the publication of LCRDC itself. This brief account is interesting (especially when read between the lines) for its account of LC practice and evolution in relation to other powerful forces in the U.S., as represented by the American Library Association. It is noteworthy that it was the ALA which represented the differences in viewpoints, and not the Association of Research Libraries, which, on the surface at least, caused the abandonment of some of the radical principles intended as a basis for AACR.

Most of the content of LCRDC has been incorporated with revision into AACR—although with some minor differences between the British and North American texts. Therefore, only a brief account of it is given here.

Considerable space is devoted to descriptive detail for monographs. There is a clear statement of its purpose, followed by quite (over?) elaborate detail on each part of the entry, including tracings.

A few pages are devoted to offprints, etc., supplements and analytical entries, the latter being carefully defined. The layouts given can be interesting and useful to the beginner and to cataloguers who are overhauling their routines.

Serials receive a great deal of attention: as with monographs, there is more than enough detail for all libraries' needs.

Particularly noteworthy for a general code, is the inclusion of rules for various types of special materials: Maps, atlases and globes; Music scores; Facsimile copies; and Incunabula. At the time, these rules were particularly useful, obviating reference to special codes where they existed, or the compilation of local rules.

There is a concluding short section on 'History cards', showing the types of information which may be needed in authority files on corporate bodies. Some of the information recommended, e.g. changes of name with relevant dates, can still be of use under AACR, even though consecutive entry may be used in the actual catalogues.

The work has appendixes on Definitions, Capitalisation, Abbreviations, and Numerals.

Nowadays, there is a partial reaction against the type and depth of detail given in LCRDC—although the use of computers for the storage and retrieval of bibliographic data may result in the rehabilitation of description, including the use of description elements as approach terms. The code itself makes it clear that not all libraries will want the amount of detail included, and that it is up to each library to take what it needs—a principle adopted by AACR. It should be pointed out finally that, had it not been for the existence of the 'raw material' in LCRDC, AACR would have been even longer in gestation.

VATICAN

This code came about as part of the reorganisation of the very extensive Vatican Library in the 1920's, when it was decided in 1927 to establish a new (dictionary) catalogue. There had been an Italian code, of 1911, and this was added to from AA 1908. With the help of mainly American librarians, the whole was reworked and consolidated, the first edition of the emergent new code being published in 1931. This edition was translated into English, but the translation was not published because of the Second World War. Meanwhile, however, a second edition was being produced, being published in 1939. The work used here is the English translation of this: but at the time of writing it is out of print.

The Foreword claims the code as 'the most complete statement of American cataloging practice' (p.v), so it is unfortunate that the code should have been unavailable for such long periods to English-speaking librarians.

The code is noteworthy as being the only really complete code in one volume for printed books of the twentieth century. It includes (*a*) Author/title entry; (*b*) Description; (*c*) Subject entry; (*d*) Filing; and (*e*) Appendixes dealing with early printed books, abbreviations, glossary, transliteration, and sample cards. It also has a very detailed index. The English-language version has been adapted to some extent to English-language needs—particularly important for subject heading work; although the examples are often not typical of English-speaking countries' library stocks, English translations are usually included.

In the 1950's one would have pleaded for a serious consideration of the whole code by English-speaking countries, especially for libraries using dictionary catalogues. However, all of the main components have since been overtaken by events: (a) We have a new author/title and description code, catering also for many special materials not included in VATICAN; (b) There has been considerable new thought and practice in the alphabetical subject field (even though a wholly convincing code has not yet appeared); and (c) There has emerged a radically simple view of dictionary catalogue filing, in the second edition of the *ALA rules for filing catalog cards*. Therefore, one must regretfully leave the Vatican code with this brief mention as not being directly relevant in this work, but in the hope that in the future it will be possible to compare it in detail and at leisure with its more recent rivals. So we must be contented with the following brutally generalised conclusions:

(a) Author/title rules correspond approximately with ALA 1949.

(b) Description rules correspond approximately with the parts of LCRDC which deal with printed materials.

(c) Subject entry rules represent a 'case' codification of LC subject heading practice. These rules are dealt with in a little more detail in Section III of this work.

(d) Filing rules correspond approximately with the first edition of *ALA rules for filing catalog cards* with a tendency towards the more classed (less alphabetical) alternatives where these exist, with one important exception: subject subdivisions are sub-arranged alphabetically.

CHAPTER 7

The New Order?

Osborn; Lubetzky; Code of Cataloging Rules 1960; International Conference on Cataloguing Principles 1961; Anglo-American Cataloguing Rules 1967

Those who look at Britain from inside may think that nothing much happened to author/title codes for half a century after AA 1908. Many British libraries seem not to have obtained the ALA 1941 draft—although the present author saw it, for example, in little Tasmania. Few librarians seem to have read, or at least been struck by, A. D. Osborn's article 'Crisis in cataloging' of 1941, even though it was reprinted in Britain's *Library assistant* in 1942. And few seem to have been impressed at the time by Lubetzky's library-world-shaking pamphlet *Cataloging rules and principles* when it came out in 1953. (People are more interested in it now, and one cannot help wondering why the Library of Congress persists in not reprinting it.) It is a chastening thought that students were passing through at least some British library schools in the later 1950's and emerging as qualified librarians without apparently receiving much of an introduction to ALA 1949, let alone Lubetzky's radical criticism of it: in contrast, one Australian cataloguing examination, at least, had a whole question on a quotation derived from the Osborn article. Perhaps some of the schools were too bedazzled by the new look in the subject approach to bother with the parallel movement in author/title work. The few indications of interest were the occasional articles on code revision which appeared in the British professional press: and of course the work behind these.

In the event, the main value of the draft code of ALA 1941 seems to have been that it stimulated the Australian Dr Osborn's outburst, which, if only it had been heeded sufficiently—in the U.S. as well as in Britain—could have advanced cataloguing usefully by at least a decade. One does not necessarily agree with all of Osborn's statements—and he makes quite a few! But the chief messages of his article, to this writer at least, are:

(*a*) 'Rules for cataloguing would be relatively few and simple, partly

77

because they would not attempt to cover exceptional and unusual cases.'

(b) 'Non-essentials would be given little attention or passed over.'

(c) 'Cataloguers would be trained to use their judgement, not to expect a rule or a precedent to guide them at all turns.'

A final factor inferred by Osborn is that if cataloguers worked more along the lines mentioned above, they would be more respected by library administrators. A current crisis in cataloguing is that some cataloguers and teachers of cataloguing exasperate other librarians by their finickiness, with the result that too few of the required type of people become cataloguers—in fact, too many librarians are made catalogue-shy by their own leaders, who themselves feel that much of cataloguing is a cul-de-sac wrapped up in abstruse terminology.

Seymour Lubetzky seems to have appreciated this danger. In his *Cataloging rules and principles* he asked three main questions about each rule:

'1. Is it necessary?

2. Is it properly related to the other rules in the code?

3. Is it consistent in purpose and principle with the other rules?'

Having applied his questions to the contents of ALA 1949, he produced the final section of his work: 'Design for a code'. This could be summarised on one page, and it seems to embody almost all that one needs to make author/title heading decisions. It may be read in Olding's *Readings in library cataloguing*, p. 248-267. Much as one respects Lubetzky, however, even his findings and opinions are open to criticism and expression of difference of opinion.

Some audio-visual forms require different treatment from printed materials, e.g. a gramophone record whose chief unifying factor is a performer could best be entered under the performer, not title as inferred by the 'Design for a code'. However, this condition was in fact catered for in Lubetzky's own CCR 1960. But a film, for example, would almost certainly go under title, in the form used in the country of the library concerned. Also, one's own preference is for an earlier abandonment of respect for 'intellectual responsibility' in the various cases of 'more than one author', and entering under title.

CCR 1960, 'an unfinished draft', was for the most part an expansion of 'Design for a code'. Its chief omissions were special rules for non-printed materials, and of course rules for description. One might have hoped that it could have been finished, approved, published—and actually put into use. But this was not to be. Some librarians obviously still preferred the 'legalistic' style of code, while others feared the quantity of recataloguing which could result from the adoption of a new, radically different, code: presumably ignoring the possibility that it might ultimately save time, perhaps, to 'close-off' their existing catalogues and then to start new ones according to the new code.

CCR 1960 got into the hands of committees, who, one fears, kicked it around until it got lost. The committees gathered momentum, and not even the International Conference on Cataloguing Principles (referred to below) with its simple truths about catalogues and codes stopped them. Lubetzky gave up being Editor of the proposed new code; he left the Library of Congress; and he took up teaching cataloguing. One hopes that one day his name will be associated with that of Cutter as the two most important codifiers we have seen to date.

The International Federation of Library Associations sponsored an International Conference on Cataloguing Principles, which was held in Paris, 1961. It is worth recalling, again, that the principles worked out by Seymour Lubetzky virtually formed the basis for the discussion and evolution of the principles which emerged from the Conference.

The most useful version of the principles for the present purpose is the *Statement of principles . . . annotated edition with commentary and examples*, by A. H. Chaplin assisted by Dorothy Anderson, published by IFLA in 1966.

Most of the principles themselves may seem quite innocuous, and even so obvious as not to be worth stating, to the more sophisticated student of today. But it should be remembered that they did in fact affect the structure of heading decisions in AACR a great deal. And, they were internationally agreed. There is the hope therefore that they will be reflected in future codes, as has already happened with the *Prussian instructions*.

The principles are not a skeleton on which a complete code could be hung. They are confined to the author (or title) headings for printed books or similar materials in large general libraries, i.e. virtually the same as Lubetzky's terms of remit.

The first important statement is that a catalogue's functions are to ascertain: (*a*) if a library has a book when specified by author and title or their equivalent; and (*b*) the range of works and their editions by an author. The inference is that the first function is more important. As has been seen in the discussion of author/title problems, this can be a very important decision: it can considerably limit the bibliographic unit hence the construction of headings for certain documents of 'diffuse authorship'.

More than one entry may be needed, depending on the types of problem discussed in Chapter 3 of this work. At this point the commentary on the Principles goes into considerable detail on, e.g., the need for references from variant spellings and transliterations, with many examples.

'Kinds of entry' mentions the need for main entries, added entries and references.

The concept of uniform headings is accepted.

The function of different kinds of entry is discussed. This topic need not be enlarged on here, since it occurs throughout this work in many forms: basically it enlarges on the kinds of entry and need for uniform headings mentioned above. Again, the commentary includes a considerable number of examples, including pseudonyms and works with variant titles.

'Choice of uniform heading' is significant, since it establishes the principle of 'most frequently used' rather than legally correct or earliest form. Uniform titles in the language of the country of the library, not of the original country, are given in the examples.

The Principles then go on to types of author and document, e.g.

(a) Single personal author.

(b) Corporate bodies including when title entry should be used and the relevance of subordinate bodies—the commentators' plentiful examples can be very useful here. Also, the acceptance of the concept of corporate authorship was revolutionary for some countries.

(c) Multiple authorship—here we have the important (but arbitrary) decision that if four or more authors are named on the title page entry is under title.

(d) Collections, preference in general being for title entry although 'a large minority' preferred some form of author entry.

(e) Summary of use of Title entry, both main and added.

(f) Change of title of serials, resulting in successive, or consecutive, entry.

(g) Form entry—limited to international treaties, etc., with non-distinctive titles.

The final Principle is that multi-word surnames of personal authors should be entered according to usage of their own countries, or failing this, according to the language which they used. This has led to the work by A. H. Chaplin, *Names of persons*, already mentioned. This work symptomises an important contradiction in current code philosophy. The Conference started off to establish broad principles. Yet an outcome of it was this 'case' enumeration (along with others on uniform titles for anonymous classics and names of countries) with more detail than has been included in any previous code.

The stage was set, then, for the new Anglo-American code. It cannot be asserted that ICCP was a turning-point in code conception. Lubetzky had reached that. But it certainly consolidated internationally some of what Lubetzky had worked for on his own.

ANGLO-AMERICAN CATALOGUING RULES 1967

Here, 'AACR' infers British Text. When the North American text is intended, this is indicated (its variations, mainly in headings decisions, are few, but important).

AACR attempts to include rules for the compilation of catalogues, other than layouts of entries, etc., and subject work and filing: i.e. it includes author/title main entry headings, added entry headings and references, uniform titles for both title and author entry, description; and all of these in relation to any materials and forms, including three-dimensional ones. It caters for the entering of all these materials into one catalogue, and although underlying it is the assumption of a completely alphabetical catalogue, it can still be applied without modification to the author/title element(s) of a classified catalogue. It is written primarily for a large research library, but it is intended also for use in other types of library, e.g. the smaller public library. In sum, it is possible for AACR to be the only cataloguing tool, other than codes or guides for subject work and filing, required in any library.

It exhibits a systematic structure, rather like a classification schedule, working from the general to the particular. So, it names cataloguing 'conditions', defines them, and then exemplifies them with 'cases'. It then gives general rules for cataloguing them followed by more specialised rules for what might be called 'sub-conditions', and for what are unashamedly 'cases' of the type found in older codes. Its general-to-particular structure also attempts to ensure that the more general and simple conditions are dealt with before the more specialised and complex ones in the code as a whole. The code is divided into coherent chapters, but the numbering of rules does not reflect the relationships between the rules themselves, e.g. 'Works with Authorship of Mixed Character' are covered by rules numbered 7 to 18 inclusive. A form of systematic notation, as is used in the Music Library Association's *Code for cataloging music and phonorecords*, would have been more complicated but it would have demonstrated the relationship between rules, on which the efficient use of the whole code depends. However, relationships are pointed out in many instances by cross-references between the rules, usually from the particular back to the more general, e.g. Chapter 13 Music, starts with a reminder that Chapter 1 applies, the composer being regarded in each case as the 'author'.

As with the use of classification schedules, one inevitably relies on the index to give a direct reference to the required section of the main work. Many cataloguers will doubtless continue to think in terms of 'cases' and so will seek these in the index. Unfortunately, not all are included, even when wholly embraced by a 'condition', e.g. thematic catalogues (referred to in the code as 'thematic indexes') feature in the index only in relation to their use in the description of music entries. They appear to belong to the condition 'Related works', Rule 19, but there is no index reference from them to this rule, and they are not even instanced at the rule itself, although 13 other cases are mentioned, e.g. concordances.

Since AACR has been long awaited as the first 'conditions' code, it is disappointing to find that there are special rules for many 'cases': i.e. not merely as examples of conditions. The much-maligned categories of corporate authors are done away with (but not wholly in the North American text by any means, despite circumlocutions), but there is still a substantial number of 'Special Rules' (Rules 20-32) for 'Certain Legal Publications' and 'Certain Religious Publications'. There is also a batch of five 'Special Rules for Names in Certain Languages'. The height (or depth) of case enumeration is reached in this section, where there is a footnote taking up nearly half a page—out of a total of 327 pages for the whole code—listing 'Indonesian titles and honorific words'. It adds an explanation that the list is incomplete 'as only some of the more commonly used titles are listed'! It seems possible that such an emphasis on oriental names reflects not only the increase in the acquisition of Oriental works (perhaps under the American 'Title II' program), but also shows an effort to internationalise the code.

In the 'conditions' versus 'cases' argument, the code is about two-thirds conditions and one-third cases. Even so, many rules seem to be superfluous as they fit into the overall conditions structure of the Code; one set of examples is found in the 'Mixed' section, which repeats the basic rules in various ways to re-assure the cataloguer—who may, nevertheless, be confused by the 20-odd pages of rules and sub-rules.

The code tries to establish a consistent bibliographic unit which on the whole should prove approachable to many catalogue users. The unit is narrower than in ALA 1949, reinforcing Lubetzky's conclusion that the catalogue's main job is to enable the user to establish readily whether or not the library has the book he wants. For a start, AACR is apparently intended for public use, since choices of heading which correspond to 'the normal usage of educated persons' are aimed at (AACR Introduction, p. 1). Occasionally a personal author unit may be split, which even Lubetzky did not countenance in his 'Design for a code'. In many cases, past corporate authors with changed names are entered consecutively. On the other hand uniform titles are established to bring together, e.g. translations and excerpts of a work. Occasionally —rather unaccountably?—exceptions are sometimes found, e.g. a few well-known parts of the Bible receive direct, specific entry: *Lord's prayer, Ten commandments,* and *Miserere* are exemplified; but they are not cited in the index. A type of work which sometimes rather surprsingly receives direct entry is the 'version' or 'adaptation'; presumably 'intellectual responsibility' has asserted itself above 'soughtness' here. Examples are children's versions of adult works. In a library which has to practise strict limited cataloguing, perhaps doing away with most added 'collaborator' entries, it would surely be more useful to have all prose versions of, say, *Robinson Crusoe* under DEFOE rather than have them all scattered. A reader is more likely to use the original author as the approach term, especially as often any abridgement is required rather than a particular one. Degrees of abridgement can then be explained in the Notes.

Before leaving the question of bibliographic and author unit, it is worth pointing out that while AACR, especially British text, tends more to direct entry for authors than any previous code, modern British subject cataloguing and indexing tends the other way, to logically constructed (indirect) headings. Finally, personal author headings are made as absolutely short as possible short of confusion with another author having a similar name, e.g. ELIOT, T. S. is now—at last—'legal'.

While AACR succeeds on the whole in establishing consistent principles —and its exceptions are recognised as such—it rarely imposes rigidity.

To some cataloguers, this may be regarded as a disadvantage, that it is hard to state categorically that a heading is absolutely right or wrong. AACR respects Osborn's plea for the cataloguer to use his own judgement. But, unlike ALA 1949, the conditions are explained carefully, and the cataloguer is offered criteria by which he can sensibly make up his own mind. One is advised to be guided by, e.g., title page layout and typography, and by basic reference sources. The disadvantage is that, although a useful decision may result, a great deal of time could be spent on consulting all works of an author in the library, or all relevant reference sources. On the other hand, we can get away from the practice of the past when a main entry might be made out to satisfy the rule and then an added entry made to provide direct access to the document! AACR caters more for limited cataloguing than past codes on the whole: an exception is the 'versions' rule mentioned above.

An example of inconsistency in AACR's principle of the bibliographic unit is that a film is entered under the release title even when this is not the same as the original.

AACR caters in general for two types of permissiveness, in which the cataloguer uses his judgement. First (as in ALA 1949) there is considerable use of terms like 'best known', 'most used', etc. And, as we have seen, we are usually shown how to reach a conclusion. Second, in a few instances, alternative rules are given, e.g. a library may decide to 'split' an author into real name and pseudonym—obviously, once the choice has been made, it must be applied rigidly, in the case of each author at least. More such alternatives might have been useful, e.g. allowing the entry of certain excerpts under their own title rather than collecting them under the entry for the parent work: this might well be useful for music and records in children's and some public libraries.

AACR is an author/title code. Yet still it perpetuates some form headings from AA 1908 and ALA 1949, examples being among the 'Special' rules for 'Certain Legal Publications', e.g. Laws (but not bills!); Constitutions; and Treaties. If the principle of 'intellectual responsibility' is to be abandoned, and if AACR really prefers direct entry, surely title, or where it is relevant, short title would have been a more useful choice.

e.g. LONDON COUNTY COUNCIL (GENERAL POWERS) ACT, 1892

rather than

GREAT BRITAIN. *Laws, statutes, etc.*
London County Council (general powers) act 1892.

If form entry is to be used for laws, etc., a slightly less cumbersome even if less accurate subheading would have been merely 'Laws'. Further, as with other sub-headings traditionally used since BM days, why italicise? As already touched upon in Chapter 4, part 5 (c), Gorman believes these are not in fact form headings: the reader should think about what form such headings would take (e.g. in a form/subject catalogue) and make up his own mind.

AACR assumes the unit entry principle, a reasonable enough assumption in these days of central and cooperative cataloguing. There is at least one rather unaccountable exception to this: e.g. a reference is to be made from the book on which a musical is based to the main entry heading used for the musical. A concomitant to the bibliographic unit used in the code is the frequent use of Author-title, or Composer-title references; the use of added entries in the many instances in which these occur would cause unnecessary lack of economy.

AACR uses a novel form of demonstrating its examples. First, a transcript of the relevant part of title page is given. This would have been useful in any code, but it is particularly necessary in AACR, which takes title pages into account to such an extent. Second, solutions are not always given in the form in which they would appear in the catalogue. One may be told, e.g. 'Main entry under Britten. Added entry (author-title) under Plomer' (p. 37), and if the cataloguer has not yet learnt how to construct the type of heading in question, he must turn to the relevant rules and find out. Probably a small amount of space is saved overall, but not enough to warrant the extra inconvenience, until one gets used to the constructions used.

SUMMARY OF AACR

It probably takes longer to get used to than previous codes. However, once it is familiar, it is easier to apply than previous codes. This is because it is more consistent in principle than other codes.

However, the great detail deplored by Osborn and Lubetzky in the past still persists. In addition to examples already mentioned, one should mention the minuteness of the rules for description. Nevertheless, these rules result in more useful information put in a more useful way than in past codes, e.g. 'Operative' date of a work is brought into the

Imprint, in the form '1960 (1962 reprint)'. Also, the detail on added entries—titles especially—is of direct practical value.

Some cataloguers will dislike the degree of permissiveness allowed. However, apart from the alternative rules, this is a matter rather of allowing cataloguers to work towards an acceptable solution using their own initiative, and it is unfair to assert that this will result in more deviations than resulted from AA 1908 and ALA 1949. But if many deviations do result, this could indeed be unfortunate in these days of closer international cooperation in shared cataloguing and similar activities.

Sometimes the splitting of the bibliographical unit may have been taken too far, as already exemplified.

Index includes some 'cases', but not others.

Solutions in examples do not always show actual form of heading.

The retention of unnecessary case enumeration has already been commented upon.

Filing rules would have been useful, especially with the formalisation of the Uniform title for say [Works] and similar collocations.

Lubetzky's plea (CCR 1960) for performer as main entry in phono-records of 'diffuse authorship' has been ignored. This can result in unsought headings and unnecessary added entries in many instances, of both 'serious' and 'pop' music.

More discussion and definition of what Lubetzky called the 'corporate complex' might have been useful. It is not wholly clear if 'groups' consisting of a few named personalities are corporate or not.

BNB's use of AACR is dealt with in Section V on Centralisation of cataloguing services.

AACR NORTH AMERICAN TEXT: THE CHIEF VARIATIONS

AACR North American Text is less radical in its approach to rules which could result in a great number of amendments in catalogues, i.e. if the old catalogue were not 'closed off'. This seems strange for a country which is so radical in its approach to physical forms of catalogues, e.g. in the introduction of computers into catalogue production.

The chief difference is in the retention of a considerable degree of the old 'institution' category, resulting in place as entry word. Another major difference is the retention of a broader bibliographic unit, hence more indirect headings than in the British Text.

In a few cases, the American choices could possibly be rationalised on grounds of soughtness, e.g. LONDON. *University* might more readily be located than the less significantly introduced UNIVERSITY OF LONDON. However, a reading of the North American variants makes one realise that in fact we are back in the old days of rules being formulated to fit not only types of bodies but even for individual names of bodies.

The North American Text makes the use of 'designations' in headings mandatory and not optional as in the British text, e.g. *ed.*, *tr.* This can be useful, since it may obviate repetition of detail in the author statement, but of course the British Text does not forbid it.

Entry for serials tends away from title entry towards corporate author entry, which seems unfortunate because, if anything, even the British Text allows too much incursion of 'diffuse authorship' factors. Here the ICCP principle is virtually negated.

In general, if it is two cheers for AACR British Text, it is only about one and a half cheers for the North American Text.

Potential revisions of both texts of AACR have been in hand right from the dates of publication of each text. At the time of writing, those from Britain have been only recommendations, made by the Cataloguing Rules Sub-Committee of the Cataloguing and Indexing Group of the Library Association. The Sub-Committee is issuing news-sheets (e.g. the first in March 1969), and announcements are made in the Group's journal *Catalogue and index*. Some additions and changes to the North American text have already been approved by the American Library Association: a substantial number appear in the Library of Congress' Cataloging Service's *Bulletin*, no. 83, Sept, 1968, for example. These range from 'legalistic' details to quite substantial amendments, e.g. that a new Chapter 12 will be issued separately entitled 'Motion pictures, filmstrips, and similar audio-visual works'. The British attitude seems to feel some disquiet at the 'inconsistent' or 'unsatisfactory solution' put forward and adopted in some American cases, as is demonstrated in 'Revising the rules', in *Catalogue and index*, no. 13, Jan. 1969, p. 3.

It is probably evident by now that the opinion of the present writer is that, if anything, AACR should be reduced, and not expanded upon detail by detail ad infinitum. Unfortunately, the Sorcerer's Apprentice is still at large.

SECTION III

SUBJECT CATALOGUING AND INDEXING

Subject Cataloguing and Indexing

As in Section II, to obviate repetitious footnotes, works cited in this section are listed here, where, with necessary, the abbreviations used when they are cited in the text. Codes and other directly relevant works are given first, followed by a second sequence of readings, both in alphabetical order. Other readings are cited in QUIGG, especially chapter 6.

Codes and readings cited

AUSTIN, DEREK. Subject retrieval in UK MARC, *in* Library Association. *Cataloguing and Indexing Group.* Seminar on MARC, Southampton University, March 1969.

BRITISH NATIONAL BIBLIOGRAPHY, 1950– .   BNB
Vital as source material for examples of all sorts.

BNB MARC Documentation service publications, no. 3.
For information on PRECIS: BNB subject descriptors.

BRITISH TECHNOLOGY INDEX, 1962– .   BTI
Pioneering example of modern 'formularised' subject approach; from 1968 includes punctuation indicating relationships between terms.

CLASSIFICATION RESEARCH GROUP. Bulletin no. 9, *in* Journal of documentation, vol. 24, no. 4, Dec. 1968; especially pages 281-290.
Background to PRECIS: BNB subject descriptors.

COATES, E. J. Subject catalogues: headings and structure. London: L.A., 1960.   COATES
Essential reading. Paperback reprint available to members of L.A. at 16s.

COATES, E. J. The use of BNB in dictionary cataloguing, *in* Library Association record, vol. 59, no. 6, June 1957, p. 197-202.

CUTTER. (Details given in readings at start of Section II.)

ENGLISH Electric thesaurofacet: faceted classification and thesaurus in engineering and related subjects, 4th ed. . . . Whetstone, Leicester: English Electric Co. Ltd., 1970.

FARRADANE, J. E. L. A scientific theory of classification and indexing and its practical applications, *in* Journal of documentation, vol. 6, no. 2, p. 83-99, and vol. 8, no. 2, p. 73-92.

FOSKETT, A. C. A guide to personal indexes, using edge-notched and peek-a-boo cards. London: Bingley, 1967.   FOSKETT

HAYKIN, D. J. Subject headings: a practical guide. Washington: U.S. Government Printing Office, 1951.   HAYKIN

KENNEDY, R. F. Classified cataloguing: a practical guide. Capetown: A. A. Balkema, 1966.

LIBRARY OF CONGRESS. Subject headings used in the Library of Congress, 7th ed. Washington: L.C., 1966.   LC

MEDICAL SUBJECT HEADINGS. Bethesda, Maryland: National Library of Medicine. (MESH); and supplementary Notes for medical cataloguers, issued occasionally.

METCALFE, JOHN. Subject classifying and indexing of libraries and literature. Sydney: Angus and Robertson, 1959.   METCALFE

   Particularly interesting when read in conjunction with COATES.

OLDING, R. K. The form of alphabetico-specific subject headings, and a brief code, *in* Australian library journal, vol. 10, no. 3, July 1961, p. 127-137.

OLDING, R. K. Readings in library cataloguing. (Details given in reading list to Section II.)   OLDING

   Especially p. 141-162: Kaiser's Systematic indexing.

PETTEE, JULIA. Subject headings: the history and theory of the alphabetical subject approach to books. New York: H. W. Wilson, 1946.

QUIGG, PATRICK. Theory of cataloguing. (Details in Section II.)
                                                                            QUIGG

SEARS list of subject headings, especially 9th ed., ed. by Barbara Marietta Westby; with Suggestions for the beginner in subject heading work, by Bertha Margaret Frick. New York: H. W. Wilson, 1965.
                                                                            SEARS

SHARP, JOHN R. Some fundamentals of information retrieval. London: Deutsch, 1965.

SHERA, JESSE H. The classified catalog: basic principles and practices, by Jesse H. Shera and Margaret E. Egan. . . . Chicago: A.L.A., 1956.
                                                                      SHERA & EGAN

THESAURUS of engineering and scientific terms: a list of engineering and related scientific terms and their relationships for use as a vocabulary reference in indexing and retrieving technical information. New York: Engineers Joint Council, 1967.

VATICAN code. (Details in Section II.)   VATICAN
WILSON, T. D. Dissemination of information, by T. D. Wilson and
J. Stephenson; 2nd ed. rev. London: Bingley, 1969. SBN 85157 062 3.

Reference may also be needed to certain classification schemes, especially DEWEY DECIMAL CLASSIFICATION (DC), UNIVERSAL DECIMAL CLASSIFICATION (UDC), and that of the Library of Congress.

Further readings

A.L.A. rules for filing catalog cards . . . Chicago: A.L.A., 1942, and 2nd ed., 1968; also 2nd ed. abridged, 1968.

ASHWORTH, WILFRED. Handbook of special librarianship and information work, 3rd ed., ed. by Wilfred Ashworth. London: ASLIB, 1967.

AUSTIN, DEREK. The new general faceted classification . . ., *in* Catalogue and index, no. 14, April 1969, p. 11-13.

AUSTIN, DEREK. Prospects for a new general classification, *in* Journal of librarianship, July 1969.

These provide useful background to PRECIS: BNB subject descriptors.

CORNWALL, G. ST C. British technology index as a basis for the subject catalogue, *in* Catalogue and index, no. 12, Oct. 1968, p. 8-10.

CORRIGAN, PHILIP R. D. An introduction to Sears List of subject headings. London: Bingley, 1967. SBN 85157 002 X.

COSTELLO, J. C. Coordinate indexing. New Brunswick: Rutgers University Press, 1966.

DOUGHTY, D. W. Chain procedure subject indexing and featuring a classified catalogue, *in* Library Association record, vol. 57, no. 5, May 1955, p. 173-178.

DUNKIN, PAUL S. Cataloging: U.S.A. Chicago: A.L.A., 1969.

Especially chapter 5: What is it about? Subject entry.

JACKSON, SIDNEY L. Long files under LC subject headings, and the LC classification, *in* Library resources and technical services, vol. 11, no. 2, Spring 1967, p. 243-245.

JOLLEY, L. The principles of cataloguing. (Details given in Section II.)

LANCASTER, F. WILFRED. Information retrieval systems: characteristics, testing, and evaluation. New York, London: John Wiley, 1968. SBN 471 51240 O.

MANN, MARGARET. Introduction to cataloging and the classification of books, 2nd ed. Chicago: A.L.A., 1943.

Useful introduction to 'conventional' dictionary catalogue, but some of the information given on the classified catalogue is suspect.

METCALFE, JOHN. Alphabetical subject indication of information. New Brunswick: Rutgers University Press, 1965.

METCALFE, JOHN. Anderson, *in* Library resources and technical services, vol. 11, no. 4, Fall 1967, p. 405-408.

Historical background on the dictionary catalogue, in Australia.

MILLS, JACK. Chain indexing and the classified catalogue, *in* Library Association record, vol. 57, no. 4, April 1955, p. 141-148.

MILLS, JACK. Guide to the use of UDC, *in* British Standards Institution. Guide to the Universal decimal classification. 1963. Especially chapter 7: The alphabetical subject index, p. 33-41.

NORRIS, DOROTHY MAY. A history of cataloguing . . . London: Grafton, 1939.

PARSONS, EDWARD ALEXANDER. The Alexandrian Library, glory of the Hellenic world . . . New York: Elsevier Publishing Co., 1952.

Especially p. 206-218, dealing with the classified catalogue of Callimachus: The Pinakes.

RECORD, P. D. Some rules for subject entry in the dictionary catalogue, *in* Association of Assistant Librarians. West Midland Division. Cataloguing and classification: some aspects. 1960.

SHERRIE, HEATHER. Short list of subject headings; compiled by Heather Sherrie and Phyllis Mander Jones. Sydney: Angus and Robertson, 1950.

A 'conventional' list; particularly noteworthy for its lists of common sub-headings.

TAUBE, MORTIMER. Studies in coordinate indexing. Washington: Documentation Inc., 1953.

CHAPTER 8

The Subject Approach: Introduction

One of the basic objects of the catalogue (including bibliographies and other records of documents), as stated by Cutter and every other author on cataloguing since, is the need for a subject approach. It is salutory to remember that subject requests in whatever type of library can be the hardest to deal with satisfactorily. Substantiation could be quoted for all types of library. For example, subject request forms in British county libraries usually need far more detail than author requests. This is mainly because there may not be a fully qualified and experienced librarian on the spot to find out: (a) the specific subject required—the enquirer wants 'British diesel-electric locomotives as used on the Southern Region' but asks for just 'locomotives' or even 'trains'; (b) the particular aspect required—building, maintenance, their influence on the economics of communication, or just 'in general'; (c) the intelligence level at which required—lay, experienced, practical, theoretical, etc.; and (d) how much information is needed. One hopes that at a fully manned service point, the reference librarian or readers' advisor would conduct a (tactful) dialogue with the enquirer to elicit exactly what is required. But the ultimate result is the same. The requirements must be matched against the library's catalogue, hence its stock, or bibliographies and indexes, with a view to obtaining what is wanted.

Basically, there are four types of subject need:

1. A specific document is wanted, and the enquirer can remember only its subject, not its author or title.

2. A specific self-contained subject is required: the enquirer will then select one or more works from the range of those indicated by the catalogue, shelves, or bibliographies.

3. A range of related subjects is required, perhaps collateral ones like 'heat', 'light', and 'sound', or histories of the countries comprising Scandinavia.

4. One subject in relation to one or more other subjects (phase relationship) may be required, say the influence of politics on the spread of the Reformation.

5. And, the qualifying and quantifying provisions already mentioned may apply. One hopes that the catalogue can be of value in sorting out all these requirements.

Coates has summed up the overall requirements of subject catalogues as the twofold objective (COATES, p. 19 ff). Briefly this comprises (*a*) the specific, and (*b*) the generic: respectively (*a*) a specific subject, although it may be complex as in item 4 above; and (*b*) a range of related subjects. It is a handy label, since it can lead directly to the two types of catalogue commonly used: (*a*) the dictionary, whose primary function is the specific approach; and (*b*) the classified, whose primary function is the generic approach. However, as will be seen later, both components of the twofold objective can be hard to define and therefore to satisfy. Ideally, one wishes to find a heading in the subject catalogue which exactly matches the requirements of the reader. Those who think that this is straightforward should try to make up a subject heading in words, or in a classification scheme notation, exactly fitting all the components of the imaginary county library subject request already mentioned—and that is one of the simpler examples. A slightly more complicated one is a research paper entitled: *Physiological response of the dairy cow to heat stress and the effect on milk consumption and equilibrium* (Tasmania. Department of Agriculture, 1964). How one attempts to meet requests like these can be used as examples to be applied to the different types of catalogue and indexing systems to be detailed later. The realist will probably soon acknowledge that not all of the qualifying components, e.g. intellectual level required, can be conveniently put into a subject heading, whether in everyday, or natural, language or in some form of code. Recourse must often be had to other information in a catalogue entry, e.g. the notes, and the operative date of publication.

A further factor to be borne in mind is that one should not think of a library as necessarily comprising a collection of books in a classified order on open-access shelves, with an adjacent conventional dictionary or classified catalogue as a key to it. If this were the case, and if all requests were extremely simple, like 'where are your books on ballet?', there would be scarcely any trouble. However, several complications arise at once concerning the physical nature and disposition of most libraries' stocks:

1. Books may be shelved in a variety of sequences, some closed access, all of which need to be located via the catalogue.

2. Certain types of document may possibly not be in classified order. Some items may be shelved in accession order, e.g. closed-access films and gramophone records. Others may be in a series of size orders, e.g. up to six sequences in a large stack or regional cooperative storage depot. Some series may be filed in series order, perhaps by arbitrary numbers put on them by their publishers as they were issued, e.g. patents, some series of reports, H.M.S.O.'s Central Youth Employment's *Careers series*; while, say, the Board of Trade's *Hints to businessmen series* may be in arbitrary alphabetical order by the first place-names in their titles. Periodicals, and possibly other serials, may possibly be filed alphabetically by title since that is how they may most often be called for; in any case the broad class marks given to a whole run of a periodical may bear little relationship to the multitude of individual, specific subjects covered by the articles in it.

It becomes apparent, then, that a variety of types of subject approach may become necessary within even one library service point:

1. Some materials may be self-indexing, e.g. fugitive material like newspaper cuttings or illustrations kept in filing cabinets. They may be in alphabetical-subject order, or they may be in classified order with an alphabetical subject index.

2. The normal subject catalogue to self-contained independent, bibliographical units, e.g. monographic works, whole periodicals.

3. The library's own subject analysis of normal bibliographical units, resulting in analytical entries, for parts of monographic works, and filed into the normal subject catalogue.

4. The library's own special indexes to certain types of materials, whether series of technical reports or sets of plays.

5. Other libraries' published catalogues, bibliographies and indexes used as substitutes for locally-compiled records.

6. Commercially or generally published bibliographies, etc., as in 5 above; and especially:

7. Analytical indexes to the contents of many periodicals, e.g. *British technology index*, *Music index;* and of monographic collections e.g. *Essay and general literature index*, and indexes to festschriften.

The methods, or media, of making the subject approach in a library or part of it may, broadly, be of two types, or a compromise of the two:

1. Pre-coordinate. In this method a subject, however complex, has just one subject entry embracing all components of the subject in its subject heading: verbal, or classification notation; i.e. the principle of

single multiple-concept entry is used. There will usually be supporting references to lead the enquirer from terms which he seeks, and which may well be relevant to the heading used but which are not 'used'. Alternatively, in the case of a heading represented by a class mark, there may be an alphabetical subject index to lead one to the required class number. In its alphabetical form, this method is claimed to be exemplified by *British technology index*.

For example, there may be a document on the reform of British secondary education, which may have an entry filed under, say, EDUCATION: SECONDARY: REFORM: GREAT BRITAIN, or other permutations of the terms (or this total subject, as represented by class numbers); with relevant references from the other components of the compound heading.

A disadvantage of this method—although it is widely used since it includes classification schemes whether enumerative (all topics and their treatment listed in the required order), or faceted (topics listed separately as 'isolates' with instructions on the order in which they are to be combined)—is that only one citation, or combination, order can be used; e.g. 'alternating current generators' must be represented as either (*a*) a branch of alternating-current engineering, or (*b*) a branch of electric generators. So, unless there is to be an unmanageable number of added entries, either (*a*) the subject will be next to alternating-current motors, and separated from other types of electric generators; or (*b*) it will be next to direct-current generators, and separated from other types of alternating-current machinery. This disadvantage applies particularly when the librarian decides on the classified catalogue approach, because it is multiplied and re-multiplied until the most general, containing, heading is reached, e.g. Technology. So in classification, the citation order and the modulation of subjects as they are arranged become the criteria by which the classified catalogue succeeds or fails. And brave is the classificationist (designer of classification schemes) who thinks he can please all of the people all the time.

2. Post-coordinate. In this method each subject, however complex, is divided into its component parts (normally isolates), and an entry is made for the document concerned under each of the components, i.e. the principle of multiple single-concept entry is used. So the document mentioned already would likely receive four entries: 1. EDUCATION; 2. SECONDARY; 3. REFORM; 4. GREAT BRITAIN. The question of permutation is irrelevant; in principle all approach, or entry, terms are of equal

standing. Also, in principle, the need for references does not arise, although, in fact, one may decide that there should be references between SECONDARY, PRIMARY, TERTIARY, etc.; and from GREAT BRITAIN to its component parts: ENGLAND; SCOTLAND; WALES; ULSTER (and even vice versa) to cater for 'subject inclusion'. The method is used in its most radical form in coordinate indexing, or uniterm indexing, and in a slightly less radical form in uniconcept indexing: dealt with in Chapter 18. A similar principle is also applied in Keyword in context listing or indexing (KWIC), which lists titles under as many terms or words as are thought necessary for tracing them.

A disadvantage of this method, if used in conventional filing systems, is that each heading may well became a 'classed' heading, i.e. it may embrace subjects which are far more specific than implied by the heading. Its advantage is that the cataloguer or indexer does not have to decide in advance the citation order likely to be most required, i.e. the bringing together (coordination) of the components is done after ('post') the indexing stage and at the search stage. In pre-coordinate subject work the bringing together, in an estimated required order, is done at the indexing stage. At the search stage, the searcher is obliged to follow the citation order decided on by the classificationist or the indexer.

Phase relations—an increasingly required part of subject work—can be recorded by both types, whether in classified or in alphabetical order.

3. Compromise of Pre-coordinate and Post-coordinate. This is a half-way mark between the two methods. It is best demonstrated by, and most practised in, the 'conventional' alphabetical-subject catalogue. Using SEARS (admittedly not the best list to demonstrate even a moderately complex subject), one gets the following headings, all of which would have to carry the bibliographic details, and location, of the document:

1. EDUCATION—GREAT BRITAIN
2. EDUCATION, SECONDARY and possibly
3. EDUCATIONAL SOCIOLOGY, this being about the nearest one can get in SEARS to 'Reform' in this context.

Each would need relevant references from the second-cited part of its heading, and from other related headings.

As has already partly been inferred, whatever method of subject record is used, some form of alphabetical approach is involved initially. There are five methods of alphabetical-subject approach, and each is dealt with appropriately in this book. These are:

1. The alphabetical-specific approach.
2. The alphabetical-classed approach.
3. The catchword subject approach.
4. The subject index component of the classified catalogue.
5. Coordinate indexing.

The two 'conventional' (accepted) methods will be dealt with first: i.e. the dictionary and the classified catalogues. A background history of their evolution then follows. This will be followed by some criticisms of 'conventional' methods. Finally we shall deal with more 'modern' approaches, including their advantages and disadvantages. Computerisation is dealt with in Section VI, on Mechanisation.

SOME TERMS AND DEFINITIONS USED IN ALPHABETICAL SUBJECT CATALOGUING

There is difference of opinion over some terms used in this Section, and the definitions used by this writer are summarised here.

Specific. A specific heading describes the subject of the document in as short and exact a term as possible. A document on the sun has the heading SUN: not SOLAR SYSTEM (too broad); not SUNSPOTS (too narrow). Similarly, a document on sunspots has the heading SUNSPOTS, not SUN which in this instance is too broad. No heading can be specific in the abstract, but only in relation to a particular document. See p. 104.

Classed. A classed heading is over-broad in relation to the exact subject of the document, and it does not specify the exact subject. An example is the use of SOLAR SYSTEM or ASTRONOMY for a document on the sun. See p. 104. Some writers use 'classed' as if it were synonymous with 'alphabetical-classed'.

Alphabetical-classed (or Alphabetico-classed). At its shortest, this is a heading which uses as entry word a classed (over-broad) term, followed by a specific 'contained' term for the specific subject of the document. A simple example is SOLAR SYSTEM–SUN, and a more complex one ASTRONOMY–SOLAR SYSTEM–SUN, for a document whose subject is confined completely to the sun. See also examples on p. 131 and 132. One suggests that a heading is alphabetical-classed if we can delete the first-cited term or terms but still be left with a complete self-contained specific heading for the subject of the document in hand.

CHAPTER 9

The 'Conventional' Dictionary Catalogue

As the name implies, all entries whether author (including collaborators), title, or subject, are filed alphabetically in one sequence. The name implies that the method is as 'easy as A B C', although even protagonists of the dictionary catalogue consider that there are complications, as will be explained later.

The main entry in the dictionary catalogue is traditionally the principal author entry. As has been seen, the main entry is noteworthy as being: (a) the fullest form of entry of a document to appear in a catalogue, although, in a unit entry catalogue, this does not apply; (b) that entry which necessarily includes the tracings of other, added, entries (these are usually on the front of the entry, but in some card catalogues may possibly be on the back of the card); and, (c) filed under the main author heading; this is very likely to affect the arrangement of the document 'within' a class number on the shelves.

Traditionally, the dictionary catalogue has title added entries—more commonly so than in the classified catalogue. The reason is not necessarily inherent in the alphabetical one-sequence arrangement of this form of catalogue, but rather it may derive from the long-established American practice of central cataloguing, which relies on unit cards combined with the fact that the U.S., and American-influenced— usually English-speaking—countries have a tradition of dictionary catalogues.

In principle, the non-subject entries and references in the classified and the dictionary catalogues can be identical and they will not be further investigated here in themselves. (But see the later part of this Section on the historical evolution of the two types of catalogue.)

Here, then, we are mainly concerned with the subject approach of the dictionary catalogue, although the interfiling of subject with other entries presents problems, commented on later, and in Chapter 24, on Filing.

Here, too, we are confining ourselves to what we shall call the 'conventional' dictionary catalogue, as derived from (general) lists of

Grease. *See* Lubrication and lubricants;
　　　Oils and fats

Great books program. *See* Discussion
　　　groups

Great Britain
　　　May be subdivided like U.S. except for
　　　History. The abbreviation Gt. Brit.
　　　may be used when followed by a
　　　subdivision. For a list of subjects
　　　which may be used under either
　　　England or Great Britain, see **Eng-
　　　land**
　　　See also Commonwealth of Nations;
　　　　England
　　　x United Kingdom
　　　xx England

Gt. Brit.—Colonies
　　　xx Colonies; Commonwealth of Nations

Gt. Brit.—History
　　　x England—History; English history

Gt. Brit.—History—To 1066
　　　See also Anglo-Saxons; Celts

Gt. Brit.—History—Norman period, 1066-
　　　1154
　　　See also Hastings, Battle of, 1066; Nor-
　　　mans

Gt. Brit.—History—Plantagenets, 1154-1399

Gt. Brit.—History—Lancaster and York,
　　　1399-1485
　　　See also Hundred Years' War, 1339-1453

Gt. Brit.—History—Wars of the Roses,
　　　1455-1485
　　　x Wars of the Roses, 1455-1485

Gt. Brit.—History—Tudors, 1485-1603
　　　See also Armada, 1588

Gt. Brit.—History—Stuarts, 1603-1714
　　　See also Gunpowder Plot, 1605; Spanish
　　　　Succession, War of, 1701-1714

Gt. Brit.—History—Civil War and Common-
　　　wealth, 1642-1660
　　　x Civil War—England; Commonwealth
　　　　of England

3. Excerpts from SEARS and LIBRARY OF CONGRESS lists of subject headings.

3 (*a*). SEARS

Grease
  See Lubrication and lubricants
      Oils and fats
Great anteater
  See Ant bear
Great auk *(QL696.A3)*
  x Gairfowl
     Garefowl
     Garfowl
Great Awakening *(BR520)*
    Here are entered works dealing with the revival of religion that occurred in the American colonies in the 18th century.
  sa Evangelical Revival
  x Awakening, Great
  xx Evangelical Revival
Great Bear
  See Ursa Major
Great books program
  See Group reading
Great Bridge, Va., Battle of, 1775
     (E241.G)
Great Britain
    Abbreviated to Gt. Brit. when followed by subdivision or subheading.
  sa Commonwealth of Nations
  Note under Commonwealth of Nations
  —Antiquities, Roman
    x Romans in Great Britain
  —Biography
  —Civilian defense
    Example under Civilian defense
  —Coast defenses
    Example under Coast defenses
  —Colonies
    sa Commonwealth of Nations
      Imperial federation
    xx Commonwealth of Nations
    Note under Commonwealth of Nations

Gentry
—History *(DA)*
  x England—Histo
—Invasions
  sa French Expec
    1796-1797
    French Expec
    1797
—Philosophy
  Example under
    Philosophy

        * *

—To 1485
—To 1066
  —Juvenile literatι
—To 449
—To 55 B.C.
—Roman period, 55
  Example under
    Romans in (
    Britain, etc.
  —Juvenile literatι
—Anglo-Saxon perio
  —Juvenile literatι
—1066-1687
—Medieval period, 1
—Norman period, 1(
  —Juvenile literatι
—Plantagenets, 115
—Angevin period, 1
—13th century
—14th century
—Peasants' Revolt,
  See Tyler's Insu
—Lancaster and Yo
  x Gt. Brit.—His
    century
—House of Lancast

3 (*b*). LC

(Relevant parts not shown here range from 'Great Britain—Colonies—Commerce' to 'Great Britain—Gentry.')

subject headings and references, such as those of the Library of Congress (LC) and of SEARS: see facsimiles on pages 102 and 103. However, it should be remembered that there are many lists confined to, or oriented towards, limited or 'special' subjects or subject groups or areas. These have in the past usually been compiled using the same principles and habits as the general lists: representative examples are mentioned in Chapters 19 to 21, on Special cataloguing.

Subject entries are made, and filed, under subject words in normal 'natural' language: differentiated from code terms or symbols—class numbers—as in the main subject file of the classified catalogue. In a 'conventional' dictionary catalogue, then, a work on education will be filed alphabetically under the word EDUCATION, after EDEN and before EFFICIENCY. In the classified catalogue the subject entry would be filed under, say, the heading 370, if the Dewey Decimal Classification (DC) is used, after 369 and before 371.

The next point, which is extremely important and must be understood intimately, is that the most specific term is chosen as the heading for a work. That is, a subject heading is chosen which, as near as reasonably possible, exactly coincides with the actual subject of the work. So, a work on the sun as a whole has the alphabetical-subject heading SUN, and not SOLAR SYSTEM, which would include the planets of the Solar system as well as the sun itself; and not ASTRONOMY, which embraces the study of all parts of the universe; and—at the other extreme—not SUNSPOTS, which is only a part of the subject sun; and not SOLAR ENERGY, which embraces that part of the study of the sun relating to the application of heat from the sun.

THE NEED FOR REFERENCES

However, SUN is part of the Solar system, which itself is part of Astronomy. Since a work on the Solar system is entered under SOLAR SYSTEM, and since a work on astronomy is entered under ASTRONOMY—all being filed alphabetically according to the words describing these subjects—these related subjects are scattered in their dictionary catalogue treatment. Nevertheless, someone who is interested in the Sun may also be interested in the Solar system. Further—and possibly more important—a person interested mainly in the sun may look in the catalogue under ASTRONOMY. Again, the sun is in fact a star, and information about stars in general may possibly be of indirect value to someone seeking information on the sun. On the other hand, a seeker of information about the sun may possibly find works about the Solar system and its constituent planets, including the earth, of fringe interest.

The long and short of all this is that the subject headings for these, and other related, topics should ideally be connected in the alphabetically arranged subject catalogue. This relating component of Coates' 'twofold' objective of the subject catalogue, is—at least, to some extent—solved by the use of references, of various types, between the headings of subjects which have some relationship with each other.

Customarily, in the 'conventional' dictionary catalogue, one is reminded to look, '*also*', under various other (related) headings, e.g. we are referred by '*see also*' references from a generic, or 'embracing', subject heading to other headings representing parts, components, or subdivisions, of the generic or 'parent' subject.

e.g. SUN *see also* SUNSPOTS, and
SUN *see also* SOLAR ENERGY.

It should be remembered, at this point, that parts of a subject do not necessarily correspond with the subdivisions as shown by any individual classification scheme, e.g. SUN in its 'Astronomy' aspect in DC 17th edition is 523.7; SUNSPOTS is 523.74. But SOLAR ENERGY (Engineering) is 621.47. If one is to savour the full advantages of the 'conventional' dictionary catalogue in relation to those of the classification scheme 'modern' chain-procedure-based dictionary catalogue, it is vital to bear in mind the apparent indifference of subject heading and subject reference construction to whatever classification scheme is used in a library. It should be borne in mind at this point, that chain procedure, as advocated by 'moderns', assumes that the type of collocation of whatever classification scheme is used in a library is best in itself, in the abstract, and in real-life practice. Whether or not this is in fact the case may, or may not, be the truth, although in many cases it probably is. For the moment, it should be remembered that one of the main advantages of the dictionary catalogue is that it can cut across the boundaries (subject disciplines, facets, etc.) of classification schemes, and enter all works about, say, Copper under COPPER as an entry word. This could possibly be subdivided by aspects, like MINING and ECONOMICS. In modern terminology one might say that the facets of the concrete COPPER are identified by qualifiers, such as MINING and ECONOMICS. In fact, SEARS—to take one example—does not consider such subdivisions are necessary, the inferred reason being that there are not enough (catalogued) bibliographic units in a library's stock to warrant subdividing COPPER: although this assumption may well be contested.

The above is a generalised justification of the use of *see also* references. There now follows a statement of the specific uses of them:

1. General to special

> e.g. PLANETS *see also* VENUS
> SUN *see also* SOLAR ENERGY.

These examples show that general to special, or 'downwards', *see also* references do not necessarily follow the hierarchy of the classification scheme (e.g. DC), as explained above. Their basic purpose is to remind the catalogue user of the more specific components of a subject which may be represented in the catalogue.

2. Collateral (sometimes called coordinate)

> e.g. DRAWING *see also* PAINTING
> WATER *see also* GLACIERS.

Again, these two examples show that collateral (equal-ranking, or 'sideways') references do not necessarily correspond with two equal-ranking classes in a classification scheme. The first examples approximately do correspond with their DC equivalents, Drawing 740 and Painting 750, each of which is one-tenth of the main class 700 Arts. However, there are no pat equivalents for 'water' and 'glaciers'. In DC, 17th edition, 'Glaciers' might go at 910.02 or 551.31, while 'Water' might go at a great variety of places too numerous to list here: examples are 546.22 in Chemistry, 910.091 in Geography, and 338.27 in Economics. The probable truth is that neither of these terms as used by SEARS has a specific meaning in the classification sense. One can only say that a reader who is interested in water as such may possibly also be interested in water not only in a particular form of it in a frozen condition, but also in a topographical or geological context.

It is noteworthy that collateral *see also* references are only rarely used between what, in a classification scheme, are likely to be adjacent, equal-ranking, divisions. References are brought into action in such cases only when the designer of the list of headings feels that a reader may need them.

Collateral *see also* references are usually made in both directions, although examples exist which unaccountably do not satisfy this 'rule'

> e.g. SEARS has OPERA *see also* BALLET

but not

> BALLET *see also* OPERA.

3. 'Inter-discipline' or 'Oblique'

> e.g. DRAWING *see also* PERSPECTIVE
> HISTORY *see also* MAN
> HISTORY *see also* ARCHEOLOGY
> HISTORY, ANCIENT *see also* NUMISMATICS
> FREEDOM OF THE PRESS *see also* LIBEL AND SLANDER.

This type of reference has something in common with the WATER *see also* GLACIERS example in category 2 above. Its chief difference is that documents under the two headings connected may have less in common with each other than those in category 2, and this is probably not only because they come from different facets, or disciplines, but further, in many cases, from different main classes. They have been called 'oblique' here because, as far as we know, they have not yet been given a name of their own: 'inter-facet' is a possibility but is only part of the story.

In the first example, both 'drawing' and 'perspective' are components of the main class 'arts', but arrived at by different characteristics: drawing is a medium while perspective is a method. A work on drawing is likely to have information in it on perspective, and a work on perspective may use the medium of drawing in its exposition of its own subject.

In the second example: we know that man is the history maker; so works on him may possibly be relevant to someone interested in history as a subject. In SEARS, this is a one-way reference; there is no MAN *see also* HISTORY.

Similar reasoning could be applied to the third example. Archeology is not part of history, but in one respect it is a tool by which history is discovered, so someone interested in one may possibly be interested in the other. However, it is part of Science in its own right.

In the fourth example, the connection between ancient history and numismatics may be felt by some to be rather tenuous. A numismatist is not necessarily a historian: he may be in it wholly to make money as a dealer. But coins can be a manifestation of part of history. It is noteworthy here, that SEARS does not directly connect PORTRAITS and NUMISMATICS, or PORTRAITS and COINS, with references.

Generally, 'inter-discipline' references go both ways.

4. Specific to general

> e.g. GIRLS *see also* CHILDREN
> ACTING *see also* THEATRE

ADULT EDUCATION *see also* SOCIAL GROUP WORK
ADVERTISING *see also* PROPAGANDA
BARBARY STATES *see also* AFRICA, NORTH
ENGLAND *see also* GREAT BRITAIN
WEAVING *see also* TEXTILE INDUSTRY AND FABRICS
FREEDOM OF THE PRESS *see also* FREEDOM OF INFORMATION.

These are 'upward' references, i.e. usually from a division of a class to the class which includes it. Books on the 'conventional' dictionary catalogue do not always acknowledge the existence of such references and the lack of them is sometimes cited as a criticism of this form of catalogue. For example, '. . . provision for references connecting used specific subjects to their containing generic subjects is omitted . . . without specific to general references the alphabetical subject catalogue cannot bear comparison with the classified catalogue as a reference tool' (COATES, p. 67). And in fact, it must be admitted that they are used rarely compared with general-to-specific references.

The need for such references is that a reader may possibly not find what he wants in a document on the specific subject but he may possibly find it in one on a broader subject. So, the information about, say, children in general may supplement and extend that found in works solely on girls. It is likely in may cases, that 'upwards' references try to be an easy substitute for analytical entries under the more specific subjects.

These references are usually given in both directions, e.g. CHILDREN *see also* GIRLS, as well as GIRLS *see also* CHILDREN, usually automatically because 'General-to-special' is the most common *see also* reference in the dictionary catalogue.

An attempt has been made here to show that *see also* references, and the headings actually connected by them, do not necessarily follow the types of collocation and hierarchy found in classification schemes. This is what is meant by the oft-quoted advantage of the dictionary catalogue over the classified catalogue: it should be truly independent of the classification scheme used for shelf location: i.e. physical collocation of documents. A scheme of references constructed solely and directly from a classification schedule could not have all of the following references:

BIRDS *see also* CAGE BIRDS
BIRDS *see also* CANARIES
CAGE BIRDS *see also* CANARIES

as allowed by SEARS, yet each is useful in its own way and cannot be dispensed with without loss of efficiency in the catalogue.

COMPOUND SUBJECTS

So far mainly 'simple' subjects have been assumed. However, two or more 'simple' subjects may possibly be dealt with combined in one document. For example, a work on the history of Britain introduces the need for two approaches: a reader may be interested in either history or Britain or the two combined. These approaches, or entry terms, must therefore be catered for, both in the chosen heading and in references leading to it.

There are several types of compound heading:

1. Two interconnected approaches to the same topic, or two topics which are usually treated together in documents.

> e.g. BOATS AND BOATING
> INFORMATION STORAGE AND RETRIEVAL SYSTEMS
> ASSES AND MULES
> LIBEL AND SLANDER.

2. Interreaction between two subjects.

> e.g. TELEVISION IN EDUCATION
> TELEVISION AND CHILDREN
> EDUCATION OF WOMEN
> CHURCH AND STATE.

The above examples are in phrase form, but sometimes these headings are given in constructed or structured form

> e.g. LABOUR AND LABOURING CLASSES—EDUCATION.

(This exemplifies both categories 1 and 2.)

3. Opposites usually treated together in the same documents, e.g. TRUTHFULNESS AND FALSEHOOD. However, THEISM and ATHEISM have their own headings, connected both ways with *see also* references, presumably because they are normally treated in documents independently from each other. Further, one heading alone may serve for two opposites, e.g. HEAT with a reference cold *see* HEAT.

4. Subject in relation to a place, or to races.

> e.g. BIRDS—WALES
> WALES—HISTORY
> CATTLE—AUSTRALIA

AUSTRALIA—DESCRIPTION AND TRAVEL
INCAS—LEGENDS
LEGENDS, JEWISH
JEWISH CHILDREN.

(Note that the next to last item uses an inverted form of construction, and the last item is in the form of a direct phrase.)

It is evident that in some instances the place (or race) is cited first and so becomes the entry word in the catalogue, while in others the subject is cited first. This syntactical inconsistency is excused because in some cases the subject is considered more significant than the place, while in others the reverse applies. This principle may lead to examples like

POLICE—U.S., but
CHICAGO—POLICE.

Generally, subject takes precedence in scientific, technical and artistic subjects. The first two are given in constructed form, while the last is given in adjectival form, e.g. PAINTING, AMERICAN. Place (or race) takes precedence in other subjects including literature and its various forms, e.g. ENGLISH POETRY; AMERICAN POETRY.

5. Form in which a subject is presented.

e.g. LIBRARY SCIENCE—DICTIONARIES
GREAT BRITAIN—DIRECTORIES
GEOLOGY—MAPS.

6. Sometimes a subject term is ambiguous, and a qualifying term is then usually added in parentheses to clarify it.

e.g. SEALS (ANIMALS)
SEALS (NUMISMATICS)
DISPLACEMENT (SHIPS)
DISPLACEMENT (PSYCHOLOGY)
COLD (DISEASE)
cold see HEAT.

However, LC uses parentheses also for a different purpose, as in COOKERY (FISH).

Summary of heading syntactical construction so far
Noun   e.g. MACHINERY
Noun—Noun   e.g. MACHINERY—MODELS
Noun, Adjective e.g. CHEMISTRY, ANALYTIC

'Direct' phrase   e.g. AGRICULTURAL CHEMISTRY
                        CHLORINE AND DERIVATIVES AS DISINFECTANTS
                        CHILDREN'S ACCIDENTS.

'SEE' REFERENCES

In addition to the *see also* references already dwelt upon at some length, *see* references also are used, and their use is simpler than that of many *see also* references. Their purpose is to redirect the user from a heading which he may seek but which is not used to that which is used. They are of three types.

1. Synonyms

    e.g. Measurement, Mental *see* PSYCHOMETRICS
         Dependencies *see* COLONIES.

The principle is, theoretically, to choose the most-used term, and to refer from less-used terms but which, nevertheless, some people may seek.

2. Near-synonyms

    Detergents *see* SOAP
    Mules *see* ASSES AND MULES
    Persia *see* IRAN
    Derricks *see* CRANES, DERRICKS, etc.

It is evident that 'near-synonym' references tend to be 'upward' or 'special-to-general'. For example, there may be an entry for one book on mules alone indiscriminately interfiled by author among entries for 19 works on asses and mules together. Again, in some cases they constitute a substitute for analytical entries on the more specific subject.

3. Construction

    e.g. Design, Industrial *see* INDUSTRIAL DESIGN
         Ireland—Folklore *see* FOLKLORE—IRELAND
         Indian folklore *see* FOLKLORE, INDIAN
         Education and television *see* TELEVISION IN EDUCATION
         Television, Closed-circuit *see* CLOSED-CIRCUIT TELEVISION.

It can be seen that some of these 'construction' *see* references more or less duplicate the function of some 'general-to-special' *see also* references, e.g. in addition to the *see* 'television' reference above, SEARS has
    TELEVISION *see also* CLOSED-CIRCUIT TELEVISION.

MULTIPLE ENTRY

'Conventional' subject headings quite often are not co-extensive with the subject of the document in hand, mainly because they rarely extend beyond two components. So a work on even a quite common subject like 'Latin epic poetry' needs to receive two entries to ensure that all its component 'isolates' are catered for.

> e.g. LATIN POETRY, and
> EPIC POETRY.

This need for multiple entry, though it keeps headings comparatively simple, can lead to quite complex work on the part of the cataloguer. For example, John and Elizabeth Newson's *Patterns of infant care in an urban community* would, strictly, need the following headings, all with their accompanying references:

> ENGLISH LANGUAGE—DIALECTS
> INFANTS—CARE AND HYGIENE
> MOTHERS
> NOTTINGHAM—SOCIAL CONDITIONS
> SOCIAL CLASSES
> SOCIOLOGY, URBAN

although most or all of the headings and references would likely be invoked also for other works. (The information used to arrive at these decisions is not all given in the title, of course; it is derived from the title, the blurb, the dedication, the Contents list, and a brief scanning of the text itself.) Even so, the headings in SEARS do not allow for complete specification; e.g. in the example cited above the dialect covered is peculiar to Nottingham, and this would have to be explained in a note in the entry. Also, it is not evident from the headings that the study is confined to infants in the first year of their lives. If thought necessary, a note would be needed for this also. Some libraries adapt standard lists of headings, which is advantageous provided the overall structure is not upset.

SHELF LIST

Libraries with dictionary catalogues usually (and should) have a shelf list. This is a file of entries, one per physical bibliographic unit, filed in the order in which books, etc., are shelved. It should therefore consist of several sequences, one of which might be, for example, reference library quarto-size works, each sub-arranged by shelf number. It is supposed to be, in fact, an inventory of stock for stock-taking purposes. However, some libraries use it as a form of substitute classified file—perhaps to such an extent that the entries for the various sequences are interfiled. Sometimes, a dictionary catalogue may even refer the user to the shelf list, e.g. under ENGLISH POETRY, there may be an explanatory reference: '*See* shelf list 821 for individual English poets'. Whether this represents a valid and useful substitute for part of a classified catalogue should be considered very carefully.

CHAPTER 10

The Classified Catalogue

As with the preceding account of the dictionary catalogue, the classified catalogue envisaged here could have identical author/title entries with the equivalent dictionary catalogue, leaving the way clear for concentration mainly on the subject approach.

The classified catalogue should have the following components:

1. Classified file

Entries here are the main entries, the historical reason being that all other approaches were originally index entries to the classified file. (It so happens, because of the use of the unit entry principle, that the chief author entry in the dictionary catalogue has become the main entry. However, this is not necessarily an inherent characteristic of the dictionary catalogue.) All entries are filed in notation order of the classification scheme used in the library, various shelf sequences, e.g. oversize or closed access symbols prefixing class numbers, being ignored. It also includes added subject—and perhaps analytical—entries filed under the added class number but indicating the shelf location of the work itself. In some more recent catalogues, feature headings are given with class numbers, 'translating' all or the most specific parts of the class numbers into their natural language equivalents: plenty of examples can be found in BNB lists (not cards).

Libraries rarely, nowadays, have shelf lists if they have classified catalogues, as the classified file can be used for stock-taking purposes fairly conveniently.

2. Alphabetical file(s)

(a) Author/title catalogue (or index, if unit entries are not used). Some libraries do not have title added, or index, entries. Other libraries may have only certain types of title entries, e.g. analytical entries for titles of plays in collections. In some libraries, again, title added entries are filed in a separate sequence from authors.

A variant is the name catalogue, which includes in one sequence not only author entries but subject entries (in dictionary catalogue form) of persons and corporate bodies. These entries need not be solely biography entries, but may include, say, critical 'subject' works on an author when the documents are shelved at 'subject' and not only 'biography' class numbers.

Occasionally one may find a 'name index', as in the Edinburgh Public Library printed catalogue, giving names of people, bodies, etc., with merely class numbers at which entries of works by, and about, them are filed in the classified file. This particular type of printed work can be most useful. As with the normal subject index, it can be used for direct access from index to shelves, as long as various sequences, e.g. oversize, are taken into account. A sample entry from it is given on page 134.

In using BNB, it should be remembered that entries under authors are reasonably full, but that title (added) entries are in brief reference form, e.g. Chrome yellow *see* Huxley, Aldous.

(b) Subject index. This may possibly be interfiled with (a) authors and titles, as in BNB. It is an essential key to the classified file, or to the classified works on the shelves. Each entry consists solely of (1) name of subject and (2) the class mark at which that subject is filed in the classified file, or shelved. It does not record details of individual books and other documents.

e.g. 1. THEOLOGY   200
    2. ASTRONOMY   520.

As in the dictionary catalogue, subject terms can get complicated, and one may find such entries as

MANGANESE: INORGANIC CHEMISTRY   546.54
MANGANESE: METALLOGRAPHY   669.95732
MANGANESE: METALLURGY   669.732

where the meanings of 'metallography' and of 'metallurgy' are not necessarily clear to the user.

Unlike the dictionary catalogue, references are not normally used, so one would expect to find

COR ANGLAIS   788.7   and
ENGLISH HORN   788.7   and not
ENGLISH HORN *see* COR ANGLAIS,

the reasons being that (a) it is just as easy for the cataloguer to give the class mark direct under synonyms, and (b) it avoids having to be referred to another part of the index before finding the class mark required.

There are various ways of constructing subject indexes, and more and more attention has been paid to them in recent years, as their full potential has been more and more appreciated, e.g. using the index to connect relationships between subjects which might theoretically be expected to be solved by double entry in the classified file. These ways are now enumerated:

(1) Instead of a 'custom-built' index for one's library, use the printed index to the classification scheme, perhaps ticking entries for topics represented in stock. Some libraries have a copy of the printed index to the scheme lying on top of the catalogue, as an incentive to its use. It should be remembered that such an index is an index to the schedules of the scheme, and not to the library's own stock. So it will include many topics not in stock, and exclude some topics which are in stock, e.g. a library may well have in stock works on the history of the British Commonwealth, but DC 17th edition's revised index does not have an entry saying, e.g. BRITISH COMMONWEALTH: HISTORY 942, or similar. Again, the only direct entry in this index under AUSTRALIA is LAW at 346. There are several under the adjectival form, but such common topics as history, geography and economics are still not included. Needless to say, the use of a classification scheme's index is not recommended.

(2) Class entry term from classification scheme with alphabetical subdivisions.

e.g. PHOTOGRAPHY   770
       AS A PROFESSION   770.232
       EQUIPMENT   771
       NEGATIVES   770.283
       POSITIVES   770.284
       [etc. etc.]

until all divisions of photography in stock have been represented. It will be seen that his method brings together in the index topics which are also brought together in the classification scheme. Therefore it is not economical. Also it does not cater directly for specific terms, i.e. in a way it tends to be alphabetico-classed.

3. Permutation, either fully or selectively.

e.g. ANCIENT GREECE: HISTORY   938   and
     GREECE, ANCIENT: HISTORY   938   and
     HISTORY: ANCIENT GREECE   938   and even
     HISTORY: GREECE, ANCIENT   938.

It is evident, from such a common example as this, that many entries for each compound subject in stock will be needed in such a system. When one gets to more complicated subjects, the number of entries per class number becomes so great as to be unmanageable, while selection of forms of permutation can be as uncertain as with the selection of 'bankers' for football pools. The method known as SLIC (Selective Listing in Context) could be applied, as this is a form of permutation; although the method was not originally devised as a method of subject indexing a classified file. It can be followed up in John R. Sharp's *Some fundamentals of information retrieval*. London: Deutsch, 1965: see the work's index.

4. Use an accepted 'conventional' list of subject headings, e.g. SEARS, possibly copying entries onto cards, and not using the original printed form. Adaptation would be required, e.g. *see* references would need to be converted into direct index entries giving synonyms and relevant class marks. Disadvantages of this method are similar to those mentioned under item 1, Index to classification scheme, plus others deriving from inconsistent constructions in the lists themselves (mentioned in Chapter 13). In addition, as already outlined, lists of subject headings should be indifferent to classification schemes, so there would be difficulty in matching the 'ready-made' terms to class marks of whatever scheme is used. However, the LC list is in fact often used as a single-sequence index to the LC classification in the absence of a specially compiled one.

5. Chain indexing. This method has emerged as the most reliable, quick and economic single method in recent years. Its basic practice is outlined here, but it is discussed in more detail in Chapter 16.

Simple subjects are entered direct.

      e.g. 1. RELIGION   200
          2. PHYSICS   530

Compound subjects are entered under the term represented by the final part of the notation, followed by that represented by the first part of the notation as a qualifying term.

      e.g. GREAT BRITAIN: ECONOMICS   330.942
           GREAT BRITAIN: GEOGRAPHY   914.2
           GREAT BRITAIN: HISTORY   942
           [etc., etc.]

This method then brings together reminders of aspects (facets) of subjects which are scattered by the classification scheme, the 'subject' here being Great Britain. In modern terminology, it collocates distributed relatives. It does not repeat divisions of a subject which are brought together in the classification scheme, as does method 2. It will be seen that the construction derives directly from the scheme used: if a scheme used a reverse citation order (sequence of constructing compound headings) from that given above, the citation order of the index would, also, be reversed. (This is discussed further in Chapter 24, on Filing.) Chain indexing is also used now as a substitute for added subject entries in the classified file, e.g. a document on the influence of the Bible on English literature might be classified at 820:22 (UDC) with some such subject index entry as

BIBLE—*influencing* ENGLISH LITERATURE   820:22.

Thus it would be accurate to say that all documents on the Bible are not classified (by main, or added, entry) at the number for Bible, 22; and the subject index then becomes necessary to illustrate, indirectly, relationships between subjects. Of course, this method of single entry cannot be used for documents dealing with two separate subjects, e.g. Trigonometry and Mechanics.

Something similar to chain procedure is recommended by SHERA AND EGAN, in the form

BEANS
583.22   (Botany)
633.3   (Field crops)
635.65   (Horticulture)

although terms like 'chain' and 'distributed relatives' are not used in their instructions on the compilation of the subject index.

Further characteristics of both the 'conventional' dictionary and the classified catalogues emerge in the comparison of the two in the next chapter.

AUTHORITY FILE

A subject authority file is necessary for the subject index of a classified catalogue. This usually consists of a file of cards in classification number order, each card bearing a tracing of all subject index entries quoting that number. Some libraries use the main (classified file) entries as authorities instead, with tracings of subject index entries at the foot of, or on the back of, the relevant class cards. Such a method is economical but not so convenient as the separate authority file. But it is useful in reminding staff to remove index entries when the last document at a number is withdrawn. Also, since documents rather than just class numbers are indexed, e.g. at points where the scheme is not specific enough, this method ensures that only the correct, specific, index entries are removed for withdrawals.

CHAPTER II

The 'Conventional' Dictionary and Classified Catalogues Compared

An attempt is made here towards objective and factual statements comparing and contrasting the two forms. Since this topic is perennial, and will probably never be settled in any case, and since the value of one form or another depends on the habits of individuals and on one's environment, no attempt is made to conclude which is 'best'. Readers should attempt to discount their environment if they are attempting to arrive at a truly objective conclusion. However, one's personal opinion is that there is little to choose between the two, and a decision to change from one to another should be considered very carefully. Account should be taken of local custom, which reflects in public usage and staff training, as well as in participation in central cataloguing services available, and other manifestations of inter-library cooperation.

DICTIONARY

1. It is alphabetical in a single sequence and so is simple to understand and use.

But the interfiling of all types of entries, and of references, makes it complex even to the point that some large libraries divide it into two sequences:

(*a*) author/title; and
(*b*) subject.

Further, the alphabetical principle is often departed from, e.g. in the groupings used by LC (see Chapter 24, on Filing: 'cookery' example).

2. It is independent of the classification scheme, and so can overcome faults in the scheme, and also the inevitable scatter of certain related materials in all schemes.

But, its form of collocation may not necessarily improve on the scheme's. Also, some knowledge, however unconscious, of the scheme is still needed, especially for vague subject interests. Also, shelf location is still usually by class mark: the classification scheme must be known to that extent.

3. Its independence of the classification scheme obviates need for extension of the scheme to cater for subjects not yet included in the scheme.

But it may include subjects under broader headings than they warrant, so concealing them and making their location time-consuming. Also, construction of new subject headings still causes difficulty because:

(a) subject headings lists do not always set consistent examples; and
(b) the complex reference system still has to be connected with new headings.

4. It leads direct to required subject at one referral (or 'use').

But the user does not necessarily think as the subject headings list used, and so is referred—perhaps several times. Use is complicated by the fact that headings are not always compiled using consistent principles or structure.

5. *See* references are easier to follow, since in natural language, than subject index entries.

But, see above, about inconsistent heading construction, too broad headings, and double referral.

6. *See also* references link related subjects which are scattered by direct-language entry and by the alphabet.

But these references may be:

(a) inconsistent and unreliable;
(b) too complex to follow through to the end until useful headings or the required documents are identified; and
(c) rarely go 'upwards', like some searches do, from specific to general.

7. Natural, direct language is often used, and, even when inverted and 'constructed', it uses forms likely to be sought by many users.

But see previous objections, since entries for documents are interposed.

8. Dictionary form is used in many trade bibliographies, in many printed catalogues, on LC and Wilson printed cards, and has apparently proved successful in many large libraries. It also follows the form of many printed periodicals indexes and quick-reference works.

But its use in library catalogues involves some empirical decisions, or delay in awaiting someone else's decisions. The pattern takes time to get used to. Since it is used by many large profit-making organisations, this militates against experiment—which is surely necessary in a method which is basically nearly 100 years old, as exemplified in some central cataloguing systems.

CLASSIFIED

1. It uses advantages of the classification scheme, e.g. general to specific; collocation by subject relevance, not by terminology.

But classification schemes are sometimes hard to get used to, and many users do not need to know the classification scheme anyway, while the principles of collocation used do not conform to all users' needs.

2. It facilitates reference to other works in the catalogue at the same class number.

But this may restrict users to the limitations of the scheme, while alphabetical-subject headings cut across time-worn disciplines. Also, some classified files do not have sufficient added entries to remind users of relevant works shelved at other class marks.

3. Subject index collocates distributed relatives.

But subject index gives only subject terms—which may be ambiguous —and class numbers, not entries for documents. Also, its terminology may be derived from the scheme (as in chain procedure) and so may omit synonyms and other sought approaches. Also, if it relies solely on chain principle it keeps users within a conventional discipline, which may restrict their searching.

4. It reproduces shelf-order and so enhances research enquiries.

But classification schemes can cater for only one citation order, and this may not be the useful one for the user. (See also item 1.)

5. It can use added class entries and *see also* references within the classified file to connect cross-discipline relationships.

But often it does not in practice.

6. Subject index can be used for simple 'subject-to-shelf' enquiries.

But it does not normally cater for parallel sequences on shelves, fugitive material, and other material out of normal shelf sequence. Also, some terms may be ambiguous (again see item 3).

7. Shelf list is not so necessary, resulting in economy.

But it is still inconvenient since it is not in order of various shelf and other sequences, for stocktaking purposes.

8. Classified file is necessary for systematic overhaul and revision of stock.

But still it reproduces faults and scatter of the classification scheme, and it may not correspond with the arrangement in bibliographies used for checking.

9. It is convenient for compiling subject lists and issuing printed sectional catalogues.

But see 8 above: it still may give a restrictive overdisciplined view of stock.

10. Classified order is used in many published bibliographies and abstracts.

But a variety of schemes, and editions of schemes, is used. Also different organisations may interpret a scheme in different ways.

11. It is easier, quicker, and more 'mechanical' (clerical) to compile than a dictionary catalogue.

But a carefully and coherently compiled dictionary catalogue can be superior for some types of use at least. It is assumed, at this point, that most enquiries are specific and not generic. However, insufficient research has been made into the nature of subject enquiries. It is doubtful, anyway, if a generalised conclusion can ever be reached because of the widely varying nature of subject needs and the way they are articulated.

CHAPTER 12

Historical Outline of the Subject Approach

The classified approach, however rudimentary, appears to be the oldest form of subject approach. More accurately, perhaps, the earliest forms of catalogues were inventories of works as they lay on the shelves, while the shelf arrangement itself was often in some sort of systematic subject, or at least grouped, order. The history of catalogues in the Ancient Near East, e.g. Egypt, Mesopotamia and later Greece, and in the Ancient Far East, is an interesting study in itself, but it would be out of place here to pursue it: some useful works for those interested are listed in the bibliography.

The first 'classified' catalogue—irrespective of shelf arrangement—showing any degree of sophistication is probably the *Pinakes* (literally 'tablets'—we could say 'records') compiled by the Macedonian-Egyptian scholar (?librarian) Callimachus, and possibly using a classification evolved by Aristotle. The *Pinakes* was a catalogue of the famous Alexandrian Library, which, since it attempted to be a research library, had copies (or the originals) of all works in Greek of its time, the third century B.C. The *Pinakes* itself is not extant, but copies of extracts, and reliable information about it, have come down to us. It seems likely that there were ten main classes (Greeks, like Dewey, liked the neatness of decimal counting), though their composition was very different from DC's. Each main class was divided logically, e.g. plays into tragedy and comedy. In some instances, existing physical bibliographical units were split up: perhaps even to fit the needs of the classification scheme. Ultimately, there was, in some cases at least, alphabetical arrangement by author. Very full information about each author was given, including his pedigree—to such an extent that the catalogue was in effect a classified catalogue combined with a bio-bibliographical guide. The catalogue was on papyrus rolls (or possibly slips); but there is no evidence to suggest the use of the unit record, as in present-day sheaf and card records. There were no author or subject indexes.

Since the time of Alexander's empire there have been various manifestations of catalogues arranged according to some form of grouping, or the present equivalent of main classes, at least. These were usually inventories of library stocks—locating works on shelves, or in chests, in, say, monasteries. Side by side, but apparently not connected, evolved classifications of knowledge, as differentiated from books and other bibliographical units. The closest connection was probably in the compilation of general encyclopaedias: works attempting to digest all information considered worth knowing in the form of many individual monographs in one great systematically compiled work. In this form, this type of work, and its name, became fully established by the sixteenth century—a period in Europe associated with learning as a whole and with attempts to interrelate the various, and expanding, branches of learning. By the seventeenth century, an alphabetical (or dictionary) arrangement was being experimented with, as a result of the growing need for individual, specific, items of information. However, the user still occasionally needed to be reminded of the existence of other, related, topics, and so, during the eighteenth century, came the alphabetically arranged encyclopaedia using cross-references, or a *syndetic* structure as the method is now called. The earliest British manifestation was Ephraim Chambers's *Cyclopaedia*: *Encyclopaedia Britannica*, at the time an attempt at a compromise between alphabetical and systematic arrangement, was first produced in the eighteenth century. Since the beginning of the nineteenth century there has been a tendency towards more and more specific, and less 'classed' or 'alphabetical-classed', entry. Since articles themselves often include a reading list on their topic, one can see how their alphabetical-specific principle could have influenced the development of the alphabetical-specific subject catalogue during the nineteenth century.

However, the 'systematic' principle still had its adherents, and the library shelf list continued to be used. In Britain, for example, it developed into the (printed) classified catalogue, often with an author index, and sometimes a subject index, perhaps referring from the briefest of 'approach terms' to page numbers as in an ordinary book's index. This type of catalogue was particularly necessary in Britain's first 60 years of public (rate-supported) libraries (1850-1910), since their stocks were (*a*) closed access, and (*b*) often shelved in accession order.

Meanwhile, U.S. public (local tax-supported) libraries, although introduced at approximately the same time as Britain's, probably worked towards open-access earlier than Britain's. In turn, open access led to shelf classification and less reliance on a classified-sequence catalogue. So, one could go direct to the shelves for the generic subject approach but use the alphabetical catalogue for the specific subject approach.

The alphabetical-subject approach warrants further investigation now, since not only is it obviously the backbone of the dictionary catalogue, but also because it is needed as a key to the classified catalogue. During the nineteenth century, trade bibliographies, e.g. the *English catalogue of books*, and library (printed) catalogues developed the principle of key subject word (or catchword) approach. The *English catalogue* might give an entry for a work called *Introduction to astronomy* under the heading ASTRONOMY, Introduction to; followed by author and other information required for ordering the work. It must be emphasised here that the approach terms were chosen from the title page of the work in hand, a practice endorsed by Panizzi (METCALFE, p. 33).

Crestadoro (Manchester Public Library) included a 'concordance of titles' as a quasi-subject approach with his (alphabetical) author catalogue of 1864. So a work with 'conchology' in its title is indexed under CONCHOLOGY, while a work with 'shells' in its title is indexed under SHELLS, even though the two words are virtually synonymous (METCALFE, p. 33-36). The title catchword approach has been revived recently under the name 'Keyword in context', or KWIC. The principle is the same, except for, probably, more entries per title, but the physical appearance is different, there being no inversion. See facsimiles on pages 127 and 128.

The essential leap from title catchword indexing to consistent subject word entry came, not directly from Cutter but, in Billings' U.S. Surgeon-General's Library catalogue in the 1880's, which also included analytical subject entries. This catalogue also used references from unused potential subject headings to used headings, and an attempt at constructed headings to ensure filing under a 'concrete' term, e.g. BRAIN, followed by qualifying terms like (Diseases of) and (Softening of) (METCALFE, p. 36).

Meanwhile, Cutter was experimenting with the consistent subject word principle in his (printed) Boston Athenaeum Library catalogue, 1874-1882.

Cutter was important for several reasons:

(*a*) He was the first to codify systematically rules for alphabetical-specific subject entry. He said (4th ed. 1904) '. . . "specific entry" is

```
I.M.E. Index
          of Current Literature on COAL Mining and Allied

          Monthly Bulletin - British COAL Utilisation Resea

                    Abstracts E. COAL PROCESSING (N.C.B

          Information Bulletin COAL PROCESSING and Co

          Information Bulletin - COAL TAR Research Asso

                   Review of COAL TAR Technology -
                                   Research Asso

     Index to Current Literature on COALMINING and Allied

                                 COBALT

                                 COKE Review

Journal of the
          Society of Dyers and COLOURISTS

Abstracts, Technical and Patent
     Publications British Internal COMBUSTION Engine R. I

                                 COMBUSTION

Information Bulletin
          Coal Processing and COMBUSTION (N.C.B.)

Monthly Technical Bulletin -
          International COMBUSTION Limited

               Electronics & COMMUNICATIONS Abstrac

          Medical Electronics and COMMUNICATIONS Abstrac

               Mathematics of COMPUTATION

                    COMPUTER Abstracts

               Cumulative COMPUTER Abstracts

Comm. Chinese
     Sci. Abst. - Cybernetics, COMPUTERS & Automation

East European
     Sci. Abst. - Cybernetics, COMPUTERS & Automation

   IEEE Transactions on Electronic COMPUTERS

USSR Scientific
     Abstracts - Cybernetics COMPUTERS & Automation
```

11

4. Excerpts from a KWIC index to the English language abstracting and indexing publications currently being received by the National Lending Library, 2nd edition, 1967. Note 'dyers and colourists' item.   [P.T.O.

Journal of DOCUMENTATION

Library Literature (DOCUMENTATION)

Library Science Abstracts (DOCUMENTATION)

Bibliography on Irrigation, DRAINAGE, river training
control

DRUG and Cosmetic Indust

F.D.A.
Clinical Experience Abstracts (DRUGS)

Unlisted DRUGS

Journal - Society of DYERS and Colourists

American DYESTUFF Reporter

Communist Chinese
Scientific Abstracts - EARTH SCIENCES

East European
Scientific Abstracts - EARTH SCIENCES

Science Abstracts of China - EARTH SCIENCES

EAST EUROPEAN Science Ab

EAST EUROPEAN Scientific
Bio-Medica

EAST EUROPEAN Scientific
Chemistry

EAST EUROPEAN Scientific
Cybernetic
& Automati

EAST EUROPEAN Scientific
Earth Scie

EAST EUROPEAN Sci. Abs.
& Electric

EAST EUROPEAN Sci. Abs.
& Equipmer

EAST EUROPEAN Sci. Abs.
Metallurgy

EAST EUROPEAN Sci. Abs.
Mathematic

14

the main distinction between the dictionary catalog and the alphabetico-classed' (CUTTER, p. 67). It is significant, and admonitory, that p. 66-82 of his Code form the basis of most that was really important in alphabetical-specific subject entry for the next 60 odd years, including LC practice and therefore SEARS practice which have been perpetuated and entrenched through the use of LC and Wilson central catalogue cards and published catalogues, bibliographies and indexes.

(b) He clearly differentiated between 'class' entry and specific entry, using the now famous example of Lady Cust's book on *The Cat*. This goes under CAT (today the plural would usually be used), and not ZOOLOGY; or MAMMALS; or DOMESTIC ANIMALS.

(c) He eschewed use of title catchword entry, using as an example, to emphasise the rule, Garnier's *Le fer*, which goes under IRON, not METALS; and not METALLURGY; and certainly not FER, which he does not even consider. Further, he specified *see* references from unused synonyms to used synonyms, e.g. Pacific Ocean *see* SOUTH SEA (or vice versa).

(d) He allowed the use of constructed headings, despite his predilection for '. . . the public's habitual way of looking at things . . .' (CUTTER, p. 6) and '. . . the convenience of the public . . .': e.g. he allowed a phrase like FERTILIZATION OF FLOWERS (which so easily could be 'constructed' into FLOWERS—FERTILIZATION) on the grounds of public usage. But, surely 'the public' does not 'look at' diseases of Cattle in the form of CATTLE-DISEASES (METCALFE on Cutter's catalogue, p. 37). On the other hand, he allowed QUEEN ANNE'S FARTHING, as a direct (i.e. non-inverted) heading (CUTTER p. 69, R. 165: examples). In his examples and rules, Cutter displayed a lack of decision (typical of the thoughtful—but uneconomic!—cataloguer) between systematic construction of headings and headings as they are used by people in everyday speech. But, 'Usage in both cases [in this case between different names] is the supreme arbiter . . . not of the cataloger but of the public [!] in speaking of subjects' (CUTTER, p. 69). In fact, colloquial usage in English tends to put the less 'significant' qualifying terms—often adjectives or adjectival nouns—before the more significant terms—often 'concrete' nouns, e.g. Farthing.

This problem—direct phraseology versus 'constructed' form—is at the very heart of alphabetical-specific catalogue construction. Whatever LC says, 'the public', in speaking of subjects, uses terms like ENGLISH ART not ART, ENGLISH. Nevertheless, Cutter tentatively suggested training the public to get used to some inverted headings, as they had already got used to the 'SURNAME, Forenames' formula.

HAYKIN (p. 2) has inferred, in effect, that if he had had his time over again, he might opt for a classified catalogue. Therefore, one suggests that inverted phrase headings, and non-alphabetical sub-grouping, as used by LC, in the past at least, symptomise a hankering after the collocation of relevant divisions, which is a basic characteristic of the classified catalogue.

(*e*) As already mentioned (item *c*), Cutter incorporated references into his practice and Code. These, as well as the *see* references already mentioned, included *see also*'s between related subjects (CUTTER, Sections 285 and 286 as well as Sections 187 and 188). In his introduction to the latter rules he made the oft-quoted assertion 'But by a well-devised net-work of cross references the mob becomes an army, of which each part is capable of assisting many other parts. The effective force of the catalog is immensely increased' (CUTTER, p. 79). His two short rules are worth quoting in full:

'187. Make references from general subjects to their various subordinate subjects and also to coordinate and illustrative subjects.

'188. Make references occasionally from specific to general subjects.'

As has already been shown in Chapter 9, and contrary to some teaching and writing, both rules are still practised in the conventional dictionary catalogue. In the discussion under section 188, he mentioned a 'synoptic table' of subjects, the nature of which has caused some discussion (COATES: *L.A. Record*, 1957; METCALFE, p. 99 and 252). He says too: 'In a way it has been done by the tables and the indexes of well-known systems of classification; the "Decimal" and the "Expansive" . . .' (CUTTER, p. 80). But his examples of references under this rule do not fit with Coates' interpretation of 'synoptic table', since they may well be 'inter-discipline' references, e.g. from CATHEDRALS to CHRISTIAN ART. Interestingly, he also stated that the 'full' catalogue needs references from, e.g. MERCHANTS to individual names of merchants; the modern catalogue usually makes do with 'general' or 'blanket' references, or even may refer one to the shelf list at a cited class mark.

(*f*) Cutter also included rules (Sections 189-192) for form entry for collections of works in a literary form.

(*g*) Cutter quietly side-stepped the vexed problem of 'country versus subject' by casually recommending double entry—only, however, to advise against this later in the rule on the obvious ground of 'profusion of entry' (CUTTER, Section 164, p. 68). However, in the next rule, he recommends such references as ORNITHOLOGY *see also* NEW ENGLAND in preference to such a phrase heading as ORNITHOLOGY OF NEW ENGLAND which, in juxtaposition with ornithology of other areas, like ORNITHOLOGY OF SCOTLAND, he regards as 'in effect class-entry' (Section 165, p. 68). This is the one instance at least where he went wrong, especially since he infers next that NEW ENGLAND BOTANY, NEW ENGLAND ORNITHOLOGY, etc. are not! Here, surely, he plays into the hands of the 'moderns' who maintain that dictionary catalogues cannot help but be 'classificatory-based'.

(*h*) Finally, Cutter catered for subject entry of works of literature. This is also catered for in LC's list of subject headings, but not practised in many libraries. One suggests, here, that there is a great deal to be said for it: or at least its possibility in various types of libraries should be considered, where it is not covered by published bibliographies.

It should be remembered that Cutter did not publish a list of subject headings as such. Criticism of him today is usually based on the 4th edition of his Rules. Only a few modern authors, notably Metcalfe, have gone to the trouble of using his actual printed catalogue as a source of examples.

During the era of the emergence of the alphabetical-specific catalogue in the U.S.—and despite Dewey's own assumption of the classified catalogue—the rival alphabetical-classed catalogue continued to exert some influence. The British Museum *Subject Index* is sometimes quoted as if it were a pat example of alphabetical-classing. In fact it is a mixture of: (*a*) specific; (*b*) classing; and (*c*) alphabetical-classing, as should be obvious from even a casual examination of it. Headings like PHILOSOPHY —METAPHYSICS—ONTOLOGY will be found, and these are pure alphabetical-classing. On the other hand, one is just as likely to come across NORTH-WEST FRONTIER, INDIA, which is as specific as one would expect in a dictionary catalogue. A comparison between BM and LC heading construction is revealing. LC, has, under PHYSICS, *see also* references to some 50 other headings, most being divisions of Physics proper. A sample BM 5-year volume has about 45, again most being divisions of Physics proper. 'Within' Physics, LC has about 20 sub-divisions; the BM volume has 10. Further, LC has about 10 headings starting with 'Physical', while the BM volume has none. In general, the chief disadvantage of the BM work is that it is even more inconsistent than the conventional dictionary catalogue. A further disadvantage is that some headings change, apparently unaccountably, between volumes, making volume-by-volume searching for a subject difficult. This work was inaugurated in the 1880's, after reasonably consistently specific examples of alphabetical subject cataloguing had emerged elsewhere. Unfortunately, lists of subject headings had not at the time been generally published: the first usually noted was the American Library Association's in 1895 (PETTEE, p. 48), although the Australian librarian H. C. L. Anderson also issued one at about the same time but completely independently.

Although alphabetical-classing is regarded as rather a 'bogey' nowadays, occasional examples can be found. One in the School of Oriental and African Studies Library, London, includes headings like

AFRICAN LANGUAGES—ABYSSINIAN LANGUAGES—AMHARIC and
AFRICAN LANGUAGES—BANTU LANGUAGES—ZULU.

The classified catalogue continued, and remains, in vogue in Britain and some European countries. However, while people like Cutter and Anderson worked out dictionary catalogue rules during the nineteenth century, very little was done towards systematising the classified catalogue until after the Second World War. The printed classified catalogues of some of the larger libraries give an indication of the contrast between the American unit entry dictionary form and the classified catalogue of pre-war years. The Glasgow Public Libraries catalogue had a classified sequence with main entries (albeit short compared with LC unit cards) under class numbers with explanatory verbal headings—the nearest equivalent to today's feature headings.

e.g. 808.81 Poetry

    Blacklaw (J.) *comp.* A garden of remembrance, poems and
       extracts. (1940)

The same catalogue includes an 'Index of subjects and author names', including entries like:

    Davies (Joseph E.)   947.084
    Davis (Forrest)   327.42; 940.5373
    Davies (Moya L.)   *See* O'Sullivan (M.)   920.

But actual titles are given under the more prolific authors.

e.g. Darwin (Bernard R. M.)
         British clubs   367

British sports and games   796.04
Golf between two wars   796.352
At odd moments   808.8
Life is sweet, brother   920
Pack clouds away   920

The following is an excerpt from the 1949 edition:

(a) Classified sequence:
   614.32 Milk and milk products
      Nichols (A) The bacteriology of canned milk products. 1936.
(b) Author entry from index:
      Nichols (Agnes A.)   614.32.
(c) Subject entries from index:
   Milk   613.3; 637.1
   [etc., etc.]
   Sale of   614.32
   Canned foods   664.8
   ['Canning' as a surname—author]
   Canning industry   664.8
   Tin cans   671; 680.

If one may generalise on the strength of the treatment of one work in this catalogue, one cannot help but conclude that the subject approach was not very coherent at the time.

Also, those who regard the unit entry as an ideal will be dissatisfied with such treatment. But (a) all forms of printed catalogues, including Cutter's, used abbreviated added entries for other approaches; and (b) card examples of British classified catalogues usually gave fuller forms of author approach, e.g. Name, title, edition, date, class number—enough information for a work to be both identified and traced on the shelves. The author approach has in fact usually been called the author catalogue, not 'index', and justifiably so. The Westminster Public Libraries' conventionally printed catalogue, initiated after the Second World War, is probably more representative of the average form of the classified catalogue. The subject index of this catalogue also uses chain procedure (explained in detail in Chapter 16).

e.g. BIRDS

BIBLIOGRAPHIES   016.5982
ORNITHOLOGY   598.2
PETS   636.2

A second example illustrates the establishment of a comprehensive works number for a subject in general, in this instance a place.

e.g. WILTSHIRE	942.31
ANTIQUITIES	913.4231
APPRENTICES: TRAINING: ECONOMICS	331.861

A further interesting manifestation of the printed catalogue is Edinburgh Public Libraries' *Subject and Name index*, issued in 1949. Example of entry:

Hardy, Thomas, English novelist	PR 4740-58
bibliography	Z 8386
novels	PR 4745-50; PV 462
poems	PR 4741; PU 462
short stories	PX 462

This index is a light, convenient volume, and so can easily be taken around the shelves to locate the various aspects and examples of an author's works.

The history of the dictionary catalogue since Cutter is mainly a matter of consolidation and expansion. The syntactical inconsistencies allowed or recommended by Cutter—and less confusing to him because of the sequential scanning allowed for by the printed page—have been multiplied and copied so much, as a result of U.S. central cataloguing, that not even computerisation, apparently, can cause any radical change in practice (BNB MARC *Record service proposals*, Section 5.2).

However, LC has departed from Cutter in two chief ways: (*a*) a semi-classed arrangement of sub-headings 'within' approach term is used; this is detailed further in Chapter 24, on Filing; and (*b*) there has possibly been a tendency towards more constructed and inverted headings than Cutter would have countenanced; however, in the past few years, it seems that there has been a reversal to direct phrase entry. Criticism of LC-type practice is dealt with in the next chapter.

THE VATICAN CODE: SUBJECT RULES

These rules are numbers 369 to 452, taking nearly 70 pages: compare this with the space given in CUTTER to subject work. The basis of VATICAN's subject approach is acknowledged as deriving from LC.

Examples are in Italian, although the subject headings derived from them are also given in English.

Choice of heading is specific in the CUTTER (not the Coates) sense, e.g. a document about the planet Mars goes under MARS (PLANET), not, e.g. PLANETS, or ASTRONOMY. Multiple entry is commonly used for relationships between subjects, and partial repetition is preferred to long complex headings. Occasionally, also, 'class' as well as specific entry are allowed for a document—a practice used by some English-speaking dictionary cataloguers whether consciously or not: e.g. A work entitled *Malaria and Greek history* receives three entries:

MALARIAL FEVER—GREECE

MEDICINE, GREEK AND ROMAN

GREECE—HISTORY—PHILOSOPHY.

These examples also demonstrate the mixtures of construction used, following conventional practice. Other examples further demonstrate the conventional mixture as before, in the use of direct phrase headings, e.g. ILLUMINATION OF BOOKS AND MANUSCRIPTS.

It can be seen that VATICAN is virtually a detailed codification of LC practice, its content and approach corresponding approximately with HAYKIN, i.e. it accepts and propounds LC practice, but probably in more detail than is available elsewhere. The only chief difference from LC is that headings are filed strictly alphabetically—there is no grouping of like subdivisions under an entry word. However, headings using chronological subdivisions are sub-arranged by date. As far as the English-speaking librarian is concerned: if he proposes to use LC-type headings, he may as well go directly to the LC list itself, rather than use a code derived from LC practice as demonstrated from the list.

The chief value of VATICAN to us is that it enumerates the many problems which are encountered in alphabetical-specific cataloguing. This enumeration could be drawn upon if a new dictionary catalogue code were being compiled, although inevitably the rules solving the problems would probably be very different, to take into account 'modern' thought. Obviously to a great extent, the equivalent of much of this has been done already by Coates, since his formulae represent a reaction against LC practice as exhibited in its list of subject headings. VATICAN, then, could be used as source material for anyone wishing to compile a code, or even a list of headings, along lines different from both LC and Coates.

CHAPTER 13

Criticism and Evaluation of 'Conventional' Subject Headings Lists

CRITICISMS OF CONVENTIONAL SUBJECT HEADINGS LISTS
Broadly, there are four.

1. Headings are not specific enough for subjects covered by many documents, especially since subjects are becoming increasingly complex. An example is the book *Patterns of infant care* already mentioned on page 112; but in fairness see also the *Medical subject headings* example on page 151.

2. Headings are not constructed systematically. This fault can lead to (*a*) lack of faith in the catalogue—assuming its users think about it to that extent, even if only unconsciously; and (*b*) cataloguers not having reliable precedents for constructing new headings as required, e.g. LC contains

    1. (*a*) FOLKLORE OF BEES
       (*b*) FOLKLORE—JEWS
       (*c*) FOLKLORE, INDIAN

and

    2. (*a*) AZTECS—LEGENDS
       (*b*) LEGENDS, JEWISH

When a document on folklore or legends of a subject or people not already listed is catalogued for the first time, the cataloguer does not know what construction to use: (*a*) Citation order—subject or race, etc., first; (*b*) NOUN-NOUN, or NOUN, ADJECTIVE; or (*c*) direct phrase.

3. References are not always constructed systematically.

(*a*) 'Chains' of *see also* references do not always modulate. For example, one finds in LC:

    1. COMMUNICATION AND TRAFFIC
       see also
       [among others]
       RADIO
       TELECOMMUNICATION
       TELEGRAPH

TELEPHONE
[but not TELEVISION] and

2. TELECOMMUNICATION
see also
RADIO
TELEGRAPH
TELEPHONE
TELEVISION

So, to reach TELEVISION one must go via TELECOMMUNICATION, but to reach TELEPHONE, RADIO, etc., one can go either direct from COMMUNICATION AND TRAFFIC, or via TELECOMMUNICATION. This cannot be because Television is regarded as a division of Radio, because there is no reference RADIO *see also* TELEVISION.

(*b*) As already mentioned, special-to-general *see also* references are used only occasionally; in some cases they are lacking where they might have been useful, and vice versa.

(*c*) A major complaint voiced by Coates (e.g. pages 70, 71) is that 'cross-discipline' *see also* references are used at all, the allegation being that where the two interconnected subjects do occur in a document, an additional or a more specific heading is needed, and not a reference. One feels that such a criticism loses sight of the fact that the conventional dictionary catalogue, being independent of any one classificatory structure (which a critic may have in his unconscious mind), is intended to have such references. One cannot claim, say, that if a work on History includes something on Man, an extra or more specific heading is needed. The two topics themselves are bound up with each other inextricably as subjects and not as represented in the literature and so cannot by their very nature be separated.

However, a valid criticism arising is that certain headings have so many *see also* references that the user is bewildered. E.g. LC under COMMUNICABLE DISEASE has *see also* references to 35 other headings. One of these is to ANIMALS AS CARRIERS OF DISEASE, yet there are also, at this same point, 13 to names of individual animals, etc., e.g. RATS AS CARRIERS OF DISEASE. Modulation could have made the list of references shorter, and therefore more likely to be used carefully, even though an additional 'referral' is made necessary if one wishes to go from COMMUNICABLE DISEASES to, say, RATS AS CARRIERS OF DISEASE.

Further, in this example, there is merely a 'general' *see also* to 'names of communicable diseases' themselves; so (*a*) the same technique could have been used for various animals as carriers of disease (as an alternative or addition to the modulation mentioned above); but (*b*), and much more important, such general references leave one unaware of which specific divisions of a topic exist in the catalogue at all.

(*d*) So, the 'general' or 'blanket' *see also* reference is a chief disadvantage of the dictionary catalogue. However, judgement is needed to decide when one will suffice and when one will not. It has been assumed here that specific *see also* references are needed in the above-mentioned example. Others may argue the other way. But if they are not used, even though possibly likely to be needed, there must be a ready alternative: some libraries refer the user to a particular classification number in the shelf list, e.g. for English poets one is referred to 821, as already mentioned in Chapter 9. In fact, this constitutes use of the shelf list as a substitute classified file, which it is not intended to be. In certain cases, general references may suffice, e.g. from HISTORY to 'names of countries, regions, etc., with the subdivision HISTORY'.

A superfluity of references may also be complained of when a list includes a *see* reference from one form of construction to another, as well as a *see also* reference from the same generic subject to the specific, e.g.

> Television, Closed-circuit *see* CLOSED-CIRCUIT TELEVISION, and TELEVISION *see also* CLOSED-CIRCUIT TELEVISION.

Provided headings were constructed as consistently as possible, and provided the user were carefully instructed (and remembered his instruction), one would suggest the use of *see also* references only in such cases, especially since LC is tending more and more towards the 'direct phrase' form of construction of headings.

4. The sub-arrangement at headings in LC, and so in libraries following this list, is not alphabetical, but is grouped which invokes in effect a form of classification. This is discussed also in Chapter 24, on Filing, although it is very relevant and should be considered at this point also. The basis of the complaint is that the erstwhile dictionary catalogue is becoming a quasi-classified file, and is therefore defeating its own object of direct, specific, alphabetically-arranged entry. However, it is untrue to say that such arrangements constitute alphabetical-classing, since all the components of the headings are necessary, e.g. COOKERY (APPLES) is no more alphabetical-classing than, say, APPLES—COOKERY.

A new—or even first!—fully explanatory code for alphabetical-subject headings and references is required if these criticisms are to be met. The various alternatives to, and improvements upon, existing practices are dealt with next. However, it is no use preaching without practising. Criticism of LC in particular has been going on for years now, and one presumes that its subject cataloguers have read such criticisms. Nevertheless, the decision has been made that the existing subject headings are to be incorporated into the U.S. computerised Project MARC, despite their blatantly obvious faults. The situation is parallel to the virtual lack of adoption by Library of Congress of even the (conservative) North American text of AACR 1967. While one appreciates that large bodies have both momentum and a day-to-day responsibility to those whom they serve, it is suggested here that ultimately the Library of Congress may prove to have done a disservice not only to American cataloguers, but even to the world of librarianship. Just as the British Museum's code was overtaken by events at the turn of the century and is now mainly library history, the time may come when another more radical centre may be needed to replace the Library of Congress as a world cataloguing centre. It is computerising, and some people still maintain that computers will make arguments about heading and reference construction unnecessary. This has not yet been proved.

For the moment, in this section, perhaps in fairness one should let the conservatives have the final say: i.e. that, despite its faults, the conventional dictionary catalogue has undoubtedly been effective; and that, again, despite its inconsistencies, people do get used to using it and finding what they want. They may maintain that nothing is ever perfect, that we are at least dealing with the devil we know: they indicate the awkwardness and artificiality of BTI—as the devil they don't know.

EVALUATING A LIST OF SUBJECT HEADINGS

1. It should be comprehensive for the library in which it is used.

2. It may be necessary to use two or more lists in combination with each other to achieve comprehensiveness, in which case lists should be compatible. Note particularly that there are many lists, dealing with various subject areas, as well as general lists like LC and SEARS. Inter-library cooperation may be very relevant here.

3. It should be up to date, including new subjects or new compounds of subjects, e.g. SEARS 9th edition does not cater for 'abstracts' as a subdivision.

4. Headings should be as consistent as possible in their construction. Deliberate inconsistencies should be explained. The list should show how two or more headings may be combined if necessary to produce compound headings. This entails (*a*) instructions, or precedents, or (*b*) statement of citation orders and how they are applied, including preferred parts of speech, e.g. noun or adjectival form.

5. New editions should delete unwanted headings and references on which documents are not normally produced, e.g. general lists produced during the Second World War included many relevant headings (with references), such as on air-raid precautions, to cope with the literature of the time; post-war editions dropped many of them. This is one reason for keeping older editions, but care should be taken to ensure consistency: see also item 6.

6. Terminology should be as up to date as possible consistent with usage, e.g. SEARS 9th edition uses SINGLE WOMEN, and not SPINSTERS, this now being a *see* reference. But care has to be taken not to include terms which may prove to have been merely colloquialisms (will SKYJACKING become an accepted term?), or which have a loose or inaccurate meaning.

7. Partly from 6: care has to be taken to ensure that headings are used according to the meanings of their own time, e.g. literally the Industrial Revolution is still happening, but in its accepted historical meaning it is past history.

8. Therefore scope notes should be included to clarify headings where necessary, e.g. the dividing line between 'ancient' and 'modern' history: SEARS uses 'modern' for general works covering the period after 1453.

9. Headings should be the most likely to be 'sought'.

10. There should be adequate and consistently constructed references to lead both the cataloguer and the user to the 'chosen' heading for the subject required by them.

11. Consistently constructed references should lead from the 'chosen' subject heading to related subjects. These (usually *see also*) references should modulate, i.e. operate one step at a time, as far as possible.

12. In general, there should be clear and comprehensive instructions on how to use the list.

13. Categories of headings to be added by the cataloguer should be clearly indicated, with instructions, or examples, showing the form they should take, and the references which should support them, e.g. SEARS,

Folk dance music (M1627)

 Here are entered collections of miscellaneous folk dance music. Music for individual dances is entered under dance form, *e.g.* Square dance music.
 If the collection also contains dance instruction, two headings are used, *e.g.* 1. Folk dancing. 2. Folk dance music.
 If the collection is for a medium other than piano, additional heading is used for the medium, *e.g.* 1. Folk dance music. 2. Orchestral music, Arranged.

 x National dances
 xx Dance music
  Folk music
  Music
Note under Folk dancing

Folk dance music, American, [French, German, etc.] (M1629-1853)

Folk dancing (Indirect) (GV1580-1799)

 Here are entered collections of miscellaneous folk dances which include instructions for the dances.
 If the collection also contains the dance music, two headings are used, *e.g.* 1. Folk dancing. 2. Folk dance music.

 sa Folk music
  Play-party
  Square dancing
 x National dances
 xx Dancing
  Dancing (in religion, folk-lore, etc.)
  Folk music
  National music
Note under Folk dance music

Folk dancing, Argentine, [French, German, etc.]
 Subdivided by locality.
 sa names of individual folk dances

Folk-drama (History, PN1008.D7)
 sa Carnival plays
  Pastoral drama
  Puppets and puppet-plays
 x Folk-plays
 xx Drama
  Pastoral drama

Folk-drama, American (Indirect)
Folk-drama, German, [Italian, etc.] (Direct)

Folk high schools
 x People's high schools

Folk-lore (Indirect)
 sa Amulets
 Animal lore
 Animals, Legends
 Animism
 Chap-books
 Charms
 Counting-out rhy
 Devil
 Divining-rod
 Dragons
 Dryads
 Dwarfs
 Elixir of life
 Evil eye
 Fables
 Fairies
 Fairy tales
 Folk music
 Folk-songs
 Folklorists
 Geographical my
 Ghosts
 Ghouls and ogres
 Giants
 Grail
 Halloween
 Incantations
 Legends
 Leopard men
 Literature, Primi
 Mandrake
 Marriage custom
 Myth
 Mythology
 Nursery rhymes
 Oral tradition
 Plant lore
 Proverbs
 Riddles
 Sacred groves
 Sagas
 Sirens (Mytholog
 Sun lore
 Sun-worship
 Superstition
 Swan-maidens
 Tales
 Tree-worship

Excerpt from LIBRARY OF CONGRESS list of subject headings showing instructions in the text: scope notes.

under BIRDS, states that 'names of birds . . . are to be added . . .': one has often known students who therefore produce, say, BIRDS—PARROTS. The situation could have been clarified by including 'at their appropriate place in the list' or similar (or are such students beyond hope?).

14. Instructions may be general, e.g. as an Introduction; or at appropriate points in the list, e.g. as shown in facsimile on page 141 from LC. It should be clear where such instructions should be expected, why, and what form they take, e.g. common subdivisions (or their equivalent) should all be at the beginning of the work, and either all or none should be repeated at their appropriate point in the main list.

15. Ways of constructing references should be clearly explained, preferably with examples, e.g. there is occasional objection to the use of 'x' and 'xx' in some lists. If this objection is valid, self-explanatory alternatives should be used, e.g. modern thesauri usually use literal mnemonics like NT for 'narrower term' or UF for 'use for'.

16. A list may include class marks, from an appropriate scheme. If this is done, they should be accurate and their purpose explained. (The conventional dictionary catalogue purist may maintain that such equivalents are impossible, since the dictionary catalogue is inherently independent of all classification schemes. SEARS 9th edition has stopped using DC numbers, but LC still includes LC Classification numbers—the purist may like to argue this out with the compilers.)

17. The list should, in turn, be both helpful to the cataloguer, and result in a catalogue which is (a) efficient, and (b) easy to use by the staff and the clientele of the library. By way of a pessimistic conclusion, it should be admitted that some librarians doubt if these conditions are compatible.

FILING AND ARRANGEMENT

Filing in the dictionary catalogue has something in common with that in the alphabetical sequence(s) of the classified catalogue, and is explained in Chapter 24, on Filing.

It could be mentioned here, though, that the one-sequence dictionary catalogue can become very complex and therefore confusing and hard to use efficiently. Therefore, some large libraries, in North America and Australia particularly, have divided or split their catalogues into two alphabetical sequences: (a) Author/Title, etc., entries with relevant references; and (b) Subject entries with relevant references.

CHAPTER 14

The 'Conventional' Subject Approach:
Two Australian Contributions

Dictionary catalogue, or alphabetical-subject catalogue, codes have been compiled since the times of Cutter and Anderson and before the theories and practices of E. J. Coates arrived in the 1950's.

The VATICAN code has been regarded as the fullest exposition of contemporary American practice, and, as an accompaniment to HAYKIN, it serves a useful purpose as a sort of 'apprenticeship' code. That is, it helps one get used to the empirical decisions manifested by conventional dictionary catalogue practice. However, it does not embody principles corresponding to those of Lubetzky in author/title cataloguing. It is dealt with as far as necessary in Chapter 12.

It is suggested here that the most trenchant criticism and comment, but still couched in 'conventional' language, and still insisting that the dictionary catalogue is inherently independent of classification schemes, has come from Australia, where perhaps 99 per cent of libraries have dictionary or divided alphabetical catalogues.

Perhaps the most noteworthy—but neglected—attempt at a code which tries to avoid the obvious inconsistencies of conventional practice, but without establishing rigid formulae, is John METCALFE's 'Tentative code of rules for alphabetico-specific entry', Appendix H in his *Subject classifying and indexing of libraries and literature*, 1959. His code is Cutter-type in its use of rules, examples and discussion, and for these reasons it warrants careful examination. Metcalfe, while admiring and being grateful to the Library of Congress for its great organisation and workmanlike cataloguing, expresses some misgivings in the Introduction to his Tentative Code: '. . . too much reliance can be placed on the apparatus of central cataloguing, on unit cards with tracing notes and subject headings lists; too much can be left to Congress, and both principles and self-reliance lost sight of' (METCALFE, p. 263). The Code was originally compiled as a teaching instrument, which may account for its occasional repetitiveness, and—for us—unfortunate lack of decision in parts.

The Code establishes several times that it aims at specific, and not 'classed'—or broader than necessary—headings. However, Metcalfe infers that 'alphabetico-classed'—as an example of 'classed'—is in effect opposite to 'alphabetico-specific', that e.g. DOMESTIC ANIMALS—DOGS is not specific. One suggests that it is specific, because it gets round to naming 'dogs', but that it is, so to speak, 'indirect-specific'. Merely DOMESTIC ANIMALS for a work on dogs is not possibly specific, of course. Elsewhere in the Code, FOOTBALL, SOCCER is suggestively allowed—although 'Soccer' is a term peculiar to football. Also, later in the Code, he implies that a Kaiser-type breaking up of a long word into component simpler words, e.g. MAPS—DRAWING rather than CARTOGRAPHY, is allowable for the sake of collocation. (Kaiser is discussed in Chapter 15.) Surely the overriding factor in a direct catalogue should be: which is the most-used form? The code also states that it can be applied to all documents, whether, say, periodical articles or whole books. Metcalfe does not differentiate in principle, but in degree, between what Ranganathan has called microthought and macrothought: and one is inclined to agree with him.

Various forms of construction are allowed, e.g. NOUN-NOUN, phrases and inverted phrases—the latter giving rise to quite a lot of justification of, say, SHEEP, MERINO as allowable even though it appears to be 'class' entry. But adjectival or conjunctive phrases are preferred to prepositional phrases. Also qualifying terms in parentheses are allowed, to clarify possible ambiguity, as in SCALES (BOTANY), SCALES (FISHES), SCALES (MUSICAL), [not (MUSIC)!], SCALES (WEIGHING). LC's other use of ( ) is deliberately eschewed as 'subdivided class entry', e.g. COOKERY (APPLES), which allegation is not substantiated. The dash, comma and parentheses are given filing significance without order: but since one might hazard that an average user would not know whether to expect, say, SHEEP, MERINO or SHEEP—MERINO, its value is possibly dubious.

Metcalfe appears to allow what Coates would probably regard as 'non-extensive' headings, e.g. Malthus' *Essay on population* goes under (a) FOOD SUPPLY and (b) POPULATION; not, say, POPULATION—INFLUENCED BY—FOOD SUPPLY.

The term 'qualification' is used for differentiating between a whole and its parts, e.g. Chairs and Legs, and is differentiated from the Genus-Species relationship. 'Qualification' can also embrace 'aspect' or 'process', as in MOTOR CARS—WASHING, and as in 'the historical form of something'.

Quite complex headings are allowed, e.g. AIR—POLLUTION—EFFECTS—CANCER, 'and/or' [!] CANCER—CAUSES—AIR POLLUTION. Also LAW—STUDY AND TEACHING—BIBLIOGRAPHY. However, elsewhere, the practice of multiple simple entry, as practised by LC is abandoned, i.e. there is a move towards pre-coordinate cataloguing: elsewhere in the Code, then, ANATOMY, COMPARATIVE—MATERIALS—FROGS is allowed: a thought-provoking one, this.

Either scientific or common terms may be used, depending on the usage of the users of the catalogue, e.g. either HORSES or EQUUS CABALLUS. However, if inaccurate terms or slang terms are colloquially used, these are not allowed as headings.

'Degree of specification' should go to at least the most specific noun. But Wall beds may go under BEDS, presumably the assumption being either that 'Wall' here is used as an adjective, or that it is not 'the most specific noun'. And elsewhere in the Code, Metcalfe allows HORSES—DISEASES alone for Strangles.

'Class' entry is not allowed in addition to specific entry, as well as not being allowed as an alternative.

'Qualification' terms must be as used in their relevant context, e.g. WOOL—CLASSING not WOOL—GRADING; but COTTON—GRADING. This rule seems to rule out the possibility of a synthetic list made up of various series of consistent terms which could be brought together in various combinations as required. Therefore, a list of headings compiled according to this code would appear to be necessarily enumerative, not synthetic, all subdivisions being listed according to accepted usage. Metcalfe does not seem to allow what one would call 'seminal semantics'.

Inverted sub-headings are allowed, e.g. FURNITURE—TRADE, RETAIL. The introduction of a second type of punctuation in one heading seems unnecessarily different from the multiple-concept headings using only the dash as a separating device exemplified above.

Metcalfe does not satisfactorily resolve the problem of the multi-component specific heading. As mentioned above, he allows HORSES—DISEASES for Strangles, which one suggests is class entry, but alternatively he allows the indirect HORSES—DISEASES—STRANGLES, and not HORSES—STRANGLES. Since the dictionary catalogue had an original ideal of direct entry, one would have expected, at least as an alternative, HORSES—STRANGLES.

The Code cannot—and perhaps, no code ever will satisfactorily—

solve the large problem of place *vs* subject. Some indication at least is given however; History *of* Australia points towards AUSTRALIA—HISTORY, while Education *in* Australia points towards EDUCATION—AUSTRALIA: a logical piece of reasoning, as well as being simple, and therefore worthy of thought.

Citation orders in other respects seem to remain confused. Following LC-type practice, and without—it seems—satisfactory justification, the Code allows ENGLISH LITERATURE, but ARCHITECTURE, SPANISH and MUSICIANS, NEGRO.

Despite what has been said already about a tendency towards pre-coordination, the old habit of multiple entry recurs later in the Code, when ART—THEORIES, PSYCHOANALYTIC and PSYCHOANALYSIS—APPLICATIONS—ART THEORY are advised for a document on Art and psychoanalysis.

'Upwards' references, either *see* or *see also*, are not allowed, except for the latter 'in some special cases' like GLACIERS *see also* GEOLOGY, with no explanation of why it is special. The main reasons given against 'upwards' are: (*a*) the enquirer may probably have only just been referred 'downwards'—a valid objection; and (*b*) it 'is generally considered to be one of the things which would take more labour and space, and make more confusion than it would be worth'. Contrast this with Coates' assertion that search processes work from special to general (COATES p. 42). Neither author substantiates his assumption, although possibly Coates assumes that the specific nature of the required subject has been ascertained in a 'search strategy' routine, while Metcalfe may assume the public's use of the catalogue.

See also references should be modulated (though Metcalfe eschews this term—too classificatory?). He emphasises that *see also* references are independent of any classification scheme, and not 'determined by the hierarchical class number of the finally specific subject in any classification, even though the number may be used for the classification of the specific literature on the shelf'. He refutes such claims by Ranganathan and Coates, and reiterates that there may be more than one sequence of references between two subjects. He seems to feel strongly about it. . . .

Collateral *see also* references are allowed between subjects which 'have something in common'. Agreed, although probably the cataloguer needs a passable amount of relevant subject knowledge to make a decision.

The Code finishes with a warning that in using lists of headings a document should not be forced under a heading which breaks the rules for alphabetico-specific entry. Practising cataloguers are likely to concur. However, it should be pointed out that SEARS, for example, gives positive instructions about when a heading may be subdivided, and how. If SEARS' rules are broken they must be done so consistently, e.g. if one decides to subdivide geographically for one document although not told to, one must do the same for other documents on such subjects in relation to places.

Metcalfe's Code seems worth quoting at length. But he has not given guidance on some of the very topics which bedevil cataloguers, especially in his rules on the construction of compound headings.

An even more neglected commentator is R. K. Olding, the author of an article which sheds some light on heading construction ('The form of alphabetico-specific subject headings, and a brief code', *Australian library journal*, July 1961, p. 127-137).

Olding derived his suggestions from an examination of the works of Cutter, Kaiser, Haykin, and Metcalfe and from experience with the LC List of headings. He states: 'Despite the great achievement of Congress's dictionary cataloguing, much of its subject practice is outdated, inconsistent, unrealistic, incomplete, and at times unnecessary'. Cutter is justifiably blamed for the inconsistency in heading construction. (Although of course, this does not mean that Cutter was stupid—it is too much to expect that the first codifier of the dictionary catalogue should at one stroke—or even in four editions—produce the perfect code, especially since this has still not been produced.) Olding contrasts, e.g., Cutter's inconsistency in his examples of CIRCULATION OF THE BLOOD and CATTLE—DISEASES. He also points out that HAYKIN does not know the meaning of 'alphabetico-classed' because he thinks a compound heading like ENGLISH LANGUAGE—VERB is an example of it. He also demands specificity, e.g. not hiding specific makes of cars (other than Fords!) under AUTOMOBILES. However, one disagrees strongly with Olding's use of the term 'class entry' for 'alphabetico-class entry': the two terms have different meanings, as Olding's own examples show.

Olding's summary Code is here summarised; reference is not made here to rules which one could take for granted, like the emphasis on the specific principle, and the numbering of items here does not follow Olding's.

1. Basically, constructed headings are preferred, using the NOUN—

NOUN structure in preference to phrase headings. However, this is not to be confused with specific subjects which are normally represented in phrase form, e.g. FIRST AID. But:

2. 'Species, kind, or variety' of subjects normally receive direct phrase entry, e.g. SIAMESE CATS, although, unfortunately, Olding cannot make up his mind, and he adds an alternative rule for inverted form, following Metcalfe.

3. However, the place *vs* subject problem is decided upon as positively as the nature of the problem allows. The formula is PLACE—SUBJECT—and far more strictly advocated than, say, by Coates. In his preamble Olding reaches the point of pushing this to its ultimate conclusion in his search for consistency by considering FRANCE—POETRY for 'poetry in French'—a solution which deserves sympathy. The heading can theoretically be misunderstood to mean 'poetry about France', but it is still no more misleading than some headings one comes across, and the chances are that users would get used to it like they have got used to inconsistent and ambiguous headings as commonly used already. Where place cannot be made to be relevant, ethnic noun is allowed, e.g. NEGROES—MUSIC. This example, of course, is itself a test of the PLACE (or RACE)—SUBJECT formula, since one can easily argue that the 'Music' element is more significant than the 'Negroes' element.

4. The use of ( ) is to be avoided, cf. LC's COOKERY (APPLES), and BTI's GAS (TOWN).

Olding's 'Code' takes just one half of a page, and it obviously cannot therefore rule for all contingencies, as he admits. But people looking for an Occam's Razor might well like to read his article as an alternative start towards a solution to the construction of headings, especially if they find the other end of the spectrum—Coates and his 20 formulae—too extreme.

CHAPTER 15

Formularised Construction of Subject Headings

By 'formularised' we mean:

(*a*) Taking care over the syntax of subject terms, e.g. preferring nouns.

(*b*) Establishing citation orders in which the components of compound subject headings are given. In general, formularised construction runs counter to direct construction. An example of 'formularised' is CHILDREN: PSYCHOLOGY; the 'direct' form is CHILD PSYCHOLOGY.

Kaiser was probably the first, though largely unsung, protagonist of the use of categories of terms, for which he prescribed a set citation or combination order. He announced his practice in *Systematic indexing*, published as long ago as 1911. For those who attach abilities to nationalities, let it be stated that he was born in Germany, spent a few years in Australia in his twenties, and from there he went to South America. Finally, he went north to U.S., and from there to Britain, eventually returning to U.S. where he worked on—and left his mark on—the *Engineering index*. He was a British subject; his works were published in London, but his main work in information retrieval took place in U.S. (METCALFE, p. 297-298).

Kaiser's methods were designed for commercial and technical indexing, and so may possibly be criticised for their lack of comprehensiveness in application. The main characteristics of his work are:

1. Selective analytical indexing took precedence over the subject cataloguing of a whole physical bibliographical unit: '. . . We do not want books: we want information . . .' (METCALFE, p. 298).

2. He devised the now familiar CONCRETE—PROCESS formula as a citation order—recognisable immediately in Coates's THING: ACTION. In implementing the formula, he went beyond the manipulation of individual whole words. If a single term represented a CONCRETE—PROCESS, then he split it, using other words to fit his formula. So 'Agriculture' became LAND—CULTIVATION, and 'Education' became CHILDREN—INSTRUCTION (METCALFE, p. 299). An obvious advantage is that all material on, say, Children, is collocated. But, as happens

sometimes with dictionary catalogue constructed headings, this type of collocation under Concretes is not necessarily useful. This assumption is perpetuated in the British Classification Research Group's Library Science Classification, which follows a similar formula, following Ranganathan. Hence Cataloguing of films, for example, is arranged at FILMS: CATALOGUING despite one's suspicions that such material is wanted, in study and research at least, by cataloguers rather than film librarians. On the other hand, Coates has mentioned an example where the collocation might be useful: when Wages and Strikes, respectively, become LABOUR—PRICE and LABOUR—WITHDRAWAL (COATES, p. 42). The snag is that most enquirers, unless well-disciplined, would use their 'habitual way of looking at things' (as Cutter would say), and instinctively turn to the more natural heading in each case.

Kaiser's CONCRETE is probably broader than Coates's THING, as it can include also places, as well as abstract nouns which in any case could be embraced by THING. Also PROCESS was interpreted rather more in the meaning of the traditional classification term aspect, or the more modern term facet; it could also include form of treatment of the concrete in the document in question.

Coates has suggested that Kaiser's analysis of words would not apply throughout a heading, e.g. Kaiser might have had PAINT—APPLICATION, but BOATS—PAINTING, where a potentially rival concrete PAINT, is turned into a process (COATES, p. 40).

3. 'Place vs subject' is solved—or sidestepped—by double entry: CONCRETE—PLACE—PROCESS and PLACE—CONCRETE—PROCESS.

4. Parts of a geographical entity are entered indirectly, e.g. BELGIUM —LIÈGE (COATES, p. 43).

5. References are made both 'upwards' and 'downwards'. The advantages and disadvantages of this method have already been touched upon. Coates has pointed out that Kaiser might well finish up with more references than actual entries (COATES, p. 40); this indeed is the tendency of BTI under the editorship of Coates, and Kaiser's example partly accounts for this unprecedented indulgence in referencing.

It is evident that Kaiser was ahead of his time, and that he has since exerted a considerable influence.

E. J. Coates, himself considerably influenced by Ranganathan, has probably exerted a more direct and practical influence on the alphabetical-subject approach than any other living person: in Britain at least, for his work is still not accepted in some other English-speaking countries. One's reading of American professional journals and one's contacts with sample American librarians gives one the impression that some American librarians at least do not recognise the existence of problems in the 'conventional' approach (e.g. LC; SEARS), and naturally they do not apprehend any need for cures. However, other Americans do recognise some faults in the CUTTER/LC heritage. One has not come across documentary evidence that E. J. Coates has been directly responsible for, say, the move towards greater specificity of headings in the U.S. National Library of Medicine's *Medical subject headings,* as shown in its more recent occasional *Notes for medical catalogers,* but evidently some thinking and amendment at least is taking place. For example, the single heading AGE DETERMINATION BY TEETH is now recommended instead of multiple entry of relevant documents under (*a*) AGEING, and (*b*) TEETH (*Notes for medical cataloguers,* vol. 2, no. 1, November 1966).

Coates's disciples may reject such a phrase heading because it is not structured according to a formula. This would produce perhaps AGE, DETERMINATION, TEETH, which is easier to file, and so to find, once one knows the method used, but whose meaning is not so obvious because the relationships between the terms is not obvious. So, the disciple of Farradane (mentioned in a little more detail later) might produce something like AGE/-DETERMINATION/;TEETH. On the other hand, a compromise could be effected verbally by leaving in explanatory terms, often prepositions, but not giving them filing significance.

e.g. AGE : DETERMINATION : (from) TEETH or
AGE : DETERMINATION : (by) TEETH.

But, to find out how we reached this situation, it is best to go back to Coates, and his investigation of 'conventional' phrase headings and other alphabetical-subject problems.

Coates's contribution itself can be examined under the following headings:

1. Heading construction as an end in itself, as in dictionary catalogues and indexes to periodicals.

2. Reference construction in relation to the headings in item 1.

3. Construction of the subject index to a classified catalogue, using the relevant classification scheme as an aid to construction. Hence:

4. The application of the principles of item 3 to dictionary catalogue subject headings and references.

5. The construction and publication of lists of subject headings as in item 4.

The use of phrase headings is analysed by Coates (e.g. COATES, p. 22). He looks at the construction ADJECTIVE NOUN (or ADJECTIVAL NOUN NOUN), and compares it with NOUN PREPOSITION NOUN. e.g. We may have CHILD PSYCHOLOGY, or PHYSCHOLOGY OF CHILDREN. Looking for the shortest consistent way of expressing such compound subjects he tries the first, but realises that it does not always work in normal speech, e.g. one uses CHILD PSYCHOLOGY, and just possibly INFANT PSYCHOLOGY, but not CHIMPANZEE PSYCHOLOGY. So, if we want both natural phraseology and consistency we must accept the longer form, e.g. PSYCHOLOGY OF CHIMPANZEES. However, again, some, even if comparatively few, subjects do not conform, e.g. FOREIGN RELATIONS would have to become RELATIONS BETWEEN FOREIGN COUNTRIES, he says. Actually, just RELATIONS BETWEEN COUNTRIES would have sufficed, but the fact remains that the phrase is unnatural, thereby contradicting the whole principle of terminology as spoken.

Inevitably, then, Coates reaches the conclusion that such subjects, if they are to be syntactically consistent, must be constructed or structured, e.g. CHILDREN, Psychology. One feels that the choice of the comma as a basic separating device was unfortunate, especially since it was used in BTI from its inception until the introduction of a variety of punctuation marks with relationship meanings in 1968 when preparations started for computerising it. The reason for one's dislike is obvious: traditionally in just about all other reference works, catalogues, bibliographies, indexes, etc., the comma has implied an inverted phrase heading, and its use in BTI has caused quite a lot of antagonism which could easily have been avoided by the use of, say, the colon which in English syntax implies a qualification or explanation of what precedes it.

Coates inevitably then has to consider more complicated subjects, e.g. he suggests OWLS, Pests, Control by, to represent 'control of pests by owls', the final preposition being needed to prevent confusion with 'control of owls as pests'. Elsewhere (COATES, p. 56) he produces FIRES, Lightning for 'fires caused by lightning', which does not seem wholly satisfactory, and MOUNTAINS, Birds, which is even less satisfactory as a self-explanatory heading.

It will be seen further, from the examples cited, that Coates prefers plurals in all cases, although he appreciates that, say, CHILDREN files at a different place from CHILD. But he has already decided that natural and direct language must be abandoned anyway, as shown, e.g. by his PILES, Driving.

Having decided on structured headings, Coates next had to decide the order in which the terms had to be combined, i.e. a citation order. The important thing is to choose the correct approach term, or term under which the subject is entered in the catalogue. The less-sought term has to be catered for by the use of references, of course. Coates here embarked on a 'grammar' of heading construction which had to be complex because it had to cater for all the possible relationships which exist between subjects. He drew up a list of 20 different 'types of compound' (table facing p. 55 of his *Subject catalogues*). In order to start to arrive at these, he first decided that compound subjects demonstrated a significance order: one part of a compound was more significant than another because 'most readily available to the memory of the enquirer' (COATES, p. 50). He decided that the most significant element was usually a thing which can be visualised as a 'static image'. 'Concrete' nouns (in the grammatical sense) are obvious examples, and he therefore cites cat as being more significant than the movement of the cat. The next most significant (in his definition), after 'thing', is whatever the thing is made of, so material too is more significant than action. He, therefore, fairly easily reaches a citation order of

THING/MATERIAL/ACTION.

This reflects a citation order already put forward by Ranganathan in his *Colon classification*, which requires components (isolates) to be combined according to the formula. PERSONALITY/MATTER/ENERGY, plus further categories; though 'personality' can be rather more complicated than a concrete object, just as Coates's 'thing' may well transpire to be an abstract noun like ASTRONOMY. It is evident, of course, that a great deal of Coates's technique derives from Ranganathan, although the Ranganathan categories cited above as used in his classification scheme are changed when applied by their author to dictionary cataloguing, and the Energy (Action) may become the first-cited term—and often with good reason. Also, the first two components correspond closely with Kaiser's CONCRETE—PROCESS formula, which of course Coates admits.

Thing/Material/Action serves quite a few purposes and may well be the most-used formula of Coates, especially since the order of any two parts from it have also been automatically decided, e.g. THING/MATERIAL, THING/ACTION and MATERIAL/ACTION.

Probably the next most important categories to decide on are the parts of a whole or thing, e.g. 'engines of aircraft', 'wheels of cars'. Coates had already discovered that a phrase in the form of 'A of B' usually finished up in reverse order, i.e. B, A; e.g. INVERTEBRATES, Exploitation (Thing/Action).

By roughly the same principle, then, we can evolve the citation order of

THING, Part
e.g. AIRCRAFT, Engines.

The same usually applies to 'A for B', e.g. 'Containers for food', which again evolves to B, A.

Another category which is liable to occur is what Coates calls PRO-PERTY. This term is not adequately defined by Coates, but only exemplified, e.g. 'fertility', 'strength', 'speed'. One might explain it as a 'weak' or less significant form of ACTION. Its 'weakness' makes it not very significant, and it is cited after the categories already mentioned.

The next type of compound subject which may be quite important is that involving an influence or reaction between two subjects, e.g. 'fires caused by lightning', 'craters caused by meteorites'. Significance is not always very obvious from the 'visual image' point of view— 'craters' and 'meteorites' may both be equally 'visual'. But the more important part of the combination is usually the result of the reaction or action, and Coates finds it straightforward to arrive usually at a 'CAUSED, Causing' solution. But if we have an ACTION caused by a THING, this could upset his basic formula of THING/ACTION, and, rather unconvincingly one feels, he allows the basic formula to triumph, despite its resulting in an opposite meaning to the 'CAUSED, Causing' formula. Unfortunately, also, he cites a weak example, which in any case results in a phrase heading: PSYCHICAL PHENOMENA.

Coates discusses the permanent problem of place *vs* subject. Cutter had side-stepped it, like Kaiser after him, by preferring double entry, but under what one now calls 'classed' (i.e. over-broad) headings, e.g. 'geology of California' under GEOLOGY and CALIFORNIA: not GEOLOGY—CALIFORNIA or vice versa (CUTTER, Rule 164, p. 68). But then Cutter relented and allowed 'a general subject with special reference to a place' to go under place. He quotes NEW ENGLAND, i.e. part of a country as his main example, and one is left with the impression that what he would probably have called a 'general' place might be excepted, and still receive double entry: country and subject. However, Coates's interpretation is simply that Cutter prefers 'locality as entry word with topic as subheading' (COATES, p. 60). Coates tries to fit 'place' into his category 'property' but acknowledges that 'place' may equally be regarded as a 'thing', with the subject being a 'part'. Ultimately, as in conventional dictionary catalogues, he has to categorise types of subject. It will be remembered that the conventional dictionary catalogue distinguishes between sizes of place, resulting in headings like POLICE—U.S., but CHICAGO—POLICE. On the other hand, Coates distinguishes between 'size' of subject, feeling that FRANCE, Animals is acceptable, but that one should decide on NIGHTINGALES, France. Eventually, and with on the whole acceptable reasoning, he decides that place should receive priority for the following: geography, geology, history, social sciences, linguistics, literature, ecology, and the names of groups of natural organisms, plant and animal. But study in these fields, like 'historiography' and 'literary criticism', should receive SUBJECT, Place treatment. Also 'locally' limited topics in 'fine arts', 'technology', 'science', 'philosophy' and 'religion' receive SUBJECT, Place treatment. As with the conventional dictionary catalogue, one wonders at the different treatment of literature and arts, as though the use of a foreign language, in literatures, must necessarily put at nought all that literary forms have in common; and in any case translations into English exist for many works for readers without fluency in other languages. Literature is an 'art': perhaps Coates is still bedevilled by, e.g., DC and UDC, which have separate main classes for Arts as distinguished from literature. Also, as with the conventional dictionary catalogue, one has to decide to which named category a smaller class belongs, e.g. DC has 'numismatics' as an Art, while LC Classification has it in History. The schemes themselves are not of direct help, since in all cases in DC, and in many in LC, for example, place is the last-cited. The only exceptions are Language and Literature, in which, language, usually inferring place, receives priority over form, treatment, etc.

Form of name is fairly quickly settled: Use adjectival form as subheading; otherwise follow conventional practice. But it is noteworthy that the adjectival form of sub-heading did not survive into BTI.

Incidentally, Coates is rather cavalier with punctuation here too. At the very place where the comma would have a generally accepted syntactical use—implying inverted headings—NOUN, Adjective—he uses the dash, e.g. RAILWAYS—Brazilian. Another device not followed up in BTI, and perhaps derived from Ranganathan, is the putting of the 'home' country at the front of the subsequence.

Finally, in the 'place—subject' problem, Coates deals with the 'Place and Event or Period' compound. The solution is given as PLACE—Event, and PLACE—Period. He cites international events as examples, resulting in FRANCE, Reformation, and FIGHTERS, Aircraft, German, World War 2, about both of which there can be considerable argument. The Reformation is probably studied as a whole just as much, if not more, in relation to one country: but this order is arrived at presumably because Coates had already decided on the PLACE, History formula. In the second example, it is possible that Ranganathan's placing of the TIME category last influenced the citation order. In any case, one feels that there is more likely to be a need for all Second World War fighters together than for all German fighters.

Only those which one regards as the more important formulae have been discussed here, and for a fuller exposition reference should be made to Coates's *Subject headings*, Chapter VI: 'Significance and term relationships in compound headings.'

Coates introduced, and apparently swears by, the principle of the heading being coextensive with the subject of the document. In principle, we cannot help but challenge this ideal, although, say, BTI headings are more coextensive than 'conventional' indexing. Short of writing an abstract it is not usually possible to get across absolutely all of the concepts, influences and so on which are often introduced into documents. The reader should apply Coates's formulae to many ordinary newspaper articles—even to simple-seeming popular paperbacks as cited on p. 112, and see how far he gets in literal and full coextensivity.

One, apparently unashamed, example in BTI is its treatment of a report on the collapse of the ferro-concrete Kings Bridge in Melbourne, which received the following two headings:

> KINGS BRIDGE, Melbourne, and
> BRIDGES, Failure.

Even if double entry is used—and this occasional practice was announced in 1962 when BTI started it—surely the 'ferro-concrete' element should have been brought in, especially since in entries for other documents BTI uses 'composite construction' to cover this. One fears that this document was indexed from its title.

One might expect *see* references also to be coextensive in the sense that the 'referred-from' part equals the 'referred-to' part, but in a different citation order, or that both parts are synonyms. Yet BTI can produce:

ORANGE FREE STATE *see* GOLD, Mining, Allanridge.

This leads to the very regrettable conclusion that Coates and BTI will not please everyone, for three main reasons:

1. The basic practice is not always what is preached: and one howler makes a field day for people disposed to criticise.

2. Citation order is not always in accordance with 'consensus'— how compound subjects are mentally associated, studied, researched into, etc., e.g. the cataloguing lecturer and student are far from happy to find their discipline as a distributed relative—ACTION—third in the queue.

3. People persist in thinking of subjects as simple-sounding 'concretes' as in the conventional dictionary catalogue. A reference librarian wanting information on the Orde River Project in Australia is not pleased to find an article under DAMS, Bandicoote Creek, without even a reference from Orde River (and 'Bandicoote' spelt incorrectly to boot).

We come back to the need for old-fashioned intuition—instinctive application of accumulated knowledge—in addition to 'modern' theory.

RANGANATHAN'S 'WALL-PICTURE' METHOD

Ranganathan's influence on Coates is readily apparent in Coates's writings, and discussion of Coates's methods infers also comment on the significance of Ranganathan. However, Ranganathan also evolved a method based on a very simple principle, as opposed to his more complex categories and their citation order. He calls it the 'Wall-picture' principle.

Where there is a choice of citation order between two, or more, components, the cataloguer establishes which component came first, or is most necessary, for the compound subject to exist. The analogy is that a wall must exist before a picture can be hung on it, thereby producing a citation order of WALL—PICTURE. Suppose one wishes to cite a compound heading for 'steel wheels'. The concept of the wheel must exist before one can say what it is made of: hence WHEELS—STEEL. But taking 'welding of steel': the steel must exist before one can weld it: hence STEEL—WELDING. The same principle is applicable to more complex subjects—almost *ad infinitum*.

Although one has not come across it used consciously in practice, it seems reasonably definite in providing a citation order for each compound subject which is 'tailor-made' to suit the document in hand, e.g. the document in BTI, mentioned previously, on the failure of the ferro-concrete Kings Bridge in Melbourne, could produce

> BRIDGES—FERRO-CONCRETE—FAILURE—MELBOURNE—KINGS BRIDGE.

Ranganathan's method can be seen to be applied here, in the way one imagines it to be envisaged. But the basic principle may be too broad: one might say that Kings Bridge itself had to exist before it could fail, yet in the heading above only the generic term BRIDGES has been used as entry term, not KINGS BRIDGE. One's own argument would be that the acts of being in Melbourne and of happening to be called 'Kings' do not necessarily affect the basic essence of the subject itself: a similar type of bridge in any other part of the world might have collapsed. Further, taking the two components BRIDGE and KINGS BRIDGE, the method can be accused of producing alphabetical-classing.

When one applies the method to a variety of compound subjects, there emerges an approximation to the formulae evolved by Coates. But, while Coates's methods are harder to learn, they are more definite than Ranganathan's 'Wall—Picture'. However, one suggests on the whole, that the two methods work towards the same objective. Therefore, the basic disadvantage applies as with Coates's formulae: although a reasonably definite citation order (and chain of references) does emerge, 'consensus' may feel that the order is not always the most helpful.

RELATIONSHIPS BETWEEN TERMS

Highly structured headings remove explanatory connecting words, usually conjunctions and prepositions, which may result in a neat-looking but ambiguous heading (the same disadvantage can apply in coordinate indexing, dealt with in Chapter 18).

EDUCATION: LIBRARIANSHIP, or LIBRARIANSHIP: EDUCATION, can mean 'education for librarianship' or the influence of 'education' on 'librarianship', or vice versa, or both. Coates appreciates this of course, and works towards citation orders which help to clarify these ambiguities to some extent, provided one knows which formula applies in a particular condition. But the uninitiated may understand DESERTS, Plants not as 'plants found in deserts', but as the 'uses of plants in deserts'.

There are various ways of reacting to possible ambiguity:

1. Ignore it, and rely on the context of the entry to clarify it. This is unsatisfactory, because it blatantly ignores the ideal of the coextensivity principle with all that that entails.

2. Revert to conventional phrases. But this of course results in clumsy and possibly unsought headings which 'moderns' are trying to get away from, e.g. GEOGRAPHICAL DISTRIBUTION OF ANIMALS AND PLANTS (SEARS). However, computers may make natural direct headings possible again.

3. Leave in explanatory but non-significant terms, but ignore them in filing. One would have constructions like EDUCATION—(for) LIBRARIANSHIP or even EDUCATION *for* LIBRARIANSHIP. Computers can be programmed to ignore italicised words in filing, which could be useful when a system is automated.

4. Use constructed headings with verbal, significant, filable connecting terms.

e.g. EDUCATION: APPLICATIONS: LIBRARIANSHIP

DUTCH: INFLUENCE: U.S. ('conventional' has DUTCH IN THE U.S.).

Terms can quite readily be found, for most situations, which are reasonably self-explanatory, and the system has the great advantage of being truly alphabetical. It can bring together related aspects without the interference of arbitrary filing orders (as in the LC 'Cookery' example, in Chapter 24, on Filing).

e.g. COOKERY: MATERIALS: APPLES

COOKERY: METHODS: BAKING

COOKERY: REGIONS: U.S.

One feels that this method warrants more investigation. It has been used occasionally in BTI, as in CARS, Types, Rovers.

5. Punctuation can be used which has been given meaning significance. Usually it will also be given filing significance to ensure the required groupings.

A simple but effective system was introduced in BTI in 1968. It did not affect filing order at the time: arrangement being alphabetically by second word (as in SEARS despite its use of (*a*) the dash, (*b*) the comma, and occasionally (*c*) parentheses). Ultimately, the objective is to use these terms in the computerisation of the production of BTI, except that heading decisions will still be made intellectually, by humans. The punctuation marks are:

. .	(Double point) Place	DAMS . . Turkey = Dams in Turkey
—	(Dash) Conjunction or composite	ALUMINIUM—COPPER = Aluminium copper alloy
;	(Semi-colon) Type or kind, designated by material	STRUCTURES; Steel = Steel structures
,	(Comma) or , , (Double comma) Type or kind designated otherwise than by material	STEEL, Welding = Steel for welding
:	(Colon) Other relationships	STEEL: Welding = Welding of steel

Of course, the (arbitrary) meanings of the items of punctuation must be learnt if one is to make full and unambiguous use of the system.

A more complicated system has been worked out by J. E. L. Farradane. The system, written on in 1950-1952, does not seem to have been practised much, and one proposes just to summarise it here. Fuller details can be found in Farradane, J. E. L., 'A scientific theory of classification and indexing', *Journal of documentation*, vol. 6, 1950, p. 83-99; vol. 8, 1952, p. 73-92; and some information is given, but not pursued, by Coates (COATES, p. 45-49). Coates summarises Farradane's work in divining nine types of relationships between terms: Causation or Functional dependence; Action upon; Distinction from, Substitution for, or Imitation; Belonging to; Dimensional (e.g. space, time); Equivalence; Association; Comparison, and Agent and activity; Copresence. Each relation is represented by a symbol consisting of two conventional items of punctuation together (with one exception, i.e. Ø), the citation order of each indicating the direction of the relationship. Examples are:

Action upon	/-		Causation	/:
Copresence	Ø		Dimension	/+
Association	/;		Belonging	/(

The citation order depends on the needs of the users of the system.

6. Simpler methods using symbols with a conventional ordinal significance are possible, especially numbers: 1, 2, 3, etc.; and letters: A, B, C, or a, b, c, etc.; and possibly punctuation itself in its likely accepted order of strength, or forcefulness, e.g. . : ; , — if agreement is reached on this order. Whenever collocation is required, but is not automatically assured by normal verbal alphabetical arrangement, numbers, letters, or punctuation could be inserted before the 'like' terms which it is required to bring together.

e.g. COOKERY—A—APPLES   material
     COOKERY—A—BREADFRUIT
     etc.
     COOKERY—B—BAKING   process
     COOKERY—B—FRYING
     etc.
     COOKERY—C—FRANCE   place
     COOKERY—C—U.S.
     etc.

If one is to insist on grouping, as in LC arrangement, one might as well use symbols with a conventionally recognised order and have done with it. Such recognised ordinal symbols could be applied too in classification: UDC has proved to be extremely useful and popular, but it is suggested that its immediacy could be increased by the use of connecting devices (facet indicators) with conventional ordinal significance as mentioned above.

PROPOSED BNB SUBJECT DESCRIPTORS

A very recent development by BNB as part of its contribution to the MARC Project—a computerisation project explained in Chapter 32— is the use of a novel form of subject 'descriptors' (which may be taken as similar to subject index entries or subject headings). The system, which is being developed experimentally by Mr Derek Austin for BNB is called PREserved Context Indexing System: PRECIS. The system is fully described in BNB MARC *Documentation service publications*, no. 3.

A method of thorough subject analysis is applied to each document. The result is a series of isolates, or single subject terms, each of which falls into one of two possible categories; it is either: (*a*) an 'entity' or (*b*) an 'attribute'. An example of an entity is 'car', and of an attribute 'weight'—adding up to 'weight of a car'. Having established a series of descriptors, the next stage is to show their relationships with each other. (It will be remembered that an objection to structured subject headings as compared with phrase headings is that connecting words, usually prepositions, are not available to show relationships between the 'kernal' terms of the heading.) PRECIS uses what are called 'relational operators' for this purpose. During the development phase, these consist of arabic numerals in parentheses, therefore having ordinal significance, as follows:

(1) Property of a system.
(2) Sub-system.
(3) Inter-reaction within system.
(4) Second system or environment related to or regulating (5).
(5) Effect produced on a system: not involving change of system.
(6) Second system or environment.
(7) Effect produced on system: system in process of change.
(8) [*not yet used*].
(9) Attribute defining a type or class.

The required number is put by the indexer between the two descriptors whose relationship it defines, e.g. one could have CAR (2) ENGINE meaning 'engine of a car': CAR is an entity, and ENGINE is a part (subsystem) of CAR. Further, relational operators can be combined to produce, say, CAR (2) ENGINE (21) HORSEPOWER, HORSEPOWER being a property, (1), of a sub-system, (2). The generic relationship ('subject inclusion' element) can potentially also be incorporated: in the above example this might be ROAD VEHICLE, producing, say, ROAD VEHICLE/CAR (2) ENGINE (21) HORSEPOWER.

It can be seen, then, that a so-called 'concept analysis string' of descriptors and their relationships can be built up, describing apparently the exact subject of a document.

Any of the descriptors in a 'string' can be made an approach term if so desired. In effect, what we conventionally call 'added subject entries' can be made under any elements of the 'string' desired by the indexer.

The whole system is designed especially for computer-manipulation, so all the indexer has to do is to decide on: (*a*) the descriptors; (*b*) the relational operators—which in turn decide the citation order; and (*c*) which descriptors are to be approach terms—if he wants a descriptor to be an approach term he simply writes 1, if not, he writes 0. The computer will then automatically produce, if required, a 'rotated' series of specific subject approaches, e.g. (to take another, complete, example):

FLOWER GARDENING
    Roses. Pests. Aphids. Control. DDT.
ROSES. Flower gardening
    Pest. Aphids. Control. DDT.
PESTS. Roses. Flower gardening
    Aphids. Control. DDT.
APHIDS. Rose pests
    Control. DDT.
DDT. Aphid control. Rose pests.

Perhaps it should be reiterated that all these permuted strings are not written by the indexer, but are machine-produced from the original string.

The method has advantages over chain procedure, because not only are all likely approaches catered for as in chain procedure, but also the specific subject of the relevant document is given at all approach terms, which is not catered for in chain procedure.

As far as Project MARC is concerned, BNB's PRECIS represents a fifth subject approach. The other four (as is shown in Chapter 32) are: (*a*) DC 17th edition; (*b*) BNB DC; (*c*) LC classification; and (*d*) LC subject headings. It may be queried whether yet another subject approach is needed. However, PRECIS is designed especially for machine generation and manipulation—this alone making it unique compared with the other subject approaches in BNB MARC—itself of course devised specifically as a computerised record. Even the most complacent librarian must surely admit that the other four methods can be improved upon. At the least, PRECIS is attempting this.

Further, in the long run, its development could be even wider-reaching. It could be linked directly with a new general classification scheme, derived from the NATO-sponsored work of the (U.K.) Classification Research Group, and now being worked upon also by Mr Derek Austin. We may hope that the new scheme—itself to consist basically of two thesauri, of entities and attributes respectively—will prove to be compatible with PRECIS, so that librarians can use it manually for the simultaneous classification and subject cataloguing of documents not covered by MARC.

These hopes may be far-fetched: to mention but one difficulty, the classification scheme's notation is likely to prove unwieldy for manual use. Nevertheless, the development of PRECIS, even in its own right, should repay careful study.

CHAPTER 16

Chain Indexing of the Classified Catalogue

The principle of this method was set by Dewey almost from the start in his 'Relative Index', which he regarded as probably more important than the schedules of his scheme. It was developed, christened and systematised by Ranganathan. It was fostered in practice, mainly by E. J. Coates, in the subject part of BNB's index, and now it is accepted by many classified cataloguers as the best single way of constructing a subject index economically and usefully. One should remember, however, that constructing it is far from being a purely clerical job, and that it has its disadvantages. Although, with careful and professional attention, these may be largely overcome.

The chain index uses three basic principles:

(*a*) It relies on the classified file to bring together entries for topics which are in fact collocated by the classification scheme used, i.e. it does not repeat, or near-repeat, the order of the classification schedules.

(*b*) It brings together reminders of topics which are related to each other but which are separated by the classification scheme. We deliberately refrain here from the oft-chanted statement that 'it collocates distributed relatives'. It merely reminds us of the existence at various parts of the scheme—or classified file—of the 'distributed relatives', but even these are not always self-explanatory, as the terminology of the scheme itself is not necessarily wholly consistent.

(*c*) It gives entries under the specific subject, as decided by the classification scheme.

BASIC CONSTRUCTION

The first, and specific, entry for a subject is ensured by using as entry word the term represented by the final component of the notation, e.g. in DC 'Economic history' is 330.9. The schedules, and knowledge of the standard subdivisions, show that the '330' element is Economics, and the '9' element, the final digit, is History. Therefore the chain index entry is

HISTORY: ECONOMICS   330.9

We could say HISTORY, ECONOMIC. However, not all names of compound subjects respond to simple inversion, and so the 'structured' form (with colons between the elements of the heading) is usually preferred, to aid consistent filing, hence use. But there are snags; there is no convenient structured colon form of 'History, Naval' which is unambiguous.

Next, we suppose that an enquirer may think of the generic, or 'containing' heading, and we cater for that. Or, to look at it another way, 'Economic history' is part of 'Economics' and we might consider offering a document on it on receiving a request for 'Economics'. So the next stage is to delete the final digit and index the remaining number.

Hence:

ECONOMICS	330	then
SOCIAL SCIENCES	300	

A card (say) is then made for each of these terms and filed in its appropriate part of the alphabet.

Similarly, 'Economic history of Australia' is 330.994, so the specific entry is

AUSTRALIA: HISTORY: ECONOMICS   330.994

where the final '94' is Australia, the middle '9' is History, and the initial '330' is Economics, i.e. where more than two components make up the subject term as used in the index, all the required elements are quoted in the reverse order from that in which they are given in the class number. Some intermediate or final terms may often be omitted provided one knows the scheme well enough to realise that a topic belongs in a certain area, e.g. in DC it is not necessary to repeat SOCIAL SCIENCES after ECONOMICS whenever the latter turns up.

When we delete the final digit we are left with 330.99—'economic history of other parts of the world', i.e. the middle '9' is used merely as a convenient device to introduce parts of the world not covered by previous numbers.

'OTHER PARTS OF THE WORLD: HISTORY: ECONOMICS' is a pointless entry since it is very unlikely indeed that anyone would look under 'other' in this context. This element constitutes an unsought link (in the 'chain') and is omitted. This is an obvious example for omission, but there are other instances about which there is doubt, e.g. if the terminal digit represents the number of a century, as in 'twentieth century English plays', some indexers may regard this as a 'sought' term, but others may not. So skill is needed to decide whether or not to include some approach or entry terms.

Further, DC 17th edition gives '991-996 history of Pacific Ocean islands'. So we have to decide whether or not, in the example given above, 'Pacific Ocean' may be taken to include 'Australia'.

On the other hand, Australia is part of Australasia, with New Zealand, etc., yet no provision for the latter is given in DC 17th edition —but an enquirer may want it as a subject, including Australia and its neighbours. One may possibly decide to take 990, or perhaps 993-995 as 'Australasia', and make index entries accordingly. In other words, a class number may include a hidden link.

If the subject were 'economic history of Britain', the problem would not arise, and the chain of entries would be:

GREAT BRITAIN: HISTORY: ECONOMICS	330.942
EUROPE: HISTORY: ECONOMICS	330.94
HISTORY: ECONOMICS	330.9
ECONOMICS	330
SOCIAL SCIENCES	300

Some librarians might wish to have also

| SCIENCES, SOCIAL | 300 |

to file immediately after

| SCIENCES, PURE | 500 |

which follows

| SCIENCES, APPLIED | 600 |

but it is doubtful if these are really necessary in practice.

Items 3, 4 and 5 would automatically apply to guide the user to quite a few other documents in most libraries.

As other documents on aspects of Australia are added to stock the index will accumulate entries like

AUSTRALIA: GEOGRAPHY	919.4
AUSTRALIA: HISTORY	994
AUSTRALIA: POLITICS	320.994
AUSTRALIA: SOCIAL CONDITIONS	309.194

It becomes rapidly obvious that 'Australia' is a distributed relative, and so reminders of it in relation to various subjects in stock are brought together in the index. However, in DC 17th edition 'Travel in Australia' goes at a subdivision of the 'geography' number, i.e. 919.404, resulting strictly in the chain index specific entry:

TRAVEL: AUSTRALIA: GEOGRAPHY   919.404

which is likely to irritate users (and staff), even if they find it at all. So, inconsistent construction of a classification scheme's schedules may lead to confusing, even if literally correct, entries according to the rules. Since librarians exist to be useful, and not to propagate a particular system, some might well decide to ignore the rule of entry word under term represented by terminal digit, and make the entry:

AUSTRALIA: TRAVEL   919.404

Or alternatively—but still breaking the rule—one might possibly put

AUSTRALIA: GEOGRAPHY   919.4
              TRAVEL   919.404

So again, chain indexing is not in this case a clerical or automatic job.

Other classification schemes, or editions of DC, may either cater for, or not throw up, hidden links and false links, e.g. DC 16th edition has both 'geography' and 'travel' at the same number; in this case, classification is not specific, resulting in an indiscriminate intermixing of, say, 'geography of Australia' and 'travel in Australia' on the shelves and in the classified file. On the other hand, UDC has a number for Australasia, (93), resulting in

AUSTRALASIA: HISTORY   993

However, never to be satisfied, there may be librarians (outside Australia) who regard this hidden link as an unsought one too!

Sometimes the classification scheme is helpful in including explanations which help in arriving at a correct chain, e.g. UDC gives '(954) Papua (Territory under Australia)', so the untutored librarian is reminded to include Australia in the chain for, say 'history of Papua'. It is evident that chain indexing relies heavily on the terminology and structure of the classification scheme to which it is hinged, e.g. DC does not remind the cataloguer that Papua is 'under' Australia.

A general difficulty is that the subject index should include synonyms, which send one straight to the required class mark, but that classification schedules and indexes (if relevant: one must know the synonym before seeking it in the index) cannot be relied upon to supply synonyms, e.g. DC 17th edition does not divulge that a synonym for Tasmania is Van Diemen's Land, although UDC does. Though strictly it is a near-synonym, as the name was changed to Tasmania in the 1850's. DC does not even acknowledge that 'New Guinea (Papua)' consists of two distinct countries, hence administrations, the western part being Indonesian and called by the Indonesians, West Irian; the eastern being in two parts, known as Papua-New Guinea. It is acknowledged that DC is geography-oriented and not politics-oriented, yet documents are produced on the two parts of New Guinea, because they are under different political jurisdictions, and so they must be catered for.

If one does not know the context of a subject, checking in reference books is needed; not only for synonyms but also for other background information. A difficulty is that one does not always know when further research is necessary. A further example: DC 17th edition gives, in class 900 History, '994.04 Australian Commonwealth, 1901-1945', then '994.05 Later 20th century, 1945-' which may infer that the 'Commonwealth' period ended in 1945: 'Later 20th century' is not indented under 'Commonwealth'.

(Australia has been deliberately chosen for examples here, because much of the English-speaking world knows very little about it and its local connections, and it is hoped that its use here will emphasise the need for some subject knowledge before chain indexing thoroughly, stage by stage.)

A further difficulty is that a complete chain according to the schedules is not necessarily relevant or useful. It is feasible to have (DC 17)

GREAT BRITAIN: HISTORY	942
EUROPE: HISTORY	940

since British history is part of, and bound up with, European history. (Though, incidentally, British history is just as connected with individual countries of its erstwhile Empire, but the DC schedules do not remind us of this—or even give a number for the Empire as a whole. Yet they include a number for the Anglo-Dutch Wars at 949.204: History of the Dutch Republic.)

However, take Social surveys of Great Britain at 309.142 ('social surveys' in the index refers to 309.1, but the schedules say just 'social situation and conditions'): we get:

GREAT BRITAIN: SOCIAL SURVEYS	309.142
[or to 'chain' very strictly—	
GREAT BRITAIN: SURVEYS: SOCIOLOGY]	
then:	
EUROPE: SOCIAL SURVEYS	309.14

But it is doubtful if any social survey of Britain or part of it can be guaranteed to be part of European social surveys. This applies particularly to small parts of Britain, say, a social survey of Nottingham, which may well have more in common with social surveys of other areas of similar size and population, than with areas in the same geographical continent. The same applies to Education, e.g. education in Britain probably has more in common with that of the U.S., Canada, Australia and New Zealand than with France and Germany, Lichtenstein and Switzerland. Also, at the moment the economy of various far-flung parts of the Commonwealth of Nations have far more in common with Britain than that of, say, France, yet the former are widely separated while the latter is quite near in the classification scheme.

One has the problem of either allowing the chain to run its course, thereby bulking the index unduly to satisfy the rule, or of deciding which links may reasonably be omitted: and this requires subject knowledge. It is emphasised that all this is not a criticism of DC as a scheme, but a warning that chain procedure has to be used carefully.

Yet another difficulty arises because the terminal digit in classification schemes may represent a form of presentation. History of a subject in relation to a country is a form, and in the examples it has been treated as a valid entry term. But other uses of History, e.g. history of cricket in an individual country, and some other form subdivisions, may not be regarded as sought or necessary headings, and their inclusion would pointlessly bulk the subject index and cause unnecessary work— typing, compiling authority file, filing, withdrawing. Such an example might be a manual of a subject: in DC 17 —020 2. However, works for specific types of users, subdivided under —024, e.g. for engineers at —024 62, may be sought headings; and so might —071 53 'radio and television classes' in a subject, and —071 2 'secondary schools'. These may be, in certain circumstances, 'sought' distributed relatives. Therefore, of course, the librarian must consider each one carefully and decide whether it is likely to be useful. In other cases, he may omit index entries altogether, or give some such general reference as

MANUALS *see* names of individual subjects.

In some well-accepted cases, he may have to break the chain rule and use some such headings as

WORKSHOP MANUALS and LOGARITHM TABLES.

Sometimes, faulty collocation in the schedules, or perhaps ambiguity in terms, may lead to works being missed if chain indexing is relied on completely, e.g. BNB 1964 listed *Beatles on Broadway* by Sam Leach. The chain indexing comprised:

1. BEATLES, The: SINGING: MUSIC	784.3[1]
	[the [1] indicates lack of specificity in the scheme]
2. SONGS: MUSIC	784.3
3. VOCAL MUSIC	784
4. MUSIC	780

But BNB 1962 includes the following:

POPULAR MUSIC	781.94[1]
SINGING	784.9

Both of the second entries lead to different numbers from that used for 'The Beatles'. But both, and the first especially since it starts with 'POP-', might be expected to have something in common with 'The Beatles'. The author heading for this work is given as 'Leach, Sam [i.e. Samuel Richard Leach]'. We cannot help feeling that the effort which went into this could have been better spent on compiling one or two 'intuition' or 'commonsense' subject index entries to supplement the chain indexing to get the enquirer from terms like POP SINGERS and POP MUSIC to the Beatles work. It would not be enough to claim that the lack of suitable entries derives from faulty classification design. Part of being a qualified librarian is using one's skill to compensate for lacks in tools; otherwise there is little point in being professionally educated as distinct from receiving training in mechanical drills or routines. Therefore, the subject index, like the dictionary catalogue, should attempt to compensate for deficiencies in a scheme, at least as it appears to some users.

Another common example is that 'Capitalism' and 'Socialism' as economic systems are separated in DC: Capitalism at around 330.1 and Socialism at around 335. DC 17th edition provides an alternative for Socialism at 330.159, but this then takes it further away from the relevant Public finance at 336.

We might then get chain index entries at

1. CAPITALISM: ECONOMICS	330.15
	[or in 17th edition perhaps 330.122]
2. SOCIALISM: ECONOMICS	335

In the classified file these two topics, which are collocated in the public mind automatically because of rival political parties, are separated by massive subjects like 'Labour', 'Finance' (e.g. Banking and Currency), 'Land economics' and 'Cooperatives'; though the last-named modulates nicely to 335. But SEARS, for all its technical faults and inconsistencies, has what one dares to call 'commonsense' *see also* references between Capitalism and Socialism. However, it does not directly connect Capitalism and Communism, which surely are intuitively contrasted in SEARS' native U.S.!

Next, the problem of unsought terms needs to be catered for, when they stand for a sought topic. One example, from DC 16 (DC 17 makes the situation even more complex) is that an enquirer may want information on methods or types of mining in general, e.g. 'underground', 'surface', 'alluvial'. A term covering these methods might be, say, WORKINGS: MINING, but many people may regard WORKINGS as too loose a term to use as an entry word; and in any case it is not in DC, which has '622.2 Underground mining', and '622.3 Types of mining'. We can do without and expect the enquirer to look up, say, MINING: ENGINEERING 622, and from that be led on by guiding in the classified file, eventually to reach the required area. But guiding is not necessarily all that it appears to be in theory. An alternative, or even addition, is to 'non-chain': e.g.

1. MINING: ENGINEERING   622
2. MINING: ENGINEERING: WORKINGS   622.2-622.3

In a few cases, BNB has resorted to non-chain entries where otherwise the enquirer might 'enter' the classified file whole drawers or pages away from his specific requirements, e.g.

HISTORY, MODERN: INDIVIDUAL COUNTRIES   940-999

More such entries are needed, based on the indexer's knowledge of the subject fields in question.

e.g. (DC 16) HISTORY   900
            HISTORY: ARCHAEOLOGY   571

This particular situation is cured in the 17th edition which relocates 'Archaeology' to 913: but now it is separated from other sciences in 500 class. So someone interested in archaeological techniques would need to be helped by some form of non-chain reminder in the subject index.

e.g. SCIENCE   500
        SCIENCE: ARCHAEOLOGY   913

because no chain procedure will get him from the broad heading
SCIENCE to 913. A more plausible solution, catering for other topics also,
might be to include a note at either SCIENCE in the index or at 500 in
the classified file. For example, 'The scientific approach to certain
subjects is classified with those subjects, e.g. Prehistoric archaeology
in History class, at 913'.

But this has the obvious disadvantage of the 'general' *see also* reference
in the dictionary catalogue. It is probably better to enumerate the
individual topics. This can apply also to forms of presentation of a
subject which may be regarded as wasted if given the full chain treatment, e.g. listing under REPORTS and similar terms, as distributed
relatives, all subjects which happen to have reports on them in stock.
One can 'non-chain' as in:

CHEMISTRY	540
CHEMISTRY: ENCYCLOPAEDIAS	540.3

Guiding and featuring are usually regarded as solutions to many of
the problems touched upon, while others are said to be solved by the
plentiful use of added subject entries in the classified file, although
only too often not included in real live cataloguing. In fact, the two
come together when 'non-document' *see also* references are included,
e.g. in the classified file:

331.5 CAPITALISM
   see also 335 SOCIALISM.

Featuring has much to recommend it, since it acknowledges that
ordinary people think in natural language terms and not class numbers.
The 'translations' of numbers, from general to specific, as laid out in
BNB's classified sequence, should be examined as probably the best,
easily available example of thorough featuring. However, a criticism
of BNB: It often happens that entries for documents are included whose
subjects go beyond the specificity allowed for by DC, especially since
BNB is still largely based on the 14th edition of the early 1940's—a whole
generation ago in the fastest moving period in recorded history. In
such cases, BNB quite rightly gives the feature heading for the document's
subject, and not merely that for the schedule's subject. Unfortunately,
the entries are then usually arranged according to an unacknowledged
systematic method. It is suggested here that where the scheme cannot
reach, and where no very obvious order emerges, it would be better to
arrange 'within' a number alphabetically by feature heading.

To scan the classified files, even the cumulated issues, of BNB shows that in many cases only one or a few documents appear under each feature heading. Apart from the objection mentioned above, this does not matter so much since BNB is a printed list allowing easy sequential scanning. However, in a card file, the pure theory is that each separate topic, however minute, has its own feature heading on its own guide card, which protrudes above the entries themselves. In practice, the ensuing bulk of the file often may preclude such luxury. In any case, where guide cards are separated by only a few entries they may obscure each other, even if their tabs are staggered. And further, staggering defeats itself when new cards are filed which do not fit the previous, carefully worked out, 'obliqueness' of tabs on, say, 'fifth-cut' guide cards. We need, therefore, to resort to selectivity of tabbed guides. But, since pure chain indexing relies absolutely on guiding and the implicit logic of a classification scheme—both of which in practice are defective—chain indexing is proved to be not quite the complete solution as was thought in the 1950's.

The conclusion then is that chain indexing is the best single method. But it must be supplemented by careful thought and commonsense on the part of the indexer, or checker, combined with the use of dictionaries, thesauri, lists of subject headings, etc., which demonstrate the relationships between subject words: synonyms, upwards, downwards, sideways, oblique, cross-discipline and so on. In fact, the interesting conclusion is that one can so add to and embellish chain indexing and the classified file that the result can combine the advantages of both the classified and the dictionary catalogues.

Note. The examples given here have followed, in general, BNB format, repeating the entry word and using colons to separate terms. In card catalogue practice, we find that sequential scanning of the index is aided by putting on to one card as many terms as possible. So the following type of layout may be more useful:

AUSTRALIA	994
[BNB would use 919.4 as a comprehensive works no.]	
Geography	919.4
History	994
Politics	320.994
Social conditions	309.194
[etc. etc.]	

Since non-chain entries have been unashamedly incorporated, we may finish up with entries like

AUSTRALIA

Geography	919.4
History	994
to 1788: British annexation	994.01
1788-1851	994.02
1851-1901: Colonial self-rule	994.03
1901- : Commonwealth	994.04

These are particularly necessary when periods do not have readily 'sought' names. Such non-chain detail becomes unnecessary under, say, GREAT BRITAIN: HISTORY, because periods do have sought names, e.g. 'Normans' or 'Hanoverians', which may therefore receive normal specific chain entry treatment.

Putting many qualifying terms on to one card involves occasional re-typing to ensure some degree of correct alphabetisation. At prolific distributed relatives, e.g. countries like Britain (and why not simply BRITAIN and not GREAT BRITAIN?), it may be useful to allocate a card for each section of the alphabet, either one per letter or one for certain blocks of letters, e.g. A-D. It may even prove necessary to include *see also* references or permuted sub-headings at some complex points where reverse citation order of schedules as used in chain procedure produces an unhelpful collocation of terms. This is especially so in a scheme like DC which sometimes changes characteristics of division in an inconsistent way. 'Group arrangement in the subject index' is Chapter XII in COATES, and this should be read carefully by anyone contemplating any radical departure from the reverse schedule order alphabetically sub-arranged which is assumed in chain indexing theory. However, an alphabetical index should surely be just that, while if qualifying terms of an entry word are included on one card as far as possible, easy scanning may help overcome unhelpful collocations.

CHAPTER 17

Chain Procedure and the Dictionary Catalogue

This was conceived by Ranganathan, and, like several other very important developments in alphabetical-subject work, has been investigated and made palatable mainly by E. J. Coates. It is a logical development from chain procedure in the subject index of the classified catalogue, and a critical knowledge of chain indexing is assumed here.

It will be remembered that the main criticisms of the conventional list of subject headings are:

(a) lack of ready-made specific headings;
(b) inconsistency in construction of headings; and
(c) inconsistency in construction of references, mainly *see also*, e.g. lack of modulation in a chain of references working from the most generic to the most specific.

There are three possible manifestations of chain procedure:

(a) Headings and attendant references can be built up as one goes along: presumably an authority file could be built up at the same time to control these 'self-generated' headings and references. Eventually one would reach the point of having compiled a list of headings. Hence—

(b) Lists of headings could be published based on chain procedure, including instructions on the construction of new headings as required, to maintain consistency. The method inevitably relies on, and is derived from, a classification. So the possibility then comes of

(c) Publication of a classification scheme complete with headings and references to suit it, in one combined work. If such a publication were successful, one can imagine what a boon it would be to dictionary cataloguers, who at present use two separate, and sometimes conflicting, tools.

It is proposed here to outline how chain procedure can try to reduce the three basic disadvantages of the conventional alphabetical-subject catalogue, viz. lack of specificity, and heading and reference inconsistency.

(a) Specificity

It is possible easily to make headings which are as specific as the classification scheme itself, e.g. LC's List of headings is, at many points, less specific than LC Classification, so the method should be advantageous using the latter. Where a scheme is very synthetic, and so capable of great specificity, subject headings can be constructed for a great variety of compounds just as class marks can. This could apply with limitations to DC, but particularly to UDC—probably the most common scheme with considerable provision for synthesis. Where the scheme is not specific enough for a document, verbal extension would have to be used as in chain indexing.

In most cases the heading is in exactly the same form as the equivalent chain index entry: usually a term representing the final component of the class mark followed by a qualifying term from further 'back' in the chain, e.g. a work classified at

621.483   Fission reactors and power plants
could receive the heading

FISSION REACTORS: NUCLEAR ENGINEERING.

(b) Heading Construction

It so happens in the example above that DC has introduced two characteristics of division simultaneously, as a single division of

621.48   Nuclear engineering

resulting in both 'fission' and 'reactors'. The heading given can still be preserved with its approachable direct terminology, or we could use

REACTORS: FISSION: NUCLEAR ENGINEERING

resulting in collocation with

REACTORS: FUSION: NUCLEAR ENGINEERING

for class mark 621.484

As with chain indexing, there may be hidden links which have to be recognised and catered for consistently.

The apologist may plead 'faulty classification design', as in chain indexing, but this is one of the occupational hazards of professional librarianship. The ultimate solution is to compile classification schemes consistently using recognised categories and citation orders of components (isolates). This has been attempted in several special schemes, so these respond more readily to chain procedure because in effect they have been designed with its principles in mind.

However, a further problem still arises, because citation orders in classification schemes, however consistent they are, do not necessarily become useful alphabetical-subject headings when translated into natural language and quoted in reverse order. A special application of this disadvantage is the fact that when certain bodies, e.g. universities, are the subject of a document the chain-produced specific entry will not necessarily be the same as that prescribed for bodies by the catalogue code used. Yet in the dictionary catalogue the two headings must be the same to ensure that entries for 'works about' are immediately adjacent to those for 'works by'. In chain indexing, countries are usually distributed relatives (but not always, as inferred by KENNEDY, p. 71: it depends on the citation order of the scheme). But even the most rigorous reformers of heading construction usually admit that in some subjects the citation order for headings must be PLACE: SUBJECT, and in others SUBJECT: PLACE. e.g. chain procedure with UDC would result in

RESEARCH: GEOGRAPHY   911.001.5

but the chain dictionary cataloguer would probably prefer

GEOGRAPHY: RESEARCH.

And as Coates admits (COATES, p. 62), one could reach very fine distinctions as to when to use one citation order and when to use the other. It is difficult to rule by main classes, where, say, in DC it might be ruled that all 500 class headings must use SUBJECT: PLACE, but all 300 class headings must use PLACE: SUBJECT. We may not even quote rules for individual sub-classes, e.g. SEARS uses U.S.—SOCIAL CONDITIONS, but SOCIAL SURVEYS—U.S. The chain-based cataloguer may possibly decide to do likewise, because in the first heading the significant subject is fairly undoubtedly the U.S., while in the second, the significant subject may well be justifiable as SOCIAL SURVEYS, because the science and method of the subject may be more important than the fact that these are exemplified by the U.S. Coates so far has not been directly confronted with the problem in practice, because his chief practical application of formulae is in BTI, which covers only those subjects in which subject is more significant than place.

So, to summarise problems (a) and (b): specificity can be positively represented as ordained by the scheme, e.g. in UDC one can get as far as

SOCIALISM: POLITICAL PARTIES: GREAT BRITAIN,

but The Labour Party (of Britain) is not specifically catered for, and verbal extension is necessary, which in such cases is little better than sensible adaptation of conventional lists; while (*b*) the old problem of citation order must still be settled empirically.

(*c*) References

See references are dealt with automatically only as far as the scheme's terminology allows; hence dictionaries, thesauri, gazetteers and conventional lists of subject headings, etc., still have to be used—selectively and critically—to ensure that all likely synonyms are catered for. However, 'upwards' *see* references are more easily done away with (assuming one regards them as unhelpful), because the process of classifying is likely to force the cataloguer to recognise hidden stages of division, or the need for extending the scheme, rather than be tempted to hide behind such references because they appear in print, with the implied authority which this carries. 'Inverted construction' *see* references can more easily seem to be replaceable, via the scheme's schedules, by traditional 'downwards' *see also*'s, e.g. TELEVISION *see also* CLOSED-CIRCUIT TELEVISION. This example is also a good demonstration of the use of natural, direct construction of specific headings, as implied by the scheme. This is useful, although it may cause difficulty for the very formula-minded cataloguer who then gets worried about the THING: PART and THING: TYPE citation order advocated or inferred by Coates (COATES, p. 54-58), i.e. one must allow for hidden, false and unsought links. With a little thought one can reasonably expect to arrive fairly quickly and accurately at the following chain, from DC 17th edition:

1. FISSION REACTORS: NUCLEAR ENGINEERING.
2. REACTORS: NUCLEAR ENGINEERING *see also*
    FISSION REACTORS: NUCLEAR ENGINEERING
      [Hidden link, needing care.]
3. NUCLEAR ENGINEERING *see also* REACTORS: NUCLEAR ENGINEERING.
4. HEAT ENGINEERING *see also* NUCLEAR ENGINEERING
      [DC 17th edition has '621.4 Heat and prime movers'; some, slight, subject knowledge is required to appreciate that in this instance 'prime movers' is not directly relevant. In fact the heat from reactors may be applied to drive, via steam, a conventional prime mover like a turbine.]

5. APPLIED PHYSICS: TECHNOLOGY *see also* HEAT ENGINEERING
   [This is the reference supplied by the system if used clerically or mechanically. A little thought helps to appreciate that the following reference is also, or more, useful.]

6. PHYSICS: APPLIED: TECHNOLOGY *see also* HEAT ENGINEERING
   [However, the dictionary catalogue does not use double entry for different constructions of one heading. Hence, we should replace *see also* reference no. 5 with the following (corrected):]

5. APPLIED PHYSICS: TECHNOLOGY *see* PHYSICS: APPLIED: TECHNOLOGY

7. ENGINEERING *see also* PHYSICS: APPLIED: TECHNOLOGY
   [The user may find it irritating to be referred via PHYSICS: APPLIED: TECHNOLOGY to the obvious, intuitively visualised, components of ENGINEERING: e.g.

   ENGINEERING *see also* HEAT ENGINEERING.

   This then seems to be a case in which classification-scheme-modulated references are not necessarily helpful. One might even advocate an even less modulated but useful form, e.g. ENGINEERING *see also* NUCLEAR ENGINEERING, but this is the heading used by old-fashioned SEARS!]

   The final link is:

8. TECHNOLOGY *see also* ENGINEERING.

The terminology of DC 16th edition would have produced a neater chain of references incorporating the following chain of terms, with *see also*'s where relevant:

TECHNOLOGY
  ENGINEERING
    MECHANICAL ENGINEERING
      HEAT ENGINEERING [from scope note]
        NUCLEAR ENGINEERING
          NUCLEAR REACTORS [but more strictly 'chain' is
                      REACTORS: NUCLEAR]

This edition is not specific enough to reach FISSION automatically, but the fact that REACTORS is cited settles the citation order for the added heading FISSION: NUCLEAR REACTORS. Whether the headings MECHANICAL ENGINEERING and HEAT ENGINEERING are useful in a chain of references towards this subject is debatable, as before.

Chain procedure can also be used to arrive at collateral (sideways) references, within a facet, e.g. if in DC 17th edition we work to the specific heading FISSION: NUCLEAR REACTORS (at 621.483) we can easily reach the reference FUSION: NUCLEAR REACTORS *see also* FISSION: NUCLEAR REACTORS (at 621.484). Also, we can arrive at SOLAR ENERGY: ENGINEERING *see also* NUCLEAR ENGINEERING (621.47 and 621.48 respectively). We could have, as well, MINING ENGINEERING *see also* APPLIED PHYSICS: TECHNOLOGY (621 and 622 respectively). This is a basic part of the 'drill' for using chain procedure and the classification scheme. But whether these are all useful references is another matter; possibly only the first one is. However, this method does not cater for the type of cross-discipline reminders which should be inherent in the dictionary catalogue, e.g. SEARS has RADIO ACTIVITY *see also* NUCLEAR PHYSICS.

Further, as we know, chain procedure brings together reminders of distributed relatives. So, in the chain dictionary catalogue, we can arrive at the real collocation of distributed relatives, since, in the dictionary catalogue, the chosen headings carry entries for actual documents, and not merely class numbers as in the subject index of the classified catalogue. Hence there will be:

FISSION: NUCLEAR ENGINEERING

followed by:

FISSION: NUCLEAR PHYSICS

a useful collocation.

This example shows the usefulness of chain procedure in a scientific and technical subject field. Depending on the critic's disposition, others could be found which show the method in either a worse or better light than has emerged here. An example of a special faceted scheme which responds well technically, and which should be available to many students, is that of the *British catalogue of music* compiled by E. J. Coates. This scheme uses non-expressive notation, yet this does not impede chain procedure, as some critics assume: hierarchy is made clear by indentation in the schedules.

SUMMARY OF CHAIN PROCEDURE DICTIONARY
CATALOGUE CONSTRUCTION

Advantages

1. It is systematic, since derived from a systematic classification scheme.

2. It complements the classification scheme: citation order in construction of headings is the reverse of the scheme.

3. It is comparatively automatic or mechanical.

4. It ensures modulation, hence reliability plus economy, in 'downward' *see also* references.

5. It can be used with quite direct natural language if desired: a scheme's citation order normally has the less significant term at the end of the notation, and this becomes the entry word. This term is usually used first when naming a subject in natural speech.

6. In general, it responds best to properly compiled faceted schemes, whose use is increasing quite rapidly.

7. It is gaining in popularity, especially in libraries whose catalogues are subject to frequent changes in any case; hence a useful body of experience can be built up.

Disadvantages

1. There is a conventional feeling against the method in some circles, especially with librarians who are more used to using conventional lists of headings, particularly since these are used in many published indexes.

2. If the principle is accepted in an existing library, the cost and inconvenience of changing over may be a deterrent.

3. *See also* references often still need professional examination and manipulation.

4. It does not usually cater automatically for all, or, in many cases, any of the *see* references required from synonyms, near-synonyms and alternative constructions.

5. In general, the resulting network of *see also* references is rather rigid since derived directly from a classification scheme—which is not perfect anyway. In particular, the method does not normally cater for cross-discipline references, by the very nature of chain procedure. Compare LC which manifests different ways of linking a generic heading to a specific one, e.g.

(*a*) SCIENCE   *and* (*b*) SCIENCE
    METEOROLOGY   ASTRONOMY
    CLIMATOLOGY   SOLAR SYSTEM
    RAIN AND RAINFALL   EARTH
                                 CLIMATOLOGY
                                   RAIN AND RAINFALL

The conclusion suggested is that chain procedure should be used as an essential part of heading construction, but that 'intuitive' headings and references—i.e. commonsense ones derived from knowledge and experience—are still necessary.

The practice of generating headings and references as one goes along seems rather chancy in some hands. This applies especially with librarians who decide on, or inherit, a dictionary catalogue structure but who do not appreciate whole-heartedly, and in detail, its main advantage over the classified in being independent, as shown by the 'loopline' or alternative chains or directions of *see also* references exemplified above. However, when chain procedure offers a logical, modulated and useful way of working from general to specific, it is pedantic to deny the value of this 'classificatory' structure as some 'conventionalists' still do.

It seems sensible that subject headings lists should continue to be constructed, but to embody both the advantages of classification and the flexibility of the traditional ideal of the dictionary catalogue. It needs to be reiterated here that the conventional dictionary catalogue is not completely independent of classification schemes. In SEARS for example, Geography of countries is 'lost' under the subheading DESCRIPTION AND TRAVEL: it is too much of a coincidence that DC up to the 16th edition did the same, especially since abridged DC numbers were given after headings in SEARS until the 8th edition.

COMBINING THE CLASSIFICATION SCHEDULES WITH THE SUBJECT HEADINGS LIST

In 1957, Coates proposed a 'Key' (*Library Association Record*, July, 1957) which in effect would embody DC, with verbal headings in the schedules being expressed as subject headings ready for use, with tracings and instructions for references built in. His suggestion was to base the key on the authority files built up by BNB over the years. The suggestion has much to recommend it, although the bulk of the combined work would inevitably be longer than the corresponding DC schedules. A disadvantage of using the present BNB authority file is that presumably it embodies its own additional classification lower case symbols, which did not prove acceptable for shelf classification in many libraries, and much of the rest of it is based on DC 14th edition. Since this edition is over 25 years old, it would be unfortunate if the new concept of wholly integrating classifying with subject cataloguing were to founder on the accident of its having an outdated scheme as its basis. Even the later editions of DC are too strict in their adherence to Dewey's outmoded principle of 'integrity of numbers', thereby dashing the hopes of some librarians who would have liked not only to relocate more numbers, but in essence to rewrite the whole scheme.

It might be that the new NATO-sponsored general classification scheme could be published in this form—to become a guide, not only for the dictionary catalogue, but also for subject indexing the classified catalogue.

This author has in fact compiled a short 'key' as an experiment, and from the results of this, it seems that the whole idea is not only feasible but practicable and useful.

The nearest approach to the ideal seems to have been reached in the *English Electric thesaurofacet for engineering and related subjects*. Whetstone, Leicestershire, England: English Electric Co., 1970. The Introduction states, 'The new publication which emerged is in the form of a "Thesaurofacet", in which a thesaurus and a faceted classification are completely integrated . . .'.

In fact, the new term 'thesaurofacet' means a combination of a thesaurus and a faceted classification scheme. ('Thesaurus' is explained in more detail in Chapter 18). It is significant that the thesaurofacet has a very wide subject coverage, although no claim is made that it could set a pattern for a future general classification/subject headings list. Basically, it consists of two interdependent components.

   (*a*) classification schedules (faceted); and
   (*b*) instead of the customary index, a thesaurus which not only gives the relevant class numbers for subjects listed, but also explains, thesaurus manner, the relationships between the terms used.

CHAPTER 18

Coordinate Indexing; Thesauri

Coordinate indexing is usually associated with the 'depth indexing' aspect of information retrieval. But it is a well-known form of alphabetical-subject approach, and so it deserves treatment in this work, even though necessarily at an introductory level. Despite its label, the method is in fact a form of post-coordinate indexing. The individual subject terms, which when combined would make up the total subject heading of the required subject, are brought together (coordinated) by the searcher, i.e. after ('post') the indexing operation itself. This is the opposite of pre-coordinate indexing in which the indexer decides in advance of ('pre') the search the order in which the various terms should be combined.

Much of the argument about subject indexing and cataloguing concerns the citation order in which a heading representing a compound subject should be combined, e.g. whether one has PRISONERS: EDUCATION or EDUCATION: PRISONERS. In coordinate indexing, the indexer is spared the agony of such decisions. All terms are treated as equal-ranking, i.e. as coordinate in the classificatory sense, as if, say, they took up collateral —side-by-side—places in a classification schedule.

However, classification in the accepted sense of assigning class numbers is not used, although it would be possible to use the method with a classified file of documents. Documents are usually arranged in accession order, i.e. in order of receipt, and are assigned accession numbers by which they are located and retrieved when required. Further, there is no classified catalogue, or other, verbal, pre-coordinated sequence of entries recording the documents themselves.

The principle of recording documents is multiple-entry under terms representing single ideas or concepts—uniconcepts or uniterms (unit-terms)—the document being recorded under as many different headings (called descriptors) as are needed to define its complete subject coverage.

The method is the same in principle as that employed in using the index of a book to trace a compound subject. Suppose, in a history of music, one wished to trace Tchaikovsky's treatment of the symphony.

One could look up in the index TCHAIKOVSKY, noting the page numbers given. One could then look up SYMPHONY, and note the page numbers given for that. The page numbers common to both topics TCHAIKOVSKY and SYMPHONY should refer to information on Tchaikovsky in relation to the symphony.

The method is normally applied to scientific and technical materials, but its principle can be applied to any field, and examples are included here in subject areas which are most likely to mean something to the average student. In fact, it is unfortunate that the method is not more widely used. e.g. a document on 'subliminal television advertising' would receive in effect three unit entries, under: (*a*) SUBLIMINAL TECHNIQUES; (*b*) TELEVISION; and (*c*) ADVERTISING. Another document, on the 'influence of television advertising on the sale of sweets' would receive four separate entries, under (*a*) TELEVISION; (*b*) ADVERTISING; (*c*) SALE; and (*d*) SWEETS; and possibly even INFLUENCE. (See diagrams on page 187.)

In searching, one looks up all the approach terms representing the required subject, so that all relevant documents under these terms are traced and so retrieved.

So where one finds a document whose accession number is given under all three headings of SUBLIMINAL TECHNIQUES; TELEVISION; and ADVERTISING, the document should deal with all of these topics (or isolates), probably in combination. Also, when the accession number of a document appears under the four headings: TELEVISION; ADVERTISING; SALE; and SWEETS, this document should deal with all four topics in combination.

If a searcher wanted all documents on 'television advertising' he would finish up with the accession numbers of both of the documents mentioned above. If he wanted merely 'Television' he would no doubt be given the accession numbers of a great number of documents, including of course those of the two mentioned above, and including, say, those dealing with 'Television' on its own, 'Television and state control', 'Television as an industry' 'Television production', 'Colour television', etc., etc. Further, if an enquirer in fact wanted 'Colour television', but asked for only 'Television', his enquiry would be answered wholly, although of course he would have to sort through more documents by hand than he really required. This would not always apply in pre-coordinate systems.

SUBLIMINAL TECHNIQUES

0	1	2	3	4	5	6	7	8	9
	1								

(a)

TELEVISION

0	1	2	3	4	5	6	7	8	9
	1	2							

(b)

ADVERTISING

0	1	2	3	4	5	6	7	8	9
	1	2							

(c)

SALE

0	1	2	3	4	5	6	7	8	9
		2							

(d)

SWEETS

0	1	2	3	4	5	6	7	8	9
		2							

(e)

6. Diagrams demonstrating principle of coordinate indexing.

MANUAL PROCEDURE IN PRINCIPLE

Normally, a card is made out for each uniterm, or descriptor as it is called, i.e. in effect a single-concept subject heading. This is the filing medium, e.g. TELEVISION. Each card has written on it the accession numbers of all documents about television, whatever may be the aspect or approach. Usually numbers are entered in columns according to their final digit to help in seeking and comparing numbers, and to ensure the even distribution of numbers as the collection grows.

In the diagrams, the examples show how the seven uniterms of the two documents in the 'television' example might look; it is assumed here that these are the first two documents to be indexed; as time went on, and as more documents were acquired, the cards would fill up.

In searching, all cards for all the uniterms required are taken from the file. The accession numbers common to all cards are noted, and the documents represented by these numbers are retrieved. This method, as it happens, is an example of item-on-term, since the item (document) is recorded on the term (uniterm, subject heading) card by its number; it is known as term entry.

MANUAL-MECHANICAL PROCEDURE

Comparison of written numbers takes time, and clerical mistakes might be made. To help offset these disadvantages, a method of optical coincidence cards for recording and searching is more commonly used. Hand-manipulated body-punched cards may be used, e.g. Peek-a-boo. The uniterm is written on to the top edge of the card. A hole is punched, accurately, into the card in a position corresponding with the number of the relevant document. Where a hole has been punched into all the cards in the same place (i.e. representing the accession number of the same document), and the cards with relevant descriptors are placed evenly in a pack and the pack placed on a light-box, light can be seen through these cards. Therefore, the holes represent the numbers of documents required by the searcher, because these are the documents in which all the subjects coincide. The positions of the holes are converted to document numbers, and so the relevant documents can be retrieved. An advantage of the light-coincidence method is that the intensity of the light source can be increased successively to ensure retrieval of documents in which say, only one, then two, of the descriptors are missing, because the light will show through these cards.

An alternative method is an application of the term-on-item, in which each card is an entry for a document, while the numbers recorded on it represent the individual subjects dealt with by that document, i.e. the subject terms are recorded on the item cards: the method is sometimes known as item entry. The method might use edge-notched cards, which are a convenient way of explaining the method. Cards are obtained with holes ready-made round their edges. To make a hole operative it is 'opened out' to the edge of the card using something like a railway ticket inspector's hand-operated clipper. Suppose there is a pack of such cards, some edge-notched at certain numbers, others not. To retrieve the required edge-numbers (i.e. documents on required subjects) a needle is inserted through the whole pack and then raised. It carries up with it the cards not required. Those required will drop off—with a little persuasion. So the number for 'television' could be needled. The 'drops' could then be needled again using the number for 'Advertising', and these would then drop, and so on until the documents were identified covering exactly the subject-compound required. One card may be able to take perhaps only 75 holes, hence code numbers for only 75 topics. So methods have been worked out to allow combinations of holes to be notched which, in combination, represent a certain single number. Methods of multiple-number coding are clearly explained and demonstrated in FOSKETT, p. 13-18. The use of combination code numbers increases the work involved. But edge-notched cards may be kept in random order, so obviating filing. Also, the description of documents pinpointed is given on the cards, and any unwanted items may possibly be able to be rejected without the labour of examining the document. The cards might even include in apertures microfilms of the documents themselves, enabling, in effect, 'self-retrieval'.

The physical systems mentioned so far are manual, even though an example of 'mechanical-manual' has been included. The principle of the method can be used in computers and other machine systems, including of course 'body'-punched card sorting machines. However, here we are mainly concerned with the intellectual value of coordinate indexing, and not the 'hardware' aspect.

ADVANTAGES OF COORDINATE INDEXING

1. Speed. Indexing can be faster than in conventional systems, because there is no classification or building up of subject headings of documents,

and because the documents themselves do not usually have to be inserted into a relative location file: they are merely added at the end of the sequence. Also, the indexer, provided he has access to an efficient thesaurus, does not have to work out references.

2. Searching. The searcher is not dependent on any predetermined citation order, and so there is no need to follow up complex subject references. He merely has to identify the terms which relate to his needs and then apply them to the system. Therefore, all approaches are catered for fully and with equal efficiency.

3. Deriving from item 2: a far greater number of approaches can more conveniently be catered for than with more traditional methods, e.g. in effect the equivalent of a subject heading with up to about 10 components might conceivably be handled.

4. The method is more flexible than conventional methods, e.g. classification scheme with subject-index. Its flexibility goes even beyond that of the dictionary catalogue, because of its use of isolates, and not compound terms, while still retaining a facility for specific retrieval.

5. The system has been developed, and made more sensitive and accurate, by the use of uniconcepts, e.g. EDUCATION FOR LIBRARIANSHIP being one term and not two: EDUCATION and LIBRARIANSHIP. This helps obviate 'false drops' (i.e. unwanted documents) in the form of 'relationship between education and librarianship' when only 'education for librarianship' is required.

6. The system can be readily mechanised in a variety of ways.

DISADVANTAGES OF COORDINATE INDEXING

1. Direct approach to the documents is not possible since they are not in a systematic order. Therefore, browsing can be made possible only by the labour of retrieving a fairly large number of documents, through citing one descriptor or a few descriptors, and which are then brought together temporarily for the current need.

2. If a manual system is used, the physical operations of needling, etc., can be time-consuming and fiddly. This usually means that only library staff operate a coordinate indexing system.

3. An efficient thesaurus is usually essential for efficiency in indexing: if title terms are used haphazardly as they crop up, this could lead to ambiguity and inefficiency. (This is expanded on below, under Thesauri.)

4. The searcher usually has to use the thesaurus to cater for related terms, as it is not usual to 'post' (mark up) these. A possible exception in some systems is when class inclusion is catered for (exemplified below under Thesauri). However, in small systems the number of descriptors used may be only a few hundreds, and reasonable control can feasibly be exercised without a highly sophisticated system.

5. Although an actual classification scheme (e.g. UDC) is not needed, a classificatory basis must exist in order to relate terms having something in common. Hence, as already mentioned, there is usually a need for a thesaurus to control the index language used.

6. In some systems groups of documents having several concepts in common have been grouped at one point, e.g. number. One feels that this defeats the basic idea of the method, which depends upon complete flexibility of all the individual concepts of all documents. On the other hand, it is too irregularly used to have the advantages of classification.

7. Generally, the system is convenient for only a comparatively small number of documents, e.g. body-punched cards may have up to 10,000 positions, and it is inefficient to add a second card for a term. Sometimes a collection has been divided into several sections, each dealing with an allegedly self-contained area of the topic as a whole. But this type of system mitigates against the complete flexibility of the method. However, the small number of documents is not necessarily a disadvantage because some special libraries wish to stop and start again every few years. It almost becomes an advantage then, because there is then an opportunity to overhaul the index vocabulary used, or even to change to a different system altogether.

8. There is usually some degree of inconvenience in having to handle each document indicated, since—at least in item-on-term entry—only an arbitrary location number, and not a description of the document, emerges from the system. So, once a document has been retrieved it may transpire not to be useful for the search in hand.

THE THESAURUS

When coordinate indexing became popular in the early 1950's, some librarians and information workers appear to have regarded it as a spontaneously created panacea for all information retrieval problems. However, it should have been appreciated at once that the terms used must be controlled as strictly as, and have the same qualities as, the subject headings in any 'conventional' dictionary catalogue. This simple fact is obvious to all students who study the history of subject cataloguing. There are two main difficulties: (a) synonymous, near-synonymous and variable constructions; and (b) such relationships as class inclusion, e.g. a document on 'Tchaikovsky' is automatically also on (one manifestation at least of) 'Russian music', and of 'Romantic period'. It rapidly became obvious, then, that lists of descriptors had to be compiled, usually showing the relationships of words with each other, and which terms were to be preferred in the case of synonyms. The lists compiled were called thesauri (singular: thesaurus), but in fact many are virtually a refined version of our old friend (or enemy) the conventional list of subject headings except that usually they list only uniterms or uniconcepts and not other compounds.

A further semantic difficulty emerged which is most manifest in coordinate indexing. In strict uniterm indexing terms are cited in isolation, since they are in fact uniterms, without the use of connecting subsidiary words such as prepositions to show their relationships. So, POLICE and STATE together may represent either (a) the (conventional) 'state police', i.e. 'police run by a state', or (b) the concept of the 'police state'. The result may be 'false drops', i.e. the retrieval of documents which are not relevant to the required compound subject. (The term derives from the mechanical techniques in which the cards representing the required topic drop out of the pack.) In turn, this means time wastage in final manual sorting, and ultimately lack of faith in the system: in fact, it means that the system can become intolerably inefficient. An attempt has been made to counteract this problem by the use of uniconcepts, i.e. terms, usually of more than one word, which express the required concept. So POLICE STATE, although related to both POLICE and STATE, would have its own place in the vocabulary of the system—or, to us, the list of subject headings used.

A thesaurus lists, as the jargon has it, controlled uniterms, and it is normally said to be a thesaurus of descriptors. But, as we have decided, to ordinary people it is in fact a type of list of subject headings. It is not essentially like the conventional thesaurus, such as Roget's, which is classified, from general to particular in large classes, although some very sophisticated examples reach Roget-like proportions in supplementary groupings of terms.

It is an alphabetically arranged list of terms recommended for use in an information retrieval system (i.e. here, index!). Usually it is confined to a particular subject—and so can include many more terms in its field than would be included in a general list of subject headings—as shown by three examples cited as follows: (*a*) Engineers Joint Council's *Thesaurus of engineering terms*. New York, 1964—or its enlarged replacement *Thesaurus of engineering and scientific terms*, 1967; (*b*) Euratom's [European Atomic Community] *Euratom thesaurus*, 2nd ed., 1967, dealing with nuclear science (it is noteworthy that both of these examples are cooperative—further demonstrating the need to control and define terms carefully); and (*c*) Gordon C. Barhydt, Charles T. Schmidt and Kee T. Chang's *Information retrieval thesaurus of education terms*, Cleveland: Western Reserve, 1968.

The basic construction and use of a thesaurus may be shown by listing the types of components which might be included at an entry. An entry, then, may have all, or some, of the following:

TERM
Scope note
UF (= used for, equivalent to 'x', or *see* 'reference from')
or USE (= *see*, i.e. do not use this term, but the one referred to)
BT (= broader term, similar to 'xx', or *see also* 'reference from')
NT (= narrower term, similar to 'downward' *see also* to a more specific heading)
RT (= related term, somewhat similar to a *see also* both ways, between approximately collateral, or equal-ranking, headings).

It will be seen that the abbreviations used have two advantages over the conventional list of subject headings: (*a*) they have literal mnemonic value, as compared with the arbitrary 'x' and 'xx' of most conventional lists; and (*b*) more exact relationships are shown, e.g. whether terms are 'broader' or 'narrower' than others to which they are related.

A further development, of some thesauri at least, as compared with conventional lists, is to list in addition groups of terms under general headings. This device obviates a great deal of repetition for related terms, since merely the number of the relevant list may be given whilst it helps in the choice of a descriptor from a list of related headings—just as Roget's thesaurus does in fact. A sophisticated example of this device is item (*c*) the education thesaurus cited above, which lists terms according to facets and sub-facets. This work further has a

'Permuted list of descriptors', in effect a KWIC (Key Word in Context) list, so that, for example, PUBLIC ADDRESS SYSTEM is found under all three words in their appropriate places in the alphabet. A further interesting feature of this work is that preferred terms are usually in direct, i.e. uninverted, form, which one cannot help feeling is what one should expect in a specific alphabetical approach. This technique is more than ever justified in this work because of the existence of the 'Faceted array' section—in effect a classified sequence but without detailed notation. For example, in the 'Alphabetical array' there is no need to group types of 'test' under TEST followed by a comma, then type, as TEST, INTEREST; TEST, MENTAL; etc., since they are listed in Facet 2 Sub-facet 2002; while in the Alphabetical array, under TEST, we have RT 2002. At the moment this type of work seems to be possibly the nearest one can get to a synthetic list of subject headings while still preserving direct, natural language, but without directly invoking the use of a set (restricting) classification scheme. However, it must be emphasised that small systems may rely on merely a simple list of preferred terms—perhaps a few hundred—and still be effective.

A thesaurus, unlike a conventional list of subject headings, is used primarily by three types of people: (a) the indexer, for obvious reasons; (b) the searcher, since the index itself will not usually include the subject references expected in the conventional dictionary catalogue; and (c) the author, to try to ensure that terminology becomes standardised: i.e. used consistently in titles, in abstracts, and if possible in the actual texts, of articles and reports.

Unfortunately, standardisation has not been achieved in all subject fields. Examples have been reported of works on related fields using different contents of entries under the same term, in this case the E. J. C. Thesaurus (1967 edition) and the U.S. Bureau of Ships' Thesaurus (WILSON AND STEPHENSON, p. 73).

Since thesauri are, at present, restricted to certain subject fields, however broad, they do not run so many risks of ambiguity as do general lists of subject headings. However, one may hope that the time may possibly come when a new systematic general list of headings may be compiled, derived in part from the best specialised thesauri available, with their terminology reconciled, and with citation orders recommended for the construction of the compound headings needed in a dictionary catalogue. A facet order of the type used in the education thesaurus discussed here, but not necessarily reproducing its order as given, might be used. Such a general list would be an alternative to the 'Key' type of list advocated in the past by Coates (see page 183). It would have the advantage of being independent of any one classification scheme or even of an edition of one scheme—which infers repeated revision of headings and references used to correspond with changes in successive new editions. Meanwhile the 'isolate' headings could conceivably be used as descriptors in Project Marc and other cooperative computerised bibliographic data activities. In this way, the flexible, natural language of the idea of coordinate indexing could be applied to large complete research libraries, and not be confined to small specialised collections as at present.

SECTION IV

OTHER TECHNICAL PROCESSES

Other Technical Processes

This section includes a variety of aspects, but for the sake of uniformity the same method of arranging the readings has been used as in other sections. Details of general codes are not repeated here; they are listed at the start of Section II.

Special codes and readings cited in the text

ASLIB. *Film Production Libraries Group. Cataloguing Committee.* Film cataloguing rules. London: ASLIB, 1963.

BRITISH FILM INSTITUTE. Rules for use in the cataloguing department of the National Film Archive. London: The Institute, 1960.

Also of interest is the Institute's Film extract catalogue (cover title: Study extract catalogue) for its examples of very full plot synopses.

BURKETT, J. Special materials in the library: a series of 14 lectures . . .; ed. by J. Burkett and T. S. Morgan. London: L.A., 1963.

CATALOGUE AND INDEX, no. 14, April 1969, p. 7-10 has the first instalment of a Register of adoptions of AACR 1967; this is of interest as an indication of recataloguing taking place in British libraries.

See also the relevant readings on AACR given in Section II.

CHAPLIN, A. H. Names of persons: national usage for entry in catalogues, definitive ed., ed. by A. H. Chaplin and Dorothy Anderson. Sevenoaks, Kent, England: International Federation of Library Associations, 1967.

COATES, E. J. Subject catalogues . . . (Details are given in Section III.)

CUTTER's Rules for a dictionary catalogue. (Details are given in Section II.) Relevant here for filing rules.

FLOWERS, E. Centralized cataloguing for Australian research libraries, *in* Library Association of Australia. *13th biennial Conference, Canberra.* Papers, vol. 1, p. 229-245. Sydney: L.A.A., 1965.

FRY, GEORGE. Catalog card reproduction: report on a study conducted by George Fry and associates. (ALA Library Technology Project.) Chicago: A.L.A., 1965.

INTERNATIONAL ASSOCIATION OF MUSIC LIBRARIES. Code international de catalogage de la musique. London, New York: C. F. Peters, 1957- (in progress).

KENNEDY, R. F. Classified cataloguing . . . (Details are given in Section III.)

KYLE, BARBARA. Notes on cataloguing in special libraries with special emphasis on author and name entries, *in* Journal of documentation, vol. 22, no. 1, March 1966, p. 13-21.

MILLARD, PATRICIA. Modern library equipment, compiled and edited by Patricia Millard. London: Crosby Lockwood, 1966.

MUSIC LIBRARY ASSOCIATION. Code for cataloging music and phonorecords; prepared by a Joint Committee of the Music Library Association and the American Library Association . . . Chicago: A.L.A., 1958.

NORRIS, DOROTHY MAY. A history of cataloguing . . . (Details are given in Section III.)

Of interest for the history of physical forms of catalogues.

PARGETER, PHILIP S. The reproduction of catalogue cards. London: L.A., 1960.

PARSONS, EDWARD ALEXANDER. The Alexandrian Library . . . (Details in Section III.)

PIETTE, J. R. F. A guide to foreign languages for science librarians and bibliographers, rev. and enl. by E. Horzelska. London: ASLIB for Welsh Plant Breeding Station, Aberystwyth, 1965.

PIGGOTT, MARY. The cataloguing of government publications, *in* Library Association record, vol. 58, no. 4, April 1956, p. 129-135.

PIGGOTT, MARY. Notes on cataloguing books in certain foreign languages, ed. by Mary Piggot. London: L.A., 1956.

PLUMBE, WILFRED J. Another appraisal of the Stripdex catalogue, *in* Library review, vol. 21, no. 5, Spring 1968, p. 234-236.

PLUMBE, WILFRED J. The Stripdex catalogue, *in* Library Association record, vol. 64, no. 4, April 1962, p. 128-131.

RUE, ELOISE. Subject headings for children's materials, by Eloise Rue and Effie La Plante. Chicago: A.L.A., 1952.

SHARP, HENRY A. Cataloguing: a textbook for use in libraries, 4th ed. London: Grafton, 1948.

Useful for some aspects of special cataloguing, including incunabula and manuscripts.

STEPHEN, PETER. The Stripdex catalogue, *in* Library review, vol. 21, no. 3, Autumn 1967, p. 137-139.

SUBJECT headings and index for a classified catalogue for post-primary school libraries: a list for use in New Zealand; prepared by the School Library Service. Wellington: National Library Service, 1965.

VOOS, HENRY. Revision of the current Library of Congress catalog card format, *in* Library resources and technical services, vol. 11, no. 2, Spring 1967, p. 167-172.

Other readings

AMERICAN LIBRARY ASSOCIATION. *Resources and Technical Services Division. Cataloging and Classification Section. Policy and Research Committee.* Catalog use study; Director's report by Sidney L. Jackson; ed. by Vaclav Mostecky. Chicago: A.L.A., 1958.

Of value in deciding how to limit cataloguing.

BOGG, S. W. Classification and cataloging of maps and atlases. New York: Special Libraries Association, 1945.

BROXIS, PETER F. Organising the arts. London: Bingley, 1968. SBN 85157 051 8.

BRYANT, E. T. Music librarianship: a practical guide. London: James Clarke, 1963.

CURWEN, A. G. Implications of the new Rules in individual libraries, *in* SEMINAR ON THE ANGLO-AMERICAN CATALOGUING RULES (details in Section II), p. 67-77.

Implications involving recataloguing.

DOCUMENTATION INCORPORATED has distributed a folder of reprints of various articles entitled Book catalogs for the library; approx. 1967.

FRIEDMAN, JOAN. Cataloguing and classification in British university libraries: a survey of practices and procedures, by Joan Friedman and Alan Jeffreys. Sheffield: University of Sheffield. Postgraduate School of Librarianship, 1967.

JOHNSON, A. F. Practical cataloguing. London: A.A.L., 1962.

JOHNSON, MARGARET FULLERTON. Manual of cataloging and classification for small school and public libraries, by Margaret Fullerton Johnson and Dorothy E. Cook, 4th ed. New York: H. W. Wilson, 1950.

Both useful for limited cataloguing; but both pre-date AACR.

KINGERY, R. E. Book catalogs, by R. E. Kingery and M. F. Tauber. New York: Scarecrow Press, 1963.

QUIGG, PATRICK. Theory of cataloguing (details in Section II), p. 92-96.

REDFERN, BRIAN. Organizing music in libraries. London: Bingley, 1966.

ROGERS, DEREK. Works of art, *in* Catalogue and index, no. 5, Jan. 1967, p. 4-6, and no. 6, April 1967, p. 10-11.

SINCLAIR, K. V. Some thoughts on the cataloguing of incunabula, *in* Australian library journal, vol. 17, no. 2, March 1968, p. 39-45.

STEPHENSON, GEORGE R. Cataloguing practice in English technical college libraries, *in* College and research libraries, vol. 25, no. 5, September 1964, p. 404-410.

VEANER, ALLEN B. Cameras for copying catalog cards: two approaches, *in* Library resources and technical services, vol. 11, no. 4, Fall 1967, p. 468-478.

WEBER, DAVID C. Book catalog trends in 1966, *in* Library trends, vol. 16, no. 1, July 1967.

Includes statistics showing the growth of popularity of book catalogues in U.S.

WEIMERSKIRCH, PHILIP J. The use of title page photography in cataloging, *in* Library resources and technical services, vol. 12, no. 1, Winter 1968, p. 37-46.

CHAPTER 19

Special Cataloguing

Introduction

'Special' cataloguing can include the usual techniques of author/title headings, added entries and references, and subject cataloguing and references or subject indexing as applied to almost any forms of materials other than monographic printed works. The term might also be applied to the cataloguing of any special or restrictive subject branch of materials. This usually means applying the usual rules to the type of condition or case most often manifested in the particular subject field. And it might further even be taken to embrace the application of 'general' techniques in various types of libraries.

It is not necessary to enumerate in detail all the 'special' categories together with all the applications of all the rules and practices as applied to these categories. This is particularly so nowadays, when the cataloguer should be educated to recognise various conditions, or symptoms even, and then apply the remedy from his generalised body of knowledge of his craft.

It is proposed here to list the various categories in the ways in which they are likely to be encountered; then to name the more common relevant factors showing to which categories they apply; and finally to go in detail through the rules and practices applicable to representative 'special' categories, including comparison of their treatment in some general and also some 'special' codes.

The need for many of the special codes has been obviated by the appearance of AACR. A skilled and sensible cataloguer, with AACR, plus subject classification, cataloguing and terminology guides and an understanding of the principles of information retrieval, should be able to tackle almost any sort of material in almost any sort of library.

Basic problems vary considerably from type to type of material: the following list attempts to identify briefly the main problems but these do not necessarily apply to all materials, and when they do, their impact may be of varying influence and importance with the different categories of material:

1. Machinery may be needed to use the documents.

2. The materials may be more fragile, rare and expensive than normal book-form materials.

3. Special subject knowledge may be needed to catalogue the materials thoroughly and quickly.

4. Special knowledge and experience of the physical form may be needed.

5. Special cataloguing tools, e.g. codes and thesauri, may be needed.

6. Hence: it may be necessary to compile one's own aids because of the rarity of the type of material.

7. Information may be harder to obtain from the documents to be catalogued than with normal monographic materials, e.g. lack of title page or adequate title-page substitute.

8. The information obtained from one source in the document may conflict with that obtained from another source in the document.

9. External sources of information, e.g. bibliographies, may have to be used, in which case there may be difficulty in thoroughly identifying documents in hand with corresponding entries in the external sources.

10. Scope of externally compiled indexes and abstracts may not correspond economically with the stock; therefore, extra internally executed indexing and abstracting may be necessary.

11. The type of material may not be covered by central cataloguing and similar services.

12. It may be harder to reach cataloguing decisions than is the case with normal monographic materials, e.g. intellectual responsibility may be more diffuse and it may be harder to find an author equivalent.

13. More variable degrees of limited cataloguing may be necessary.

14. The bibliographic unit may be less easily defined, ranging from mere collocation to the incidence of separately issued excerpts and the need for more analysis of individual physical units.

15. A single document may include a mixture of different forms of material, e.g. audio-visual and printed.

16. If the collection is part of a larger system, there may be a conflict between the case for separate catalogues for the various materials and that for incorporating entries for them into the library's general catalogue.

17. Some materials are confidential, e.g. some research data in private industry. This can militate against the whole concept of library science, which implies mutual sharing of information and materials.

18. In some forms of material, forgery or inadvertent misinterpretation of the information content is more likely to be encountered than with printed book form materials.

19. Some materials are more international and so a knowledge of foreign languages may be more necessary than in dealing with more routine forms of material.

In the chapters on special materials, general codes are cited by the abbreviations used at the beginning of Section II.

CHAPTER 20

Special Cataloguing

Physical Forms of Material

It will be appreciated that quite a lot of cross-classification applies. This is to be expected, and is in fact part of the treatment. Where two or more general conditions intersect, at that point will emerge the special cataloguing need for that job. For example, suppose the essence in cataloguing for primary school libraries is simplification, and the essence of the cataloguing of film strips is the subject approach, the emergent factor is simplified subject cataloguing.

1. *Manuscripts*

Pre-printing era. Occasionally one may have to catalogue a real extant classical period or medieval manuscript. But the likelihood is rare enough for us to leave instructions for such a job to a combination of specialist works and a specialist apprenticeship. Facsimile copies may more frequently be acquired: these need a combination of rules for manuscripts, e.g. AACR Chapter 10, and those for photographic and other reproductions, e.g. AACR Chapter 9.

Post-printing era. These will be:

(a) Items which have been written specially with a view to publication, e.g. the MS of an author's novel; or

(b) Those items in (a) but which never have been published; or

(c) Miscellaneous collections of items, perhaps correspondence, some or all of which may have been published, in various forms, fullness and sequences.

The last group is usually the more important to the academic librarian since it is essentially primary source material and scholars will need to find out quickly and efficiently what a collection contains, if possible without overmuch handling of the material itself. Again, AACR Chapter 10 is of value. In addition, some older cataloguing works may be useful e.g. CUTTER (p. 135 ff.), which includes instructions for calendaring (detailing of each piece in a collection), and H. A. Sharp's *Cataloguing*

AA 1908 and ALA 1949 have been overtaken and more than embraced by AACR.

One may reach the point of being in charge of a collection of archives, in which case the average librarian should do nothing until he has sought the advice of an archivist.

Manuscripts are likely to be encountered in librarianship mostly in local history collections, other specialised history collections, e.g. the private papers of a statesman, and in collections of literature or music scores.

2. *Printed Letterpress*

Monographic works

(i) Pamphlets (applicable to some extent also to paperbacks)

Those which are valuable and large enough may be bound and then treated like any other monographic works. More ephemeral ones may receive merely a subject heading and kept in a file, which of course needs to be weeded out regularly. Some libraries keep a selection of extremely ephemeral or unoriginal material in a browsing corner or room, in which case it is likely that no record at all may be kept. (See also Chapter 22, on Limited Cataloguing.) Some pamphlet-type material may also belong to the government publications category, dealt with below. Others may be music scores, dealt with later.

(ii) Government publications

Treatment of these varies depending on whether a library acquires only occasional items, e.g. a small public or a school library, or whether it acquires complete or nearly complete sets, and from a variety of countries.

In the former case, the fact that items are government publications is immaterial: they are treated like other, usually monographic, works, depending on their physical form and ephemerality or permanence. In such libraries, the cataloguer might well contemplate some of the simplifications of author/title entry mentioned in Chapter 4, e.g. simple titles for main entry.

In the latter case, there may even be a special government publica-tions department, usually under the care of a qualified librarian with a suitable academic qualification. In such a department, two basic courses are open:

(*a*) All the material may be fully catalogued, complete with analyticals and the resulting records integrated irrespective of country of origin.

(*b*) If the material is normally sought because of its country of origin, separate sets of records may be kept, using the official lists and catalogues from the respective official publishing offices as far as possible. H.M.S.O. publications are particularly well served in this respect, with their cumulating indexes and even central card service, while contents of relevant Australian publications are well indexed in *Australian public affairs information service* (APAIS) compiled in the National Library of Australia. A special department may include also non-official publications, e.g. from political parties, and again treatment of such material may depend on the efficiency of lists and catalogues issued by the publishing body. In any case, *ad hoc* indexes may have to be compiled, depending on the type of use made of the collection. Simple title indexes may well be needed to cut through the complexities of diffuse corporate authorship. A knowledge of a variety of languages may be particularly useful, including Welsh for dealing with vernacular Plaid Cymru documents.

Code treatment. As already inferred, if one wished to accept a ready-made formula, AACR is the most comprehensive source of consistent rules. The other general codes are mainly of academic interest now. The chief advantage of AACR is that it can be made to cater for publications of all modern governments. It uses a rather narrower bibliographic unit than, say, ALA 1949, and so should be reasonably helpful in locating the entry for a required document, while still preserving a reasonable degree of collocation likely to be useful in research. Also, in its rules for 'mixed' authorship, it offers palatable solutions to the vexed problem of corporate versus personal entry. Two possible variations on AACR may be worth considering: (*a*) To enter executive departments directly, and even under their operative (subject) terms, instead of indirectly via names of countries, etc.; and (*b*) To use English forms for names of such departments. Names of countries would then become the second-cited filing terms. Also, there should be a liberal use of conventional title added entries. Alternatively, main entries could be under conventional titles, with reliance on the library's catalogue's subject approach, or on official lists and catalogues for the 'departmental' approach.

There will come a time when the shared cataloguing and MARC projects become really international, and when BNB's hope for a computerised analytical approach is realised. When this happens, a great deal of local cataloguing and indexing will become unnecessary. For, when countries begin central cataloguing and information retrieval services, what better material is there to start on than their own government publications? Already, many non-U.S. government publications are being covered by Library of Congress cataloguing, in the printed *National union catalog* and on cards.

(iii) Research reports

Many research reports are of a scientific and technical nature, and so are as well covered as any material by published indexes. Author/title problems include the types of conditions identified in AACR, the chief being the various manifestations of mixed authorship. Some information scientists show exasperation with what they may regard as cumbersome corporate authorship treatment, and they may prefer to emphasise more direct entry. Reliance can be made in some instances on lists of series and 'semi-serials' issued by various research establishments, whether government, nationalised, or private-industrial. But the chief emphasis is on subject approach, and with probably an increasing interest in bibliographic coupling (knowing which documents are cited in other documents). Manual methods in rising favour are exhaustive or systematically selective subject indexing in depth, perhaps appended to a specially constructed (often faceted) classification scheme, and coordinate indexing. However, testing of these and other modern methods, whether manual or automated, has still some way to go. The subject element is dealt with, as far as this book allows, in Section III.

(iv) Incunabula

This category is about as far apart from the preceding topic as it is possible to get. Since, by definition, it is a question of cataloguing works printed before 1500, methods have long since been worked out, tested and agreed upon. The only real disadvantage is in finding the time to practise these techniques. AACR of course has a chapter, 8, working along the now conventionally accepted lines that the owning library normally has only to identify its copy in hand with the much fuller bibliographic description which will be found in an existing printed catalogue or bibliography. Various symbols and typographical devices are used to save space, and therefore the cataloguer should get to know these in order to identify the work described and to collate this description with the copy in hand. Some relevant sources are also mentioned in AACR. The category might also include music, in which case one needs to find the relevant 'co-ordinates' between AACR Chapter 8, already mentioned, and AACR Chapter 13, Music.

(v) 'Sets' (multiple copies), e.g. plays, and choral music

These categories may be encountered mainly in large public, especially county, libraries. Multiple copies—the number depending on the number of characters in plays and size of choral group in music—are loaned for long periods. Borrowing organisations may be distant from the library, especially a county headquarters, and so there is a particular need for printed catalogues or check lists.

Choral works can probably be covered adequately by check lists giving only sufficient detail to identify a work, since one may often rely on the knowledge of those running the choral society to know whether a particular work is suitable for them. Lists could be compiled according to sex and types of music, since these will normally be the first characteristics used by choirs in selecting their wants. In the case of little-known works, dates of composers and brief annotations could also be useful—annotations could be fairly subjective if compiled by a librarian who knows the type of clientele for which he is catering.

Sets of orchestral, etc., 'parts', although different bibliographically since the parts are unique, might also be maintained by the same department. Information about these is given under Music, below. But in addition, librarians may compile lists of works not normally for sale but which are available on commercial hire, giving name and address of firm, and if possible charges.

Plays are normally listed by author alphabetically. Vital information is: Title; Number of acts and scenes; Estimated running time; Numbers and sexes of characters; Idea of plot or theme, and location. Since shorter plays—perhaps those most likely to be wanted by amateurs—are often most cheaply, even though not so conveniently, obtained in collections, analytical entries will be needed. Indexes are necessary, e.g. Title; Subject; Location; Number of cast including sex; and Playing time.

It may be useful to indicate also in catalogues if the library stocks gramophone records of the works in stock.

(vi) Serials, including multi-annual works, annuals, periodicals, and newspapers (complete, not cuttings)

The treatment of these categories may vary slightly, but together they form what might be called a 'case-condition', since they constitute a 'form'; in fact they may warrant special rules. However, if one wished, one could divide them into real 'conditions', e.g. shared authorship, collections under editorial direction, works without named authors, etc.

As with government publications, some libraries maintain a separate serials department. If in this case, separate records are kept, continual care must be exercised to ensure that inexperienced assistants on subject searches do not overlook such a department's existence.

There is a growing tendency, especially in large libraries, not to classify periodicals, and therefore cataloguing and shelf-location may be simpler. (The reason against classifying is that the subject of a sought article is very often so far narrower than the class mark given to the periodical as a whole that it is pointless having the latter. Approach is almost always via indexes which index many periodicals, e.g. *British technology index*, and what any cataloguer thinks of the general class number of a periodical is therefore immaterial; the class mark is used solely as an arbitrary shelving device.)

Most of the effort in recording serials goes into maintaining some form of register to ensure prompt receipt and to supervise payment of accounts, all of which does not concern us here.

As far as actual catalogues are concerned, opinion is divided as to whether entries should be filed into the general (monographic works) catalogue, or whether a separate catalogue of serials should be maintained. Where a separate department is maintained, a separate catalogue is more convenient for stock-checking purposes. However, many serials of the multi-annual or annual type, either directories or surveys of subjects over a period of time, may not be thought of as serials. In fact, some, like the *Libraries museums and art galleries yearbook*, are mis-named. Further, when a new directory is started, it is not always readily apparent, or even known by the publishers, if it is in fact going to be a serial. Rather than maintain duplicate records, the best compromise is to rely on the register for stock-checking and marking off purposes, while interfiling brief 'open' entries, author/title and subject, in the main catalogue, giving precise location. 'Continuations', where such a category exists ('semi-serials' and series going on for a long time but probably with an end in mind), can receive similar treatment as if serials, but they will almost certainly require individual monographic-type treatment too. If a separate catalogue of serials is maintained, one would seriously consider excluding from it works which are usually thought of by users in 'non-serial' terminology, e.g. British Railways' timetables, *Yearbook of education*, and various Kellys directories.

Codes

BM (1) Basic rule: enter according to the formula:

> [1] PERIODICAL PUBLICATIONS. [2] Town of publication. [3] Title; earliest form (i.e. not treated as Anonymous works);

except (2) For allegedly corporate authorship periodicals:

> [1] Heading appropriate for the organisation. [2] Title.

Extensive use of references is needed, but is not always given, in the BM printed catalogue.

Certain other categories, e.g. almanacs, ephemerides, are given their own broad form entries.

PI Always treated as PI's anonymous works, i.e. entered under constructed real title. Earliest form is used as basis for real title.

CUTTER (1) Basic rule: first word of title not an article, including journals published by a society and newspapers;

except (2) Transactions of a society: under society.

Provision for inverted title references, except where covered by subject entry.

AA 1908 (1) Basic rule: first word of title not an article; earliest form (ALA exception: latest form). Applies to all 'serials';

except (2) Corporate entry under society if its name appears significantly in title.

ALA 1949 Considerable catering for various types of complexity of title, but approximately same as AA 1908 incorporating ALA alternative for title change.

CCR 1960 (1) Title, with choice for changed title: earliest, or latest, or successive;

except (2) Title starting with name of corporate body: corporate entry; and (3) Transactions: as (2).

ICCP 1961 Basically preference for title in as many cases as possible. Changed title: successive entry.

AACR (1) Basically title;

except (2) If main title includes name of body: corporate entry;

and (3) If by a personal author: personal author entry. Change of title: successive entry;

i.e. AACR in effect repeats application of its 'conditions' under the 'case' heading Serials.

One's own preference is for title entry but with generic (and often changeable) initial words like 'proceedings' and 'bulletin' in brackets and ignored in filing; for substantial changes in title: successive entry is preferred. It is noteworthy that the National Lending Library for Science and Technology uses strict title entry, including the use of insignificant words.

One would normally recommend shelving alphabetically by main title entry, reliance on subject approach being via indexes and abstracts.

3. *Graphic materials* including atlases and maps, including globes and relief maps (i.e. 3-dimensional forms), pictures and other objects of art value and illustrations of subject value.

Some of these materials might be in a special Art Department in which case the question of separate catalogue versus inclusion in main catalogue arises. The same principles apply if atlases and maps are housed in a separate, e.g. Social studies or History, Department.

(i) Atlases, Maps

It is felt that too much differential treatment is given to these two categories because of their accidental physical form. Since they have a common function they should be given uniform catalogue treatment as far as possible, which need not reflect their shelf location if this is decided by physical form.

A clear distinction should be drawn between author/title and subject/form cataloguing. Some writers and codes assume, perhaps rightly, that author entry is not required, then give rules for place entry, and in an avowedly author/title code or chapter in a book. This is confusing for students who are trying to learn the principles of cataloguing. If the compilers of an author/title code decide that author/title entries are not required, this can be stated, and the topic left at that. If the compiler establishes a precedent by substituting subject/form treatment, surely he should give rules for the subject/form treatment of other materials, too.

Author/title entry will probably in fact be required, as with most other library materials. With older works, this is usually the cartographer; with modern works it is more likely to be a corporate body, e.g. a government department, or an academic body, or a commercial publisher, or an editor's name may be most prominent. If authorship is too 'diffuse', the most sought term may be the title.

Maps do not have title pages, of course, so a title page substitute should be sought, e.g. information within the borders of a map, or in a cartouche, as probably being the most distinctive and complete. Complete series of modern maps, e.g. British one-inch Ordnance Survey, could be given, in effect, merely a 'group-series' entry, being treated as a multi-volume work but without the 'contents list' part of note. The library should have an 'index-map' to identify which maps are required for a particular purpose. Older maps, e.g. Speed's, should preferably receive individual entries.

Subject/form entry presents, in some cases, a three-part conflict: Place *vs* Subject *vs* Form. Form can usually be regarded as the least sought. So it could be represented in a dictionary catalogue in the form of general *see also* references. In a classified catalogue, the scheme used will decide its place in the order in which the class mark is constructed, and the subject index can accordingly reflect this order. But if the form 'map' or 'atlas' is not always given a constant place in the way in which the class mark is constructed, explanatory notes or references could be used in the subject index, e.g. in UDC 'subject' maps are usually classified with the citation order (1) Subject, (2) Map, but topographical maps usually have the citation order (1) Map, (2) Locality. Therefore one might have, say:

> MAPS: ECONOMICS   33(084.3)
> MAPS: GEOLOGY   55(084.3)

> For topographical maps see names of localities, e.g.
> AUSTRALIA: MAPS.

In the case of Place *vs* Subject, the list of subject headings may decide citation order.

> e.g. GEOLOGY—AUSTRALIA and
> GEOLOGY—MAPS.

If one is constructing one's own subject headings and references according to chain procedure, as reflected by the classification scheme in use, the citation order of headings and construction of references are usually decided automatically, e.g. from UDC, one would get from 55(94) (083):

> MAPS: AUSTRALIA: GEOLOGY
>
> AUSTRALIA: GEOLOGY *see also* MAPS: AUSTRALIA: GEOLOGY
>
> GEOLOGY *see also* AUSTRALIA: GEOLOGY [or a general *see also* might be made].

However, as was discussed in Section III, cataloguers may still want to change the citation order from that decided by the chain.

Codes

BM Main entry under specific English name of locality; added references for engravers, compilers, etc.

CUTTER (p. 140) Multiple unit entry under authors and subjects, 'subject' including place-names. Commercial publisher is allowed as author. Analyticals are given for insets. Considerable description is prescribed.

AA 1908 Cartographer; if not known: publisher.

ALA 1949 Rather similar to AA 1908, but with order of priority for choice of entry, final choice being title. ATLASES as form entry for comprehensive works.

AACR, Chapter 8. Eight pages are given to Maps, Relief Models, Globes and Atlases, including 'planetary and astronomical aspects as well as terrestrial', and including rules for both entry and description. Generally, the principle of intellectual responsibility governs entry, examples being given to show how this is decided upon. In some instances, entry under commercial publisher is prescribed. In the description rules, the basic AACR description rules are consistently applied, so as to produce information such as scale, size, series statement, and the type of notes likely to be useful, e.g. source from which map is derived, and additional material such as insets.

ROYAL GEOGRAPHICAL SOCIETY. (Summarised in Burkett and Morgan, pages 89-96.)

This uses basically a logical-topographical system, e.g. first World; then Continents, followed by Sub-continents; then individual Countries, and their divisions; fourthly Oceans. Subject of maps is treated as a distributed relative.

One's preference would be for (*a*) Subject arrangement according to a flexible synthetic classification scheme, like UDC, which could be manipulated consistently, with either a classified catalogue with a subject index, or alphabetical-subject approach reflecting UDC citation order, and (*b*) AACR-type decisions for author/title approach.

(ii) Art works

Lack of space and immediate demand precludes detailed study of this category. AACR Chapter 15 devotes 12 pages to the author/title and descriptive cataloguing of Pictures, Designs and Other Two-Dimensional Representations (including slides and film strips). These rules are carefully designed for the non-expert, technical terms being explained, and the rules seem to be consistent with the basic principle of intellectual responsibility used elsewhere in the Code. One's only doubt over this set of rules is that author entries are prescribed for illustrative material used for its informational content, and there may be some doubt about whether such entries are necessary at all.

Illustrations of subject value, including slides and film strips.

The main and perhaps only interest here is in the subject treatment. One would recommend that an illustrations collection should be arranged consistently with that of the library's subject catalogue. If this is classified, the subject index entries could possibly be incorporated into the main subject index, using some such prefixes as I or ILLUS to indicate the medium of information, hence sequence to be used.

e.g. KENT: DESCRIPTION   914.223 [for normal material]
     and
     KENT: DESCRIPTION   ILLUS. 914.223 [for illustrations collection].

The reason for this is that an enquirer does not necessarily know that he needs an illustration; his request may be, say, for the colour of the Lord Mayor of London's robes.

However, if a separate Illustrations (or similar) Department is maintained, as in most larger general libraries, it is plainly more convenient to rely on inservice training and staff supervision to ensure that the material is adequately exploited, rather than have mass duplication of entries in general catalogues.

(iii) Other fugitive material of subject value, including cuttings

Similar treatment to that recommended for illustrations could be followed with, again, a preference for a common index to all forms of material.

If very minute specification were required a general synthetic and flexible classification scheme like UDC could be used. However, many newspaper libraries use alphabetical-subject arrangement of cuttings. The usual pros and cons of alphabetical versus classified apply.

4. Music Scores

Music is quite common in library stocks, yet it is one of the harder materials to catalogue. Therefore considerable detail is given here but in compressed form. Most of this information applies also to gramophone records of music, and this section should be used in conjunction with that under Audio-Visual Materials.

Music is often in 'fugitive material' form, e.g. items of four pages are not uncommon. Therefore binding together could be considered for say works of one composer for one form, and the resulting unit given a collective title with a detailed contents list. A better alternative is to buy complete works in the first place, for standard composers.

Music is used for varying purposes, e.g. playing, singing, 'following' a performance, and additional approaches may be needed to cater for these uses.

Title pages may give incomplete or even inaccurate information; or they may be non-existent, in which case a title page substitute must be found, e.g. a caption title, cover title, information in a bibliography or other reference work, or a combination of all or some of these. An example of a fairly typical caption title for a song is shown on page 218.

Arrangements are made from originals for a variety of instruments and voices, and words are put to music thereby multiplying the number of possible approaches, whether composer, librettist, form, instrument and even title.

Music is international and therefore it is likely that more aquaintance with foreign languages will be needed than with many other types of material. Further, non-roman alphabets may well be encountered. Composers' names, titles of works, names of musical forms and instruments, key signatures and instructions within a score must be recognised whatever their language, to ensure that entries for different editions, etc., of the same work are not accidentally separated.

The 'sought' term in 'pop' music scores is often not the name of the composer, but more likely the group whose record causes the demand for it, though in some cases the composer is one of the group. A

Pris 8c.

Y Cerddor N.S. 119

I Gwenda Mair

YR OEN BACH
(LITTLE LAMB)
a
Y GWANWYN
(THE SPRING)

Caneuon Unsain i Blant
(Unison Songs for Children)

J. M. EDWARDS
O CERDDI'R PLANT LLEIAF
trwy ganiatâd Hughes a'i Fab, Caerdydd
English Translations by
J. M. EDWARDS
By kind permission

W. ALBERT WILLIAMS

I. YR OEN BACH
(LITTLE LAMB)

7. Example of a fairly typical song score, from which catalogue entries have to be compiled.

convenient entry for, say, *Jumping Jack Flash* by Mick Jagger and Keith Richard is probably ROLLING STONES, with no other entries.

Excerpting happens more with music than with normal books, and a decision has to be made whether or not to enter under the parent title or direct. Collections of excerpts or of small self-contained pieces raise further problems.

Description details do not always have the same relevance, or equivalents, or importance, as with other documents, e.g. opus numbers are unique to music, as well as being one of the best ways of identifying a work, and so they must be incorporated, and in an appropriate place. On the other hand the original date of publication of certain music works is not particularly important in, say, popular libraries, and so variations in Imprint may be necessary to obviate a great deal of pointless bibliographical searching. One particularly wearing example, one recalls, was a set of 12 Haydn symphonies for 2 pianos 4 hands, the symphonies being merely numbered 1 to 12. Haydn composed 104 symphonies, so the necessary bibliographic searching and comparison of key signatures and names of movements to identify each of the 12 selected can be imagined. Compare such an example with its nearest equivalent: say, an anthology of short stories based on 12 selected poems by one poet—and the extra work involved in cataloguing the music item is the more striking.

An example from the *British catalogue of music* is shown on page 220.

Codes

All codes state or imply that the composer of a work is an author-equivalent, and their basic rules about main entry being under composer are not repeated here. Also variations are usually put by all the codes under the later composer.

BM 'Added-references' are used for many of the alternative approaches, e.g. arrangers, editors, first words of title of songs, operas, oratorios, etc. Anonymous works: Title. If no title: under 'class' (i.e. form) of music if relevant, except that songs go under first word of first line (!). Collections with no compiler: under relevant 'class'. Periodicals: as BM general rule for periodicals. Programmes: 'class' (form) heading PROGRAMMES. These rules are of practical importance since several useful catalogues of music are published by the British Museum.

PI Decisions are approximately as in AA 1908, but with fewer 'added references'.

MUSIC SCORES AND PARTS

E — CHORAL WORKS WITH ACCOMPANIMENT OTHER THAN KEYBOARD INSTRUMENT

EM — With orchestra
EMDE — *Cantatas*
   BACH, Johann Sebastian
   Tonet, ihr Pauken! Erschallet, Trompeten! Congratulatory cantata for the Queen's birthday. [S.]214; edited by Werner Neumann. [Miniature score]. Cassel, Bärenreiter; London, [Novello], 11/-. c 1963. *v,65p. 8vo. (Taschenpartitur—no.183)*

(B64-50500)

   BACH, Johann Sebastian
   Vereinigte Zwietracht der wechselnden Saiten: congratulatory cantata for the installation of Professor Gottlieb Kortte. [S].207; edited by Werner Neumann. [Miniature score]. Cassel, Bärenreiter; London, Novello, 13/-. c 1963. *vii,79p. 8vo. (Taschenpartitur—no.84)*

(B64-50501)

   BERIO, Luciano
   Passaggio: messa in scena di Luciano Berio e di Edoardo Sanguineti. [Score]. Milan, London, Universal Edition, 84/-. c 1963. *56p. fol.*

(B64-50502)

EMDG — *Masses*
   BEETHOVEN, Ludwig van
   Missa solemnis [in] D major: for four solo parts, orchestra and organ; edited from the original sources by Willy Hess. Op.123. [Miniature score]. London, Eulenburg, 26/-. c 1964. *xxix,390p. facsims. 8vo.*

(B64-50503)

ENW — With wind & keyboard ensemble
ENWS — *With recorder & keyboard*
ENWSDW/XC — *Rounds*
ENWSDW/XC/AY — *Collections*
   FLAY, Alfred Leonard, *arranger*
   Follow me; traditional rounds arranged for equal voices, descant, treble and tenor recorders and piano. Full score [and parts]. London, Chappell, 6/-. c 1964. *4pt. 4to.*
   Chorus ed., 1/-.

(B64-50504)

8. Sample from classified section of *British catalogue of music*.

Librettos: composer; references from author. Title references are not mentioned. The usual PI rules for anonymous works, including periodicals, apply. There are a few additional instructions for description of music in Incunabula (Appendix IV: 22).

CUTTER (supplement) Added entries under authors of librettos, etc. But librettos alone go under librettist with composer added entry. Much of CUTTER deals with minutiae of description which today would be of value only in an academic library if that. (In the body of the Code, we are told to enter 'doubly'—author and composer, but 'Short' and 'Medium' catalogues need enter only under composer, with occasional references for author if they are important.)

AA 1908 Librettos: librettist. Thematic catalogues: Composer—these two cases represent a good example of contradictions in principles used. Although the Code includes description, music description is not dealt with specifically or by implication.

ALA 1949 Music is dealt with in more detail than in AA 1908. Intellectual responsibility is usually used as a basic principle, except that librettos go under composer, and cadenzas go under the original composer in whose work they are played.

Music Library Association. *Code for cataloging music and phonorecords*: prepared by a Joint Committee of the Music Library Association and the American Library Association Division of Cataloging and Classification. Chicago: ALA, 1958. (MLA) This is the most important code completed to date dealing solely with music scores and records. It absorbed, and expanded on, the music rules from ALA 1949 and LCRDC. Subsequently, the bulk of its rules were in turn taken with little change into AACR. However, MLA includes two important features excluded from AACR: (a) a Simplified code which could be useful in a small public or a children's library; and (b) a Filing code, which is referred to in Chapter 24 of this book, on Filing. MLA is therefore still worth acquiring to be used in conjunction with AACR. A most important part of MLA is the refinement of the 'conventional' title introduced in LCRDC. The Uniform title feature of AACR derives from this, and is made applicable to any relevant documents, not only music and records.

AACR: Chapter 13. The usual AACR conditions apply, necessitating referral back to more general rules, but in turn of course the overall coherence of the Code allows interfiling of music entries into the general catalogue.

In Chapter 13, AACR conditions are applied specifically to music, e.g. works of mixed character including operas and songs. Basic decisions are similar to those in ALA 1949, as stated above, including librettos under librettist; but there is an alternative rule allowing entry under composer. The usual AACR rules for fullness of names result in more realistic and time-saving forms of names than ALA 1949 and MLA expected.

The main entry decisions include, of course, composer as equivalent of author. Ballad operas go under dramatist, if their music already existed, but in the case of specially composed music the basic rule for Shared authorship applies, resulting usually in a choice of one of the composers, but possibly title. A poet's works set by various composers are entered under general editor; failing that under title: i.e. not under the poet. Incidental music: composer. But Liturgical music: name of church with form sub-heading. Arrangements of anonymous works: original title; but of folk songs: arranger. Variations: later composer. Cadenzas: later composer.

Uniform titles are established, as explained in Section II of this book. They are particularly useful for music, especially those for 'form' items like symphonies—which do not necessarily have distinctive titles. A citation formula is worked out using English terms, to ensure consistent bibliographic units, which may range from complete works to titles for individual opuses. They are also used for works with distinctive titles whose title varies or is translated: generally the original is preferred. Unfortunately the wording of conventionally constructed titles (e.g. for works and for forms) as uniform titles does not exactly correspond with the terms used in MLA's Filing code, but a little effort could reconcile the two.

Description is over-complete for most purposes, e.g. a great deal of emphasis is placed on plate numbers and publishers' numbers—probably of interest mainly or only to a research scholar. However, the types of notes seem particularly useful and well exemplified. The full use of AACR in the *British catalogue of music* would enhance this already useful bibliography.

There is yet another music code. *Code international de catalogage de la musique*, by the International Association of Music Libraries. London, New York: C. F. Peters, 1957- . This code is worth a full study of course, but it has been decided to defer a full study in this book until a later edition, when the code is completed. One published part which does stand out on its own is vol. 2: *Limited code*, 1961, which, with parallel texts in French, English and German, runs to 54 pages. In general, this code is similar to AACR in its respect for intellectual responsibility, but, in construction, it allows brief references instead of full added unit entries. It pays too little attention to the need for uniform titles. It is acceptably brief in descriptive detail. It stipulates multiple subject/form entry, generally under single terms, e.g. a piano sonata receives two entries: 1. PIANO; 2. SONATA. Such a method is simple to operate; it obviates a great deal of heart-searching over citation order, e.g. which comes first, form or instrument, and so might be satisfactory in a very small library. However, on the whole, one prefers the approach of AACR, and the slight information on the subject approach does not seem, to the librarian whose home language is English, to make this Code an acceptable substitute for AACR or MLA. One useful part of its contents is a very short but up-to-date list of recommended music bibliographies. Librarians of English-speaking libraries who wish to practise simplified cataloguing may still prefer MLA: it contains a simplified code, but in case of need the cataloguer can refer back to fuller rules; also the code has a more comprehensive filing code than I.A.M.L. vol. 2.

An example of how minute some cataloguers feel it necessary to go in instructions and guidance is Donald L. Foster's *Notes used on music and phonorecord catalog cards*, Occasional paper no. 66, Dec., 1962, of the University of Illinois Graduate School of Library Science. Admittedly, notes are an important part of music cataloguing, but we may well query whether a whole work of 39 pages is needed to tell us that we may need to include in an entry, for example, 'For orchestra'.

5. *Reprographic reproductions*

This category can apply to any two-dimensional library materials, but the main points to remember are few and belong to the description. It must be made clear what type of reproduction it is, and its size and shape must be described in terms appropriate to the type of reproduction, e.g. size and number of microcards. Sufficient details for most purposes are given in AACR Chapter 9.

6. *Local history*

This is included here as a reminder that most or all of the categories dealt with in this chapter may be encountered, plus the possibility of archives and museum specimens. As one might expect, AACR is the best single code because of the compatibility of its rules for such a wide variety of types of materials.

Subject work is likely to call for the most original cataloguing. As described in Section III of this book, subject headings and indexing can be tackled from scratch provided certain basic rules are observed. Part of the subject work may entail the compilation of a special classification scheme; this in turn can simplify the construction of subject index entries or alphabetical subject headings and references. Special indexes, e.g. to local newspapers, may be needed.

Some public libraries in Britain are official repositories for local archives. As already mentioned, it is vital that expert advice should be sought or hired before the original sequence of any archival collection is disturbed. Facsimile copies of the 'plums' can be made and subdivided, classified and indexed to the heart's content of the exploitation-minded public librarian without violating the sacred 'respect des fonds' of the originals.

7. *Audio-Visual Materials*

These comprise:

(*a*) Moving films. Documentary (or educational); and possibly Newsreels and Fiction films if one works in the relevant types of libraries. They may be silent or sound; and if sound, they may have dialogue, commentary, or be dubbed into the home language.

(*b*) Film strips. Usually documentary or educational; possibly with an accompanying sound-recorded or printed commentary.

(*c*) Slides. Various sizes; black-and-white or coloured.

(*d*) Illustrations: opaque. These have already been mentioned under item 3. However, subject cataloguing or indexing should be consistent with that of other similar forms, preferably so that retrieval of them can be coordinated irrespective of medium.

Slides may often be supplied in sets, and a decision must be made as to whether to subject catalogue the set as a whole, or slide by slide. A similar principle applies to illustrations collections, of course. Quite a lot of cross-referring or multiple entry may be required, depending on demand. Slides should not normally be self-indexing, because of their physical form, unless there are very few in stock, in which case habit and human memory can obviate a great deal of indexing and listing.

(*e*) Sound recordings. (Note AACR's consistent use of terms: phono-record, phonodisc, phonotape, etc.)

Physical forms—Disc: various speeds; mono-aural or stereophonic. Tape: perhaps in easily handled cassettes, especially for the blind; speed; 2-track or 4-track; Wire; Cylinder; Roll.

Types of content:

Music of all types and genres, including instruction, which also include 'minus one' recordings which are supplied with a leading part lacking to be filled in by the home performer from the accompanying score.

Sound effects: also connected with sound moving films.

Spoken records:

'Talking books' for the blind.

Language-learning, including sets.

Literary forms: plays, poems; various languages.

Accompanying printed material, usually letterpress.

Audio-visual materials: General problems

Audio-visual media are rapidly increasing in importance, but space is available here to deal in any sort of detail with only the types most likely to be encountered in practice.

A most important factor is that mechanical apparatus is normally needed to use these media, whether by users of the library—the equivalent of browsing through graphic and printed material—or by the cataloguer. Such apparatus presupposes a sound-proof room, and the time to hear or screen a work in its entirety.

Because of their fragility, and expense, and perhaps rarity, handling of these materials should be reduced to a minimum. This in turn presupposes greater detail in catalogue entries than with 'browsable' materials. Often they are kept under 'closed access', although a substitute for display purposes exists in many L.P. record sleeves and some accompanying printed material, e.g. the text in Chaucerian English with a record of parts of *Canterbury tales* in the 'vernacular'.

These items are often shelved in accession order, and so more reliance than ever is placed on the catalogue. The catalogue may be further complicated in some libraries, mainly public record-lending libraries, by having to serve also as an 'indicator', i.e. indicating, usually at the main entry, whether a record is 'in' or 'out'. So, the physical form of a catalogue may be at least partly dictated by non-cataloguing factors. Such a use makes it more important than ever for the main entry to be the most 'sought' by most users of the library.

Audio-visual materials do not have a title page, and various other sources have to be used as title page-substitutes, e.g. with phonodiscs: a combination of the label, the sleeve, any accompanying textual matter, and external sources such as bibliographies; with phonotapes: a combination of information on the reel, the container, and perhaps a spoken introduction; and with films: a combination of the credits, the label on the metal or cardboard container, and again external sources. Some of these are not permanently attached to the physical bibliographic unit and so may get lost or interchanged. Yet further complications, especially with records, is that vital cataloguing information from the various sources may be contradictory or absent altogether. It is not all that unusual for a conscientious record cataloguer to have to play a disc all through, using authoritative catalogues, thematic catalogues of composers' works, and perhaps scores, in order to identify accurately all the items on the record equivalent of an anthology.

One final and most important factor is the performer element.

Moving films

Documentaries are those most likely to be encountered, and most of the discussion here centres round these; additional account has to be taken of 'stars' in fiction films.

Films are the ultimate example of 'diffuse authorship', and cataloguing treatment of them is in advance of book-cataloguing because it has long been acknowledged that they should be entered under title. Even title entry as a principle is often complicated by the existence of several titles for one film, depending often on the country of release, which often has to do with language of dialogue or commentary, although U.S. and Britain sometimes release a film under different titles. The chief choice is between the original, vernacular—academically the more accurate, e.g. *Tirer sur le pianist*—and the 'home' title—often the more sought, e.g. *Shoot the pianist*. A problem arising, if two or more 'releases' are to be entered in one catalogue or bibliography, is the extent of the bibliographic unit—separate entry for different titles or all under one collocating heading.

Another factor is that the sound track alone may also be published as a record. A further complication is that of trailers.

Films have many other approaches, including one—or often more—scenario authors, editors, translators, etc., perhaps the author and title of a book on which the film is based, distributor, producer(s), director, sometimes cameramen, commentator(s), or actors in fiction films, and composer and/or arranger(s) and performer(s) of incidental music, e.g. The Seekers in *Georgie girl* as a fiction film example.

Finally, for documentaries, is the subject approach: the film may set out to deal specifically with one subject—itself possibly complex—but incidental, background, subjects may become significant enough to warrant entries, e.g. a film about hovercraft may also be useful because it includes shots of land and sea scenery in a certain place or of a certain type.

Not all of the potential approaches will receive entries, but perhaps so many are required that it may be decided to abandon the unit entry principle and revert to a main entry plus very brief added entries or indexes. The catalogue could take the form of a main classified sequence, e.g. in UDC order, with other approaches covered by index entries, perhaps with one index per type of approach—titles, producers, etc.—or with one complete interfiled index. *The British national film catalogue* is an example of a classified file (UDC) with several indexes: two examples from it—one from the Classified sequence and one from the Index—are shown on pages 228 and 229.

Whether or not all the collaborators named are used as approaches, they, with other details, will need to be considered for inclusion in the description. Some films have a 'colophon-equivalent', e.g. 'Filmed at Pinewood Studios, England', which may be useful. Details include Imprint-equivalent: including place of manufacture and/or release, names of distributor and production company, possibly two dates: original and later releases; Collation-equivalent: length in time and in reels, gauge of film—35, 16, 9.5 or 8 mm., black-and-white or colour, including type of colour, e.g. Technicolor, Sound or silent; Notes including treatment, intellectual level, if animated, perhaps if copy in hand has been bowdlerised, possibly contents, plot if a fiction film. In addition, personalities and other items, already mentioned, may warrant noting.

As in book-cataloguing, one has to decide not only what has to be included, but where in the entry, and in what form.

Newsreels are a particular category, usually warranting special treatment. The cameraman is very important, usually being his own

528—GEODESY. SURVEYING
528.9—Cartography. Mapping
The MAP AND THE GROUND; parts 1 & 2
dist. : Rank Film Library, Hire. 1965. *p.c.*, *sp.* :
Surrey Education Committee.
10 mins. each. sd. col. 16mm.
Credits : p. J. Newsome. *ph.* C. R. Lawrence. *sc.* J. H.
Boait. *comm.s.* Kenneth Kendall.
A geographical study showing how map work can be studied
practically during fieldwork, emphasising the need for careful planning and the correlation of the map with the ground.
Part 1 illustrates this method used by a primary school. Part
2 shows a secondary and a grammar school and directs
attention to teachers' activities, particularly with a voluntary
fieldwork society.

53 PHYSICS

531—Mechanics
PHYSICAL SCIENCE FOR THE PRIMARY SCHOOL:
MAKING THINGS MOVE
dist. : Rank Film Library, Hire. 1965. *p.c.* : Encyclo-
paedia Britannica, *U.S.A.*/Rank Film Library.
10 mins. sd. col. 16mm.
Credits (English version): sc. J. Newsome. *comm.s.*
Frank Phillips.
The concepts of force and motion and the connection between
them showing the effects of inertia, gravity and friction. Seen
through the eyes of a small boy in a farm environment.
Intended for children aged 9-11 years.

532—Fluid mechanics
PHYSICAL SCIENCE FOR THE PRIMARY SCHOOL:
WATER AND WHAT IT DOES
dist. : Rank Film Library, Hire. 1965. *p.c.* : Encyclopaedia Britannica, *U.S.A.*/Rank Film Library.
8 mins. sd. col. 16mm.
Credits (English version): sc. J. Newsome. *comm.s.*
Frank Phillips.
The nature and properties of water and illustrations of its
three states of solid, liquid and gas using animation and time
lapse photography. Intended for children aged 9-11 years.

9. Extracts from *British national film catalogue.*

9 (*a*). Classified sequence.

28

9 (*b*). Index.

producer/director. The subject(s) and the time of shooting are also particularly important. The time approach may conveniently be catered for by shelving the films in chronological order. A newsreel usually consists of several 'segments', each having one or more significant subjects, say an event and a leading personality; these can be catered for by analyticals referring to the manufacturer, e.g. Movietone, the date and the position in the reel.

Television films need similar treatment to documentaries and newsreels. But since clips may be needed at very short notice and on minute subjects and personalities, the need for many approaches is more urgent. Normal 'still' illustrations must also be readily accessible, so that a news or current commentary programme editor, for example, can decide quickly between a moving film illustration or a still. A further manifestation of the television film is the videotape. These are subject to the same rules as other audio-visual media: the time may not be far off when they are commercially viable and therefore potentially part of general libraries' stocks.

Stockshots may be important, especially in historical documentaries and fiction films. (The perceptive cinema-goer may recognise the same shot in several films, e.g. a view of a bomb's impact from the bombing plane.) Three important factors are: Subject; Source (for what film or purpose originally made); and Time of supposed event. Stockshots have a great deal in common with sound-effects: in fact, perhaps the best rules for cataloguing sound-effects are those in Aslib's *Film cataloguing rules*, Chapter 4.

Filmstrips

Relevant information about the problems of this type of material can be extracted from the information on moving films. The main differences are: (*a*) statement of number of frames; (*b*) whether the strip is in loop-form for easy repeat performances; and (*c*) notes are required on accompanying materials, either printed commentary, or teachers' guides, or a sound recording.

Since filmstrips are in effect series of slides fixed together in a set order, the cataloguing of slides can be paralleled with that of filmstrips.

Codes

BM, CUTTER and AA 1908 not surprisingly do not cater specifically for film cataloguing.

ALA 1949's Rule 15 Scenarios (Motion picture) is the only relevant rule, which states that scenarios go under title of the film plus sub-heading *Motion picture*; it does not specifically mention an added entry under scenarist(s), though Rule 157 Added entries could be invoked.

AACR Chapter 12 devotes some 10 pages to Motion Pictures and Filmstrips (plus a rule in chapter 15, Rule 262 Motion picture stills, which gives main entry according to intellectual responsibility). Chapter 12 includes, as one might expect, a useful introductory section on the characteristics of moving films. Main entry is under title under which released, plus designation *(Motion picture)* or *(Film)*. Short descriptive titles may be supplied if lacking, in the form [Aviation activities in the A.E.F.] *(Motion picture)*. Another rule provides for two main entries of the 'bound with' type, using the terms 'on reel with'. A great number of added entries is catered for. These include author and title of work on which the film is based (Rule 21); this is inconsistent with the rule allowing merely a reference from book on which a musical is based—Rule 230A. Added entries (not references) complete the bibliographic unit in their use for 'Variant titles' including the original. Change of title of a continuation results in collocation under latest title, though a footnote allows consecutive entry as for serials, therefore being more consistent with the bibliographic unit principle of other AACR rules. Other aspects of description cater for mention of 'operative' date, i.e. date of making of film, as well as date of release, and other details such as width (gauge), silent or sound, speed, and running time or number of reels, or number of frames for filmstrips, and colour or black-and-white or sepia. Notes cater, among other items, for accompanying (usually printed) material, and source of film, e.g. book from which derived.

There are several useful codes compiled especially for films:

(*a*) Aslib. Film Production Libraries Group. Cataloguing Committee. *Film cataloguing rules*. London: Aslib, 1963. This recommendable and comprehensive work includes rules for: (*a*) Complete films; (*b*) Newsfilms; (*c*) Picture material other than complete films; (*d*) Sound material including effects and dubbed tracks; (*e*) Added entries; (*f*) Capitalisation, etc.; (*g*) Definitions; (*h*) Abbreviations; (*i*) Specimen entries. The main difference between this and most other codes (apart from its comprehensiveness) is that the main entry goes under title of original release, and in the language of origin; references (not added entries—a useful economy) connect the main heading with later forms.

'Imprint' date, consistent with the rule for main entry, is that of original release; later dates of release may be recorded in a note. Country of origin can be important in assessing the slant of a film, and this is therefore catered for. Description, detail, layout and degree of catering for alternative approaches can be deduced from the specimen entries reproduced here on page 233. (Also given in the British Film Institute code, described below.) It will be seen that the Aslib code is an academic, thorough and painstaking set of rules.

(b) British Film Institute. *Rules for use in the Cataloguing Departments of the National Film Archive.* London: The Institute, 1960. An example of a code designed for one library but which is potentially applicable in other libraries, it has apparently been translated into other languages. This code, rather in conventional printed catalogue tradition, caters for a long main entry for each work, with a series of indexes covering other approaches. Its main sections comprise: (a) Title (i.e. Main entry) catalogue; (b) Newsfilms; (c) a variety of Indexes; (d) Style, including alphabetical-arrangement preferring on the whole literal rather than inferred logical arrangement, and capitalisation. Appendixes include Sample cards, some of which are reproduced here to obviate a great deal of verbal description. Subject approach is by a 'classed index' using UDC and chain procedure, and the need for analytical entries is mentioned.

Main entry is, like Aslib, under original title, in vernacular language. The Uniform title principle is used to implement a broad bibliographic unit. Supplied titles, i.e. by cataloguer, when the title is missing, are given within brackets [ ].

Another code worthy of consideration is the UNESCO code of 1956.

Sound recordings

Music. All the problems encountered in music scores apply, but with several important additions. Performer is the chief one. This element may range from one person to hundreds, and a decision must be made as to which receive added entries and which are merely cited in the entry itself—if that. Sometimes the performers, and composers and authors, coincide, or nearly so, especially with 'pop' records. (Whether or not a library should stock these is an interesting question, but which is outside the scope of this book.) As already mentioned in such cases in relation to scores, corporate entry under group may be the answer, and also has the advantage of consistency, especially if record and

TITLE: (8th February, 1912) PATHE [GAZETTE]   LOCATION NO. 8271 A(h)

BELFAST: THE CHURCHILL MEETING. Scenes and incidents of Mr. Churchill's visit to Belfast. A shot of mounted troops wearing capes (6–19); a contingent of the Irish Guards form fours and march off (41); policemen at a street corner search and check the identity of passers-by (50); a queue of people waiting to gain admittance to the hall (57). Arrival of Lord Pirrie and Mr. and Mrs. Winston Churchill. Lord and Lady Pirrie in close shot leaving their car (61–68); a similar shot of Mr. Churchill who is immediately followed by Mrs. Churchill (81).

35mm./st./pos.   Scottish Film Council

SUBJECT REFS.
941.61[1]: 323.17   Belfast – Anti-Home Rule Meeting
PIRRIE, William James, 1st Viscount
PIRRIE, Margaret Montgomery, 1st Viscountess
CHURCHILL, Sir Winston Leonard Spencer
CHURCHILL, Lady Clementine

10. Specimen entries from ASLIB film catalogue.

music score catalogue entries are interfiled. In another case, the performer may be the chief unifying factor, as was realised by Lubetzky in CCR 1960, Rule 1. The type of record concerned might be of the 'Joan Sutherland sings' type, including extracts from, or short pieces of, many composers. A rather similar type would be an 'anthology' whose chief unifying factor is the orchestra, or possibly the conductor who might well have been the selector-editor: an example might be a selection of Sir Thomas Beecham's so-called 'Lollipops'.

Performer as main entry heading is obviously intellectually inconsistent with the usual rule of entry under author-equivalent, and it may be almost as illogical and heretical as entering a festschrift under the person honoured, especially if the latter includes some biographical information as in the McColvin work exemplified in Section II of this work.

A rather parallel example is exemplified by a record called *Foggy mountain breakdown*. Its composer and performers become immaterial when one is told that it is the theme tune of the film *Bonnie and Clyde*. In this case the film title becomes the unifying factor.

Couplings. Two or more dissimilar works by dissimilar composers are issued on the same disc far more often than two dissimilar printed works are issued in one volume. Often one part, say a side, cannot be regarded as the chief work. So, double entry is called for, but the decision as to which is the main entry (e.g. for use in an indicator system) may have to be arbitrary, e.g. which is named first on the sleeve. Sometimes, many short works are combined, but by one composer; this poses a question of sub-filing term, e.g. first-named on sleeve, or what the cataloguer considers to be the most important or sought, or the construction of a uniform title, e.g. [Selections]. A further question is whether or not there shall be added Author-title entries, or references, or neither, reliance being placed on a contents list on the main entry. Another type of collection is exemplified by a record called *Themes from James Bond films*, with no common factor (orchestra, composer, etc.) other than a fictional character. The obvious cataloguer's solution is title entry, but how many people will look in the first place under 'Themes' when confronted with such a highly sought (after) counter-attraction? Suppose one gives in: is the filing word 'James' or 'Bond'? One could reach the point of making a *see* reference from '007'. (One can imagine the length of a new edition of CUTTER, if he were alive today!)

Occasionally a short item is thrown in as a fill-in, without its even being mentioned on the label.

Excerpts. This problem may overlap that of couplings. But in addition is the main question of whether, under composer, it gets direct entry under title of excerpt, or indirect entry via title of parent work. This is another manifestation of the problem of bibliographic unit. How many popular library users know that the *Sabre dance* comes from *Gayane* (with its various spellings as a further complication), or even that the composer is Khatchaturian? Such thoughts if acted upon could revolutionise the whole concept of 'author unit' and 'bibliographic unit': remember the basic assumption that a library's catalogue's chief purpose is to answer the question: 'Has the library a named work'.

Sound track of a film. This problem has already been mentioned under Films. Possibilities in choice of a heading are mainly title of film and author of music, and possibly subject of film, but sleeves may feature names having no connection with the record, such as producer and 'stars'. Again, which is more sought: *Lawrence of Arabia* or Maurice Jarre, who composed the music?

Some records are of the 'minus one' type; the part of a prominent instrument is omitted, to be fitted in by the listener. Scores are essential supplementary material to such records, and the 'minus one' factor must be made quite clear in the entry.

Items mentioned may, or may not, be chosen as added entry headings. But they must also be considered in relation to description.

'Spoken' records

These have the approaches of the printed equivalent, but in addition performers, directors, etc., in the way that films have. These may be approaches and/or parts of description.

Accompanying printed matter is usually particularly important, certainly warranting mention in notes, and possibly even an occasional added entry. It may need added entries in the general catalogue, in its own right as a text of the work in question.

Language record courses are rather similar to serials as cataloguing problems. The cataloguing is slight; it is the organisation of use which is more complicated, especially for long courses. However, added entries for such records in the relevant language sections of catalogues of books may be particularly important: a mere short reminder of their existence and a recommendation to ask the staff may be important.

Some libraries sponsor local history recordings, perhaps of the 'oldest inhabitants' reminiscences' type or of folk music of local significance. The minutest detail of such records is vital.

Sound effects

The subject approach is the most important. It may take the form of specific entries, with location, e.g. which record and which band of record. Or there may be a class entry 'Sound effects', followed by a listing of the contents of records in stock. In some cases, the source may be important, including if a sound is counterfeited. Great detail is important: a heading like 'Train' is not helpful to a dramatic society which wants a 1930's British branch line steam locomotive of the Southern Railway.

Description of records includes Imprint-equivalent: name of recording company is the most important, while place may be unnecessary and date of release so difficult to ascertain that only record archivists may think it worth going to the trouble of finding it out.

Collation-equivalent includes size of record, speed, and number of sides. If the library never buys 7" '45's' it may, then, not be worth differentiating between 10" and 12" except if necessary as a guide to shelf location. Collation-equivalent in tapes includes size of reel, number of reels and speed in inches per second, and whether 2-track or 4-track. All recordings of music require a statement of 'mono' or 'stereo', unless the library stocks only one type. Nowadays it seems pointless to state 'microgroove' as the older shellac broader groove are rarities—if they are in stock their speed (78 for most, 80 for older) should be sufficient indication of their other physical characteristics.

A brief reminder is given here that other information such as soloists, orchestras, conductors—as mentioned under possible approaches—will need to be incorporated into the description.

One type of information which cataloguers do not normally have time to ascertain is whether any abridgement has been made, and then, if it has, if it is worth noting. Some feed-back from irate connoisseur members of the library may help supplement the information in the catalogue.

As with notes in all descriptive cataloguing, it is risky to express subjective judgements about quality of performance or recording. But objective information, from which conclusions on quality may be inferred, should be included, e.g. a note that a recording (even though the copy in hand was released recently) was first recorded acoustically in, say, 1925.

Useful codes are (*a*) AACR Chapter 14 Phonorecords; and (*b*) MLA, mentioned under Music.

CHAPTER 21

Special Cataloguing

Subject Collections; Types of Libraries

SUBJECT COLLECTIONS

The first requirement is an exact knowledge of the scope and size of the collection, including of course basic subject knowledge. Scope includes subject area covered and physical form of material. Next, one needs to make an inventory of all the cataloguing aids—codes, headings lists, periodical indexes and abstracts, practical articles and books, etc., and central cataloguing agency cards which may be of use. Organisations like the Library Association, Aslib, and the (U.S.) Special Libraries Association may have copies of or may know of relevant tools which have not been officially published or reviewed. Then one's requirements must be compared with what is available. (Classification schemes will also be relevant but they are outside the scope of this book.) For example:

Author/Title and Descriptive cataloguing. One may take a representative selection of documents and make out headings according to AACR. These will then be examined critically to see how they fit with expected approaches. A code may be locally derived from the relevant parts of AACR, with decisions over alternatives, amendments, limitations, etc., clearly laid down. Time will thereby be saved both in day-to-day cataloguing and in inservice training of staff.

Subject cataloguing. A similar procedure may be applied to existing lists of subject headings. As already mentioned in Section III, subject headings may be accepted ready-made from general or special existing lists, or thesauri: it may be necessary to add more specific headings with appropriate *see also* references and some synonyms with appropriate *see* references. Or they may be compiled by chain procedure, or modified chain precedure, from the classification scheme used.

The extent of local analytical cataloguing, indexing and abstracting will depend on externally published tools. The department may take part in cooperative activities, e.g. contributing to a union list of periodicals in the subject field covered.

Examples of the cases of catalogue problem which may be encountered in
LAW, *as a representative example of a subject*

Solutions are available in AACR, but, as mentioned in the general comments above, consistent variations could be made if carefully thought out, and if practised as a trial on a representative cross-section of documents from the collection.

1. Bills, Laws, etc.

(*a*) Can be entered under name of country, with a choice of sub-headings, or more directly.

(*b*) Choice of sub-headings: Legislative body; Relevant executive department; Form, e.g. *Laws, statutes, etc.* Hence:

(*c*) Construction of complex headings, citation order, hence filing, hence bibliographic unit.

(*d*) Direct entry: any of (*b*) but with a need for suffixed qualifying term indicating country if more than one country is represented in stock or if a single country is a federal system. Feasibility of short-title entry of acts may be considered.

Acts of local application. Can be treated as above or (inconsistently) using local names as quasi-subject entry.

Commentaries on laws: corporate *vs* personal, possibly either or both *vs* title.

2. Constitutions: Charters, Treaties

(*a*) Form *vs* corporate authorship, as above.

(*b*) When granted to, or negotiated with, a colony or colonising company, additional choice between parent country and colony (AACR technically is inconsistent: author is parent but entry is local).

3. Local authorities

By-laws; Departments: equivalent of legislative body. Similar conflicts as in state legislation and constitutions above. Charters are also applicable to localities and to trade associations.

4. Edicts of rulers

Personal *vs* corporate. If corporate: construction of heading needs to ensure that citation order results in desired bibliographic units. In constitutional monarchies: possible overlap and inconsistency over choice between name of monarch and prime minister or other régime or constitution. (Cf. DC, which divides 942 History of Britain according to monarch, but other monarchies of the Commonwealth of Nations according to local constitutional conditions.)

5. Administration of law; Legal cases

(a) Conflict between plaintiff, defendant and name of court for main entry. Bibliographic unit relevant here also. Subject approach is also relevant.

(b) Commentaries on laws and cases: additional complication of commentator as possible personal author.

(c) Appeals: more additional complication: higher court.

(d) Judges, barristers: need for mention in description, or even for added entries possibly.

6. Changes of names of, and amalgamations of, departments, etc.

Dealt with in Section II, on Codes.

7. 'Semi-government', nationalised, or government-financed organisations

Conflict of country name *vs* direct entry—latter either as written, or possibly inverted to bring sought word to front.

8. Serials

Title entry *vs* corporate; latter in various constructions, as mentioned under *Laws, statutes, etc.*; plus extra complication of non-government corporate bodies.

9. Reports: Routine and special

Personal *vs* corporate, possibly *vs* title. Bibliographic unit: degree of collocation desired.

Difference between treatment of routine and special, especially relevant to application of 'bibliographic unit'.

10. Textbooks

Original author *vs* revisers and editors. Intellectual responsibility (academic accuracy) *vs* 'sought' name.

11. Subject entry

Subject entry in all instances; not to be confused with form entry, as in AACR.

12. Language

Language used for entry, notes, etc.

See also part of Chapter 20 dealing with Government publications.

Representative examples of aids in various types of special cataloguing

EARNSHAW, VIRGINIA W. Aviation subject headings and classification guide, compiled by Virginia W. Earnshaw and Agnes A. Gautriaux. New York: Special Libraries Association, 1966.

NATIONAL LIBRARY OF MEDICINE. Notes for medical catalogers. Issued occasionally. Mainly devoted to subject cataloguing and classification; supplementing *Medical subject headings* (MESH).

PIETTE, J. R. F. A guide to foreign languages for science librarians and bibliographers, compiled by J. R. F. Piette; revised and enlarged by E. Horzelska. London: Aslib, on behalf of Welsh Plant Breeding Station, Aberystwyth, 1965.

PIGGOTT, MARY. Notes on cataloguing books in certain foreign languages, ed. by Mary Piggott. London: L.A., 1956 (L.A. Pamphlet no. 15).

CHAPLIN, A. H. Names of persons: national usages for entry in catalogues, definitive edition edited by A. H. Chaplin and Dorothy Anderson. Sevenoaks, England: IFLA, 1967.

BROXIS, Peter F. Organising the arts. London: Bingley, 1968.

TYPES OF LIBRARIES

A great deal can be inferred from a detailed study of the literature on the type in question: objectives, administrative basis, needs, intellectual level, and numbers of users; whether or not the users normally use the catalogues and supporting bibliographies themselves, or if they trust such searching activities to staff of the library. A student taking professional examinations should have learnt or will be learning such information independently of the cataloguing aspect, and the information can be applied to cataloguing just as to any other branch of a library's activities.

Also, previous information in this chapter and Chapter 20 can be applied, usually quite directly; it is the intelligent selection of the information which is important.

In some libraries training in use of catalogues and bibliographies is an important part of the academic discipline of the institution as a coherent whole, e.g. school, college or university undergraduate

libraries. This is dealt with in greater detail in Section VII, on Administration.

CHILDREN'S LIBRARIES: PUBLIC AND SCHOOL

Many of the problems are to some extent common to both types of
library. The main difference is that some children use a school library
because they are obliged to, whereas use of a public library's children's
department is voluntary. Its relevance here is that children at a school
with an active library and an interested and informed librarian or
teacher librarian will receive training in the use of the catalogue. This
in turn implies that considerable trouble is taken to make the catalogue
useful as a training medium. Perhaps, then, there may be a greater
emphasis on printed introductions to the catalogue and more attention
paid to adequate guiding. Apart from altruistic motives, the more a child
can use a catalogue, the less time does the librarian have to spend on
using it for him.

The chief governing factor in a children's library, then, may be that
of the catalogue being user-oriented. For this reason children's catalogues are simpler in almost all respects—one possible exception in an
active library being the number of subject analytical entries, including
selective indexing of some periodicals, to cater for projects and similar
activities.

Choice of type of catalogue is regarded by some librarians as important.

Physical form (see also Chapter 25, on Physical forms of catalogues).
A card catalogue has its basic advantage of flexibility, a particularly
necessary quality in a children's library, which has a high rate of turnover of stock. The card form, as a unit record system, is also useful for
training purposes, as samples can be distributed, handled and identified
individually. Cards are easier to handle in use than sheaf slips; further, a
card catalogue can be more adequately guided than a sheaf form. Printed
lists may also be useful as the result of research projects, lists of readings
selected from the catalogue, etc.: these can be derived from cards made
out and copied by children.

Internal arrangement. Traditionally the dictionary catalogue is
supposed to be simpler to use than classified, especially in a small
library. It is suggested here that the choice is not so important as the
quality of compilation going into whatever kind is chosen. One has seen,
for example, young trained schoolchildren making successful use of

the subject index to a classified catalogue, including applying it to the allegedly hard-to-understand classified file. However, if a classified catalogue is decided upon, one would recommend a name catalogue as an adjunct since many enquiries relate to books both by and about people. Also, any special supplementary 'information source' entries might be incorporated into the subject index.

Children's libraries are acquiring increasing stocks of initial teaching alphabet books. Preferably these should be entered in the main catalogue, as well as in a sequence of their own. If a choice has to be made, one would suggest the latter, assuming that the books are sought primarily as examples of i.t.a. The problem is rather parallel to large-print books for the short-sighted, and again this characteristic is usually the primary one; it should be remembered that some such works are produced for children as well as for adults.

Tools. Simplified versions of classification schemes, of cataloguing codes, and of lists of subject headings will probably be needed. But it must be remembered that the age range in a school may be up to 7 or 8 years, and in a public library it may be 10 or 11 years. Also, widely varying ranges of intelligence must be catered for. If in doubt one would prefer less simplicity rather than more, e.g. the very simplified DC for British schools seems too simplified for almost any school use; yet despite this oversimplification it does not cater for subjects such as countries as 'concretes', i.e. it does not give a comprehensive works place despite the fact that many children's works deal with a subject as a whole, and may not be confined to one aspect or facet of it. Therefore one would advocate the normal Abridged DC, the local cataloguer further simplifying, consistently, when required.

Simplified cataloguing tools and instruction manuals are also available. Some are produced by local libraries which are particularly aware of their responsibilities towards schools as part of their service to children as a whole in their area. One example is Nottinghamshire County Library's *Simple rules for school library catalogues* which deals mainly with author/title and description, but which incorporates subject indexing, assuming a classified catalogue, and layouts. The rules include some commonsense variations from AA 1908, including use of better known pseudonyms and including societies and institutions in the same rule. A very simplified version of AA 1908 was made by SAUNDERS and FURLONG: *Cataloguing rules*, School Library Association, 1966. The introduction of AACR could stimulate the compilation of a similar—preferably longer—abridgement of its relevant rules for children's libraries, but to date one has not been mentioned in the professional literature.

Dictionary cataloguers could possibly use *Sears list of subject headings* although it would require considerable abridgement. One existing American list by E. Rue—*Subject headings for children's materials*—seems not to be satisfactory mainly because of its use of unduly complex headings like DUTCH IN THE U.S., which could cause filing troubles, hence detracting from their ready location. The best officially published subject aid which one has encountered to date is *Subject headings and index for a classified catalogue for post-primary school libraries*, 2nd ed., 1965, issued by the National Library Service of New Zealand. This work has two main sections: first, an alphabetical subject index; second, classification schedules selected from DC. Similar works might well be compiled for use in other countries, or there might be considered a potentially international list along the same lines. The New Zealand work is not, as it stands, suitable for the dictionary catalogue. Synonyms are included in the index, but the preferred form of each is not indicated, so there is no guide to choice of used headings; also the alphabetical sequence lacks *see also* references.

Another, rather similar, work but basically intended for dictionary catalogues, and with relevant *see* and *see also* references, is the present author's *Classification schedules and subject headings: a combined key for school librarians*, a draft of which was used experimentally in teacher-librarian inservice training courses run by the State Library of Tasmania in 1965. This is an example of a single work combining the purposes of both a classification scheme and a list of subject headings, the construction of which is explained in Section III on Subject work.

Various textbooks and manuals explain the techniques required in school and similar libraries. A British example is A. F. Johnson's *Practical cataloguing*, London: A.A.L., 1962. An American one for dictionary catalogues is Margaret Fullerton Johnson's *Manual of cataloging and classification for small school and public libraries*, 4th ed., New York: H. W. Wilson, 1950. There are numerous other works; however, some are by people in charge of school libraries who have had little or no education in librarianship themselves, and to quote them would merely tend to perpetuate a 'how I done it good' habit which is only too prevalent already.

U.S. children's librarians may well prefer to use one of the central cataloguing agencies rather than bother overmuch with technical practical details themselves. So the information given in the chapters on Central cataloguing may be relevant here. Much as BNB has done to widen its appeal, it still does not equal the direct value of the H. W. Wilson dictionary catalogue services in U.S.

PUBLIC LIBRARIES

It is impossible to generalise about this type, as it ranges from library systems serving only a few thousands of people to those serving a million or more whose central libraries give a more 'research' than 'popular' service.

Children's services are dealt with under that heading, above, while the academic aspect will be dealt with below.

If we can posit such an institution as an average, medium-sized public library system, whether municipal or county, with a central or headquarters and several branch libraries, perhaps the following generalisations may apply.

Almost all cataloguing for the whole system should be centralised internally, and external national schemes should be taken advantage of, e.g. BNB, H.M.S.O., and with the minimum of amendment. If possible, library suppliers should be used which obtain central agency cards and match them with the relevant books, while also doing the physical processing—governed to some extent by cataloguing decisions—as well.

Otherwise, principles of limited cataloguing, as outlined in Chapter 23 of this work, should be applied, the moral being 'if in doubt, don't', as long as reliance can be placed on published bibliographies, indexes, etc. One exception is that one feels that the 'purposive' uses of fiction and to a lesser extent of children's works as a whole are not exploited enough.

There is a case for doing away with branch library catalogues, but this should not be contemplated unless a fully adequate substitute exists, e.g. 'real time' (i.e. instantaneous)—perhaps teleprinter—contact with headquarters to produce, say, lists of recommended reading on various subjects. This all presupposes an efficient union catalogue, both author and subject, at the headquarters which is suitable for 'telecommunication' whenever any libraries in the system are open.

An alternative is a frequently updated printed (e.g. computer-

produced) union catalogue at all major service points, which then have
the authority and mechanical facilities to contact other service points.

Service should not be confined to monographic material only:
information requests should be answerable by telephone, teleprinter or
even—ultimately—telefacsimile, from the central library, at the time
of, or as soon as possible after, receipt. All of this presupposes an
adequately equipped bibliographic centre at the central library.

The regional interlending systems rely on public libraries more than
others on the whole, with a consequent delay, and lack of full and
efficient service. With the launching of the British MARC project
(explained in Chapter 32), and the ultimate hope of computerisation,
it may be hoped that in the future all important libraries will have
access to the information in each other's stocks more readily and quickly
than at present.

It is suggested that any independent public library system which is
too small and poor to play its part in future useful mechanisation may
well be too small and poor to be an autonomous service at all.

UNIVERSITY LIBRARIES AND COLLEGE LIBRARIES

The functions of these can be divided into two: teaching and research
although the learning process should involve real research even if not
particularly original or extensive. Libraries other than Central are of
two basic types: (a) subject collections; and (b) general college collections for undergraduate use. Some libraries have special undergraduate
central libraries. The basic pattern then is of a central with perhaps
many branch-equivalents. With the present-day increase in cross-
discipline teaching and research, a central union catalogue seems an
essential, with both author and subject approaches. 'On line' or immediate communication between branches and Central is a requirement for
thoroughly efficient information and document location and retrieval
as is outlined for public libraries, above. For depth research, the type
of documentation service required by most special libraries (described
below) is a necessity.

National central cataloguing should obviate a great deal of repetitive
cataloguing. However, BNB items comprise possibly under 50 per cent
of average British university library acquisitions; foreign language
works, whether or not produced in Britain, may form a high proportion
of total stocks. Also, not as high a proportion of libraries use DC as is

the case with public libraries, other quite common schemes being LC and UDC, for all or parts of a total stock. With the growth of the technological university, UDC may well become even more favoured. For these reasons, BNB cards are not used much in British university libraries. What is more surprising, LC cards are used even less, due to (a) possible conservatism; (b) the assumption of the dictionary catalogue in added approaches, though surprisingly few Australian libraries use LC cards; and (c) the much higher cost of LC cards as compared with BNB's, which British libraries, whether or not they use them, may regard as a recommended price. With the increased sharing of data arising from the combination of LC Shared cataloguing and project MARC, British university libraries may well find it quick and easy to partake indirectly of LC cataloguing.

Catalogue detail, e.g. imprint, collation and contents lists, is normally supposed to receive extra emphasis in academic libraries, but observation makes one think that this is not necessarily so: author, title, edition, place of publication and date seem to be made to suffice in some libraries at least. This may be because catalogues are used mainly as finding lists, more reliance being placed on published bibliographies, indexes and abstracts, e.g. a university central library may well sport all the British Museum and Bibliothèque nationale printed catalogues available, plus many special bibliographies to help with the subject approach. This latter may account for the lack of care over, or even existence of, subject approach in some British academic libraries. One has even come across a university library of high repute which has a classified file but whose subject index is compiled from a 'suggestions book' left on the catalogue cabinet for the casual use of users of the catalogue. A further reason for lack of attention to subject cataloguing may be the subjugation of library science techniques to academic qualifications in the selection of staff. Possibly, more technical expertise is evident in some of the newly 'promoted' ex-technical college libraries, which to date have more chartered librarians than graduates in high places in their libraries. The introduction of joint library science/ 'academic' subject degrees, as in the College of Librarianship Wales, may help to kill both birds with one well-aimed stone.

Notes and annotations are said sometimes to be less necessary in academic libraries than in popular libraries because most basic reading by students is done from recommended author-title lists. Such an assumption could presuppose an alarming lack of curiosity in people of supposedly above-average intelligence, especially since U.S. and Australian academic libraries apparently need subject catalogues. Some cataloguing is, wisely, done by subject experts from subject departments, and these people seem to be in a most favourable position to compile useful annotations during their cataloguing of books in their subject areas. They are also in a position to initiate more subject analyticals than they sometimes seem to at present.

Much of the above comment has revolved around university libraries, but some of it is also applicable to college libraries. However, a subjective judgement is that the criticisms suggested seem less applicable to technical colleges and colleges of education.

Much also applies to national and other very large general libraries, but from the broad research rather than the specific research viewpoint. Again, the relevant parts can be recognised from the information given above. It may be claimed that a great deal of valuable research is done in older British academic and research libraries which use outdated techniques according to the attitudes of 1970. This is true: but possibly more valuable research might be done in these libraries if more modern techniques were used. There are indications that the British Museum, for example, is evolving towards more direct entry for periodicals than in the past. This seems laudable, for reasons given in Chapter 4, and one can only hope that this is a real trend and not an isolated instance. There is no logical reason why the older libraries should remain aloof from current newly-introduced principles of cataloguing. But this seems to be the case, whether it is a matter of U.S. research libraries perpetuating ALA 1949, or the British Museum and the older academic libraries perpetuating BM-type codification. Surely, these prominent libraries, with their wide use and influence, should be in the vanguard of new ideas, not in the guard's van.

SPECIAL LIBRARIES

Of all types of libraries, this group is the hardest to generalise about. In addition to comparing the libraries of government departments, industrial and commercial firms, and various industrial and professional research establishments, it should also be taken to include certain university and college library departments, as far as their cataloguing is concerned anyway. A common characteristic of the group is the small proportion of normal book-form materials compared with periodicals, scientific and technical reports, trade catalogues, short-lived pamphlets and similar items, and other materials in the fugitive material category. The special needs of such libraries have been favoured by an extra emphasis into investigation and equipment in subject and bibliographic-coupling techniques than in, say, conventional author/title and descriptive cataloguing. The computer project of the Massachusetts Institute of Technology, the MEDLARS project, and the publication *Science citation index* are symptomatic of the great investment of energy and funds into this area of librarianship. The field itself has probably generated more new or newly applied terminology than all other aspects of librarianship put together—to the point that even 'librarianship' has been giving way to terms like 'documentation' and 'information science'.

Knotty problems like 'corporate authorship' and 'bibliographic unit' are virtually side-stepped in favour of 'facet-analysis' and SLIC, KWIC, other cyclic, and various other forms of indexing. One regrets that the generation of a non-self-explanatory jargon—however necessary its inventors believe it to be—has raised a barrier between the generic field of 'depth' information retrieval on the one hand, and the rest of library science on the other. However, one hopes for a feed-back of the useful outcome of such experiments into 'humanities' librarianship; and this indeed is happening, as the introduction of RILM [Music] *Abstracts* in 1967 demonstrates.

Since most of the library science techniques of most special libraries revolves around the subject approach, it is not proposed to reiterate information about it here, but merely to refer the reader to Section III, on the Subject approach, and Section VI, on Mechanisation.

An exception is shown by the article of the late Barbara Kyle on 'Notes on cataloguing in special libraries with special emphasis on author and name entries' (*Journal of documentation*, vol. 22, no. 1, March 1966, p. 13-21), which touches partly on the author approach. See also the article by F. Ayres cited in Chapter 4.

CHAPTER 22

Limited Cataloguing

'Limited cataloguing' is an omnibus term comprising what in the past has been known as simplified and selective cataloguing. The term is used here to embrace also any limiting of classification. In general, it means the reduction of any cataloguing processes from what might be called standard cataloguing. This item itself may be taken as meaning full cataloguing as laid down by recognised cataloguing codes both as to contents of entries and as to the number of entries required for each document, plus full subject treatment. Few codes have provided directly for degrees of limitation in cataloguing. CUTTER goes the furthest in recognising from the start what he called 'short', 'medium', and 'full', although, characteristically, he used 'the three words Short, Medium and Full . . . with the preliminary caution that the Short family are not all of the same size, that there is more than one Medium, and that Full may be Fuller and Fullest' (p. 11). Most other codes allow for occasional variations in fullness of cataloguing, although if any generalisation is applicable perhaps it is in the direction of fuller than the standard set by the code, e.g. the English language codes have rules from time to time offering *carte blanche* for additional references and/or added entries under which a work might be sought.

It should be remembered then that 'limited' can only apply to a particular standard, and that standard is shorter in, say, the British Museum than the two Anglo-American and the ALA codes. Here, it is assumed that the standard from which we may deviate is that of AACR 1967 British text.

Basically, economies may be practised in six main areas:

(*a*) Fullness of heading (usually author).

(*b*) Fullness of description, in both main and added entries.

(*c*) Number of added entries, whether author, title or subject.

(*d*) Number of references, from unused forms of headings, whether author, title, or subject.

(*e*) Number of *see also* subject references in a dictionary catalogue.

(*f*) (An extreme form) omitting completely certain types of entries, e.g. in some British libraries, title added entries. Or even not having a subject catalogue. Or—the most extreme—not having a catalogue at all, at some service points at least, e.g. in branches of a public library.

These possible economies should be considered in relation to the potential of 'catalogue-substitutes' considered later in this chapter.

A more conventional view of limited cataloguing, as already stated, is to divide it into 'simplified' and 'selective'. Although these two terms overlap, it is now proposed to attempt to define, describe, and differentiate between them.

Simplified cataloguing is basically omitting parts of an entry, and/or omitting certain added and analytical entries. A further component might be the adoption of simpler filing rules than in the conventional filing codes.

Selective cataloguing is, in effect, the application of simplified cataloguing to certain categories of documents. Conventionally it has been described as giving some documents fuller treatment than others, and even not cataloguing some documents at all: i.e. selecting documents in relation to fullness of cataloguing.

Both of these components of limited cataloguing are explained in more detail below, but before going further it should be borne in mind that certain other factors can be very relevant. One is staff salaries: economies are achieved if it is possible to 'inservice-train' clerical assistants to do work previously done by qualified librarians. Perhaps better this than to be forced to cut out catalogue approaches or information which merely shifts work from the cataloguing department to the readers advisors' desk, or which—far worse—lower the library's standard of service. A further—major—aspect of economising is to reconsider the physical form of, and production of, catalogue in one's library. Mechanisation, taking part in a central cataloguing scheme, conducting a careful 'O and M' (i.e. organisation and methods survey) on procedures—any of these may result in being able to retain the required fullness of cataloguing without increasing expense.

DETAILS OF SIMPLIFIED CATALOGUING

Heading

An application of AACR, in preference to ALA 1949, would immediately effect economies, since the latter works towards an academic ideal of an author's full used names and dates of birth and death. Surely a heading such as 'MOZART, Wolfgang Amadeus, 1756-1791' repeated time after time at the top of perhaps hundreds of entries is incredible (ALA 1949, Rule 12A(9)).

In fact, AACR has gone as far as—perhaps further than—many libraries wish in its fullness of author headings: in effect, it allows the shortest used form of authors' names consistent with no conflict with different, but similarly-named authors.

A regional union catalogue could allow confusion between similar names since its basic objective is identification of a work and not the range of works by an author: it can ignore forenames and have title's first word as the second filing characteristic. However, the extra data will probably already be on the entry, so this economy may be more apposite as a simplification of filing.

The cutting down of bibliographic searching is an obvious economy in time. However, AACR frequently requires a cataloguer to search for the commonest form of an author's name, an operation which necessarily entails several consultations. A way round this possibly superfluous searching would be for certain reference works to be named as authorities in the instruction manual—perhaps a later edition of AACR might include a short recommended list.

In the case of voluminous authors with long (cataloguing) names, a single guide card bearing the long form could go at the front of all that author's entries; all others would bear only a shortened form. One would then rely on the filing assistant to insert entries in their correct place. There is a lot to be said to having merely BACH for *the* Bach, with initials and/or forenames only, as commonly used, for the less illustrious members of that family.

Description

AACR has gone quite a long way in obviating the rashes of . . .'s and [ ]'s which emerge from AA 1908 and ALA 1949 when rigidly applied. However, one might go further and make it unnecessary ever to use the marks of omission or to explain sources of information like 'cover title'—more honoured in the breach in many libraries in any case.

The basic title itself is obviously necessary, and one favours much of the use of the Uniform title introduced in AACR as helping not only to collocate but also to identify editions of works produced under a variety of titles. In many cases, sub-titles and alternative titles could be omitted, but not where their omission would necessitate the use of annotations to explain the subject-matter of a book. It is quicker to retain the full title of Robin Borwick's *People with long ears: a practical guide to donkey-keeping* than to omit the sub-title and then have to insert a virtual repetition of it lower in the entry—or to leave the catalogue user ignorant of the subject of the book. Relevant in this context is the subject heading in a dictionary catalogue and the feature heading in the classified catalogue: their use can often obviate more long-winded but possibly not more useful descriptions thought up at great length by the 'literary' cataloguer.

AACR frequently permits the omission of a great number of collaborators. Provided one can sink one's 'academic responsibility' scruples, even more can be left out. Illustrators, editors and so on are perhaps not as 'sought' as some cataloguers may imagine. They could be omitted unless necessary to distinguish between editions. However, if a collaborator is deemed worthy of an added entry, then he must be mentioned in the description itself.

Cataloguers who were never weaned from AA 1908 on to ALA 1949 may never have known that repetition of author's name in the author statement could often 'legally' be omitted. Unfortunately one optional economy in AACR British text—the omission of *ed.*, *tr.* and the like after a heading—may necessitate repetition of the author statement to clarify the function of the person named in the heading in relation to the document. In such cases it is quicker to put the designation into the heading: it can still be ignored in filing.

The imprint has traditionally been shortened in many libraries. Place of publication may well be omitted, especially if it is in the home country of the library. It may possibly indicate a national slant in a text—although in these days of simultaneous publication of a work in several countries by different publishers this use is less valid. If it does mean anything, the solution would be to name country of origin, not town of publication. The catalogue is not inherently a source of information for re-ordering a document, but if it is used as such there is then a case for retaining place of publication.

The name of publisher has always been omitted in some academic libraries without apparent ill effect. Its main function may be an oblique indication of quality or intellectual level. But, as with place of publication as a possible indication of national slant, such information, if required, could be more explicitly given in an annotation. Again, name of publisher may be retained if the catalogue is used as a source of information for re-ordering a document. If it is retained, it could in some cases be abbreviated. However, while a cataloguer may feel confident that the meaning of O.U.P. is self-evident, he may have doubts about A. & U. for Allen and Unwin, while A. & R. for Angus and Robertson is even more doubtful. If in doubt, rather than waste time thinking or asking about imponderables, the best solution is probably to give the longer form, though U.P. might be permanently acceptable for University Press. The device [etc.] to indicate omissions is probably of little value except to the compiler of scholarly bibliographies—and in any case he should probably examine the document himself.

The date of publication supposedly indicates the degree of up-to-dateness of information. But until AACR, date of imprint of copy in hand, not the operative date, held pride of place high up in the description. The really useful information had to be given in a note—if the cataloguer got round to it, e.g. 'This edition first published 1897'. Some libraries long since used some such device as 1897 (1968), and AACR has now legalised a similar fairly economical solution using the device 1897 (1968 reprint).

Of the three components of the imprint, operative date of the document should be the last to be dispensed with. However, its place in the description is open to discussion. Common usage and parlance tend to put it next to edition statement—perhaps a future revision of AACR will cater for, say, '5th ed. rev. 1968' immediately at the end of the title (and author and collaborator if any) statement.

The collation is probably the most suspect of all the parts of the description. Presumably the number of pages and the size taken together can give some idea of how much information a document contains (irrespective of quality). If so, they should surely be juxtaposed, not separated by statements of illustrative material. Even so, though, no account is taken of variables like type size, measure, and leading. Therefore, one may doubt their value. A rough and ready indication of size can be given by, say, P (for pamphlet), prefixing the class mark, which also infers useful information for helping identify a work—it is likely to be unbound and flimsy, and it serves too as a shelf sequence symbol, whose meaning should be prominently indicated in the pictographic instruction on how to use the catalogue which is displayed on top of the catalogue or shelving. If we are going to retain size-spine height, we may as well retain now its metric measure—despite its uselessness in British-oriented countries for the last century because of

Melville Dewey's whim—in anticipation of the coming acceptance of metric measure. AACR logically includes number of plates in pagination, since plates by definition are on additional leaves. Illustrative material in general has a dubious claim to be recorded, especially in the stereo-typed formulae of all codes—even AACR perhaps. It is superfluous and even irritating to find 'illus' or 'plates' in the description of a work entitled, say, *A selection of the printed work of H. A. Murch*, or *Japan: a history in art*, while one would be astounded not to find 'illus' in, shall we say, *Examples in trigonometry*. (These are random examples from BNB 1965.) In other words, the cataloguer might reserve the illustrations part of collation solely for noting anything unusual or unexpected in the presence or absence of illustrative material in a document. But again, as already mentioned, if in doubt, rather than spend time meditating in mediaeval-type way along the lines of the number of angels who can squat on a pinhead, he could if in doubt put it in.

Series statement (or 'note' in pre-AACR codes) may be usefully retained as being easily and therefore quickly expressed, especially if other information like height in centimetres or quality of edition are omitted. 'Everyman', for example, conjures up a visual image to many people obviating just about all of the conventional imprint and collation except for operative date of edition. There is doubt about whether one needs repeat 'series', or 'ser', and almost all of AACR's examples omit it. A useful extension of series in AACR reminds us that here at last we have a useful place for naming Command paper, British Standard, etc., numbers. One would say that these are useful since such works are frequently identified by them, including distinguishing between similar-sounding documents.

Notes and/or annotations can be the most time-consuming component of the description, probably because it is difficult to squeeze them into set formulae. Here, at last, the descriptive cataloguer has a chance to use his initiative—or demonstrate his lack of perception—as the case may be. The most formularised, e.g. 'Spiral binding', are probably the least useful. Some others, e.g. 'This ed. first published 1904', may be eclipsed by an imaginative use of the earlier parts of the description. Probably the least dispensable are of the type which describe the text itself, e.g. stating languages of text if not apparent from title, or pointing out that the document was previously published under another title. Sequels notes are useful but may be obviated by F. M. Gardners' useful and easy-to-use *Sequels* or some of the 'British writers' series.

Complex and popular sequences of novels, e.g. Galsworthy's Forsytes, can most easily be covered once for all by an extra entry at the start of the sequence listing in reading order all the components and including omnibus titles, connecting episodes and so on.

The annotation, one suggests, is at once the most neglected and the most abused part of the description. First—length: some sort of guide is useful for the beginner, but with the result that some cataloguers tend to eke out their annotations to the 'regulation' 30 words. Others merely paraphrase the title, sub-title, subject heading, feature heading, etc., with mere blurbs like 'reminiscences of the famous cricketer'. It is suggested here that annotations are useful for the following purposes, if they do not merely repeat information elsewhere in the entry (from heading to tracings): subject of work; type of treatment—e.g. systematic, discursive; intellectual level; connection with other works—e.g. 'parody', 'reply', sequel in certain cases (e.g. Galsworthy example above). Some public libraries include a brief outline of locale, period, and general theme or cateogry of fiction: one's sympathy goes out to these people if only they can find the time. Finally, the source of a review, with indication of whether favourable or not, certainly helps realise the oft-apostrophised 'purposive' value of reading from libraries.

In the library of a teaching institution, a great deal of this information can be omitted when students are issued with lists by teaching staff, especially if these lists are themselves annotated with a slant towards local needs.

Tracings, at the foot of a catalogue card, are necessary to ensure control of additions to, amendments to, and withdrawal of, entries. The subject index tracing, or subject heading tracing, if prominent, may help obviate part or all of the annotation, as already inferred.

A final, general reminder of an economy practicable in almost all libraries is to try to obviate any time-consuming searching for catalogue data, e.g. beyond the document itself, the library's own catalogue, and one most likely published source—BNB for recent British works, U.S. NUC for other current American works, BM catalogue for older works.

ADDED ENTRIES

The time-saving advantage of following a code is that in many cases the cataloguer is saved thinking time in deciding whether or not to implement certain added entries, while a reasonable degree of consistency is maintained fairly automatically. Against this is the cost of time and materials in making the added entries, possibly having to check them, e.g. if headings or the whole entries are typed individually, and time in filing in, checking filing, or withdrawing entries when documents are withdrawn or have their location changed or when amendments are required to the catalogue itself. Finally, a clinching factor may be the ensuing bulk of the catalogue leading to considerable expense, use of floor space and even confusion, through too many entries which may rarely be used but which must be scanned and considered in a search.

One might consider the extreme of allowing only one author/title type entry per document. In Gilbert/Sullivan and Beaumont/Fletcher type cases, a single explanatory reference may be put in at the unused entry point, e.g. under Gilbert 'for works in which Gilbert collaborated with Sullivan *see* SULLIVAN, Arthur (or, SULLIVAN, *Sir* Arthur Seymour, if one insists on being 'pukka').

The next stage is to throw responsibility on to the cataloguer, and indirectly on to his superior, by having an instruction that joint author, collaborator, title and series entries are made when likely to be 'sought'. Such a course may result in time and bulk saving, but from this must be subtracted time spent checking the catalogue to ensure consistency, e.g. to prevent making series entries for some Oxford history of England monographs but not for others in the same series. One would suggest that significant title not revealing subjects of documents should be the last to be cut out—perhaps both readers and librarians remember titles above author rather more than we have been accustomed to thinking.

Many added entries may be replaced by one reference in cases where many editions of a work are in stock, e.g.

HAMLET *see* SHAKESPEARE, William. [Hamlet.]

It should be remembered, as will be mentioned again later in this chapter, that it is unhelpful to leave out entries which a reference librarian will need to check through several sequences of bibliographies at the time of an enquiry. Readers' advisory staff must be brought into any decision-making over any economies in cataloguing.

In some cases a series of monographs could be treated as one multi-volumed work—the Oxford history of England is one example. Each author and title appears merely as part of a contents list.

Analytical entries, e.g. for plays, poems, essays, and conference papers in collections may be omitted if 'catalogue-substitutes' are available very near to or on the catalogue.

Subsidiary and analytical subject entries are probably used too sparingly already—if one can go by one's own experience with certain catalogues, especially classified catalogues, and random sampling of BNB. Published bibliographies are more likely to provide alternative author, and title, approaches than subject. Therefore, one would suggest using some of the time saved in reducing descriptive and 'collaborator' cataloguing to making more, even if short, subject entries. No rules can be laid down, but SEARS has found apparently that a need for up to 3 alphabetical-subject entries for a book is not unusual. (But some of these may in fact be multiple single-topic entries rather than single multiple-topic entries, as discussed in Section III, Chapters 9 and 13.)

Detailed contents lists, combined with a flexible and imaginative subject approach to the catalogue, may however obviate a great number of analyticals, especially when the analyticals would go into the catalogue very near the main subject entry.

REFERENCES

A wise choice of a main entry heading may well obviate many references. There is something wrong when one decides on a certain main entry heading to satisfy the code, knowing that a reference must go in to enable the user of the catalogue—staff or public—to find that main entry heading.

Many specific-name references may be reasonably replaced by one explanatory reference, e.g. 'DEPARTMNET OF . . . *see* names of countries, states and similar organisations'. Even these may be obviated by suitable general instructions on top of the catalogue and tactfully insistent but unassuming indoctrination of the public by readers' advisory staff.

There is great doubt about the value of references between similar forms of an author's name which will in any case file adjacent to, or very near each other, in the catalogue, e.g.

SHAKESPER, William *see* SHAKESPEARE, William.

If an author's works are split between real name and pseudonym, explanatory *see also* references both ways are necessary.

As with added entries, the responsibility for economising on references must usually be left to the judgement of cataloguing staff, but who keep their ears open for oaths from their colleagues in the act of using the catalogues: not all deficiencies are reported formally even when a 'complaints' notebook is kept on the catalogue.

Subject references are dealt with in Section III, but a brief reminder here is apposite. Some dictionary catalogue libraries have experimented with great pruning of, especially, *see also* references, while having a copy of the list of subject headings available at the catalogue. But even if catalogue users can be drilled into always using the list, the double referral necessitated must necessarily detract from speed in use of the catalogue.

DEGREES OF SELECTIVE CATALOGUING

The fullness of cataloguing could be varied with the various categories of material. Choice of categories could be according to arbitrary physical principles, e.g. the number of pages in a work, whether a work has a hard cover or is a paperback, whether it is stapled, spirally bound or sewn. Or the choice could be made according to categories of material, e.g. fiction or non-fiction, recreational or research, or a commonplace subject or unique, or even a naked qualitative differentiation could be made—the trivial *vs* the serious, nuclear physics *vs* soccer, and so on. It can be seen that some decisions are objective—hence easier to make, while others are subjective—hence liable to cause differences of opinion. The moral is that there is a risk of spending more time on deciding how simplified will be the treatment of certain works than one might spend on giving them the full treatment. The Library of Congress practised selective cataloguing for a time, but eventually its strict categories system was modified, with more autonomy being left to the cataloguer: apparently the risk of subjective inconsistency was considered a preferable evil to the time necessarily spent on fitting documents into this or that category.

All of this background must be kept in mind when considering the following suggested categories. And of course, there is no doubt that inconsistent cataloguing—as to fullness, etc.—will certainly result, and users of catalogues may be confused by finding, say, individual author entries for some documents but only a collective author or series entry for certain other documents.

1. No cataloguing at all of certain documents, e.g. ephemeral works such as 'pop' records and reprint paperback novels of passing interest or with allegedly no individual literary value but only as a category such as Romance. Such works are not expected to stay in stock very long and if not catalogued they could not be included safely in a reservation system. A rough and ready stock statistical record would be achieved

by marking them off automatically after, say, one year. The inclusion in this category of pamphlets, e.g. unbound works with fewer than 50 pages, is of doubtful value, as no account is taken of information value. Propaganda pamphlets, leaflets and magazines from religious sects or political parties, if within the library's stock selection policy, might be included in the category. Some form of symbol would have to be stamped on to their corners or title pages, e.g. UC for 'uncatalogued' to obviate futile checking for catalogue entries when the time came to discard them.

A relevant event under this heading is the National Lending Library which boasts of no general catalogue, and manifestly shelves books by titles. This is discussed in more detail in Section II on Author/title problems and codes.

A further example of this category would be where only one complete catalogue was maintained at the Headquarters and no catalogues were maintained at branches. Rapid and reliable communication between branches and H.Q. would be prerequisites.

2. Classified only, and put into boxes or temporary bindings such as spring-loaded covers, usually with general subject index entries or subject entries. e.g. 'CAREERS: uncatalogued leaflets shelved in pamphlet boxes at P371.425 UC'. The same principle might be applied to holiday guides, the primary location symbol being perhaps H for holidays with instructions that such material is available in either a browsing area of the library or on a certain display rack.

3. Specific subject cataloguing only, if authors are unimportant, or whose names imply the subject coverage, e.g. International Wool Secretariat; Department of Education and Science: 'Reports on education' series. There would be subject treatment for each item, e.g. D.E.S.'s *The Certificate of secondary education:* class number with specific subject indexing for classified catalogue; or SECONDARY EDUCA-TION—EXAMINATIONS—GREAT BRITAIN, with attendant references, for a dictionary catalogue.

4. Specific subject cataloguing plus general author entry probably referring to examples of types of subject entry. A midway point could be a general subject entry as well as for the author approach. This would sacrifice the specific subject approach of item 3, but since there is a belief that enquirers tend to enter the catalogue at a more generic point than they really want, the generalised approach need not be too great a handicap. At the subject point minute specification could be practised,

e.g. in a UDC classified catalogue using a colon to introduce the 'species', or in an alphabetical subject sequence committing the theoretical heresy of alphabetical-classing. Staff inservice training would be necessary to account for the blatant inconsistency of alphabetical-classing at one point for slight material while preserving direct specific entry for the same topic in hardback form for other documents.

5. General subject entry, with or without specific author approaches. A variation on item 4 could apply where, say, a popular library had many documents, probably popular outlines, on 'saturation' subjects like gardening or horse-riding. At the subject entry—whether under class mark or alphabetical subject heading—there would be specific, annotated entries for the alleged unique documents; but in addition there would be a general entry reminding the user that there were many books on the subject, shelved at, say, 635, which were not individually recorded in the subject catalogue. Such documents could not be reserved specifically, and the success of the system would depend on saturation selection of such works—so that there were always several items to choose from on the shelves at any time, even of unusually heavy demand. An alternative—in fact a book selection and not a cataloguing problem— would be to stock many copies of a very few best-quality works on the subject, which would receive individual subject entry and therefore be reservable. In such cases, annotations, contents lists, etc., would be needed to differentiate between the items in a range of books for reservation purposes (one of Cutter's oft-quoted objects of the catalogue).

6. Author (or title) only entry. In this category would be standard texts, e.g. in an educational institution library, which were normally recommended and listed by teachers by author and therefore usually sought as such: e.g. 'reserve' collections, especially for school and undergraduate use. The choice of heading would need to be decided upon between academics or teachers and cataloguers, in which cases added author or title entries would be superfluous—whatever the code said. The same principle could be applied to old works kept in stacks and which were so well known as to be (almost) always sought by author. The books themselves might even be shelved in alphabetical-author order, as with current 'reserve' collections, thereby enabling the catalogue to be short-circuited when demand arose. Periodicals could come into this category, especially since the necessarily generalised subject entry for many would be fairly meaningless, and shelf arrangement might therefore be by main (usually title or corporate author) entry.

7. One author (or title) entry, and one subject entry. Most of a library's stock might come into this category. Selection for it might be dictated by layout of title page and whether or not the content of a document conformed to conventional subject disciplines. In some libraries this category might become confused with category 6 above, especially when academics are not as up to date as one would wish in evaluating new books and editions. Periodicals would normally come into this category. But if 'consecutive' entry were used for changed titles they might more accurately belong to item 8 below.

8. Full standard cataloguing according to the code, etc., used in the library. Here, all the usual entries, analyticals, references and descriptive detail would be implemented. Nowadays, only a small proportion of a library's intake would belong here, unless a central cataloguing agency were relied upon uncritically for supply of entries, including decisions for numbers and types of added entries.

THE INFLUENCE OF PUBLISHED BIBLIOGRAPHIES, CATALOGUES, AND INDEXES ON A LIBRARY'S CATALOGUING

Four types of published works are concerned here:

1. Published library catalogues which are normally printed in sufficient quantity to ensure that they are as readily available as published bibliographies. Since these catalogues are used mainly, in other libraries, for checking of bibliographic data—for reservations or ordering purposes, say, as well as for cataloguing—they are referred to here as bibliographic catalogues. They are particularly important in some libraries as raw material for pre-cataloguing.

It is important that libraries producing these catalogues can 'break even' so that their continued publication can be assured. Ideally there should be national—or similar—subsidies for such catalogues if there is a real demand for them but if their publication would run at a loss.

Part of the cost of purchase of such tools should be taken into account in catalogue-costing in a library.

As with bibliographies these can be general, e.g. British Museum's Catalogue of printed books; or special, e.g. Lewis's Medical, Scientific and Technical Lending Library catalogue.

2. Published bibliographies, which may be either general, e.g. *Cumulative book index*—which attempts to list all works published in the English language; or national, e.g. *British national bibliography*; or special, e.g. *British catalogue of music*.

To be useful as cataloguing aids, these works should give standard catalogue entries, preferably compiled by qualified librarians according to a stated code.

3. Standard catalogues are bibliographies of works of a certain category, e.g. fiction, or for a certain type of library, e.g. children's, whose entries are presented in a form and fullness which could be copied directly by cataloguers: clerically, or even by facsimile copying. The most common examples are those issued by H. W. Wilson Co. and therefore they are of most use to libraries in the U.S., or those whose stock is predominantly American. A typical example is *Standard catalog for public libraries*, currently in its fourth edition, with supplements. The main sequence is in Dewey Decimal Classification order, with prominent class numbers and feature headings. Each work recorded has a standard catalogue entry, with SEARS subject tracings for a dictionary catalogue, and with extensive bibliographical notes and descriptive annotations. There is, also, an Author, title, subject, and analytical index.

One disadvantage of over-reliance on standard catalogues is that a librarian may—perhaps unconsciously—allow his book selection to be confined to books, etc., included in such works, especially since—these being Wilson publications—a tendency to rely on Wilson printed cards may become built into the catalogue organisation.

4. Indexes, usually to periodicals, but in some cases analysing the contents of monographic works. Use of these works is taken for granted in much reference work. However, their connection with cataloguing is manifest, since local libraries' catalogues may also make analytical entries as an alternative to, or substitute for, published indexes. Some indexes, e.g. *Engineering index*, issue entries in card form, ready for filing into one's own catalogue or perhaps into a separate Information file.

USES MADE OF PRINTED CATALOGUES, ETC.

1. Data may be copied from them. Provided the cataloguing is of a high quality and relevant to the needs of the local library, all important cataloguing decisions could be taken from the printed aid. When advance collection of the 'raw' cataloguing material is practised before the relevant document comes into stock, the process is known as pre-cataloguing and it can help shorten the time between receipt of a document and its availability for use.

If no amendments are made and if the entries are acceptable physically, they can be facsimile-copied: such a method is particularly feasible for entries which are themselves 'card-oriented', e.g. BNB; BCM (especially since its scores do not have cards); LC's NUC. If the library's policy demands amendments the printed aids can be used as basic working copy on to which amendments are written by the cataloguer, the corrected form then being passed to the typist.

Compatibility between various sources used and between the sources themselves and the local practice should be a prerequisite. However, a suggestion was once made that an Australian central cataloguing system could be based on a mixture of BNB and LC entries to cater for Australia's mixed intake of books from both the U.S. and Britain (FLOWERS: L.A.A. Canberra Conference, 1965, p. 229-246).

2. Bibliographic checking of certain items of information, e.g. full names of authors to be incorporated into the library's own catalogue entry. This use is common, and need not be expanded upon here, except that a warning may be necessary that such an activity should not be overindulged. There are cases of cataloguers spending hours in trying to ascertain, say, the dates of birth and death or the full forenames of an author simply because the library provides a fertile hunting ground for such activities. So, if in doubt—don't.

However, a particular value of published bibliographies and indexes is for guidance in establishing new headings, especially in the use of indexes to periodicals in deciding on the form of new subject headings. LC entries' subject tracings and BNB's feature headings may be used for the same purpose. Thinking time is cut down, while, further, the hope of uniformity is increased. Care has to be taken in this use of indexes to periodicals, otherwise inconsistency may result. For example, headings from IBZ, BTI and the Wilson indexes may often be incompatible. One index should be chosen as arbiter, and of course this has itself to be consistent with whatever other headings go into the library's files.

3. As substitutes for library catalogue entries: added and analytical. The extreme example is in the case of indexes to periodicals: reference staff commonly use indexes in conjunction with catalogue-searching, perhaps even without realising that they are in effect practising a form of limited cataloguing. What has been said in 2 above about compatibility of subject headings is especially relevant here. This may account for some of the resistance to BTI's headings in libraries where 'conventional' headings are accepted as normal.

Similar examples, but of the analysis of books and not of periodicals, are found in the use of works like Sears' *Song index* and Granger's *Index to poetry*—the latter especially for its subject approach to poetry, a rare practice in library cataloguing.

It can be seen that a library's selection policy, e.g. which anthologies of poetry are acquired and which periodicals are regularly subscribed to, has an effect on the quantity of local indexing which will be required in order to offer a full service.

Trade and similar bibliographies are customarily used in conjunction with libraries' catalogues as substitute added entries, especially for the title approach, but also for, say, joint authors, editors and series. The Whitaker bibliographies' inverted title (quasi-subject) entries are particularly useful. The basic problem is whether cataloguers should anticipate enquiries with a multiplicity of approaches (many of which may never be used), or whether the readers' adviser should be saddled with time spent on bibliographic searching after receiving the enquiry, and perhaps at a time when he is already inundated by requests. The situation is somewhat analogous to the pre-coordinate *vs* post-coordinate indexing problem.

4. Substitutes for the library's catalogue itself. The ultimate is the existence of a bibliography, or of bibliographies, whose entries for documents which are in the library's stock are marked up in some way, perhaps with an accession number and with branch or department location symbol. Such a policy presupposes (*a*) the existence of one or few bibliographies whose listings completely embrace the library's stock; (*b*) compatibility between bibliographies if more than one are needed; and (*c*) the labour of accurately copying out accession and location symbols when new cumulations of the bibliography are obtained.

A rather more feasible practice would be to have normal catalogue entries for works not in the basic bibliography but merely a brief reference to the bibliography entry for works which are listed in it. However, if such a policy were hinged to BNB there would be a risk of neglecting selection of works not in BNB.

Some libraries practise the bibliography substitute policy for their British Government publications, holdings being marked up in the relevant H.M.S.O. 'catalogues'. Other libraries might possibly consider the policy if H.M.S.O. cataloguing were more compatible with common library practice. The idea could conceivably be applied to other government publications which are well documented, e.g. U.S.,

Australia, and U.N., although this would lead to an ever-increasing number of sequences to search and is probably feasible only in a library with a very large collection of government publications and in which these publications are usually asked for primarily by their issuing country, and not, say, by subject whatever their country of origin.

It is apparent that an economical use of published lists as substitute catalogues or as cataloguing guidance is best effected when uniformity exists between the aids themselves and between them and the library's catalogue. The same principle applies as decisions over whether or not to take part in central cataloguing.

It is suggested that more attention should be paid to the compilation and use of published bibliographies and indexes. The problem exemplifies the need for a coming together of reference work and cataloguing: future examination syllabuses might well reflect the common ground between these two component disciplines of library science.

CONCLUSION

A policy of limited cataloguing should not be drifted into casually or undertaken lightly. Vital factors can be summarised as:

1. Basic object(s) of catalogues, especially the consumer point of view.

2. Catalogue-substitutes available, including their physical availability near the catalogue and staff using the catalogue; also their recurring cost, the increasing space taken up by them, the increasing amount of time spent using them as number of sequences and supplements grows, and the lack of control exercised over their editorial policy or even over their continued viability—many of them are profit-oriented.

3. Flexibility of attitude of all catalogue users—staff at all levels, and public also at all levels. In turn—training of staff, and of public if feasible—to take into account the varying amounts of information yielded by a catalogue.

4. External responsibilities, especially contributions to union catalogues.

5. Possible impact of current and future physical means of producing catalogues and the varying forms of central cataloguing.

6. From all other points mentioned: cost in relation to efficiency of the resulting catalogue.

CHAPTER 23

Recataloguing

This topic can range from occasional minor alterations and corrections, through a permanent process of catalogue overhaul, to all that could be involved in complete adoption of a new code. The latter makes the topic very relevant at the present time. Also to be borne in mind, in Britain particularly, is the amalgamation of local authorities with a consequent amalgamation of catalogues. It may—and should—be decided that such an occasion should be made one for complete overhaul, not only of techniques, including cataloguing, but also of the complete administrative structure of the library services resulting from amalgamations, and taking advantage of new, sophisticated methods of mechanisation.

On the other hand, the advice of F. M. Gardner should be borne in mind too (*Letters to a younger librarian.* London: J. Clarke, 1951):

(*a*) What do we want to achieve?

(*b*) Have we the means to achieve it?

(*c*) Is the result going to be worth the time and effort?

Even within one existing system—and discounting amalgamations, and overhaul of the whole library's structure—the decision to change from one catalogue code or classification scheme to another can be a very big decision. Even to change from the first edition of the *ALA Rules for filing* to the second edition could involve a major upheaval in staff use. It is worth considering, for any major once-for-all job, the temporary employment of suitable extra staff for the period of change. This would usually entail long-term planning, to ensure that funds are made available. Further, the planning would have to be particularly exact if it were separately budgeted for.

To help decide on whether a change will prove worth while or economically feasible, a 'trial run' of some sort might be advisable. A small but representative cross-section of stock could be recatalogued, reclassified, etc., under strict conditions of costing, temporary inconvenience to the service, but also—the ultimate test—observation of extra convenience for staff and users in the resulting product. The trial could be a full-scale one, as implied above; or, to prevent too much inconvenience, purely the technical (not economic) aspects could be tested by, say, pencilling in and refiling relevant catalogue entries in the master catalogue. On the other hand, it may be that most people, including library staffs and of course cataloguers, are rather conservative and automatically suspicious of change. This would have to be allowed for where it existed.

If a large-scale and full change is embarked upon, all of its implications need to be appreciated in advance, and relevant decisions made. It seems a minor point to decide whether to correct existing entries or to make out new ones, but such a decision may involve, ultimately, a lot of time or materials. Checking of work may be time-consuming also. There must be storage space for books where spine markings, etc., are being amended. Relevant works in lending libraries must be 'flagged' in issues to ensure that they are sent in for re-marking.

But the most important part of advance planning is to ensure that all staff, and especially cataloguers, are fully acquainted with, and where necessary have practised on, whatever new system or method is to be implemented; i.e. inservice retraining is very relevant. Sometimes, professional organisations run 'workshops' and seminars, and attendance at suitable such meetings should repay the time involved.

The following further comments assume the new AACR as a vehicle for decision making, but similar principles would apply for, say, a new much-changed edition of a classification scheme, say the 17th, or proposed 18th, edition of DC compared with the 14th: a decision facing BNB-oriented libraries currently and in the near future.

1. Whether or not the catalogue code is to be adopted (*a*) entirely, and if so (*b*) all of it simultaneously.

2. A part-way decision would be possibly (regrettably?) not, say, to change to the new direct rules for corporate authors, but to implement only the rules for shorter entry of persons.

3. Another sort of part-way decision would be to implement the whole code, but very gradually, perhaps over several years. But this would involve the confusion of cataloguers and others using two dissimilar codes at the same time, with additionally the frustration of knowing that some current work would be changed within a short time.

4. A reason for item 3, however, might be that the existing catalogues could continue in use as if 'normal'. The possibility of confusion has

been mentioned above. It should be admitted that users anyway may not particularly notice a mixture of code philosophies; they are more likely to be irritated superficially by syntactical inconsistencies of the type exemplified in the section of this work on Codes.

5. A slightly more radical policy is to institute a form of 'no-conflict' superimposition policy but combined with potential application of the new code to all new stock. This is the policy practised for the most part by the Library of Congress with the new code. If a new author is entered for the first time, the new code is used. But existing headings are not changed. It is suggested here that this is a rather timid policy, and ultimately merely postpones the time of reckoning.

6. An alternative is to make entries for all new stock according to the new code, to file them into their correct place, to leave the different headings for existing authors in the old place, and to make explanatory references both ways.

7. The next most radical policy is what might be called 'attrition'; i.e. a gradual wearing down of the influence of the old code. This is the policy being practised by BNB. All new intake is catalogued according to the new code. Where a new heading conflicts with an old one, the old one is changed to conform to new practice. But the catalogue is kept in one sequence still. BNB's policy is to be admired, as setting a practical example showing faith in the new code but which is reasonably practicable. Actual libraries are faced with a larger problem, admittedly, as they must amend not only all relevant catalogue entries, e.g. in departments and branches, but very likely too markings on books themselves. However, the latter job could be postponed provided the actual shelf location is left clearly indicated on the catalogue entries and distinguished from main entry filing heading. A possible compromise might be to re-mark only the books on open access.

8. The ultimate is to 'close-off' the old catalogue and to start a new one. We should bear in mind that in most libraries this potentially entails two sequences at every service point which has its own catalogue. The thought of two sequences of author/title approach seems to daunt some librarians unduly. In fact, if the new file is more approachable and if there is a rapid turnover of stock, the system may soon possibly prove positively advantageous. In any case, in many libraries the time may soon come when the old sequence has shrivelled to the point that a rapid *coup de grâce* can be executed and the headings for remaining old entries amended and filed into the new sequence.

It has been assumed throughout that attention will be paid only to headings, and the institution of uniform titles where relevant.

Libraries subscribing to BNB cards, or using its listed data as a basis for cataloguing, will find it worth their while at least to accept BNB rulings as from its adoption of the new code in 1968. However, they need to allow for the fact that BNB cards made up to the end of 1967 will still be according to BNB's adaptation of AA 1908, although, as was stated in the section on Codes, BNB anticipated the new code in some of its pre-1968 practices.

CHAPTER 24

Filing; including Inter-reaction between Classification and Cataloguing

Filing is not merely a matter of following rules laid down in certain filing codes—although this itself can be confusing enough. It also influences, and is influenced by, classification. This chapter will, therefore, incorporate inter-reaction between classification and cataloguing.

Basically, there are two manifestations:

(*a*) how to arrange catalogue entries at an entry word, which may be the usual author, title and subject, and including both alphabetical and classification symbols where applicable; and

(*b*) how to arrange documents themselves, on shelves or in files at a class number or at an author's name—perhaps itself already a division at a class number.

Certain catalogue codes also include filing rules. Others, especially AACR, do not. Since this code in particular reaches the point of constructing uniform titles, the omission of the next logical stage—how to arrange them—seems unfortunate.

MINOR PROBLEMS: EXAMPLES

1. Prefixed terms

There are two sorts of prefixed headings, for example:

(*a*) DE LA ROCHE or AP GRUFFYDD as proper names; and
(*b*) ANTI-SEMITISM.

Generally both types are filed letter by letter, ignoring spaces and hyphens, i.e. using the opposite of the usual library catalogue method of word-by-word. Logic seems to demand this apparent contradiction. The only radical solution would be spelling reform—closing up spaces, omitting hyphens and transforming such terms into single words. The M', Mc, Mac problem is usually solved by filing all as though spelt MAC. But it is difficult to see why only these names should be made uniform and inaccurate, while SMYTH is filed apart from SMITH.

2. Numerals

The entry term of a heading, or even a complete heading, may be a number, e.g.:

> Welensky's 4,000 days
> 1812: a solemn overture (Tchaikovsky)
> 1,001 nights
> 1066 and all that.

The treatment of these in filing, assuming that they are interfiled with alphabetical terms, conventionally depends on how each number is spoken, often in turn dependent on whether it is a date or some other form. The examples given are normally spoken as:

> Four thousand
> Eighteen twelve
> A thousand and one
> Ten sixty-six

Some libraries put numerals in a separate sequence: possibly roman separate from arabic also. In this case, a word form and a numeral form title of the same work would be in different sequences. And to file by roman or arabic is less desirable still. A few Swedish libraries use double entry:

(*a*) in the alphabetical sequence; and
(*b*) in a separate numerical sequence following the alphabetical sequence.

In general, all entries should be in one sequence, even though this may need explanatory references between different forms of numerals as spoken. The opposite point of view, but in relation to union catalogues, is presented in the work by WILLEMIN cited in the reading list.

In addition to the cardinal numerals, ordinal numerals (1st, 4th) must be catered for. These are less ambiguous and may usually be filed as though written out: FIRST; FOURTH.

If necessary, to aid filing and the understanding of filing, a uniformly understood, verbal filing term in brackets could prefix the title page form.

> e.g.: [FOUR THOUSAND] 4,000 days
> [TEN SIXTY-SIX] 1066 and all that
> [SECOND] 2nd international conference . . .

3. Initials; Abbreviations; Contractions

Initials are not necessarily abbreviations in the sense that they could theoretically be spelt out, e.g. E. T. is a pseudonym of a biographer of D. H. Lawrence and means nothing beyond the title page on which it appears. But it is a potential entry point into a catalogue and so must be given filing significance.

Other initials stand for known words, so there is an opinion that they should be filed as if the full version appeared in the heading, e.g. A.A. filed as if AUTOMOBILE ASSOCIATION or ALCOHOLICS ANONYMOUS were given in full.

However, other abbreviations may be spoken as if they were words and so there is a case for filing them as though they are words in their own right, e.g. UNESCO, EURATOM—which, in fact, some have come to be. AACR is being realistic in allowing such terms to be used as headings, inferring that they be filed as real words. There is little doubt that all such terms, when entry or filing terms, should be used at face value. Filing codes nowadays sensibly cater for this.

Another form is the contraction (Dr, St). Conventionally these have been filed as if spelt out, e.g. Mr as Mister, presumably because one caters for them as spoken. But A.A. is usually spoken as such, and so we cannot but query filing rules which differentiate between sets of initials and contractions. Further, rules can become complicated, and possibly pedantic; how many people would look for 'Mrs' as though it were MISTRESS, or 'Dr' in a German title as though it were DOKTOR? (The new ALA filing rules now allows MRS as an exception, to be filed as spelt, but it still insists on other contractions being filed as spoken.) Therefore, there is something to be said for filing these—and all abbreviations, acronyms, contractions, etc., exactly, letter by letter, as represented in the catalogue heading itself. General explanatory references could be used at the appropriate, but unused, entry points.

For the sake of economy, provision could be made for representing much-used headings in an abbreviated form but filed as though given in full, e.g. G.B. or U.S., filed as GREAT BRITAIN and UNITED STATES. But here, such an accepted abbreviation as 'U.S.S.R.' might be sought under initials for the simple reason that the exact meaning is not known.

4. Initial articles

These may be encountered in titles of some serials and other works, and in some corporate names. They may be found in any language in addition to English. Normally, they are ignored in filing, whatever language they are in, and whether or not the user—or cataloguer—knows all the languages concerned. Confusion can result, e.g. a work may be entitled DIE CASTING, and distinction must be made between this and, say, DIE MEISTERSINGER. Easy solutions would be to have the (ignored) article in parentheses, or in lower case, or in italics, or even to omit it altogether.

> e.g. DIE CASTING
>   (Die) MEISTERSINGER   or
>   *Die* MEISTERSINGER   or
>   MEISTERSINGER.

The use of parentheses is supported here, since the method can be applied to any words to be ignored in filing.

> e.g. (Board of) EDUCATION
>   (Ministry of) EDUCATION
>   (Department of) EDUCATION AND SCIENCE.

The principle is really the same: ensuring entry under what is considered to be the first significant word of the entry. But—very important—care must be taken, or we are back in the morass exemplified by the BM rule for entering anonymous works. Italicising the words without filing significance cannot be wholly recommended because most catalogue codes have italicised terms in some headings with filing significance.

> e.g. AACR, p. 105: GERMANY (*Democratic Republic*)   and
>   GERMANY (*Federal Republic*).

5. Operative part of heading: Punctuation

Conventionally, parts of titles following punctuation are ignored in filing. This condition should be isolated from a personal author surname. A surname may belong to two or more different people, and it must therefore be distinguished by forenames following a comma, or by other distinguishing terms. Also, distinction must be made between accidental identical entry terms.

> e.g. LONDON, *City*   and
>   LONDON, Jack.

Certain parts of a heading could be rendered inoperative for filing purposes by the use of parentheses. But it should be remembered that some catalogue codes and libraries, e.g. BM, use parenthetical terms for forenames with filing significance. Personal names are further discussed as such under Major problems later.

The filing of inverted headings can be relevant here. With titles, some librarians ignore punctuation inferring inversion. But with subject headings, they may allow the punctuation—usually a comma as in inverted titles—to have filing significance. So there may be doubt as to the sequence of, say, CHEMISTRY, INORGANIC and CHEMISTRY, INTRODUCTION TO. Parts of a heading to be ignored in filing should have a punctuation of their own, e.g. italics or parentheses, as has already been suggested.

Punctuation can also be very important in preventing ambiguities, e.g. POLICE, STATE (inversion for STATE POLICE in SEARS) has a very different meaning from POLICE STATE.

MAJOR PROBLEMS

The basic problem here is that an entry word may be all, or some, of a personal author's surname, or a corporate author's entry word, or a subject term with varying uses. A common example is LONDON, which, in addition to the problems mentioned above, could be different places in various countries, and different entities in one country (e.g. City, County). Such highly multifarious uses of one term are comparatively rare, but must still be catered for.

1. Personal surnames

One surname commonly applies to several different people. Usually such names are subdivided alphabetically by the forename, following a comma. If all the known or used forenames of two or more different people are common, a further characteristic of separation is needed. Conventionally, dates of birth and death are used. But forenames or initials and dates are not necessarily the most useful means of differentiating between such people, though the type of library may be relevant. In a children's library more workmanlike methods might be considered. For example, LAWRENCE OF ARABIA instead of, or qualifying, LAWRENCE, Thomas Edward.

However, few names have such convenient qualifying terms, so we must usually fall back on full forenames. AACR allows use of initials alone in uncommon cases, e.g. ELIOT, T. S. (cf. ELIOT, George), when initials only are used in documents. (Filing rules normally stipulate that initials are filed before spelt-out names.) But it reinstates full forenames in cases of potential confusion, e.g. LAWRENCE, Daniel H. precedes LAWRENCE, David Herbert—even though the public think of 'D. H. Lawrence', and not 'David Herbert Lawrence'. Some libraries, and certainly BNB, continue to spell out all forenames in full when easily ascertained. Fuller forms of names could be quoted in catalogue headings for identification purposes, even though they may possibly be ignored for filing purposes.

The situation may arise when a surname plus nickname or designation must be considered in conjunction with forenames, e.g. where

BEDE, *the Venerable*

is filed in relationship with BEDE, Cuthbert—even if the latter is merely a reference to the real name: Bradley. Conventionally, all 'appellative' qualifiers precede forenames (e.g. ALA filing rules, 1st edition). So BEDE, *Venerable* would file before BEDE, Cuthbert. Such a distinction is arbitrary and unhelpful, and pure alphabetical sub-arrangement might be more useful.

Finally, we come to parts of personal names which are helpful to identify a person, but which are not used in arrangement. AACR allows the use of *Sir*, for example, but not *General*. Such personal qualifying terms can be useful to distinguish between otherwise identical names, e.g. between Thomas *the Rhymer* and Thomas, *Saint*. In this case, qualifying terms are more useful than dates and the revised ALA filing rules wisely give such terms filing significance (Rule 20).

The bibliographical status of a personal author's heading has in the past sometimes been regarded as important, e.g. an author as such has been filed before the name of the same person as a subsidiary bibliographic entity, e.g. as editor or reviser. But even the first edition of the ALA filing rules ignored the difference between 'main' and 'secondary' entries for any one person. With the advent of AACR and its optional rule about the use of such designations as 'editor', and BNB's decision to omit them, the time has surely come to question the value of such designations. Who really cares about intellectual responsibility between Quiller-Couch as author of *On the art of writing* and as compiler of the *Oxford book of English verse*?

Occasionally, no differentiation at all is made between authors with the same surname, the second characteristic for filing purposes being the first word of title not an article. This method is especially useful in a union catalogue whose only function is the location of a named work, i.e. whose bibliographic unit is a work—or even an edition of a work, and not an author. This method, part of the Berghöffer system, is advocated in the work by WILLEMIN cited in the reading list.

The Berghöffer system is sometimes carried further to allow filing under the first noun of the title, though any noun is not necessarily more significant than any adjective. Unorthodox filing, for recall of a document, might be carried to the extent that a work of established joint authors might be filed first by the surnames, then by the title, e.g. Jesse H. Shera and Margaret E. Egan's *The classified catalog* might be filed as SHERA AND EGAN: The CLASSIFIED CATALOG. In fact it probably should be catalogued as such, if the first purpose of a catalogue is to decide whether or not a cited work is in stock.

2. 'By' and 'About'

The relationship between the entries for works by and about an entity can apply to both personal and corporate entities. Since there is an important distinction in approach between a person or body as author and as subject, a distinction in catalogue arrangement is necessary, e.g. a heading as author can be typographically different from the same as a subject—perhaps authors in black and subjects in red; or authors in lower case and subjects in upper case. Conventionally, dictionary and name catalogues file entries for works 'by' before those for works 'about'. But BNB's alphabetical sequence reverses this order: subject entries, using the colon, file before author entries, using the full stop. Entries for documents about a specific work of an author file immediately after the entries for the work itself, e.g. an entry for a document about Shakespeare's *Hamlet* files before entries for the actual texts of, say, *King Lear*. Such a precedent can become complicated when seeking all commentaries on a named play: whole monographs are entered immediately after the text, while those in a more comprehensive document—say on Shakespeare's tragedies as a whole—will come later in the sequence.

3. Voluminous authors and works

Filing in an alphabetical catalogue, e.g. of authors, should be as simple as ABC. However, some element of non-alphabetical grouping is allowed for in the 'by' and 'about' combination, and this precedent is often carried further, to provide for groupings of works by an author at the bibliographic unit of the author as such. Even before AACR officially provided for such collective forms as 'plays' and 'poems', the ALA filing rules catered for the collocation in various sequences of works, whether or not designated as such in the actual entries.

A basic arrangement for entries for works of voluminous or prolific authors is given in the ALA *filing rules*, 1st edition, Rule 26, summarised and commented on as follows:

(*a*) Complete works in sets;
      possibly sub-arranged by editor.
(*b*) Selections of works;
      sub-arranged by title of selection.

In each of the above groups, further arrangement could be publisher or date: i.e. by data which comes a long way down the entry. This adds substance to the argument in favour of systematically compiled full uniform titles according to whatever arrangement is desired, rather than leaving it to the filer (and user!) to pick out the required information, perhaps from underlined parts of the description.

(*c*) Single works;
      alphabetically by best known titles, with author-title references
      from other forms of titles as required.

What is the best known title may well vary from library to library. Note here that AACR's rules for uniform titles should apply, and do provide for the sensible bringing to its appropriate place in the entry of the desired form of title for filing purposes. So it is up to the cataloguer to decide whether to use either *City of God* or *Civitas Dei*—a public library, or a school library, may well decide on the English form. Whatever characteristic is used, this should be incorporated into the uniform title to facilitate both filing and use.

(*d*) Finally come works about the author as a whole—those on individual works follow the entries for the texts of the works. Sub-arrangement is by main entry heading, usually author; further arrangement would usually be by title.

The BM printed catalogue uses a somewhat similar type of grouped arrangement, which varies as required from author to author. It can get rather complicated, but the catalogue gains from being in book form, making sequential scanning easier. Further, it most helpfully gives a layout before the entries for authors, and for such titles as Bible

The MLA/ALA *Code for cataloging music and phonorecords* also cater for a degree of non-alphabetical grouped filing, e.g. the conventiona (i.e. uniform) title [Works] precedes all others at a composer's name. This is followed immediately by all other complete works for an instrument, resulting in:

> [Works]
> [Works, organ]
> [Works, piano]
> [Works, violin]

followed then by individual works arranged alphabetically by their conventional titles. But, interfiled, come other collective conventional titles, e.g. [Concertos, organ].

Conventional titles are built up meticulously, including the use of punctuation with a named filing significance, i.e.:

(*a*) Closing bracket   (as at the end of a conventional title).
(*b*) Semicolon   (preceding statement of arrangement).
(*c*) Period   (between title of whole work and that of excerpt).
(*d*) Parentheses   (enclosing later form of title).
(*e*) Comma   (between opus number and key signature).
(*f*) No punctuation   (longer titles).

Fuller details, with examples, are given in the Code itself, which should be read carefully by anyone contemplating using it. Such details as given here are included to show that:

(*a*) music can present one of the most complex needs for filing to ensure useful collocation; but

(*b*) rules can get so complicated as to be incomprehensible to an untrained catalogue user, whether on the staff or not.

It would surely have been at least a little more helpful to devise a method using an understood ordinal significance, either of ordinary numbers or letters interposed between the parts of the title, or of punctuation in order of 'strength'. In any case, clear instructions and sample layouts are needed on the catalogue, even if not at each voluminous author or composer. What this amounts to is that, in fact, the cataloguing rules are wasteful—they force one into double entry, i.e. both

(*a*) alphabetical-classed—BIBLE, etc.; and

(*b*) specific entry, MOFFAT, etc., as added entries.

There should be alternative rules, for specific entry, when compiling the alphabetical subsidiaries of the classified catalogue.

AACR rules for Uniform titles cater for any works and can include terms which can be used for sub-filing alphabetically, e.g. when *English* follows a title in its vernacular. But most complications are found with what the ALA Catalog code of 1949 calls anonymous classics, which, because of their very nature, may be excerpted and translated in a great variety of ways. Examples are religious scriptures, e.g. Bible, and long-standing legendary collections of stories, e.g. Arabian nights.

Conventionally these are entered indirectly, e.g. BIBLE. O.T. *Ecclesiastes*, which is why the filing problems arise of course. There is potentially a choice between:

(a) A wholly systematic, or canonical, arrangement, e.g.

> BIBLE. O.T. *Genesis* preceding BIBLE. O.T. *Exodus*; and
> BIBLE. O.T. preceding BIBLE. N.T.; and

(b) An alphabetical arrangement, word by word.

The latter is usually practised. Even so, the ensuring grouping and sub-grouping seems to be an attempt at near-reproducing, at least, the truly systematic order of the classification scheme, e.g. 220's in DC. So, taking the classified catalogue, we have (a) classified file: grouping—systematic, e.g. 220's; and (b) author/title file: grouping—alphabetical, i.e. alphabetical classing, since we know, for example, that Exodus is a part of the Old Testament, itself a part of the Bible. The dictionary catalogue, because of its very nature, does not suffer from this near-duplication: it simply has its only Bible entries under BIBLE. Now, the filing code used is one compiled by Americans for the dictionary catalogue. But it seems wasteful merely to copy this in Britain, with its predominance of classified catalogues. The author-title approach and the subject index should surely complement, not duplicate, the classified file. So specific versions and excerpts from the BIBLE could, one suggests, be entered in the author-title sequence specifically, e.g. under MOFFAT for his translation. Also, the subject index will give the specific class numbers for excerpts.

e.g. GENESIS: BIBLE   222.11

4. Sub-arrangement at a class number

It has been assumed that basic rules are intended for nominally alphabetical catalogues. However, since classification schemes rarely provide systematic notation for all possible detail, the arrangements mentioned may be applied within the classified catalogue at the class mark allocated to an author, e.g. in DC, 822.33 for Shakespeare. But it should be noted that, for example, DC 17th edition does list a sub-arrangement for Shakespeare, using roman capitals. This files works about the plays in general before the texts themselves. However, the order is reversed for individual texts and works on them. So, texts of *Hamlet* go at 822.33 S 7, and works on Hamlet at 822.33 S 8. The edition of DC, or other scheme, used may not go into such detail. Therefore, other methods have been created to give works as specific class numbers as possible. So the Cutter-Sanborn tables would allocate the symbol M64 to John Milton; *Paradise lost* is represented by M64 P. and the 1667 edition of this poem is represented by M64 P. 1667, a reprint being M64 P. 1667.2. *Paradise regained* is M64 R., followed by similar detail for various editions and reprints. DC 17th edition does not cater specifically for Milton's poetry, since the closest one can get is 821.4, i.e. 1625-1702, although, up till the 14th edition, individual numbers were given to specific 'major' writers of a period, the -9 being allocated to 'others' or even 'minor' in early editions, disregarding their period. It is little wonder that some libraries quickly gave up use of DC's full numbers, and arranged both entries and documents alphabetically by name of writer. LC classification also caters for some standard authors and other people down to giving individual titles their own notation—and even giving death masks of Abraham Lincoln their own class mark.

It is reasonable to expect that a catalogue should clarify, in its class marks, the means of arranging entries at any number: e.g. if by alphabetical subject, the subject term, or abbreviation of it, should follow; if by author, the author's name, or first three letters, should follow. If necessary, classification notation should differentiate between the generic and more specific, e.g. DC could be adapted so that cars in general go at 629.22 subdivided by author, and specific makes at 629.221 subdivided by make. For example, 629.22 ABB for a general work by Abbey on cars, and 629.221 FOR for a work on Fords by Abbey. Such distinctions should be registered in the subject index, of course.

e.g. 1. FORDS: CARS   629.221
                              FOR
     2. CARS: ENGINEERING   629.22
        Individual makes   629.221 [*pace* chain indexing!]

There seems to be an underlying attitude that alphabetical sub-arrangement, other than by author, in the classified catalogue is almost something to be ashamed of. In fact, it can be more intelligible than some of the hidden, unobvious, sequences which we find in BNB after the specificity of DC has been exhausted.

5. Subject sub-arrangement in the dictionary catalogue

Complications can ensue when a common subject term is followed by a great variety of types of qualifying or subdividing terms, and when attempts are made to group these types of heading irrespective of their apparent alphabetical place.

Probably greatest complexity is encountered in Rule 34 of the first edition of the ALA filing rules, and as exemplified by the Library of Congress. The dictionary catalogue in such cases seems to be trying to combine the alphabetical advantages of the dictionary catalogue with the collocation expected in the classified catalogue. The following example illustrates the contention:

Heading	*Corresponding DC16 ed. class no.*
Cookery	641.5
Cookery—Bibliography	641.5016 (OR 016.6415)
Early works to 1800	641.509 (nearest no. ?)
Cookery (Apples)	641.6411
(Cereals)	641.631
(Oysters)	641.6941
Cookery, American	641.5973
Mexican	641.5972
Military	641.573
Spanish	641.5946
Cookery for institutions	641.57
Cookery for the sick	641.563

Rearranged in DC order—obvious ordinal arrangement by notation:

641.5	Cookery	
641.5016	Bibliographies	⎫ Form
641.509	Early works (?history)	⎭
641.563	For the sick	⎫
641.573	Military	⎬ Quantity. Type of consumer
641.577	For institutions	⎭
641.5946	Spanish	⎫
641.5972	Mexican	⎬ National origin
641.5973	American	⎭

641.631	Cereals	
641.6411	Apples	Type of material cooked
641.6941	Oysters	

(There is no DC equivalent of COOKERY—EARLY WORKS TO 1800, which apparently was devised as an aid to easy weeding of Library of Congress stock for relegation to stack. One cannot help wondering how many other libraries have unthinkingly reproduced this purely domestic device.)

Ultimately, such a formula can lead to the following type of construction:

SCIENCE—YEARBOOKS

SCIENCE—U.S.

SCIENCE, MEDIEVAL

SCIENCE FICTION

i.e. on the face of it, reverse alphabetical order.

If it is necessary to introduce such complex groupings into an alphabetical catalogue, then verbal relationship terms, with a conventionally known order, should replace the completely arbitrary punctuation used in Rule 34.

e.g. —FORM—

—MATERIAL—

—REGIONS—

Or letters or numerals with known ordinal significance could be used to decide the required citation order.

e.g. —A—   (1)

—B— or (2)

—C—   (3)

etc. etc.

At this point, if necessary, reference should be made back to the parts of this book dealing with subject headings. For example, Farradane's and BTI's use of punctuation marks with filing significance are very relevant.

Strangely, long ago Cutter advocated 'classifying' (i.e. grouping) *see also* references under a heading when they reached unwieldy proportions, rather than arranging them in purely alphabetical order, e.g. under ARCHITECTURE they would be arranged in several sequences by, first, 'things built'; second, 'methods of building'; third, 'cities whose buildings are described'; fourth, 'countries whose architecture is described' (Rule 342). In principle, he was anticipating the thesauri compilers of this century who try to differentiate between references, but not according to topic or facet but by hierarchy, e.g. 'broader' or 'narrower' terms. It might have proved useful if the LC headings list had followed Cutter's example, providing the methods of subdivision were more clearly indicated than they were by Cutter.

SEARS is more alphabetical in its sub-arrangement, but even so, it is not purely alphabetical. Structured headings form a first single sequence, whatever punctuation is used.

> e.g. LAW
>> LAW—AUSTRALIA
>> LAW, CRIMINAL (a *see* reference to CRIMINAL LAW)
>> LAW—U.S.

There follows a second sequence of phrase headings.

> e.g. LAW AS A PROFESSION
>> LAW REFORM.

A personal name, e.g. LAW, Bonar, would precede both subject sequences, while titles, etc., as phrases, would interfile with the LAW phrase subject headings, following Rule 35 of the 1st edition of the ALA filing rules.

Under HISTORY divisions at names of countries, both styles of filing, following Cutter, depart from alphabetical and use a chronological sequence. Chronological subdivision is also used for national literatures, e.g. ENGLISH LITERATURE. But the sub-sequences are introduced first by names of periods, if they exist, then followed by dates. It would be more useful to have dates first, since those are the filing terms, followed by explanatory verbal terms where relevant. Also, an explanatory guide is needed in the catalogue at the start of each chronological sequence, outlining its main divisions.

> e.g. *now*   U.S.—HISTORY—COLONIAL PERIOD—to 1776
>> U.S.—HISTORY—COLONIAL PERIOD—KING WILLIAM'S WAR, 1689-1697
> *preferred*   U.S.—HISTORY—to 1776—COLONIAL PERIOD
>> U.S.—HISTORY—1689-1697—COLONIAL PERIOD—KING WILLIAM'S WAR.

Probably COLONIAL PERIOD could be omitted in any case, especially if given on the preceding guide card. The simple and obvious need to cite components in the order in which they are used is becoming more obvious as attempts at computerisation are made.

AUTHOR, TITLE, SUBJECT

The problem of interfiling a variety of types of heading is notoriously encountered in the single-sequence dictionary catalogue. However, it can also apply in the classified catalogue's alphabetical approaches, especially if subject index entries are interfiled with entries for authors and titles as in BNB and *British catalogue of music*. It is worth noting that in BCM the alphabetical approaches are no longer called merely 'index' and that the alphabetical section now precedes the classified sequence.

The basic problem is best exemplified by place-names. There may possibly be eleven types of heading to be considered.

1. Personal name as author, e.g. LONDON, Jack. Perhaps, even, different people with same surname, e.g. LONDON, Alexander. (Also some form of grouping may be used for voluminous authors, although the possibility of a really prolific author's coinciding with the groups mentioned here is remote.)

2. Personal name as subject, whether or not the person is an author.

3. Place-name as entry word for corporate name as author, e.g. LONDON. County Council; LONDON. City.

4. Place-name as entry word for corporate name as subject. But problems 3 and 4 will diminish in libraries and bibliographies adopting AACR British text, although they will persist in reference construction.

5. Place-name as subject alone, e.g. LONDON.

6. Place-name as subject; entry word for compound heading, e.g. LONDON—ANTIQUITIES.

7. Same place-name, but different place, potentially applicable to items 3, 4, 5 and 6, e.g. LONDON, ONTARIO.

8. Other complications, like the same name as name of a ship, radio station, etc., e.g. LONDON, H.M.S.

9. Place-name as title; alone, or preceding punctuation with filing significance, e.g. LONDON: a guide.

10. Phrases starting with the name, sometimes a title, e.g. The LONDON I love; sometimes subject, e.g. LONDON BRIDGE.

11. Finally, the word may feature as an inverted heading, although this may often be in the form of a reference, e.g. LONDON, FIRE OF.

We could adopt a completely arbitrary word-by-word (or even letter-by-letter) rule for filing. So, for example, all subdivisions of London as a subject would be interfiled between people and bodies whose names started with London, and other places called London would also interfile with the main London subject subdivisions.

e.g. LONDON—ANTIQUITIES

LONDON BRIDGE

LONDON. CITY

LONDON. COUNTY COUNCIL

LONDON—DESCRIPTION

LONDON, Jack

LONDON, OHIO

LONDON—POPULATION

LONDON UNIVERSITY

LONDON—WATER SUPPLY

[etc.]

But even the most literally alphabetical catalogues put personal names first in their own sequence, sub-arranged by forenames or other designations if necessary. The next group chosen for segregation is usually the corporate author, which precedes the name as subject.

The most complex form advocated is that used by the Library of Congress, and as codified in the first edition of the ALA filing rules, Rules 24, 27, 31 and 32.

Summarised, the order emerges as:

PERSON A as author

PERSON A as subject

PERSON B as author

PERSON B as subject

CORPORATE BODY A as author

CORPORATE BODY A as subject

CORPORATE BODY B as author

CORPORATE BODY B as subject

PLACE A as subject

PLACE B (same subdivision as PLACE A)

TITLE, PHRASE, etc.

Full details, with examples, are given in the filing code itself, which must be consulted if it is to be used as a working tool. It should be borne in mind that the same filing code also includes alternatives, providing for fewer sequences. Despite the very high degree of grouping, there is still no distinction between phrases representing subjects and titles. As has been suggested previously in other circumstances, if grouping is desired, it would be helpful if ordinal symbols could be intercalated to make more obvious the method of sub-arrangement. As things are, one sympathises with students who try to rationalise the punctuation used as a mnemonic.

    e.g. 1. Comma (Personal)
       2. Full stop (Corporate)
       3. Dash (Subject)
       4. Nothing (Phrase)

although this does not cater for all circumstances.

BNB INDEX

In general, it has been seen that the conventional dictionary catalogue files complex headings in the order Person; Place; Subject; Title, with added complications caused by the use of different punctuation marks with an arbitrary filing order, e.g.

    WAR (INTERNATIONAL LAW)   [Why not use a dash—?]
    WAR, DECLARATION OF   [Why not WAR—DECLARATION?]
    WAR AND RELIGION   [Why not WAR—RELATIONSHIP—RELIGION?]

BNB has attempted to solve some of these apparent inconsistencies, though possibly not fully, and at the expense of reversing the conventional citation order of: (*a*) 'by'; then (*b*) 'about'. But it has the advantage of giving punctuation consistent significance.

    e.g. (BNB 1965): Dickens, Charles: Fiction: Criticism   823.8
                 Dickens, Charles: Lives   928.238
                 Dickens, Charles. A Christmas carol [etc.]
                 Dickens, Charles. The cricket on the hearth [etc.]

giving a filing order of

    1.   ,   :
    2.   ,   .

A more complex example from BNB (before AACR) is:

    London, Alexander Louis [etc.]
    London: Art: Professional education   378.997d21
    London: Assault: Interrogation methods:
        Criminal investigation [etc. etc.]   351.54rgmd21

London: Town planning   711.4d21
London. *Bishops.* see [etc.]
London. Building Centre [etc.]
London. *City*: History   942.12[1]
London. *County Council* [etc.]
London. National Portrait Gallery [etc.]
London. Whitehall Banqueting House. See [etc.]
London (Red guides). See [etc.]
London and county trades directory. See [etc.]
London Baptist Association   286.d21bp
London in colour. See [etc.]
Londonderry. *County*   914.162

The basic citation order is therefore:

1. Personal author: 'about'
2. Personal author. 'by'
3. Place: subject
4. Place. Corporate author
5. Series as designated by ( )
6. Phrases, e.g. titles and corporate authors.

(Also, overall word-by-word alphabetisation is used, as commonly found elsewhere.)

Bearing in mind the sequential scanning advantage of the printed catalogue form, BNB offers a plausible arrangement. The chief reservation, as with other grouped methods, is that some users may prefer a more strictly alphabetical arrangement.

POSITION OF REFERENCES

In the dictionary catalogue in the past, *see also* references have normally come after all the entries for documents at a heading, but before sub-headings of the simple heading.

e.g. CROWDS
     [entry for document]
     CROWDS *see also* RIOTS.

A complaint against this is that one might have to turn over (assuming cards) many entries at a certain heading before coming to the reference one is really seeking. Therefore, the references might be filed before the entries. But the argument against this method is that the novice is referred away from a heading before even knowing what is actually entered under that heading. The first edition of the ALA filing rules preferred the former. However, the second edition has decided that *see also* references shall now precede entries under the same term (Rule 35c).

    e.g. CHILDREN   *see also* [etc.]
        CHILDREN
        CHILDREN, ADOPTED
        CHILDREN—CARE AND HYGIENE   *see also* [etc.]
        CHILDREN—CARE AND HYGIENE
        [etc.]

A solution would be to follow the second edition ruling, but that a 'weaker' term than 'see also' should be used, e.g. 'related headings' as in modern thesauri.

ALA RULES FOR FILING CATALOG CARDS, 2ND EDITION

Examples so far have been taken for the most part from codes and catalogues or bibliographies which are easily accessible—and which should be referred to by the student to get his own examples for criticism.

But a new filing code appeared in 1968, unheralded and perhaps unnoticed through being overshadowed by the more epoch-making AACR. This 2nd edition of the ALA rules is available as a full version of 260 pages, or as an abridged version of 94 pages. The latter 'mini' edition should be all that is necessary for most purposes of study—and even of use—as the rules themselves are the same in both editions. The code is as yet comparatively unknown, and a brief summary of its general attitude is given here, because it is revolutionary in its own quiet way.

Throughout, a much more directly alphabetical principle is followed. At last, it seems, the dictionary catalogue (for which basically the code is intended) has thrown off the classified catalogue complex which bedevilled the first edition, especially in its more 'grouped' alternative rules. In fact, 60 per cent of the rules in the first edition allowed alternatives. The later edition, unlike the permissive AACR, allows very few alternatives. Librarians who dislike its strict alphabetical flavour will presumably ignore it. As the Preface says (p. iv): 'From the filer's point of view, the simpler arrangements of the straight alphabetical order should result in more accurately filed catalogues; from the user's point of view, the inflexible order of the alphabet presents a uniform order that can easily be understood'. However, inflexible order is unhelpful if it is followed for its own sake, and it seems that the Preface misses the point of strict alphabetical entry. The real reason for direct alphabetical arrangement is the same reason for having the dictionary catalogue. Any sort of non-alphabetical grouping gets away from the basic primary objective of the dictionary catalogue and shows lack of faith in it.

One non-alphabetical principle allowed in the new code is that where a name is a surname of both a person and of non-personal entities, the personal headings are filed in their own sub-sequence before other uses of the word, which then form a second sub-sequence. The full edition of the code explains why: complete names (presumably forenames) may not be known, and 'a small number of surname entries would be rather lost scattered through long files of subject place-name and/or other entries beginning with the same word' (p. 93).

One other basic factor—also potentially disputable—is that the code is intended primarily for manual filing, and so takes little account of mechanisation of catalogue data. This seems particularly unfortunate, especially since the code was published in the same year in which the Library of Congress initiated its experimental Project MARC. Surely it would be more useful to accommodate the very fast but unreasoning characteristics of the computer than to bother to tell us that 'The +mas star for the poor' is filed as 'The Christmas star for the poor' (full edition, p. 38).

Most of the code consists of exemplifications of how alphabetical arrangement is applied: possibly as a reaction against the old code spelt out in black and white, e.g. having stated that strict alphabetical arrangement under surname is the rule, it should not really be necessary to demonstrate that SMITH, Captain, files after SMITH, Adam, and before SMITH, Chester. However, bearing in mind the basic assumption of 'nothing before something', it is surprising to find that HOMER, Winslow, files before HOMER alone, because it includes a comma, while HOMER alone is not a surname—although we must expect it to come before HOMER AND HISTORY, since personal names are in a separate sub-sequence from other entries.

The following example demonstrates the effect of the strict alphabetical sub-arrangement, demonstrated by the code on the whole:

GERMANY—BIBLIOGRAPHY
GERMANY (DEMOCRATIC REPUBLIC)
GERMANY—DESCRIPTION AND TRAVEL
GERMANY, EASTERN—DESCRIPTION AND TRAVEL
GERMANY (FEDERAL REPUBLIC)—DESCRIPTION AND TRAVEL
GERMANY, NORTHERN
GERMANY (TERRITORY UNDER ALLIED OCCUPATION, 1945-1955)—
    POLITICS AND GOVERNMENT.

As might be expected, the second edition reverses the highly grouped rulings of the first edition, resulting in:

COOKERY
COOKERY, AMERICAN
COOKERY (APPLES)
COOKERY, CHINESE
COOKERY—DICTIONARIES
COOKERY FOR DIABETICS
COOKERY, INTERNATIONAL
COOKERY—YEARBOOKS.

Though we may not complain about this rule in itself, it seems pointless to retain the different types of punctuation, e.g. ( ); —; and , . Though it is occasionally necessary, as in the example given earlier of POLICE, STATE and POLICE STATE. In fact, this problem could be obviated by using a *see also* reference, i.e. POLICE *see also* STATE POLICE. If consistently structured headings were used, ambiguity would not often be encountered; would any but a pedant regard COOKERY—DIABETICS as meaning how to cook diabetics? (Or cannibals?)

There is one exception to the alphabetical sub-arrangement of subject headings: a sub-heading consisting of a number precedes verbal ones.

    e.g. EDUCATION—1975-
then EDUCATION—AFRICA

This is notwithstanding the rules that numerals as entry words are filed as spoken, which if applied consistently here would give

    EDUCATION—AFRICA
then EDUCATION—[NINETEEN SEVENTY-FIVE-] 1975-

Another, more used, example of non-alphabetical arrangement is that historical periods following HISTORY as a sub-heading are still arranged chronologically. Unfortunately, the conventional practice is still followed of assuming that the citation order of the components of such headings need not coincide with the used order, i.e. sub-filing is by dates, but these follow the verbal name for the period. While sympathising with the codifiers that they do not decide heading structure, surely before the code was compiled, cataloguers could have redesigned such headings. Again, this perpetuation of illogical practices makes it that much harder to computerise catalogue compilation.

A final point, this time in favour, is the recommendation in the code that explanatory cards should be included at the start of a sequence to clarify the fact that references precede a heading alone.

Almost all that has been said here about the new filing code could apply to the one-sequence alphabetical auxiliaries of the classified catalogue.

A general conclusion is that the new code is to be welcomed, because it should result in a catalogue which is straightforward to use. However, advance collaboration in the future between codifiers of filing rules, compilers of subject headings, and codifiers of author-title rules, could result in tools of all types which are even more straightforward both to apply and to use. The time has long since arrived when there should be one code which gives rules for both construction of headings and of filing, and which caters at the same time for computerisation of catalogue data.

FILING AS AFFECTED BY CLASSIFICATION: CHAIN INDEXING

The chain index reflects the classification scheme from which it is derived, but in reverse order: as a student once put it, the citation order of the index terms is a mirror image of the notation. So, using UDC for a document on research in geography in the twentieth century, one has:

(a) TWENTIETH CENTURY: RESEARCH: GEOGRAPHY   911.001.5"19"
(b) RESEARCH: GEOGRAPHY   911.001.5
(c) GEOGRAPHY   911

TWENTIETH CENTURY and RESEARCH may not be helpful entry terms in this particular context, and we may prefer:

GEOGRAPHY   911
RESEARCH   911.001.5
TWENTIETH CENTURY   911.001.5"19"

all on the same entry card, filed at GEOGRAPHY. Examples like this— needing manipulation of the 'mechanical' order—could be multiplied infinitely, especially using chain procedure in constructing a dictionary catalogue, or in indexing periodical articles in the abstract, i.e. with no overt dependence on a classification scheme.

This problem, although fairly simple in this example, can become very complex when considering the great number of possible entries under common entry terms. The problem may be pursued in COATES, chapters XI and XII.

In particular, citation and hence filing of index terms may vary for the same subject, but when classified by different classification schemes.

e.g. (*a*) LC produces:

> DU 112.4   History—Australia—Naval

while

> (*b*) DC produces:
> 359.00994 Public administration—Navies—History—Australia

resulting respectively in:

> (*a*) LC: NAVIES: AUSTRALIA: HISTORY   DU 112.4

and

> (*b*) DC: AUSTRALIA: HISTORY: NAVIES: ADMINISTRATION [!]
>   359.00994

or, say,

> AUSTRALIA: HISTORY, NAVAL   359.00994

since the 'Public administration' element is irrelevant. Obviously, the rest of the chain, hence filing, is affected.

Note, incidentally, that KENNEDY is at variance with the entry word which emerges from the LC-dictated entry—see his Rule 29 (page 71): '. . . place may not be indexed as a sub-heading under a subject'. Presumably his rule assumes that place is always a distributed relative. This does not always apply in LC, although scrutiny of its classification schedules implies that the ultimate citation order emerged (like the British Empire) in a fit of absentmindedness.

The perceptive cataloguer may advantageously manipulate filing and citation orders, but he should remember that he is not immortal, and his variations from 'mechanical' production of chain index entries should be recorded and specifically pin-pointed for the benefit of successors.

A final reminder: a classification scheme may be inconsistent in its degree of specificity for, say, individual literary authors. DC gives Shakespeare his own number at 822.33, but Dylan Thomas gets as far as only 821.91—modern English poetry. Hence in the subject index we may have:

SHAKESPEARE, WILLIAM: PLAYS: ENGLISH LITERATURE   822.33

but

THOMAS, DYLAN: POETRY: ENGLISH LITERATURE   821.91
                                                          THO

(or perhaps ANGLO-WELSH LITERATURE, since Dylan Thomas was a Welsh poet writing in English).

These are examples of the ways in which a classification scheme can affect cataloguing and indexing and filing. Others have been mentioned in previous sections of this chapter and further examples may be worked out by the student.

CHAPTER 25

Physical Forms of Catalogues

The term 'physical form' of a catalogue can be as narrow or as broad as one wishes: it could range from (*a*) an exercise book written up by a teacher acting as spare-time 'librarian' in a small school library, to (*b*) a computer storage unit, with users being 'on line' to it via the use of consols. However, what is not relevant here is the internal arrangement of the entries in a catalogue. It is evident, therefore, that this section is relevant in all types and sizes of library, but that it must be interpreted realistically depending on which library is postulated either in practice or in an examination question.

It is proposed: (*a*) to name the criteria in assessing physical forms of catalogue; (*b*) to name and describe the main forms available; then (*c*) to compare (*a*) and (*b*).

POSSIBLE REQUIREMENTS OF A PHYSICAL FORM OF CATALOGUE

Some of these contradict each other, so a compromise is necessary in the ultimate choice of physical form.

1. Flexibility:
    (*a*) inserting new entries;
    (*b*) removing old entries;
    (*c*) removing and reinserting for:
        (i) change of stock from one location to another;
        (ii) amendments, which may be infrequent and so insignificant, or which may be a large-scale operation, e.g. adopting a new catalogue code.

2. Not occupy much space: there should be room for expansion of the catalogue during the library's estimated life.

3. Be easily accessible to all users, however many wish to use it at once, and wherever they may be.

4. Portable.

5. Be available in multiple copies (see also 3).

6. Be convenient, quick and cheap to reproduce.

7. If required, copies for use by users of the library in their houses and offices, and for use in other libraries.

8. Quick, easy, accurate and convenient to use.

9. Inexpensive to maintain: as to staff time, permanent and consumable equipment; space occupied is also relevant here.

10. Facilitate inter-library and intra-library cooperation, e.g. allow for physical interfiling of entries with those of other libraries.

11. Usable in conjunction with bibliographies and indexes, whether individually compiled or published. (Possible overlap here with internal arrangement.)

A basic contradiction seems to be emerging at the moment. Some library systems are tending towards having a copy of a full union catalogue at all major service points. Conversely, other systems are tending towards a single union catalogue at the Central or Headquarters library, combined with a quite sophisticated means of receiving enquiries quickly and accurately, e.g. by teleprinter, from major service points. The latter form is more akin in principle to what is usually assumed will happen ultimately: that of service points being 'on line' with computer storage catalogues.

PHYSICAL FORMS COMMONLY AVAILABLE FOR EXAMINATION

Summary, as dealt with here.

1. Printed conventionally: bound book form.
2. Printed: looseleaf.
3. Printed: guardbook or pasted slip.
4. Sheaf.
5. Card.
6. Visible index: all of each entry visible.
7. Visible index: other.

1. Printed: Bound book form

One of the best known examples is the British Museum's *General catalogue of printed books*. This catalogue in the past was printed from normal relief type. In the mid-1950's it was realised that this method was impossibly slow, and, in mid-edition, a change was made to a new method. This entailed photographing the B.M.'s guardbook catalogue slips, manipulating the entries to make their appearance neat and uniform, and then printing them (conventionally) by litho-offset. The facsimile on page 298 demonstrates the excellence of the method. Unfortunately the catalogue of 263 volumes is now out of print, and present-day purchasers must make do with the *Readex Compact* edition—a much-reduced facsimile copy of the original: see facsimile, page 299.

The printed form in general was customary until about 1900-1910, after which it was rapidly replaced in many libraries by the card, or sometimes sheaf, catalogue. Some libraries continued producing printed forms of their catalogues through the period of their being out of fashion, only to realise in the mid-1940's that they were in fashion again: the Library of Congress had produced a printed and bound catalogue of its stock, although from cards, and this of course made printed catalogues 'in' in all libraries which bought copies—throughout the world. (See facsimile on page 300.) Since then, many libraries have produced printed catalogues, often from cards, and often by a photo-litho-offset process. At present, there is a growing tendency towards computer-printed catalogues. Although the method of producing the 'master' copy is not 'conventional', the off-printing of the number of copies required usually employs conventional methods, e.g. photo-litho-offset, or today's near-conventional methods, e.g. xerographic printing. So this category of printed catalogue can be included in this section if one wishes. It is further expanded on in Section VI, on Mechanisation.

The bibliographic value of printed catalogues is usually taken for granted—this is why libraries buy them—but one feels it should be emphasised, even to the point of using the term 'bibliographic catalogues' to cover printed catalogues intended for sale to other libraries for use as bibliographies. A great deal of space can, of course, be taken up by the great catalogues—the B.M. one, with its 4 million entries in 263 volumes, is one of the largest single publications in the world. Yet large research libraries may well need both the B.M. and the Library of Congress printed catalogues, since there is only about a 25 per cent overlap between the two. In addition, many special libraries' printed catalogues may also be needed if they are relevant to a library's activities. The supply, and need for, bibliographic catalogues is likely to increase, and librarians will find themselves faced by the increasing cost of purchase, of space, and of use, of these tools. One could mention, in passing,

367

GERMANY. [Laws, etc.—i. General.]

—— Traité sistematique touchant la connoissance de l'état du saint Empire Romain de la nation Allemande, ou le droit public de cet empire, tiré des loix fondamentales de la jurisprudence politique, *etc.* [By C. L. Scheidt.] tom. I.–III. *Hanovre,* 1751, 52. 8°.   **501. c. 18–20.** *Imperfect; wanting tom. 4.*

—— Le Droit Public Germanique.   Où l'on voit l'état présent de l'Empire, ses principales loix et constitutions, *etc.*   Avec une dissertation sur la jurisdiction de l'Empereur, une autre sur la forme du gouvernement du corps Germanique, et une troisième sur le Ban de l'Empire. [By E. De Mauvillon.] 2 tom. *Amsterdam,* 1756. 12°.   **229. b. 6.**

—— Johann Jacob Schmaussens ... Corpus Juris Publici S. R. Imperii Academicum, enthaltend des heil. Röm. Reichs deutscher Nation Grund-Gesetze, nebst einem Auszuge der Reichs-Abschiede, anderer Reichs-Schlüsse und Vergleiche. Neue . . . vermehrte Auflage, durch H. G. Franken und G Schumann. *Leipzig,* 1774. 8°.   **1234. f. 7.**

—— Johann Heinrich Ludwig Bergius Sammlung auserlesener teutschen Landesgesetze, welche das Policey- und Cameralwesen zum Gegenstande haben. (Fortgesetzt von Johann Beckmann.) Erstes (–elftes) Alphabet. *Frankfurt,* 1781–89. 4°.   **28. i. 2.** *Imperfect ; wanting Alphabets* 12–14.

—— Repertorium des Teutschen Staats und Lehnrechts, ehemals von einer Gesellschaft ungenannter Gelehrten mit einer Vorrede des Herrn Buders herausgegeben, nunmehro aber mit Zusäzzen und neuen Artikeln weit über die Hälfte vermehrt und durchaus verbessert. (Tl. 1, 2. Von D. Heinrich Godfried Scheidemantel. Tl. 3, 4. Von D. Carl Friedrich Häberlin.) 4 Tl. *Leipzig,* 1782–95. 4°.   **1234. i. 1–4.**

—— Codice, ossia collezione sistematica di tutti le leggi ed ordinanze emanate sotto il regno di Sua Maestà Imperiale Giuseppe II., tanto in affari secolari, quanto ecclesiastici

11. Extracts from British Museum printed catalogue.

11 (*a*). Full size.

367

GERMANY. [Laws, etc.—i. General.]

—— Traité sistematique touchant la connoissance de l'état du saint Empire Romain de la nation Allemande, ou le droit public de cet empire, tiré des loix fondamentales de la jurisprudence politique, *etc.* [By C. L. Scheidt.] tom i.-iii. *Hanover*, 1751, 52. 8°. **501.** c. **16-30.** *Imperfect; wanting tom.* 4.

—— Le Droit Public Germanique. Où l'on voit l'état présent de l'Empire, ses principales loix et constitutions, *etc.* Avec une dissertation sur la juridiction de l'Empereur, une autre sur la forme du gouvernement du corps Germanique, et une troisième sur le Ban de l'Empire. [By E. De Mauvillon.] 2 tom. *Amsterdam*, 1756. 12°. **228.** b. **6.**

—— Johann Jacob Schmaussens ... Corpus Juris Publici S. R. Imperii Academicum, enthaltend die Röm. Reichs deutscher Nation Grund-Gesetze, nebst einem Auszuge der Reichs-Abschiede, anderer Reichs-Schlüsse und Vergleiche. Neue . . . vermehrte Auflage, durch H. G. Franken und G. Schumann. *Leipzig*, 1774. 8°. **1234.** f. **7.**

—— Johann Heinrich Ludwig Bergius Sammlung auserlesener teutschen Landesgesetze, welche das Policey- und Cameralwesen zum Gegenstand haben (Fortgesetzt von Johann Beckmann.) Erstes (-elftes) Alphabet. *Frankfurt*, 1781-89. 4°. **28.** i. **2.** *Imperfect; wanting Alphabete* 12-14.

—— Repertorium des Teutschen Staats und Lehnrechts, ehemals von einer Gesellschaft ungenannter Gelehrten mit einer Vorrede des Herrn Ruders herausgegeben, nunmehro aber mit Zusätzen und neuen Artikeln weit über die Hälfte vermehrt und durchaus verbessert. (Tl. 1, 2. Von D. Heinrich Godfried Scheidemantel. Tl. 3, 4. Von D. Carl Friedrich Haberlin.) 4 Tl. *Leipzig*, 1782-95. 4°. **1234.** i. **1-4.**

—— Codice, ossia collezione sistematica di tutti le leggi ed ordinanze emanate sotto il regno di Sua Maestà Imperiale Giuseppe ii., tanto in affari secolari, quanto ecclesiastici per tutti gli Stati ereditarj, . . . tradotta dal Tedesco da B. Borroni. (Appendice.— Continuazione. Tom. 1.) 9 tom. *Milano*, 1786-89. 8°. **504.** a. **21-23.**

—— [Another copy of tom. 1.] **230.** i. **25.**

—— Recueil, précieux et unique, des loix fondamentales de l'Empire, servant à l'illustration du droit public d'Allemagne, *etc.* 2 tom. *Strasbourg*, 1787. 8°. **230.** a. **21, 22.**

—— Epistolæ Imperatorum, et Regum Hungariæ Ferdinandi primi et Maximiliani secundi ad suos in Porta Ottomanica Oratores Antonium Verantium, Franciscum Zay, Augerium Busbek, Albertium Wiss et Christophorum Teuffenpach. [1553-1572.] Quas ex autographis edidit J. F. de Miller. pp. 454. *Pestini*, 1808. 8°. **10910.** g. **20.**

—— Francorum Regum, Imperatorum, divi-o Imperio, capitularia Au. 840-921. *See* Misne (J. P.) Patrologiæ Cursus Completus, *etc.* tom. 138. (Appendix.) 1844, *etc.* 4°. **2000.** c.

—— Das Keyserrecht, nach der Handschrift von 1372 in Vergleichung mit andern Handschriften und mit erläuternden Anmerkungen herausgegeben von Dr H. E. Endemann . . . und mit einer Vorrede versehen von Dr B. Hildebrand. pp. lxii. 256. *Cassel*, 1846. 8°. **5510.** d. **7.**

—— Historia diplomatica Frederici Secundi, sive constitutiones, privilegia, mandata . . . que superaunt istius Imperatoris et filiorum ejus, *etc.* 1852, *etc.* 4°. *See* Huillard-Bréholles (J. L. A.) **10705.** h.

368

GERMANY. [Laws, etc.—i. General.]

—— Der Congress von Soissons. Nach den Instructionen des Kaiserlichen Cabinetes und den Berichten des Kaiserl. Botschafters Stefan Grafen Kinsky. [1729-32.] Herausgegeben von C. Höfler. 1871-76. *Oesterreichische See* Vienna.—*Akademie der Wissenschaften.* Fontes Rerum Austriacarum, *etc.* Abth. 2. Bde. 32 & 38. 1843, *etc.* 8°. Ac. **810/9.**

—— Reichs-Gesetzblatt. 1871. no. 19(-1944. Tl. 1 no. 58, Tl. 2 no. 19). [1871-1944.] 4°. *See infra: Reichskanzler-Amt.* 8. **506.** e.

—— Gesetz-Sammlung für das Deutsche Reich. 1867 bis 1871 incl. Chronologische Zusammenstellung der in den Bundes-Gesetzblatte des Norddeutschen Bundes und dem Reichs-Gesetzblatte des Deutschen Reiches für die Jahre 1867 bis eins-hliesslich 1871 enthaltenen Gesetze, Verordnungen, Erlasse und Publikanda. Mit vollständigem alphabetischem Sach-Register. *Berlin*, 1872. 4°. **5605.** f. **27.**

—— Recueil des traités, conventions . . . et autres actes relatifs à la paix avec l'Allemagne. 1872, *etc.* 8°. *See* France. [Collections of Laws, *etc.* n] **9078** a 1.

—— Traités de la France avec l'Allemagne. Janvier 1871 à Octobre, 1873. 1873. 8°. *See* France. [Collections of Laws, *etc.*] **9078.** f. **27.**

—— Die Gesetze und Verordnungen nebst den sonstigen Erlassen für den preussischen Staat und das deutsche Reich . . . Chronologisch Zusammengestellt . . . von G. A. Grotefend. (Das gesammte preuss-isch-deutsche Gesetzgebungs-Material.—Das gesamte deutsche und preussische Gesetzgebungs-Material. Herausgegeben von Dr. C. Cretschmar, 1903, *etc.*) *Cöln & Neuss*, 1876, *etc.* 8°.

—— —— General-Register, 1876-1895, [*etc.*] *Düsseldorf*, [187-] 8°. **05604.bb.**

—— Die Gesetzgebung des Deutschen Reiches mit Erläuterungen In Verbindung mit Prof. Dr. Endemann, Dr. v. Holtzendorff . . . und Anderen herausgegeben von Dr. Ernst Bezold (Tl. 2 Bd. 2, Tl. 3. Bd. 6 von Oscar Meves). 3 Tl.

Tl. 1. Bürgerliche Recht	11 Bd.	4 Ergänzungshft. 1879 [1875]-1904
Tl. 2. Staats- und Verwaltungsrecht.	3 Bd.	1881 [1874]-90.
Tl. 3. Strafrecht	6 Bd.	1877 [1874]-89.

Erlangen, 1877 [1874]-1904. 8°. [MISSING]

—— Die Urkunden der deutschen Könige und Kaiser. *See* Germany.—*Gesellschaft für ältere deutsche Geschichtskunde.* Monumenta Germaniae historica, *etc.* Diplomatum Regum et Imperatorum Germaniae tomus 1, *etc.* **2017.b.** 1877, *etc.* 4°.

—— Denkschrift und Aktenstücke, betreffend zwei bewaffnete Angriffe auf Kaiserliche Konsularbeamte in Leon, Nicaragua, im Oktober und November 1876. pp. 36. [1878] fol. **5510.** f. **15.**

—— Reichsgesetze [which modify and amplify the Code Civil of France]. *See* France.4 Der Code Civil, *etc.* 1883. 8°. **5606.** aaa. **9.** [Laws, etc.—i.—Code Civil.]

—— Guttentag'sche Sammlung deutscher Reichsgesetze. Text-Ausgaben mit Anmerkungen. *Berlin*, 1883- 8° & 16°. **2227.** b. 1. *etc.* & **05656.** e. 1, *etc.* *The volumes are of various editions.*

11 (*b*). Compact edition. (Readex Microprint Ltd.)

Actual size of text.

:ари от старо

ори")

vreme.

aravelov i nego-
ot staro vreme."
66–92373

академия на

Етнографски

—Plovdiv.

ovdivski tavani.
66–86935

оск ва, Совет-

: Svetlye goroda.
66–94280

думка, 1965.

СР. Институт
тного. А. А.

eet sugar.

aGi11 sakhara.
66–88861

osudar-
i. Ukaza-
›itel'nykh

tures. 2. Chyzhevs'kyĭ, Dmytro, 1894–
I. Weintraub, Wiktor, ed. II. Winkel, Hans
Jürgen zum, ed. III. Chyzhevs'kyĭ, Dmytro,
1894–
CtY NNC NjR ICU   NUC67–1056
CtW MCM NIC

Gerigk, Wolfgang, 1934–
    Die vollziehende Gewalt in der Staatstheorie Lorenz v.
Steins; ein Beitrag zur Bestimmung der vollziehenden
Gewalt im modernen Staat. München, 1966.
    ₁14₁, 81 p. 21 cm.
    Inaug.-Diss.—Münster.
    Vita.
    Bibliography: prelim. p. ₁5₁–₁13₁
    1. Stein, Lorenz Jacob von, 1815–1890. 2. Executive power.
I. Title.
    JC234.S724G4   66–31624

Gering, Leonard, joint author
    see Cowen, Denis Victor. Cowen on the law
of negotiable instruments in South Africa.
4th ed. Cape Town, Juta, 1966.

Gerke, Friedrich, 1900–
    Das Christusmosaik in der Laurentius-Kapelle der Galla
Placidia in Ravenna. Stuttgart, Reclam (1965)
    32 p. with illus., ₁12₁ leaves of illus. 16 cm. (Werkmonographien
zur bildenden Kunst, Nr. 104) DM 1.80
                                               (GDB 66–A25–236)
    Reclams Universal-Bibliothek, Nr. B9104.
    "Daten und Quellenhinweise": p. 28–32.
    1. Ravenna. Mausoleo di Galla Placidia. I. Title.
    NA6167.R3G4   66–66311
    MH

Germain, François, ed.
    see Balzac, Honoré de, 1799–1850. L'Enfant
maudit. Paris, les Belles lettres, 1965.

Germany (Democratic Republic, 1949–   )
    Fachstelle für Heimatmuseen
    see Fachlich-methodische Anleitungen für die
Arbeit in den Heimatmuseen. Halle (Saale)

Germany (Democratic Republic, 1949–   )
    Institut für Fachschulwesen
    see Reusch, Karl. Lehrbuch der Elektro-
technik. Berlin, Verlag Technik, 1966–

Germany (*Democratic Republic, 1949–*   ) *Laws, statutes,
etc.*
    Baurecht; Arbeitsschutz im Bauwesen; gesetzliche Be-
stimmungen. Bearbeiter: Kurt Linkhorst. Berlin, Verlag
für Bauwesen, 1965.
    180 p. 30 cm. (Deutsche Bau-Enzyklopädie)
    At head of title: Ministerium für Bauwesen. Deutsche Bauakademie.
    Running title: Arbeitsschutz im Bauwesen.
    Bibliographical footnotes.
    1. Construction industry—Safety regulations—Germany (Democratic Republic, 1949–   ) I. Linkhorst, Kurt, ed. II. Title.
    III. Title: Arbeitsschutz im Bauwesen.
                                               66–91219

Staucebau unu Rau
see Weigler, Hel:
Berlin, Vertrieb (

Germany (Federal Re
    Bundesverfassung:
    des Bundesverfass
    see Hofmann, Kla
gen des Bundesver
    Bundesverwaltung:
chen u. Berlin, B(

Germany (Federal Re
    Bundesverwaltung:
    (Indexes)
    see Hofmann, Kla
gen des Bundesver
    Bundesverwaltung:
chen u. Berlin, B(

Germany (*Federal Repi*
    Aktiengesetz 1965.
    übersetzt und eingelei
    Galbraith. Frankfur
    502 p. 21 cm. DM 49.

    Added t.-p. : The Germa
    Label mounted on adde
    Fred B. Rothman & Co., S
    1. Corporation law—G(
    Müller, Rudolf, 1904–
    IV. Title: The German sto(

Germany (*Federal Repu*
    Arbeitsschutzgesetze,
    schluss, Jugendarbeits
    schutz. Textausg. mit
    Sachverzeichnis. 9., v
    gesetz in den beiden, f
    sungen. Stand vom 1
    Beck, 1966.
    181 p. 20 cm. (Beck's(

    1. Hours of labor—G
    2. Labor laws and legisl(
) I. Title.

Germany (*Federal Repu*
    Das Ausländergesetz
    lichen Vorschriften.
    München u. Berlin, Be(
    xx, 817 p. 23 cm. DM

    Bibliography: p. xix–₁x₁
    1. Aliens—Germany (F.
    Political — Legal status,
    1949–   ) I. Kanein, V

12. Extract from Library of Congress printed catalog: *National union catalog.*

13. 'Rotadex' rotary card catalogue.

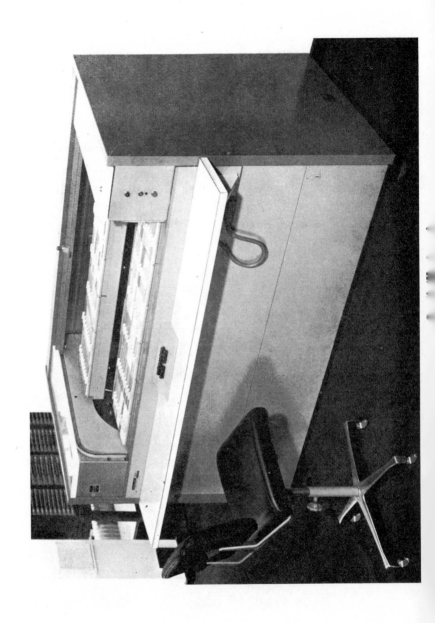

the bibliographic value of certain old manuscript-compiled catalogues, sometimes available in facsimile or printed form, though their use is usually confined to the study of the history of libraries and their collections, and so is not directly relevant here.

Characteristics of the printed catalogue

1. It is the least flexible of all physical forms. Insertions, deletions, and corrections of entries in a volume itself are virtually impossible, except when a library's own copies are corrected by hand. Even then, the results would be untidy. The only practical solutions are (a) the issue of supplementary volumes—entailing in use repeat-checking under the required heading in all sequences; or (b) frequent revised editions—entailing a great deal of waste of materials and expense. It may be that some libraries will get into the habit of very short entries, even a 'title-a-line' annual version and cumulation, and computer compilation and printing. The capital outlay in such cases would be great, and the whole situation may possibly be completely overtaken by a more sophisticated use of computers—especially in the large research libraries which one has in mind for the type of use of printed catalogues envisaged here. Also, the form is useful for comparatively static collections, like many film and record libraries.

2. This form is the most economical of space, with the possible exception of a computer magnetic tape or similar machine-readable record—but with all that that implies in making ready use of it. For example, one volume of the full-size B.M. catalogue contains some 15,000 entries, the equivalent of perhaps 15 average card catalogue drawers. (We are ignoring here the number of entries per document.)

3. It can be easily accessible to all users, especially when made available in multiple copies. It can be the most physically convenient form to use, since one can sit at a table or desk and read it like a book, since it is one.

4. It is portable in principle. However, the validity of portability has to be practical: both as to number of volumes in the catalogue, and as to size of each volume. However, even a heavy volume can be more easily taken to the shelves than, say, a card drawer.

5. This form is more easily made available in multiple copies than any other form. The fact that a large number of copies can be printed and sold itself makes the production of bibliographic catalogues

feasible. A printed, or duplicated, subject index can be made available at several points within a library.

6. This form can be the most convenient and economical to reproduce, although the production of the original master may be inconvenient and expensive, whether in time and skill or machinery. Ultimate economy is directly related to item 5, above.

7. The question of having copies available outside the 'home' library is parallel with portability—as far as individuals are concerned, and with economy, as mentioned in items 5 and 6 above. Some printed catalogues are produced specifically for individual members who use the library by post, e.g. the catalogue of Lewis's Medical, Scientific and Technical Lending Library.

8. The well-produced printed catalogue is the best for convenience in use. As already mentioned (item 3) the user can sit or stand comfortably at a desk—compare this with the contortions necessary to read the last card in a bottom drawer of a card catalogue, especially if someone equally impatient is already using a nearby drawer. However, until very recently, computer-printed catalogues have been ugly and hard to read compared with a conventional type-printed surface. Also, some computer catalogues use the print-out from the computer full-size, with a resultant bulky oblong format, with each entry taking up one very long line of type. Some libraries have experimented with photographically reducing the surface, and then reproducing it, e.g. Aston University Library, Birmingham. This process may result in a more pleasing and legible image, since unwanted gaps and irregularities in the image are thereby closed up. With computer-photo-typesetting the computer-compiled catalogue has access to the variety of size, styles and formats available in other printing. This method is already in use in the medical indexing service MEDLARS and is being experimented with (1969) in the Newcastle University Computer Unit in Britain.

An important factor is the ability to scan many entries, one after the other, quickly, if possible at one glance. This, sequential scanning, is achieved better by the printed catalogue than any other form, perhaps even if the lines of type are overlong and not very clear.

9. In maintenance, the printed catalogue can be the least convenient, for reasons already mentioned. However, once plant and programmes have been established, computer-catalogues at least may prove ultimately to be more economical than some members of the profession realise. Hard-headed, practical librarians are already claiming great savings in

staff time, even when compiling copies only for 'home' library use. As the years go by, it may well be that the only way of maintaining a 'hard-copy' catalogue effectively will be to partake of centrally produced computer-readable data as a basis for local catalogues, and, likely for the next few years, these will be in printed-book form.

10. The entries in a conventionally printed catalogue are the least convenient for use in inter-library cooperation if interfiling of entries is necessary, say in a card or sheaf catalogue. However, at the other end of the spectrum, some union catalogues, e.g. the Library of Congress's *National union catalog* and the *British union catalogue of periodicals*, could not conveniently be used in the way they are if they were not in book form. NUC in printed form was specifically designed to replace, and enlarge on, the sets of cards previously deposited at major library and cooperation centres throughout the world, e.g. the National Central Library in London and the University of Sydney Library.

11. The book form catalogue is probably the most convenient to use in conjunction with bibliographies, indexes, etc., because they too are almost always in book form. They can be shelved adjacent to each other and sequentially scanned side by side. But the internal arrangement of entries can be relevant, although details need not be enlarged upon here.

Summary and prognosis

The printed book catalogue has a longer and more successful history than any other form, its only major disadvantage in comparison with other forms being its lack of flexibility. It is now having a renaissance, and its renewed popularity is likely to increase more and more until this form starts to be replaced by catalogues in the form of computer storage units.

2. Printed: looseleaf

This form usually consists of separate pages, probably produced by some form of documentary reproduction, e.g. wax stencil or litho stencil duplicator, and with entries made by normal typewriter or more sophisticated form such as a Varietyper. Or the pages could be produced by less conventional means. The pages are held in the cover by a temporary or 'near-binding' method, the simplest being ring-binding as in ordinary notebooks, or by 'posts' as in the sheaf catalogue—similar to the method used in *Keesing's contemporary archives*. Ring-binding facilitates flat-lying and use of all the surface of a page, but is less secure and neat than post-binding, which, however, does not usually permit flat opening and which necessitates wide inner margins.

The looseleaf form has been used in the past in libraries with many service points, e.g. the late Middlesex County Library, and at one time in the State Library of Western Australia. It may be used for union catalogues, e.g. for the two national union catalogues of serials in Australia: one for scientific and technical, the other for humanities and social sciences. In general, it is decreasing in popularity, partly because of the increasing use of short-life computer-printed catalogues with cheap, non-sewn (so-called 'perfect') bindings.

Characteristics of the looseleaf catalogue

1. More flexible than the bound printed form, since it can be up-dated page by page, and not only as a whole.

2. Occupies slightly more space than bound printed form, but less than other forms.

3. It can be easily accessible to all users, especially if available at one service point in multiple copies. It is rather less physically convenient to use, especially in the 'post'-bound form, but is more convenient than other forms.

4. Portability: heavier and bulkier than printed bound form. Otherwise similar to it.

5. Easily available in multiple copies.

6. Probably more convenient to produce than printed bound form, since it can be produced, or revised, page by page. In itself, it is cheaper to produce because plant and labour are cheaper, as compared with the printed bound form. Typing stencils for pages is easier than typing cards or slips, with their inconvenience of handling of unit records. Most libraries have duplicators, while they do not have their own type-setting machinery or computers, so the looseleaf form does not have to be a special 'batch job' with an extra-mural or parent organisation.

7. Copies can be made available to individual users. See also item 7 under 'Printed bound book form'.

8. Nearly as convenient to use as printed bound form, e.g. for sequential scanning. But the form can be physically inconvenient, through weight and bulk, and especially if of the 'post' sort. Sequential

scanning may be less convenient when a page has been split, resulting in only half-filled pages.

9. Very convenient to maintain, since (*a*) page-by-page work is possible and (*b*) local plant is usually available.

10. Most of what is said in item 10 under 'Printed bound book form' applies. Note too that some of the examples mentioned in the introduction to this form are union catalogues.

11. Nearly as convenient as the printed bound book form for use in conjunction with bibliographies, etc.

3. Printed: guardbook or pasted slip

The basis of this form is the looseleaf book, with particularly tough pages. The entries are printed, usually conventionally, and starting life as lists of accessions which are cut up to form unit records. The resulting flimsy slips are 'tipped-in' (pasted at the corners) in the required order, perhaps only down the left-hand column of a page. New entries are tipped in opposite their appropriate place. When a page is full, it can be split to form two pages, and so on, as with the looseleaf catalogue; a volume also can in turn be split to form two, and so on. The method is very rarely used now, the British Museum Reading Room form of its *Catalogue of printed books* being the best known example. A few of the older British university libraries also use guardbook catalogues. It is understandable that some of these older libraries have this form, especially since it probably evolved from the idea of cutting up an existing printed catalogue, which, as we have seen, is probably the most standard form in library history.

Characteristics of the guardbook form

1. It is very flexible physically; but see also item 9 below.

2. Space occupied is greater than other forms of printed but smaller than other unit record forms. Judging by the B.M., with its thousand-odd volumes of guardbook volumes, the form is about three times as voluminous as the printed bound book form.

3. It is usually no more easily accessible, since usually only one copy is available at any one time (although the B.M. in fact maintains three copies since one or two are always being worked on). It is more accessible than other printed forms because of its greater spread through a larger number of volumes.

4. Less conveniently portable than other printed forms because of its greater bulk.

5. Rarely, if ever, publicly available in multiple copies (see also item 3 above). But, as with the B.M. it can form a basis from which very pleasing multiple copies can be produced.

6. Requires a considerable staff to produce it; but, as mentioned above, it can form a basis for quite convenient reproduction.

7. Not normally available outside the library.

8. More convenient to use than other unit record forms. But, compared with other printed forms, sequential scanning can be impaired by new entries being slightly out of place, until the next grand reshuffle takes place.

9. It usually relies on contract printers for its basic copy, which could cause delay—but the typing of cards, say, could also be in arrears. It is probably quite expensive to maintain in staff labour—not to mention patience and dedication to duty—as compared with, say, the card catalogue.

10. It is not amenable directly to interfiling with other catalogues, but entries could be cut up and stuck onto cards, as was expected to happen with BNB when it started.

11. Comparable with other printed forms.

Summary and prognosis

In its standard form, it is obsolescent, having been replaced decades ago by card catalogues in newer research libraries. However, its principle has, in the past few years, been revived through one type of the visible index form, dealt with later.

4. Sheaf

Entries are typed, or duplicated, onto slips, and the slips are temporarily bound into loose-leaf type of binders, usually fixed by posts passing through with 'open' or 'closed' holes in the slips and which are probably held in place by screws. In some forms, two posts are fixed to each cover, front and back, and the slips have four holes. This ensures that a binder can be 'broken' into two without danger of individual slips becoming loose. Usually each slip, say, $4'' \times 8''$, contains only one entry, although some libraries using a sheaf subject index may have several entries per slip. One has discovered by experiment that the sheaf form can be used quite conveniently for a title-a-line index to song collections, the slightly larger format, compared with 5″ × 3″ cards, usually being sufficient to take a short entry of song title plus brief shelf location on one line.

This form seems to be peculiar to Britain, and is far less popular than the card form. It is used in most of the British regional union catalogues.

Characteristics of the sheaf catalogue

1. It is infinitely flexible, like the card catalogue, provided the unit record principle is maintained. When a volume becomes full, it can be split to make two, and the other volumes moved round to make room for them. But see also item 9.

2. It is space-saving compared with the card catalogue, but less so than the printed forms. But since the volumes are shelved and are not free-standing furniture, like card cabinets, the space-saving is particularly evident compared with card catalogues. A 2″ thick volume can hold about 500 slips—an average card drawer a foot or more long may hold about 1,000 cards. Like the card, each unit is space-wasting—only a small part of only one side of a slip is used for many entries.

3. It is more accessible than the card catalogue, since volumes can be taken away from the catalogue shelves or pigeon holes and consulted in a comfortable position for the user, e.g. at a table or away from a crowd, or at the shelves.

4. It is portable, volume by volume. This can be advantageous, as mentioned above, but it can result in volumes being replaced out of position and perhaps even among the library's book stock, where they may evade recapture for some time.

5. Multiple copies are available by carbon copy or stencil, and by any facsimile copying method, e.g. xerography.

6. As already mentioned, copies of entries can be quite conveniently reproduced. BNB in the past has printed entries on to slips supplied by libraries. Also BNB prints slips for some regional union catalogues, also entering on the slips the symbols for libraries which have bought BNB cards for a work, this meaning that these libraries have the work in stock. Such a system is capable of considerable sophistication, with suitable cooperation.

7. Usually, a service point has only one copy of the catalogue. But, being unit records, slips, or copies of them, could be used in a selective dissemination of information service, by which individuals are notified of new accessions in which they are likely to be interested.

8. It is fairly convenient to use, but less so than printed forms since sequential scanning (of separate unit entries) is not possible. Opinion varies about whether it is slower or faster than the card catalogue; certainly it cannot be guided so visibly.

9. It is rather time-consuming and fiddly to maintain: how much depends on the type of binder and slips used. Some examples do not hold the slips firmly, which then get dog-eared and may have to be replaced. At least, withdrawals can be easy—one can simply tear out the relevant slip: a tip preferably not mentioned to schoolchildren in tours of the library.

10. Regional and similar union catalogues could not conveniently be directly compiled by interfiling, even if this were required, because of the variety of sheaf catalogues available. But see item 6 above, again.

11. It is not particularly convenient for use with other records, although the lightness and portability of individual volumes means that it can be taken to heavy or long runs of bibliographies.

Summary and prognosis

It is not a popular form, despite its book-like appearance, and it is probably obsolescent in spite of its flexibility and its space-saving compared with the card catalogue. One presumes that the present regional union catalogues in Britain will ultimately be replaced by computer records, that is if the regional bureaux themselves survive.

5. Card

The conventional manual card is usually about $5'' \times 3''$ (or $12 \cdot 5 \times 7 \cdot 5$ cm. for the accurately minded, or $12 \cdot 8 \times 7 \cdot 7$ cm. for the very accurately minded). It is filed vertically in drawers, usually wooden but sometimes metal. The drawers are housed in cabinets, usually being held in by gravity-action catches which can be lifted to allow complete removal of drawers. Cards usually have a circular hole punched near their base, through which a rod can be passed from the front of the drawer to prevent—or at least delay—their unofficial removal. (One has occasionally come across students who think these are therefore 'punched cards', which literally it must be conceded they are.) Some libraries use larger cards, say $8'' \times 5''$ (or their metric equivalent), for the unit-recording of abstracts. One Australian library finished up with $5'' \times 2\frac{3}{4}''$ approx. cards for the most part, since its librarian decided to cut off the tops of

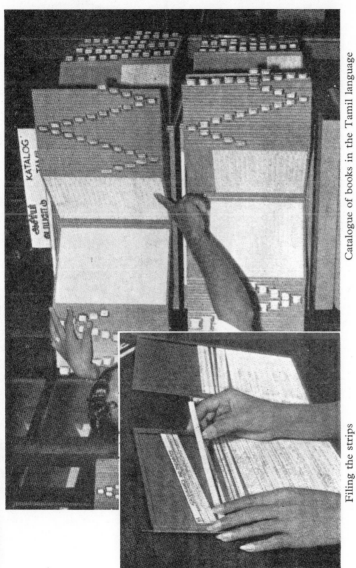

Filing the strips

Catalogue of books in the Tamil language

15. Visible index catalogue: 'Stripdex'.

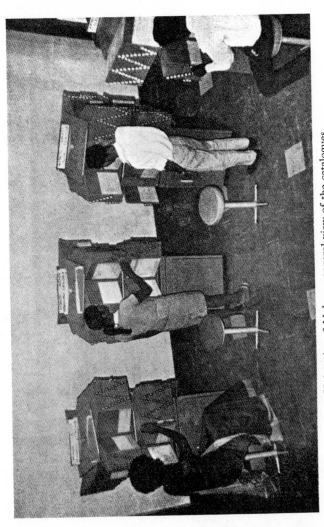

University of Malaya : general view of the catalogues
15. Visible index catalogue: 'Stripdex'.

all entries which repeated the heading of the card before it, therefore making the (dictionary) catalogue in effect self-guiding. Usually one entry per card is recorded, and the card catalogue is the standard form of unit record. The card catalogue is by far the most popular in libraries; even other forms of catalogues are often based on cards, or slips, drafted by the cataloguers.

The conventional card drawer has been mechanised to some extent. Machines are available, at which the operator can sit comfortably, and which produces the appropriate drawer or row of drawers at the press of one or more buttons. Sample trade names are Kard-veyer and Lectriever. See illustration 14 facing p. 301.

One has seen a whole card catalogue on wheels—product of the ingenuity of the staff of the Hellyer Regional Library in Tasmania. A manually operated version has the card drawers as radials (like wheel spokes) on revolving platforms; the operator sits at the catalogue and swivels the whole platform to bring the required drawer to the front It can be a single, or a multiple, deck form. See illustration 13 facing p. 300.

Punched cards and edge-notched cards can be used for mechanical sorting. These may sometimes be used as a basis for the automatic compilation of printed lists, as in the Fotolist process.

Magnetic cards as well as punched cards are sometimes used as unit records, for convenience, for manipulation by computer.

Aperture cards can also be used as both the entry and document combined—the latter being in microfilm form and framed in the card. It can be retrieved mechanically and printed full-size on demand.

Characteristics of the (mainly manual) card catalogue

1. It is infinitely flexible, when used as a unit record. It is sometimes said that librarians invented card records for this reason, though it seems likely that they were first used in France soon after the French Revolution for recording Napoleon's new legal code. They have been in common use in libraries since around the beginning of the twentieth century, when the Library of Congress started its central card cataloguing service.

2. It occupies more space than any other form of catalogue, not only in volume but in obtrusiveness and floor area.

3. It can be reasonably accessible, especially when it is allowed to spread sideways rather than upwards. But see again item 2 on space occupied. Some forms of cabinet allow alternate drawers to enter on

opposite sides of the cabinet; this spreads use, and so is more convenient for users, but it necessitates 'island' cabinets, with even more use of floor space. The mechanical retriever type of machine permits only one person to use the whole unit (of perhaps 500,000 records) at a time.

4. It is the least portable of catalogues (excepting on-line computers). Some libraries allow users to remove drawers and sit comfortably at tables while using the catalogue. Even when drawers are removed, it is inconvenient to use a card catalogue at the shelves.

5. It is almost never available in multiple copies.

6. It is very expensive to initiate and to maintain. Cabinets—especially aesthetically pleasing ones—are expensive. Cards are, in many applications, too durable and therefore uneconomic. However, there are several quick and reasonably cheap ways of reproducing entries: dealt with in the next chapter. Also ready-printed cards are available for purchase from several central sources, whether cataloguing agencies, or from or via commercial library suppliers. These are dealt with in Section V on Centralisation. Filing, although tedious, is probably as quick as, if not quicker than, that in other manual forms.

7. Copies are virtually never available outside the library. But, as with sheaf slips, copies of cards can be used in a selective dissemination of information service. Occasionally, one has come across research libraries which issue their new acquisitions lists on perforated card stock. The individual required cards can easily be torn off and filed by the academic or research worker—if he can be bothered to do this. Also, the stencils used to produce entries for locally compiled index entries and abstracts can be manipulated to use as entries in a (usually special) library's information bulletin.

8. It is not very convenient to use; see again item 3. Sequential scanning is not possible, although its form permits a potentially quite efficient guiding system. Because the form is common, and because cards are thick enough to handle with dexterity, people can get used to the form, despite its inherent handicaps.

9. See item 6.

10. Since the form is so common, it is very convenient as a means of notifying, and if necessary interfiling, entries in a union catalogue. It was used in the past by the then *London union catalogue* of the then London Metropolitan libraries. Interfiling has become necessary because of amalgamations of various British local authorities. In many cases it appears that card catalogues have responded reasonably well to this,

although a minority of libraries took advantage of the upheaval to change to computer-compiled and printed catalogues.

11. It is physically inconvenient to use in conjunction with bibliographies, lists, etc., even though this is a very common occurrence. Some cabinets have retractable shelves between certain drawers on which the user can rest bibliographies, etc., and writing equipment.

Summary and prognosis

The only virtue of the card catalogue really is its flexibility. As soon as librarians perfect other media of flexibility they are likely to try to rid themselves of the cumbersome and expanding piece of furniture known as the card catalogue. This is happening with computers now, and the trend is gathering momentum.

However, manual cards are likely to remain for small files which are not worth mechanising.

'Mechanical' (punched) cards may continue in use for a long time yet, especially for the periodical running off automatically of lists for which it is not yet economical to use computers and for the sorting of fairly small files. They may also persist in some cases as input for computers.

6. Visible index: all of entries visible

The earliest form warranting this term was probably the *Rudolph Indexer* in the 1890's, a panoramic type of catalogue and similar in principle to the oriental 'book-wheel'. Entries were fixed to an endless belt. The operator wound a handle and peered through a window, waiting for the desired entries to appear below it. One might best describe this as a 'what-the-butler-saw' form of catalogue (*Library resources and technical services*, Fall 1961, p. 259-266).

Today, this form of visible index catalogue is, in effect, a modern and more convenient manifestation of the principle of the guardbook catalogue. Each entry is typed on one strip, or on to two strips fixed together, each perhaps $\frac{1}{2}''$ high and about 6″ long—the strips are used as continuous stock, with perforations for tearing off. The entry may then be sheathed or covered in plastic to preserve it. It is filed in a metal tray, usually vertical, with flanged edges to hold the strips. The file of strips is prevented from falling out by, usually, a spring-loaded base-piece, which can be moved up or down within the flanges. See illustration 15, facing pages 308 and 309.

The metal trays are suspended vertically in racks, so that they can swivel—in effect be turned over like the leaf of a book, the racks being fixed to a wall; or they are attached to a free-standing spindle, so that the whole can be spun round in addition to allowing the trays to swivel.

This form is used as the main catalogue of the Institute of Electrical Engineers' Library in London. It was introduced into the University of Malaya Library, but this Library has apparently reverted to the card catalogue. It has also been introduced into the Ahmadu Bello University Library in Nigeria, and into the University of Malawi Library. Many libraries use this form as a finding or location guide for periodicals, and some use it as a subject index to a classified catalogue. Also, many libraries use it as a visible index method of recording reservations when 'flagging' the issue is not possible or desired. A trade name is Stripdex.

Characteristics of this form of visible index

1. As a unit record form, it is infinitely flexible, with the usual provisos about the inconvenience of moving round, 'splitting' contents of trays, etc.

2. It occupies more space than printed book-type catalogues, and probably even more when it is used fixed to a wall, although this aids ease of use and access. It spreads more than the card catalogue, e.g. along a wall. For all these reasons, it occupies a great deal of floor space. Each entry is almost as economical of space as the printed forms, as it can take as few or as many strips as required, e.g. one very narrow strip can be used for references, while a whole $5'' \times 3''$ card is needed in the card catalogue.

3. It is easily accessible, especially when it spreads along a wall. If the rotary-spindle form is used, some trays may be inaccessible when required because they may be obstructed by people using adjacent trays.

4. It is not conveniently portable, although trays can usually be unhooked quite easily from their racks if necessary, say for inserting and removing entries.

5. Individual strips or trays of made-up strips can be facsimile reproduced, e.g. by xerography although there may be some loss of clarity if the image being reproduced is held too far from the xerographic 'screen' by the metal flanges.

6. It is comparable with the card catalogue in convenience, speed and expense in the production of individual entries.

7. From item 5, it can be seen that in principle multiple copies could

be produced, including ones for sale to individuals and other libraries. Since the form is not widely used yet as a normal library catalogue, this aspect has not yet been fully investigated and experimented with.

8. It is probably the most convenient form to use for sequential scanning, both in selecting the required entry from a wide range since it is rather like a printed catalogue open at several pages at once, as well as in ease of reading a whole entry. This is undoubtedly the great advantage of this form.

9. Expense of maintenance in materials and time is comparable with the card catalogue.

10. Because of its minority use and its physical format, it does not allow interfiling with more conventional forms, like cards. But entries could presumably be facsimile-copied onto card stock if required.

11. It is not convenient to use in conjunction with book-form bibliographies, etc., for similar reasons as apply to the card catalogue. One has to stand to use it (unless trays are unhooked), with the attendant physical difficulty of holding a printed list and writing at the same time. However, as with the card catalogue, shelves could be made along the 'run' of catalogue as 'leaners'.

Summary and prognosis

Despite its ease of use, this form has not caught on as quickly as one might expect. Certainly no really large library has used it as its main catalogue; the largest library one can find records of is Ahmadu Bello University with, at the time, a book stock of 55,000, with author and subject approaches each taking some 45,000 entries (Plumbe, W. J., 'Another appraisal of the Stripdex catalogue': *Library review* vol. 21, no. 5, Spring 1968, p. 236). It seems likely that this form will remain mainly for smaller libraries and for such ancillary functions as location lists of periodicals and subject indexes—for which purposes it is ideal.

7. Visible index: other forms

Several types are included here, all of which provide for easy or fairly easy scanning of headings, but not directly of complete entries without turning over cards.

In one form, entries are made on cards filed in metal trays which may be hung vertically or filed horizontally like drawers. The cards overlap (or rather 'underlap') so that only the lower $\frac{1}{4}''$ or so of each card is visible. To consult the whole entry a sequence of cards has to be raised up or flipped over. Cards are usually larger than the standard $5'' \times 3''$ size, because this form is often used for fuller records than normal catalogue entries, e.g. (*a*) for marking up arrival of serials; or (*b*) as a main entry catalogue combined with indicator ('in' or 'out') for closed access gramophone record libraries, in which case the catalogue entry must include a pocket of some sort to hold an issue card.

Another version is in the form of a drum. Cards are held on peripheral rods, rather like the rotary blades of a turbine. The 'drum' is revolved to bring the required section to the top. A batch of cards can be fanned out by pressing them down, thereby giving a temporary visible index effect for the headings typed on to their outer edges. Up to about 8,000 cards can be contained in one unit. As with the tray type explained above, cards are larger than the usual $5'' \times 3''$, and are therefore used for similar purposes as the tray type. One has come across the revolving-drum type used as serials registers and as a main-entry catalogue combined with booking records in a library of moving films. Trade names are Rotadex and Cardwheel.

Characteristics of these forms of visible index

1. They are infinitely flexible, as unit entry records, but with the usual provisos about expansion, moving round, splitting one unit into two, etc.

2. They occupy about as much space as card catalogues on the whole: the tray sort rather less, the drum sort perhaps more.

3. The tray type is similar to the card catalogue for access. The drum type necessarily restricts access to one person per unit, though where two or more smaller drums are used side by side, access is improved.

4. Neither type is portable. Trays can be removed, like card drawers can. The drum type is usually supplied on wheels and so is transportable, e.g. from desk to desk, or from desk to shelves provided there is room for manoevrability. (The time may yet come when a motor and a driver's seat are fitted.)

5. Multiple copies are not conveniently available, and are not normally required for the double uses to which these types are put.

6. Convenience in production is similar to other forms of card record.

7. Copies for external use cannot conveniently be supplied, and are not usually required.

8. Both types are quite convenient to use. The tray sort is best,

because: (a) of its ready and permanent visibility of headings; and (b) trays can be pulled out and then allowed to rest downwards on to the bench on which the whole cabinet is housed, for convenient reference to and writing on cards. With the drum type, if one gets too enthusiastic over splaying entries, a whole run of cards (which are the open-hole type) may be forced off the rods and will either spray across the room or drop into the fairly inaccessible bottom of the unit.

9. Basic equipment is about as expensive as with normal card units made of metal. Cards themselves are dearer, and justifiably so because of their greater size and varieties of use.

10. See item 10 under no. 6, the first form of visible index.

11. Both types are quite convenient to use in conjunction with other records, the tray type because bibliographies, etc., can be laid on the bench beside the trays, and the drum type because it can be put alongside a desk and because it is about desk height for this purpose.

Summary and prognosis

These types are not intended as normal catalogues, and so probably will never become widely accepted. But one feels that they could be used more for unit record files of abstracts instead of the more common 8" × 5" conventional card-type files. Their use as stock and booking records of various sorts in large libraries will probably diminish, because the computerisation of such records is increasing.

SUMMARY OF HISTORICAL EVOLUTION OF FORMS OF CATALOGUE

1. None; or the human memory.
2. Engraved on walls: e.g. Ancient Egypt.
3. Manuscript clay tablet form: potentially flexible, but not in fact used as unit records: e.g. Ancient Near East.
4. Manuscript papyrus: e.g. Ancient Egypt.
5. Manuscript parchment: e.g. Ancient Near East.
6. Manuscript paper: e.g. Mediaeval Europe.
7. Printed bound book form.
8. Cards and sheaf slips.
9. Looseleaf, perhaps borrowed from the use of looseleaf ledgers.
10. Visible index forms.
11. Mechanised manipulation of conventional card form.
12. Mechanised printed, first from punched cards, then by computer.

13. Long-range access, by teleprinter, to a central conventional or other form, i.e. as opposed to having a copy at each service point.
14. Machine-readable computer store; access by 'dialogues', resulting in print-out to suit individual needs.
15. As 14, but with the actual required data, not merely citation of bibliographical units, being printed out or facsimile-produced.

THE CATALOGUE ENTRY: PHYSICAL LAYOUT

This continues from the point reached in Chapter 2 in which it was assumed for the sake of explanation that the layout of the entry is static. Criticisms may be made of the type and form of detail in entries, and some is included in Chapter 22, on Limited cataloguing. But here we are concerned with more radical criticism of the layout of entries, especially in relation to the traditional card.

Occasionally, librarians have tried to break away from the traditional method of entry compilation, i.e. extracting information from the title page of books, or the caption-title of periodicals and some music, adding to this items of information from elsewhere in the document, manipulating it and then presenting it in a particular way as laid down by a code and/or local instructions. An alternative has been used, usually as part of a 'crash' programme aimed at cutting out refinements and producing usable entries quickly. The basis of this is making a facsimile-copy of the title page of a document, reducing it in size, superimposing suitable headings, putting the whole onto cards, and using these as entries. The assumption is that title pages carry sufficient information for a work to be identified and to be distinguished from other, similar works. There is a great deal to be said for this, from the author/title and description viewpoint, although rarely so from the sub-ject approach—except for those with ultimate faith in title-word indexing.

The facsimile cataloguing method has been discussed by various authorities, but it seems to deserve more practical experiment. The time may even come when it can be applied in computerisation programmes, and incorporating analysis of periodicals from their contents lists, especially those which incorporate abstracts of articles, and more practicable than at present if optical character recognition becomes applicable to the variety of type faces and type sizes used in letterpress printing.

Other suggestions have been made, but confined to accepting the form of catalogue data as produced according to codes. In particular, the use of the unit entry and the tracings resulting in the filing of the unit entry in appropriate places in catalogues has been investigated. In some cases, sets of cards, for dictionary catalogues, with the appropriate headings ready-printed, are available, as explained in Section V on Central cataloguing services. Where this is not the case, librarians have for many years now experimented with physical layouts which facilitate the recognition of parts of an entry, often an added or analytical for author, or title, or subject approach. AA 1908 included an Appendix with examples of how parts of a unit entry can be marked to focus attention on the part of an entry which is, in effect, the justification for filing a copy of an entry into the catalogue at that point. See facsimile on page 318 (AA 1908, p. 79).

This type of indication has become commonly known. But in the past there has been feeling against it because some librarians tried to maintain a higher standard of neatness in their catalogue than is exemplified by ruling lines across entries. Nowadays, under the influence of poor computer print-out, economical but far from perfect BNB cards, and through the use of near-print, we are beginning to put speed and economy before physical perfection. Recently, suggestions have been made for using the tracings on unit entries directly as headings. Examples are shown in the facsimiles on pages 318-19, and little further explanation is required. With tracings at the top of the entry, or in a clear margin down the side, the relevant added entry headings can be quickly underlined, therefore made prominent, and so made significant in themselves as filing terms. This type of manipulation is so obvious and simple that one can only marvel that it has not been practised before—or if it has been practised, that it has not become better known. A detailed explanation, if required, can be seen in the article from which the facsimiles here are reproduced (Voos, Henry, 'Revision of the current Library of Congress catalog card format': *Library resources and technical services*, vol. 11, no. 2, Spring 1967, p. 167-172).

AS36   Wallace, Charles William.
N2   ... The newly-discovered Shakespeare
 v.5   documents.   (In Nebraska.University.
       University studies. 1905. v. 5, p. 347-
       356)

*   Wister, Owen, 1860-

 813   Stories of the colleges; being tales of life at the great Ameri-
 St55   can universities told by noted graduates. Philadelphia &
          London, J. B. Lippincott company, 1901.

       353 p. 19½ᶜᵐ·

          CONTENTS. — Harvard: Philosophy 4. by O. Wister. — Yale: A bachelor of
       arts, by R. Holbrook. — Princeton : Rah, rah, rah, Murray, by B. E. Stevenson.
       — Pennsylvania : Smith of " Pennsylvania," by F. C. Williams. — Columbia : A
       lightning change, by A. P. Terhune. — West Point : The code of the corps, by
       General C. King. — Annapolis : A hazing interregnum, by C. T. Brady. — Cor-
       nell : The personal equation, by J. G. Sanderson. — Chicago : The head marshal
       of the University of Chicago, by J. W. Linn.

16. Excerpt from AA 1908 code: specimen entries.

McFadden, Dorothy Loa (Mausolff) 1902–
     Touring the gardens of Europe, by Dorothy Loa McFad-
den. Wheel tour maps by Winfield Barnes. New York,
D. McKay [1965]

     xii, 306 p. illus., maps. 22 cm.

     1. Gardens—Europe. 2. Europe—Descr. & trav.—Guide-books.
I. Title.

SB466.E9M3   712.094   65–18547

Library of Congress   [⁵]

Exhibit 1

17. Possible revised catalogue card layouts. 'Exhibits' 2 and 3 illustrate possible
methods of amending the conventional unit card entry.

McFadden, Dorothy Loa (Mausolff) 1902–
    Touring the gardens of Europe, by
    Dorothy Loa McFadden. Wheel tour
    maps by Winfield Barnes. New York,
    D. McKay [1965]

       xii, 306 p. illus., maps. 22 cm.

1. Gardens–
   Europe
2. Europe–Descr.
   & trav.–Guide-
   books

I. Title

SB466.E9M3   712.094   65–18547

Library of Congress   [5]

Exhibit 2

1. Gardens—Europe. 2. Europe—Descr. & trav.—Guide-books.
I. Title.

McFadden, Dorothy Loa (Mausolff) 1902–
    Touring the gardens of Europe, by Dorothy Loa McFad-
    den. Wheel tour maps by Winfield Barnes. New York,
    D. McKay [1965]

       xiii, 306 p. illus., maps. 22 cm.

SB466.E9M3   712.094   65–18547

Library of Congress   [5]

Exhibit 3

CHAPTER 26

Catalogue Card Reproduction

Despite the widespread use of central catalogue services, and despite the rapid encroachment of the computer as a catalogue filing and printing device, many libraries still reproduce their own catalogue cards and, in a few cases, sheaf slips. However, it is likely that the wide variety of methods available will become increasingly of only academic interest, so only a brief summary of the more common methods is included here. Details of the methods current up to the late 1950's can be found in a useful and concise British pamphlet (Pargeter, Philip S., *The reproduction of catalogue cards*. London: L.A. 1960), while more comprehensive and up-to-date information, including statistics, is given in a more recent American work (ALA Library Technology Project. *Catalog card reproduction: report on a study conducted by George Fry & Associates*. Chicago: A.L.A. 1965).

CRITERIA FOR EVALUATING METHODS OF CARD REPRODUCTION: A SUMMARY

1. Economy: cost of equipment, and of expendable materials.
2. Speed in operation: staff salaries; keeping catalogues up to date.
3. Skill in operation: salaries, again; able to be operated by 'relief' staff.

In general, one wants a cheap machine, which can be operated easily, intermittently, quickly, and without much training.

4. Number of copies before the master (stencil, etc.) wears out must exceed average requirement of one's own library. (Photographic and xerographic copying do not affect the master copy and therefore can be used for an indefinite number of copies.)
5. Space taken up by plant, materials, and especially masters, if these are to be retained indefinitely.
6. Image quality: suitable for permanent black (plus red if required), well-defined printing on smooth white, or off-white, card stock. Quick-drying, or dry all through operation.

7. Ease of correction of master.

8. Adaptation of master for different types of entry, taking into account also non-catalogue records if relevant.

9. Cater for typing in additions—headings, etc.—if required, to match original.

10. Accurate registration on card stock.

THE METHODS OF REPRODUCTION

1. Letterpress

This method is still used for the original printing of entries in the British Museum printed catalogue and for Library of Congress and H. W. Wilson printed cards. It is economical, in general, only when a great number of copies is required, and is therefore not directly relevant here, except that some libraries may make facsimile copies from standard bibliographies and bibliographic catalogues. It should be remembered that a central cataloguing agency is, in effect, a method of reproducing catalogue cards.

2. Typewriters

When only 5 or 6 copies of an entry are required, it may still be economical to use the ordinary typewriter. It should be remembered that carbon copies for sheaf slips are possible. Electric typewriters are faster and give a more even impression than conventional machines, especially when operated by skilled typists. A basic disadvantage of repeat-typing is that all copies must be checked for clerical accuracy.

3. Automatic typewriters (Trade names: Flexowriter, Ultronic)

A 'hard copy' is typed, for convenient checking, while at the same time a punched tape (usually paper) is produced. Corrections are provided for, and easily made. The tape can be fed back into the same machine to produce automatically as many copies of entries as required, using continuous card stock which is perforated to allow the individual cards to be torn off. The machine can be programmed to stop automatically at pre-set points, e.g. at the top of a fresh copy, so that added entry headings can be typed in manually. Apart from the obvious advantages of speed and lack of checking, the manually-typed additions match the unit copy, and so have a better appearance than, say, when typing headings on to a central cataloguing agency card, which is probably produced by a different method. Individual tapes can be preserved, e.g. in envelopes which themselves can form a main entry in a union catalogue (as in Shropshire County Library), and used again as often as required, whether for repeat cards or for the production of reading lists. Tapes which are used so often that they might get damaged may be made of plastic rather than paper. A further advantage of this method is that the punched tapes may be used as computer input, either directly or indirectly through 'converters' which transpose the data into magnetic tape form.

4. Wax stencil duplicator (Trade names: Gestetner; Roneo)

These may be used on the rotary type of duplicator normally found in offices, or in small flat-bed machines made especially for the production of catalogue card-sized copy. Stencils are usually capable of producing many more copies than are normally required for one library system, and stencils can be preserved for future re-use. A disadvantage is that the duplicators have to be inked and may be slightly messy in certain (not very smooth) operators' hands, while some types of ink do not dry very quickly on catalogue card stock. An advantage is the cheapness of some models of the machinery: a library can have, say, its own little flat-bed duplicator, always ready for use. Also, catalogue cards produced direct on the same typewriter that is used for producing the stencils will match the duplicated ones. Corrections may easily be made by using a special fluid on the master.

5. Spirit duplicator (Trade names: Banda; Ditto)

A master is made by typing on to a special type of paper backed by a special carbon, producing a reversed image on the back of the master, while providing a 'straight' copy on the front for checking. By retyping on to the original paper with a different-coloured stencil, multi-coloured masters can be made. Corrections are made by using a special fluid on the master. In printing, a spirit dissolves a small amount of the dye from the master and deposits it on the card. The early versions used purple ink, but later black became possible. However, the image tends to be ill-defined, and it also fades. But sufficient copies for most library catalogue purposes can be produced before the deposit of dye on the master is used up.

A slightly similar method, in principle, is the dyeline (trade name:

Diazo) process, relying on the reaction of ultraviolet light on sensitised paper.

6. Offset lithography (Trade names: Multilith; Rotaprint)

This is a lithographic process in which a master is made which attracts ink on to its 'image' surface but repels it on its 'non-image' surface. The method is sometimes used in conjunction with a Varietyper (trade name) which allows a greater variety of type than the usual typewriter. The method is too expensive for small runs, but it produces a clearly defined image for runs up to thousands.

7. Metal plate 'addressing' method (Trade name: Addressograph)

A metal plate embossed (relief) master is produced from a special typewriter. This is used as a relief printing surface using an inked ribbon like that on a typewriter, or in the Dickman issue charging machine (a mechanical version of the Newark charging system used in some lending libraries, in which the reader's number is printed on to the book card). The method may entail sending out 'batch jobs' to a contractor, which may possibly cause delays, although some libraries purchase their own machines. A further disadvantage is that the storage of the master plates takes a lot of space. An advantage is that the method is clean, and parts of the entry may quite easily be masked for added entries, etc.

8. Xerography (Trade name: Xerox)

An image is transmitted from the master—which may be in any form, e.g. printed, typed or manuscript—using an electrostatic principle which causes black powder to be attracted to, and then fuse onto, ordinary card stock. The result is usually on foolscap or A4 size which is then cut up to the usual 5″ × 3″ size. This is a quick and, mercifully, dry method which produces a clear image without fuss or skill. Xerographic machines are increasingly common in libraries for normal documentary reproduction purposes, and are quite cheap to operate compared with most methods. One disadvantage is that some machines cannot cope with card stock of average thickness. Another is that preferably a 'jig' or positioning framework should be used to ensure that the original cards are kept in their correct place.

9. Silk screen

Little need be said about this, since it is the medium used for past BNB cards (facsimiles of which are shown in Section V, on Centralisation of catalogue services). The ink is pressed through a screen on to the card stock, the screen therefore accounting for the slightly 'fuzzy' effect of the image. However, as is well known from BNB cards, the method is quick and cheap, and the masters may be stored for a long time without ill effects. BNB's past method is explained by A. J. Wells in 'Printed catalogue cards', *Journal of documentation*, vol. 13, no. 2, 1957, p. 67-71.

When passing judgement on BNB cards, it should be remembered that the size of type has been increased from that used in its early days, while the cost of cards has only marginally increased during a period of considerable inflation in Britain.

10. Microphotography

This method has been used in North America and Australia for the mass copying of catalogue entries in research libraries with a view to ultimate full-size reprinting, by xerography, to make entries for union catalogues. Essentially, it is a camera method, involving reduction, then enlargement, of the image, and it is not likely to be used for day-by-day local library card reproduction. Its two main advantages are: (*a*) saving in postage charges for transmission from the local library to the national bibliographic centre; and (*b*) saving in storage space pending full-size reprinting.

SECTION V

CENTRALISATION OF CATALOGUING SERVICES

Centralisation of Cataloguing Services

Readings, including works cited in the text
BRITISH NATIONAL BIBLIOGRAPHY questionnaire: a report, *in* Library Association record, vol. 67, no. 2, February 1965, p. 52-57.
  Comments by users of BNB.
BRUMMEL, L. Union catalogues, Paris: UNESCO, 1956.
CATALOGUE AND INDEX, no. 11, July 1968, initiated a series: Studies in central cataloguing, the first dealing with Rotherham Public Library.
CRONIN, J. W. The Library of Congress National Program for Acquisition and Cataloging, *in* Libri, vol. 16, no. 2, p. 113.
FLOWERS, E. Centralized cataloguing for Australian research libraries. (Details are given in Section IV.)
GILJAREVSKIJ, R. S. International distribution of catalogue cards: present situation and future prospects. Paris: UNESCO, 1969.
HOWARD, RITA. Standard book numbers at Greenwich, *in* Catalogue and index, no. 11, July 1968, p. 4-5.
LEWIS, PETER R. British national bibliography provision in public libraries, *in* Library Association record, vol. 70, no. 1, January 1968, p. 14-16, 22.
  Further reported on *in* Catalogue and index, no. 12, October 1968, p. 1.
LIBRARY OF CONGRESS. The cataloging-in-source experiment: a report to the Librarian of Congress by the Director of the Processing Department. Washington: L.C., 1960.
  Also summarised *in* Library journal, 15th April 1960, p. 1535-1537.
LIBRARY OF CONGRESS's Processing Department issues an occasional Bulletin. This should be watched for announcements concerning Library of Congress's central cataloguing services.
LIBRI, vol. 17, no. 4, 1967, included several articles on shared cataloguing.
LODEWYCKS, K. The self-cataloguing book, *in* Australian library journal, April 1953, p. 29-34.
LODEWYCKS, K. Cataloguing in source experiment: an appraisal, *in* Australian library journal, July 1961, p. 157-160.

NATIONAL LIBRARY OF AUSTRALIA. Catalogue card service for Australian publications, *in* Australian library journal, vol. 18, no. 3, April 1969, p. 80-82.

QUIGG, PATRICK. How to make a union catalogue: a review article, *in* Catalogue and index, no. 13, January 1969, p. 14-15.

STANDARD BOOK NUMBERING AGENCY. Standard book numbering, incorporating the recommendations of the Publishers Association for implementing the Standard Book Numbering scheme. London: The Agency, 1967.

STEVENS, NORMAN D. The National Program for Acquisitions and Cataloging . . ., *in* Library resources and technical services, vol. 12, no. 1, Winter 1968, p. 17-29.

WILLEMIN, SIVERE. Technique of union catalogues: a practical guide. Paris: UNESCO, 1966. Reprinted from UNESCO Bulletin for libraries, January-February 1966.

CHAPTER 27

Definitions; Evaluation of Central Catalogue Services

This section embraces all forms of cataloguing in which there is a sharing of any form of catalogue data between libraries, or between libraries and a coordinating agency. The agency may, or may not, be a library itself. Mechanisation aspects are dealt with in Section VI, Mechanisation.

DEFINITIONS

Central cataloguing, or (earlier term) Centralised Cataloguing

Cataloguing for a service point is done, wholly or partly, at some place other than the service point itself and which serves several service points or libraries. The basic object is economy: to obviate cataloguing the same material in different places. In addition, the quality of cataloguing at the central point should be higher than it is locally, while useful uniformity can result from centralisation. Sometimes the term is used generically, and so it may embrace other terms given below.

Usually it is said that there are two types of central cataloguing; either national central cataloguing, or centralisation of cataloguing within a library system. However, in fact, there are five possible levels of centralisation. It may be practised within a library system; or in a region; or in the catchment area of a commercial or other organisation; or at national level; or at international level. Also, one library can possibly take part in several levels simultaneously.

The method of using the service may vary:

(a) Unit entries as Cards; or (in one service: BNB) slips may be supplied, in multiple copies for the local library to type in relevant headings, and possibly amend to local needs.

(b) Cards may be supplied, as unit entries, with required headings already printed in, in which case the subscribing library allows the suppliers to decide which added, including analytical, entries will be needed.

(c) Cards may be supplied as part of a complete (technical and 'physical') processing service, usually in the form of cards with books; in this case the cards may have been supplied initially from some other, usually more central, agency.

(d) One copy of the catalogue data for each work may be obtained. This can be either (a) adapted and clerically copied; or (b) facsimile copied; then it would be treated as a unit entry as already described.

Some libraries practise pre-cataloguing. That is, catalogue data is copied from reliable bibliographies or bibliographic catalogues, usually by clerical assistants, at the time of selection and ordering. This data is then used by the professional cataloguer, either before or after receipt of the document, in drafting entries.

2. Cooperative cataloguing. A more recent, associated, term is Shared cataloguing

The cataloguing data produced internally by a library or service point for its own stock may be interchanged with data from other libraries produced for their stocks. The basic object is economy, as in central cataloguing. The method may become, or may develop as, part of a central cataloguing system, as in Library of Congress's Shared cataloguing. The method may be associated with the maintenance of a union catalogue, as has happened in some libraries with many, widely separated, service points. A past example has been Australia's C.S.I.R.O. (Commonwealth Scientific and Industrial Research Organization). An inter-library example is the American *National union catalog*.

A similar principle applies in the compilation of certain indexes and abstracts, R.I.L.M. [Music] *Abstracts* being an example.

3. Cataloguing in source. Other terms: Pre-natal cataloguing (Ranganathan); The Self-cataloguing book (Lodewycks)

A standard entry, including tracings for added entries, is printed in the book itself, usually on the back of the title page. The entry may be adapted and clerically copied, or—theoretically at least—it may be facsimile-copied.

A recommendation by Ranganathan is relevant here, even though it does not approach the completeness of the basic definition. This is that an author's name should be printed on the back of the title page of his book in the form in which he wishes it to be used. Today, the practice could facilitate the application of AACR rules for choice and form of name. One example of the practice is Palmer and Wells' *Fundamentals of library classification*.

4. Standard catalogues, e.g. as published by the H. W. Wilson Company

These are bibliographies of 'standard' works, i.e. likely to be required in a library's stock. They may be used as stock selection or stock overhaul guides, but their chief value here is that works receive full catalogue entries, and so the entries may be adapted and clerically copied by libraries. Certain 'bibliographic' catalogues are often used in the same way, of course, basic examples being the various Library of Congress printed catalogues. An advantage of some of the Wilson standard catalogues is that they may serve as bases for either classified or dictionary catalogues. As mentioned in Chapter 22 on Limited cataloguing, they may be used as 'catalogue-substitutes' in varying degrees when their entries are fuller, or when they have more approaches, than in the catalogues of the library in which they are used.

5. Union catalogue

This term should be recapitulated here, since it may be associated with various forms of centralisation and cooperation. A union catalogue lists, in one sequence, the holdings of various libraries, whether service points and/or departments of one system, or of various systems, and it gives locations of items in libraries.

It should be appreciated that there may be a considerable intermixing of these methods in some libraries—whether or not the staff realises it. The county branch assistant, in a library with no title catalogue, who looks up a title in BNB for an enquirer, is, in effect, partaking of a form of central cataloguing service in its broadest sense.

Also, it should be remembered throughout that there is a great variety of types and degrees of service: libraries' own bibliographic centres, national libraries, other non-commercial agencies, commercial agencies, and so on.

EVALUATION OF CENTRAL CATALOGUE SERVICES

These criteria apply particularly to card services, but they may be extended where relevant to all forms of centralisation and cooperation in cataloguing and indexing services. The criteria are applied to some actual services in the next chapter.

1. Library's stock intake should be compared with the scope of the service

(a) National coverage. The national origin of the service will probably be reflected in the works catalogued. Works in the 'home' language may also be emphasised in the service. A disadvantage is that if a library becomes very dependent on a service, its selection policy may come to be restricted more and more to items included in that service, especially since the agencies usually issue lists which can be used for selection and ordering.

(b) Retrospective coverage. The basic question is: How long has the service been running? But additional factors are

(i) entries may not be permanently kept in print, to be supplied immediately on demand; and

(ii) an 'axe' may be applied by which entries before a certain period are no longer made available. e.g. The Danish agency has several times proposed getting rid of its old cards (it has stocks of every title catalogued since its inception in 1938), but this has always been squashed because of users who want: (1) to have cards for books bought second-hand; and (2) new cards to replace worn ones.

(c) 'Special' materials. Some services include materials like moving films and gramophone records. In such a case, a library may actually be encouraged to initiate services covering these materials, because they are notoriously more difficult to catalogue than most other materials. Some services apply solely to certain special materials, two diverse examples being British government publications, and L.P. records available in Britain.

2. Technical processes

(a) Catalogue code.

(b) Classification scheme, and edition.

(c) Agency's interpretation of, and amendments to, codes and schemes.

(d) Detail and fullness of entries, including whether or not entries include tracings, which indicate need for added entries.

(e) Internal arrangement of catalogue assumed by the service.

(f) The local library's use of bibliographies: to what extent they correspond with decisions made by the agency. Pre-cataloguing may be relevant here.

There are two overriding factors: (*a*) How different are the library's requirements? and (*b*) How much does it cost to make additions, deletions and changes? These may be critical decisions. One fears that alleged local needs have sometimes been used as an excuse to avoid the temporary inconvenience of changing to what may in fact be a superior cataloguing service. If many changes are insisted upon, then the cost of making professional decisions and the clerical execution of these may be more than the money saved on ready-made entries.

It is even possible for a library to subscribe to a service not having the same scheme or code yet still to find that it pays. On the other hand, an attractive service may influence a library to change to its scheme and/or code. This condition might possibly lead to conservatism and a non-critical acceptance of a service which itself then develops a 'vested interest' in self-perpetuation and lack of experiment.

However extensive the coverage of a scheme, a library will still have to catalogue some of its intake. It may have decided to omit certain parts of entries which are included in the agency's service. In this case, inconsistencies in details may result: what these are, and hence whether or not they matter, may be open to doubt.

3. Cost of service compared with the cost of cataloguing the same material in the library

This is obviously related to item 2 above.

(*a*) Basic entries themselves.

(*b*) Administering the service: checking, ordering, receiving, filing, storage, retrieving, and matching with the correct documents.

(*c*) Technical service changes; clerical execution of these.

(*d*) Plant already invested in in local library. A library may use equipment for duplicating entries, e.g. a Xerox machine, which is essential for other services but still is not fully occupied.

4. Administration. Affects cost

(*a*) Ease of ordering. Whether the agency allows a variety of ways, depending on the varying needs of its subscribers.

(*b*) Additional services, e.g. 'cards with books', 'physical' processing. A few publishers supply books with the required number of cards already inserted in them in envelopes. But the practice of these services usually involves a library supplier who obtains the cards from the relevant agency. Such sophistication usually entails giving up to the supplier the decision as to how many entries are required per document. These cards would usually be supplied with added headings ready-printed on cards.

(c) Stability of agency may be relevant in 'small-time' or newly established services, especially if they are private-enterprise services. If they do not make a profit, they may be discontinued (as happened with the Harrods service started in the later 1940's in Britain), and perhaps after a library has reorganised to fit the service. But others may run as 'loss-leaders' to encourage libraries to use their other services. Australia had two unsuccessful attempts at small, pilot, card services soon after the Second World War, one being cards with books. Their failure may have indirectly caused the postponement of attempts at larger scale enterprises. After considerable planning a service did emerge in 1968.

(d) Promptness of supply for both newly-published works and past items. 'Arrearages' in a library responsible for its own cataloguing should be taken honestly into account: then, alleged delays in central services may not seem so bad. In any case, the entries may still be received before the books, especially when these are ordered after publication.

(e) Not a criterion, but a hope: there is possibly a need for a national —even an international—coordinating centre to match orders for cards with those of the most suitable agencies. Such an agency could include a 'cards with books' and a 'physical' processing service.

A proposal was made for a similar service in Australia, which would use data from BNB, LC and the agency itself, to produce cards for books included in all three services. Soon after this proposal, Shared cataloguing started and so it seems likely that the proposal may not materialise (FLOWERS, L.A.A. Conference, 1965).

5. Physical appearance, etc., of entries

Includes clarity of reproduction, sizes and variety of type, method of printing, durability: all in comparison with whatever forms the library produces.

Some examples of agency cards are reproduced in facsimile, together with a locally-produced card, on pages 351-356.

In evaluating quality, account must be taken in each case of cost of entries, and the comparative cost of producing the same entries for the same types of works in the local library.

If the data is copied clerically, physical appearance is immaterial.

Durability of card stock could be a final factor, but this is not a common criticism.

A service may be slightly marred by defects in layout and detail because it is a by-product of another service, e.g. a national bibliography or a large library's own cataloguing service.

CHAPTER 28

Representative Central Catalogue Services

British National Bibliography; Library of Congress; Wilson;
H.M.S.O.; Long Playing Record Library

BRITISH NATIONAL BIBLIOGRAPHY
CARD SERVICE

1. Coverage

Includes British copyright material, i.e. all printed material produced in Britain, although it excludes: Periodicals other than the first issue of a new one, or a re-titled existing one; Many, slight, government publications; Some reprints; Maps; Music scores; Some ephemeral fiction considered unlikely to be stocked by public libraries. Audio-visual materials are excluded since, anyway, they are not covered by U.K. copyright law.

Most of the material is English-language, and so a research library's intake coincides less with BNB coverage than that of the average public library. It is possible that as much as half of a British university library's stock, for example, would not be covered by the service.

Children's material is included automatically, subject to the exceptions mentioned above. Usually a note 'For children' is included in the entry, but such material does not receive special treatment as LC and WILSON cards do (but see later information on 'segmentation' of class numbers).

Retrospective coverage is limited to the last full 10 years, although the service started in 1956. At the time of writing (1969) this 'axe' is interpreted liberally, and cards back to 1957 are still available. Some students seem to think that BNB incorporates all of the British Museum's acquisitions. This underlines the opportunity missed by the B.M. in the past—if only it had started a central cataloguing service when AA 1908 came out . . .

2. Technical processes

Code: AA 1908 with modifications (detailed later) to 1967. AACR with declared minor modifications and options (detailed later) from 1968.

Classification: Basically DC 14th edition, with varying modifications. Chief modifications are: own common form and common subject subdivisions using lower-case letters; expansions at various points throughout the scheme using lower-case letters. These will be dropped as from 1971. It is probably true to say that BNB's own modifications, whatever their inherent value, have not been popular, or even advisable, from the card service viewpoint. A personal opinion is that it is unfortunate that new DC editions, especially 16th edition, have not been more readily and fully adopted. However, from 1969, DC 17th edition numbers were included in addition to 'BNB DC'. Also, from 1969, DC 'segmentation' has been introduced: explained under 'Library of Congress', which was the first to introduce the service. To this extent, then, BNB now caters for smaller public and children's libraries.

Arrangement. Main sequence of printed list is classified order, with full feature headings, and BNB serial numbers for card ordering. Alphabetical index is in one sequence: a full description of this is not relevant here, except to state that author entries include BNB serial numbers for ordering purposes, and standard book numbers where they exist, but that the title approach consists of simple *see* references to the author entry.

Tracings. Generally these are not given, e.g. for collaborators and for analyticals for authors and titles. In the past, feature headings were given at the foot of cards, but this practice was discontinued. From 1969, tracings are given in the weekly lists, but not normally on cards, so these lists must be retained for catalogue guidance even when supplanted by cumulations. However, at the time of writing a special 'full set' service is available, whose cards include tracings. There is, unfortunately, some doubt about whether this service will continue unless it receives fuller support.

Fullness. As full as expected from AA 1908 or AACR. A few bibliographical notes; very few annotations. Unit entries.

3. Cost

By the card: Minimum payment per title is 6d. for one, two or three cards, thereafter an additional 2d. per card is added. There is a minimum charge of 10s. per order, which includes postage within Britain or to overseas subscribers by surface mail; air mail is extra (but worth the cost). Cards are despatched daily.

Sets of cards: One copy of each card produced by BNB (1969:

approximately 26,000) may be obtained at £200 per year. Cards are despatched weekly. These are the cards which are of improved appearance, but the future of which is uncertain.

When magnetic tapes become generally available under the U.K. Project MARC, these will possibly cost very approximately £200 a year, but they will consist of 'raw' data to be processed by subscribing libraries.

4. Administration

Cards must be ordered by serial numbers: not necessarily listed in numerical order except by years. At present these numbers are available only in BNB lists. But increasingly the use of Standard book numbers should, it is hoped, facilitate ordering since these should appear in all books.

Some British suppliers will supply 'cards with books'. BNB is financially viable and there is no fear of its services being severely curtailed or of its going out of business. It is not a commercial organisation, and it does not have to make a profit. BNB will notify regional library bureaux of cards ordered by libraries—indicating that the books represented by these cards are in their stocks. Such a service can be extremely useful to a subscribing library in obviating delays and inconvenience. BNB also prints entries on to sheaf slips for bureaux if required.

BNB supplies copies of its entries to LC under the latter's Shared cataloguing programme (National Program for Acquisitions and Cataloging), and so its description data will be found in some LC cards. (But LC supplies all its own headings and DC numbers.) This aspect of the service is not reciprocal; however, the eventual consolidation of Project MARC may render the interchange of 'hard copy' unnecessary.

Promptness. Within the 'ten year axe' (in 1969 in fact a 12-year period), and provided a work has been catalogued by BNB, cards are supplied to British libraries within about a week. BNB has, over the years, made considerable efforts to keep its listing up to date by encouraging publishers to deposit their works on or in advance of publication. In general, the service may well be more prompt than LC's.

5. Physical factors

Until 1968 a photo-sensitive silk-screen process was used, resulting in rather less clear definition compared with normal relief type. Since

1968 the method of producing the stencils has been automated, using punched paper tape, as a by-product of MARC processing, but this does not affect the appearance of the cards. These comments do not apply to the complete sets of cards: see the facsimiles at the end of this chapter for comparison with the 'daily' cards.

BNB has printed unit entries on to sheaf slips supplied by subscribing libraries, but this service is ceasing at the end of 1970.

Class numbers are given at the bottom of the card, so classification alterations need not be obtrusive. There is room at the top of entries for added headings and feature headings to be typed in.

BNB AND THE CODES

AA 1908: up to the end of 1967

The (British) code's rigid earliest and real form of personal name was departed from in many cases. Examples: Pseudonyms (one author with several pseudonyms received separate entries, with explanatory references between headings used); Noblemen; Married women; various other changes of name: under the name normally used in their books, i.e. generally, the best known form. Instances when the academically accurate name was not the best known form included certain saints, classical authors, and oriental authors. In these cases, English form was generally used, except that the vernacular form was used for saints canonised after 1850.

Concordances were entered under compiler, as in the American exception to the rule.

Publishers' names were used for entry of certain works, e.g. certain directories and atlases, when the works were estimated to be best known by these names.

Periodicals issued by societies were entered under the societies if these names were prominent in titles and if the work had no distinctive title otherwise.

The author's name was not repeated in the description if it was the same as in the heading. Unused forenames, however, were included in the heading but in brackets.

Some of these practices follow ALA 1949 (published the year before BNB started) and anticipate AACR.

AACR: 1968 forwards

BNB started using AACR British text from the beginning of 1968, almost while it was still wet from the press. (AACR itself was the first document catalogued, according to AACR, in 1968.) This contrasts, in BNB's favour, with Library of Congress, which virtually uses AACR North American text only for completely new headings, one strange exception apparently being Catholic Liturgies. (Meanwhile, Australia's newly instituted central cataloguing system has used AACR North American text from its inception, the apparent reason being that the British text was not available at the time.)

BNB, like many British libraries, had long since departed from AA 1908 in some important respects, and, as a central catalogue agency, had possibly caused such changes to be accepted by other libraries. Its adoption of AACR will very likely have similar far-reaching effects, and its interpretation of AACR may well become standard, in many British libraries at least. For this reason, its interpretation of AACR is particularly important. There follows a summary of BNB's AACR practice:

1. Designations, like *ed.* and *tr.* are not used.
2. Librettos are entered under librettist.
3. Pseudonyms are used, linked by explanatory references.
4. Non-roman alphabet names are given in a commonly accepted English form when there is one.
5. Non-Western language corporate authors are given in the English form.
6. Unlike AACR, BNB will continue spelling out forenames when known, even though only initials are used in documents.
7. When works are entered under pseudonyms, the real name of the author is given as a tracing in the weekly printed list and on 'set' cards.
8. Uniform titles are used less than in AACR, being limited to pre-1900 titles.
9. Collation includes 'bibl.' and 'index' although these forms are not catered for in collation in AACR.

Most of these decisions seem acceptable to the libraries which mainly use BNB's services, especially since BNB's anticipation of AACR means that there will be comparatively few important changes in headings between pre-1968 and 1968 forwards. However, the usefulness of the librettos decision may be doubtful.

The continued spelling out of forenames causes some extra work for BNB cataloguers, and the extra work may not be worth it, except for large research libraries. From the commonsense point of view it seems unfortunate that the 'Priestley, John Boynton' type of artificiality will continue to irritate users and subscribers in many libraries. It may be that AACR's Uniform title rules would be well worth adopting more fully. The incorporation of information about a bibliography and an index in a document are of dubious value in some catalogues, although such information may be of value in the use of BNB lists as a selection tool, as it may give some idea of scholarliness and authority in a work.

The main disadvantages of the BNB card service stem from its essential reliance on British copyright law, and from its being a by-product of a national bibliographic service. One could theoretically suggest ways in which improvements might be effected, such as BNB's buying advance copies of all documents—book and non-book, British and non-British—for which libraries might need cards. However, such radical changes would result in a completely different organisation, and no doubt in a greatly increased cost to subscribers. In conclusion, we might remember that BNB's card service—whatever its faults and limitations—is increasingly used, and probably the least expensive in the English-speaking world.

LIBRARY OF CONGRESS

1. Coverage

Very wide—possibly at the rate of over 200,000 documents a year. Not confined to U.S. copyright material, or even to only Library of Congress acquisitions. Scope extended even further from 1966 with the inauguration of shared cataloguing, e.g. allowing access to and use of BNB entries.

Retrospective coverage is nominally complete back to the inception of the service in 1901. However, cards go out of print from time to time and apparently are reprinted only when demand seems to justify this; data on cards is not normally updated at reprint times. It has to be remembered that the LC card service started as a by-product of one library's own cataloguing needs, and this fact obtrudes frequently.

Children's books. See item 2, below.

Special materials. Audio-visual materials, and atlases and maps are included in the service. A really complete service is given for the (usually American-produced) films covered, including for example, sets of cards with added entry headings ready-printed-in.

2. Technical processes

Codes. Virtually, the service still uses ALA 1949, which it anticipated, and to which its practice contributed, following on from the U.S. alternatives in AA 1908, and its own rules. AACR North American text has officially been adopted but to date has been for the most part invoked only for headings not already in the LC catalogues. This perpetuation of poorer author headings than those derived from AACR, even its North American text, will undoubtedly, one suggests, set back American and American-influenced cataloguing a great deal, especially since these headings are now being fossilised in MARC data.

Classification. On many entries DC as well as LC class marks are given. A very important refinement of the service's DC classification is a method of shortening numbers called 'segmentation'. DC numbers cannot be arbitrarily shortened while still preserving a consistent logic, e.g. a 3-figure or a 6-figure minimum may often result in, in effect, cutting an isolate into halves. So DC numbers are now marked at one or two points to show how they may be logically and consistently abbreviated, through the use of apostrophes put at the suitable 'break-off' points, e.g. a history of music in Kent would be given as 780.9'42'23. So, depending on a library's closeness of classification the number can be adjusted to represent (a) history of music 780.9; or (b) history of music in Britain 780.942; or (c), its full number, history of music in Kent, as part of Britain. It is up to the local library to use this device consistently, e.g. at a certain subject whether or not to use . . . 03 for dictionary of that subject.

One has a suspicion that in the past the service has sometimes been less academic in its interpretation of DC than has BNB, but it is difficult to draw close comparisons because LC tends to use the later editions of DC. In any case, the 17th edition—drawn up in effect under the control of Library of Congress—is itself one feels more academic in the sense that it obviously discourages 'slotification'—the use of a number as a comprehensive works place, or as a 'concrete', for a subject. Symbolically perhaps, the Introduction to DC 17th edition uses Jews and Judaism as an example—sending all facets of them wandering throughout the whole schedules. There are indications that DC 18th edition will again allow for 'comprehensive works' numbers. There are no idiosyncratic extensions or modifications in LC's use of DC, as some may allege applies to BNB. However, since DC is revised by Library of Congress, a watch can be kept on the development of subjects with a view to incorporation of expansions and relocations in later editions of DC.

Children's books. Special entries, suitable for use by children, are now used, thus attempting to compete with the Wilson service. These include suitable DC numbers (9th abridged edition) and subject headings, and often annotations.

Fullness and detail correspond with conventional code usage. One feels that LC gives more notes and contents lists than does BNB. However, one has come across criticisms of LC cards on this count; that they are cluttered up with unwanted detail. On the other hand, a contents list can be far more useful than pernickety collation data, and it would be unfortunate if LC were prevailed upon to give up such a degree of sophistication. One of these years, when Project MARC reaches the point of analysis of documents, such data could be invaluable, although presumably it will have to make its peace with such conventional printed services as the *Essay and general literature index*.

Tracings are given in conventional American pattern at the foot of the unit entry, along with class marks, and distinguishing between collaborator (roman numbered) and subject (arabic numbered).

The dictionary catalogue is assumed, using of course Library of Congress' own subject headings. The LC card service has without doubt contributed to the widespread, uniform adoption of the 'conventional' dictionary catalogue throughout North America. In turn, the service may account for the fact that the LC subject headings list is Library of Congress' best-seller, since it is vital to have it in subscribing libraries to ensure insertion of appropriate references to back up headings traced on cards. Subscribers have the added advantage that when a new heading is needed, the LC service will include one which will become integrated into supplements to, and later editions of, the list of headings. But LC subject headings and references provide the supreme example of how a far-from-perfect system becomes entrenched—even to the point now that they, with all their blatant imperfections, are being perpetuated in Project MARC.

Use with bibliographies. Libraries using LC cards tend to use the Library of Congress' own printed catalogues, which are made from facsimiles of the card entries. The LC catalogues represent the most comprehensive current service in the world to English-speaking countries, and are therefore indispensable to all research libraries, whether national, public or university. Headings are usually similar enough to those in H. W. Wilson's catalogues to enable these to be used alongside LC-card catalogues and LC's printed catalogues.

3. Cost

It is not possible to give exact figures because charges vary with different types of document, e.g. cards for a Korean work are more expensive than those for an American work. Very approximately, the cost of a card may range from 6 to 10 cents, and the set of entries for the average book will be about 20 cents. On average, it can be seen that one has to pay extra for any superiority which the service has over BNB's. However, there is little doubt that American libraries in particular—which may spend $2 or $3 or more cataloguing a book—and as near as possible identically with LC practice anyway—gain by using the service. Libraries which wish to partake of LC cataloguing, but which wish to reproduce their own cards, can subscribe to the rapid service available through LC 'proofsheets'. These are intended as a basis for facsimile reproduction as well as clerical copying, and cost up to $210 a year.

4. Administration, which, in this case particularly, is very much interlinked with cost.

It is very easy to order LC cards. Many books themselves, American and some other countries', carry an LC card number on the back of the title page; LC issues blocks of numbers to publishers in advance so that if a book is received before publication, or even LC cataloguing, card-ordering can be put in hand. A disadvantage is that a librarian may receive the idea that the existence of the LC number means that cards are ready and waiting. Also LC numbers appear not only in LC's own advance lists but also in many U.S. trade bibliographies, e.g. the Wilson lists.

Cards with books is very widely practised in the United States by a variety of commercial processing agencies, regional cooperative schemes, and increasingly by some publishers even. One is approaching, then, the advantages of cataloguing in source without its disadvantages.

The LC service is the most stable service available in the English-speaking world. The *Annual reports of the Librarian of Congress* reveal the extent of the income derived from the sale of cards, so the service would be very unlikely to suffer from any economic axes, whatever political party or administration is in power. In fact, at the moment it is making a profit. Perhaps it is too stable in its monopoly, which may account for the lack of progress in entry, whether author or subject, of LC cataloguing.

Promptness. Generally, cards are received within three weeks of ordering. In the 1950's there were some allegations of lateness of receipt, or even non-receipt, of cards, either through tardiness in the processing or because the relevant works were never catalogued by LC, or because cards were out of print. Shared cataloguing will help remove fears of LC's never cataloguing a work, and the service may well become as near complete as one can reasonably expect. However, because of its international complexities, one may justifiably retain fears that promptness may not be improved: it remains to be seen. It should be emphasised that LC does not exercise copyright control over its data, and other, local or commercial, services can therefore produce their own entries from the data given in LC lists, especially its advance proofsheets, which can be facsimile-copied, to be incorporated into a complete processing service.

Library of Congress itself has become an international agency for the processing of data, via Shared cataloguing, although, as already mentioned, the headings—the most vital components, one suggests—are amended to conform to LC practice.

5. Physical appearance, etc.

This has already been touched on in item 2 in relation to fullness of entries. LC cards have more indentations than BNB's, and so particular parts of entries may be found more readily.

Up to the present, conventional relief type has been used, with its customary variety of bold type, lightface type, italics, and smaller sizes if required, e.g. for contents lists. In general, and despite allegations of over-fullness, one feels that LC cards are satisfactory, assuming the present layout: criticisms of the latter are included at the end of Chapter 25, Physical forms of catalogue.

When ready-printed-in sets are available and obtained, the overall appearance is enhanced because the added headings match the rest of the entry typographically.

Recently, LC cards have been slightly off-white in colour, and very likely this makes them less trying to the eyes than the 'blank-white' of most other cards.

LC cards are thicker than BNB's, and presumably more durable—assuming this is necessary.

More space has been devoted to LC cards here than is customary in works of British origin. The main reason is that the scope of the service should be regarded as a challenge by the British library profession. This, as has already been mentioned, is not solely the responsibility of BNB by any means. Practising librarians must invest both money and faith. There are signs that BNB itself is increasingly sensitive to consumer pressure. One hopes for the time when such materials as music scores, sound recordings and moving films are common enough in British libraries for their inclusion in a national central catalogue card service to be viable. (BCM cards were produced by BNB in 1957-58, but support of the service did not warrant its continuance.) Second, one feels that the LC service as it is could be profitably considered by more British libraries—and certainly more Australian (dictionary catalogue) libraries—especially the large and expanding, and new, university libraries. Suitable and sizable pressure, from potential non-American subscribers, especially those using LC classification, might stimulate LC to bring its cataloguing techniques more into line with current thought, rather than remaining in the 1940's in author and title work and in the early 1900's in subject work. Third, Shared cataloguing will bring about more and more interchange of catalogue data, not only between Britain and the United States, but throughout the world. So willy-nilly, libraries outside the present LC sphere of influence may find themselves partaking more and more of catalogue data originating in, or passing through, the Library of Congress.

H. W. WILSON CO.

Wilson does not seem to compete with the gargantuan LC service. It sets out to serve children's libraries and the smaller public libraries, a large proportion of which are small systems, compared with Britain, although increasingly they receive technical services from commercial cooperative schemes or via state libraries.

Because of the lack of application of Wilson cards outside North America, the system is dealt with briefly here.

1. Coverage

The Company's own bibliographical publications are automatically included in the service, and these are likely to be needed in any English-speaking library in the world. In general, however, the service is confined to only a few thousand American books a year.

2. Technical services

Only DC numbers are given, and these in a short form to suit the nature of the subscribing libraries. The service is dictionary catalogue oriented. Sears subject headings are used. Author work seems to be slightly more ambitious than LC's, the new Code even being anticipated in some respects. Description is adequate for the purpose, some omissions being apparent and justifiable. Notes and annotations are comparatively plentiful, and in laymen's (or children's) language. Conventional tracings are included at the foot of cards.

3. Cost

Cost is lower than LC's, at approximately 10 cents per set.

4. Administration

As already mentioned, the cards may be incorporated into a cards-with-books complete service. Cards are ordered from Wilson lists—the practice carrying with it the temptation to use these as 'pre-selection' tools. The service shows no signs of discontinuance, and so may be regarded as stable. Cards are normally received on a weekly basis, the inference being that the service is prompt. When sets of cards are ordered for a work, one receives the full complement of added entries according to the tracings plus an additional card for the shelf list. The local library must make any references required.

5. Physical appearance, etc.

The cards are printed from relief type, catering for a variety of sizes, e.g. collation and long notes are usually in a smaller type than headings and titles. Wilson cards seem to have the best appearance of the central cataloguing cards examined in this chapter.

Card stock seems to be thick enough and durable.

Even taking into account the narrow coverage of the service, Wilson cards set an example to the rest of the English-speaking world.

H.M.S.O.

Even some British librarians seem to be unaware of the existence of H.M.S.O.'s catalogue card service. The service is an approach to cataloguing in source in the sense that the cataloguing is undertaken by the publisher.

1. Coverage

All items included in the *Daily list of government publications*, i.e. including also works sold by but not published by H.M.S.O. The service has been running since 1950.

2. Technical processes

Entries do not conform to any generally used code, and no conventional class numbers are given. But full information about each document is given on each card, and space is left at the top of each card for a library to type in its own heading and uniform title if required. Details correspond with those in H.M.S.O.'s own 'catalogues' of publications (which some libraries 'mark up' and use as a catalogue-substitute), including prices of documents, with their postage charges.

3. Cost

Cards may not be bought individually, but are sold by the set, i.e. one card for each work published. Cost of the first set is £12 10s. a year; subsequent sets cost £9 10s. a year. Sets excluding statutory instruments are £10 and £7 respectively. Cards are sent out daily, and the prices include postage. However, if cards are posted weekly only, rates are reduced by £2 10s. on the first set and 10s. on subsequent sets.

4. Administration

As already inferred, ordering is simple, since one automatically takes a complete set. Even if a library does not use the cards as catalogue entries, it can use them as a selection and ordering medium, using two sets, obviating the labour of making out order and record cards.

5. Physical appearance, etc.

The cards do not match, in layout, any other agency cards. However, they are clearly printed and their unorthodox layout would simply have to be tolerated if they were to be interfiled with cards produced in the library or obtained from another central source. They are on quite thick card and seem to be durable.

LONG PLAYING RECORD LIBRARY
'LPRL (unit entry) catalogue cards'

This service is included as an example of a little-known service, and which is restricted to a particular type of special material.

1. Coverage

All L.P.s currently available through normal commercial channels in Britain, including approximately 4,000 basic repertoire recordings. Thus, non-music records within these categories are also included. Jazz and 'pop' are excluded. All sizes of records—12″, 10″ and 7″—are included, although 7″ records are not strictly L.P.s.

2. Technical processes

Generally, conventional cataloguing is followed, composer being the author-equivalent. But in a few occasions, e.g. where the unifying factor is a performer (performing several works by a variety of composers), the performer's name is taken as the main entry heading. The service started before AACR was published and does not seem to have been influenced by it. Uniform titles are not used, despite the need for them previously shown in the ALA/MLA code (dealt with in Chapter 20, on Special materials).

No class numbers are given, which is justifiable at the moment, since records are not usually minutely classified. However, one does not see why a card service should not try to cause innovation if this enhances its value to a library. No tracings are given. In fact, then, a record librarian must still construct his own added entry headings and subject catalogue.

Detail included seems generally sufficient, as can be seen from the facsimile reproduced at the end of this chapter. Manufacturers' names and serial numbers are included, for the benefit of libraries whose records are arranged in serial number order, and to help identification.

A cause for doubt is that some records appear to be catalogued from sleeves obtained from manufacturers.

3. Cost

6d. per card, plus 3d. for each additional copy of a card. To this, as with many unit card services, one must add the cost of professional and clerical work involved in typing in added headings, etc.

4. Administration

Cards are preferably ordered from LPRL's own record catalogue, since it is then known in advance which cards are available. The catalogue costs only 7s. 6d. and so libraries not buying records from LPRL have inexpensive access to the service. The cards could be particularly time-saving when a record library is initiated. In this case, selection would tend to be guided by what LPRL had thought worth stocking. However, this might be an advantage in some cases, where the library concerned did not have the expertise or time to do its own selection from scratch.

Promptness seems open to doubt to some extent. But, as in other central catalogue services, one must compare the service honestly with how long a document would await technical processing in a local library.

5. Physical appearance, etc.

The entries are produced from embossed metal plates produced on a typewriter, and so they have the appearance of normal typewriting. But the local alternative might well be a similar typewriter, or duplicated form from typewritten masters.

There is no indentation, which makes it difficult to find certain elements of information, especially since the title runs straight on into contents list where relevant.

A similar service is run by Record Specialities, another commerical organisation catering particularly for libraries. Prices are similar to LPRL's. See facsimile at the end of this chapter.

BRITISH STANDARDS INSTITUTION
  Methods for the analysis of nickel for use in
  electronic tubes and valves. London, British
  Standards Institution.
  Part 16: Determination of combined and free magnesium.
  4/-. Feb 1966. 7p. 21cm. Sd. (British standard 3727: Part
  15: 1966)
                                        (B66-23836)

621.381pmNf

   18. Examples of cards from central catalogue agencies.

   18 (a). British National Bibliography card: 1966.

[NORTH Wales, southern section]. Aberystwyth and
  North Wales (southern section): Borth, Machynlleth,
  Towyn, Barmouth, Pwllheli, Criccieth, 16th ed.;
  edited by Reginald J.W. Hammond. London: Ward,
  Lock, 9/6. 1968.
  159p, 16plates; illus,maps(incl 4col). 19cm. (Red
  guides)
914.291/3(1)   (B68-03304)

   18 (b). British National Bibliography card: 1968.

CARAVAN and camping sites and farmhouse
accommodation.
1969. London: British Travel Association. (1969).
3/6. (2), 60p; illus. map. 21cm. Sd.
Cover title: Britain: caravan and camping sites and
farmhouse accommodation. 'Abbreviations and
terms' in English, French, German, Dutch,
Swedish, Spanish and Italian.
*647. 97(1)

647. 94   sbn 900225 26 2   (B69-07948)

18 (c). British National Bibliography 'daily' card: 1969.

CARBERY, Thomas F
Consumers in politics: a history and general
review of the Co-operative Party, by Thomas F.
Carbery. Manchester: Manchester U.P., 1969.
50/-. sbn 7190 0347 4
vii, 276p. 23cm. bibl p264-268; index.
          329.9'42
                                        (B69-07030)
1. Ti

18 (d). British National Bibliography card: 'weekly set' 1969.

Skrobucha, Heinz.

Sinai; with photographs by George W. Allan, translated by Geoffrey Hunt. London, New York, Oxford U. P., 1966.

viii, 120 p.   illus., 28 plates (some col.)   maps, plan, facsims. 19½ cm.   70/-

(B 67-2272)

Bibliography: p. 110-113.

1. Sinai, Saint Catherine (Basilian monastery)   ɪ. Allan, George W.   ɪɪ. Title.

DS110.5.S513   915.3'1'03   67-76663

Library of Congress   ₁3₁

18 (*e*). Library of Congress card incorporating British National Bibliography description.

Roorbach, Orville Augustus, 1803-1861.

Bibliotheca Americana: catalogue of American publications, including reprints and original works, from 1820 to ₁Jan. 1861₁ ...   Metuchen, N. J., Mini-Print Corp., 1967.

1 v. (various pagings)   28 cm.

First published in New York, 1852-61 in 4 v.
Bound with Kelly, James.   The American catalogue of books. Metuchen, N. J., 1967.
Photocopy in reduced size.

1. U. S.—Imprints.   2. Law—U. S.—Bibl.   3. American periodicals— Bibl.   ɪ. Title.

Z1215.A3   1967   015.73   67-8332

Library of Congress   ₁5₁

18 (*f*). Library of Congress card.

COMPOSERS—DICTIONARIES

920.03   Ewen, David, ed.
    Great composers, 1300-1900; a biographical and critical
guide.   Wilson, H.W. 1966
    429p illus
        This volume "is a replacement for 'Composers of Yesterday,' published in
    1937." Introduction
        A reference book which furnishes biographical, critical, analytical, and
    historical information on about 200 composers of the past, both the musical
    giants, and lesser masters. Entries, alphabetically arranged by composer,
    incorporate principal works and bibliographies. Appendixes offer a chrono-
    logical listing of composers, and a listing by nationality

    1 Composers—Dictionaries   I Title   920.03

                                    (W)   The H. W. Wilson Company
                       18 (g). Wilson card.

U.S.—HISTORY—REVOLUTION—FICTION

         Bowen, Richard M
Bo   Nails, a boy at Bunker Hill and
         Valley Forge, by Richard M. Bowen.
         With illus. by Nathan Goldstein.
         Barre 1967
            44p   illus

         1.U.S.—History—Revolution—Fiction
         I.Title

    18 (h). Typical U.S. commercial agency card as part of complete book-
                          processing kit.

UNITED KINGDOM ATOMIC ENERGY AUTHORITY

A.E.R.E.:
  Bib. 148 List of Unclassified Documents, Lectures, etc.
            by the Staff of the Chemistry Division, A.E.R.E.,
            Harwell, 1965. Jan. 1966. 26pp., 11.1/2 x
            8.1/8in. (30 x 21cm.).

                                    Placed on Sale 8.2.66

Sold but not published by H.M.S.O.

                              PRICE   4s.(4s.6d.)

H.M. Stationery Office
  17 **London**
                    18 (*i*). HMSO card.

MENDELSSOHN,Felix:Symphony no.4 in A ma.
("Italian") op.90 (1 side)
SCHUBERT,Franz: Symphony no.5 in Bb ma.
(1 side)

Israel Philharmonic Orchestra cond.Georg Solti

Decca (m) ADD 121 (s) SDD 121

                18 (*j*). Long Playing Record Library card.

MAHLER, Gustav

Lieder Eines Fahrenden Gesellen
(Fischer-Dieskau; Philharmonia/Furtwangler)

Kindertotenlieder.
(Fischer-Dieskau; Berlin Phil.Orch/Kempe)

(2 sides)   HMV XLP 30044   (mono)

18 (*k*). Record Specialities card.

LONDON UNIVERSITY. Institute of education.
    ... The problems of secondary education today.
London, Evans bros. limited, [1955]
    viii, 153p. 18cm. (Studies in education. 6)
    This edition first published 1954.

                                         373.42
                                         373.42
                                         373.5(41)

    Britain only.

18 (*l*). Locally produced litho offset card (College of Librarianship Wales)
for comparison. (AA 1908.)

CHAPTER 29

Shared Cataloguing; Cataloguing in Source; Union Catalogue Compilation; Standard Book Numbers

SHARED CATALOGUING

Literally 'shared cataloguing' means 'cooperative cataloguing', defined at the beginning of this section. But the term was coined to represent an unprecedentedly large scheme of international cooperative cataloguing based on the Library of Congress.

The skeleton of the scheme is that the cataloguing of a country is based upon, or coordinated by, the national library or the national bibliographic centre of that country. The centre sends copies of its catalogue entries to the Library of Congress. LC processes the data to make it conform to LC practice, or at least near enough as to make no substantial difference. LC then is in a position to make available catalogue entries—as cards and in its *National union catalog*—to libraries requiring them.

The basic theory presupposes that all countries have a centre with:

(a) immediate access to all worthwhile material produced in that country, and

(b) the skill and facilities to produce catalogue entries which are informative enough to enable LC cataloguers to fit the entries into its own cataloguing scheme, i.e. not merely to identify a document, but also to classify and subject catalogue it.

Also, the whole scheme, to be effective, must operate at an unprecedentedly fast rate: entries should be available in time to obviate a participating library's having to catalogue works itself. A refinement of the scheme—but essential for its success—is that material should be catalogued in the 'home' country before publication, otherwise the LC output will arrive too late, presumably even if expected only in LC's 'proofsheets' (in advance of NUC) from which subscribers can make facsimile copies of entries for local reproduction.

'*Title II*'

To understand this formidable scheme, one must go back to before 1965, when it became forcibly apparent that LC central cataloguing, even though the most extensive in the English-speaking world, could not keep pace with the needs of the major U.S. research libraries. Estimates have varied, but possibly 30 to 40 per cent of the stock intake of some libraries was not covered by the LC service, even though the service already incorporated cooperative cataloguing from other North American libraries.

Also, it had become obvious—despite the ambitious Farmington Plan for the mass acquisition of non-American materials—that U.S. research libraries were deficient in research materials from outside the U.S. Consequently the federal *Higher education act 1965* included a section—Title II—making available funds to obtain all research materials of the world which could be of value in U.S. tertiary education and research. This material could not be used effectively if it were not exploited—hence the need for cataloguing it in a way which brought it to the notice of all interested American libraries, the obvious vehicle being the American printed *National union catalog*. The cataloguing programme emanating from this need therefore became known as *Title II*, and it was started in 1966. In the first place, a catalogue entry is supplied by the supplying country to LC agents in the country, and these are used as a selection medium. If the material described is then selected, the *Title II* cataloguing procedure goes into action, resulting in an entry in NUC and the acquisition of the material by LC for itself or to be deposited with another research library, the location appearing in NUC. One important proviso has to be made: material receiving the full treatment at present is generally monographic research material only.

So far the advantage would seem to apply mainly to the U.S. But if the scheme were operated fast enough, and if libraries throughout the world were willing to accept LC cataloguing, it becomes apparent that all libraries would be assured of the existence of a prompt central catalogue card service for, theoretically, all noteworthy research monographs of the world.

The earliest foreign agencies to cooperate in *Title II* and Shared cataloguing were BNB and the National Library of Australia, and by 1966 LC cards were appearing, including BNB description, this reflecting 'British practice, which is considered to be as comprehensive as current LC practice or more so' (L.C. *Bulletin* 75, May 1966). However, it is

noteworthy that all entry terms (the most important elements in cataloguing) were transformed into LC practice: i.e. main and added author
headings, subject headings, and DC numbers.

If a British library wants to partake of Shared cataloguing it has to do
so via NUC or LC cards; there is no reciprocal appearance of LC entries in
BNB lists or as BNB cards. It seems at present that British government
publications are not part of the scheme. The apparent reason is that
H.M.S.O. lists are sufficient for LC selection purposes. This brings
home to non-American participants in shared cataloguing the fact that
shared cataloguing is, in fact, a by-product of American book selection
policy; it is not geared towards an altruistic world-wide central cataloguing system. We must continue to wait—or work—for this.

Shared cataloguing dovetails into Operation MARC, and this obvious
and logical conclusion is dealt with in Chapter 32.

CATALOGUING IN SOURCE

A work which is catalogued in source is catalogued before publication
so that the basic entry, including tracings, may be printed into the book.
An example is shown on pages 360 and 361, but excluding subject
approach. Therefore, the book carries with it its own catalogue data,
hence K. Lodewyck's term 'self-cataloguing book'. Ranganathan's term
'pre-natal cataloguing', though rather fanciful, is probably more
accurate. However, Ranganathan's term appears to apply also to the
mere inclusion of a card order number in books, and so could apparently
apply to most of LC cataloguing as at present.

It is salutory to recall that, although the general practice has still
not been realised, it was suggested at least as long ago as 1876, and experiments were made during that decade by the American firm of Bowkers.

In the early 1950's a noteworthy Australian experiment was made by
the publishers Cheshires of Melbourne and the Melbourne University
Press in conjunction with Melbourne University Library. A 'pre-natal
cataloguing' experiment was also conducted by the Australian publishers
Angus and Robertson with the then Commonwealth National Library
(now National Library of Australia), the idea being that the publishers
would print and issue cards with books.

The most far-reaching experiment was run by Library of Congress
during 1958, financed by the Council on Library Resources, and involving the cataloguing in source of some 1,000 books from a total of 230
publishers.

Seminar on the Anglo-American Cataloguing Rules (1967)

Proceedings of the Seminar
organized by the Cataloguing and Indexing Group
of the Library Association
at the University of Nottingham
22nd–25th March 1968

Edited by
J. C. DOWNING, F.L.A.
and
N. F. SHARP, B.A., F.L.A.

London
The Library Association
1969

19. Cataloguing in source.
19 (*a*). Title page.

SᴇᴍɪɴᴀR ᴏɴ ᴛʜᴇ Aɴɢʟᴏ-Aᴍᴇʀɪᴄᴀɴ Cᴀᴛᴀʟᴏɢᴜɪɴɢ Rᴜʟᴇs (1967), *University of Nottingham, 1968*

Seminar on the Anglo-American Cataloguing Rules (1967): proceedings of the Seminar organised by the Cataloguing & Indexing Group of the Library Association at the University of Nottingham, 22nd–25th March 1968; edited by J. C. Downing and N. F. Sharp. London: Library Association, 1969.

xii, 104 p. 30 cm. *Pbk.*

1. Downing, J. C. 2. Sharp, N. F. 3. Library Association. *Cataloguing & Indexing Group.*

---

19 (*b*). From verso of title page.

All of these experiments ended in failure. The only viable forms of the method are those of: (*a*) H. W. Wilson, mentioned before, whose published reference works include relevant sets of Wilson cards; and (*b*) British government publications cards which are compiled in effect by the publishers. But in neither case is the entry printed in the book itself, and so—according to the strict definition—these practices do not belong to cataloguing in source.

Therefore, we must conclude, however reluctantly, that for various reasons, the method has not yet proved practicable, at least on a large scale. So it is dealt with quite summarily here.

Advantages

1. A book carries with it its own catalogue entry, which can be copied in any way a library chooses. So whatever library orders a book, whether operated by professional staff or not, the book can be catalogued accurately on receipt.

2. A book carries with it its own details for tracing it in a catalogue.

3. The system has all the advantages of uniformity as central cataloguing, e.g. lack of duplication of effort of cataloguers all over the world.

4. In certain circumstances, and especially if changes are not insisted upon, facsimile copies may be made, thus obviating checking for accuracy in clerical copying.

Disadvantages (emerging mainly from the Library of Congress experiment) (*a*) From publishers:

1. Delay in publication.

2. Unsightliness of the full catalogue entry in the book, usually on the back of the title page. (Alternatives have been suggested from time to time, such as having the entry at the back of the book, or even on the dust-wrapper.)

3. Technical difficulties in reproducing entry on back of title page, including some resultant 'show through'.

4. Extra cost.

5. In some cases, apparently, disagreement with the librarian's mundane representation of the book in the catalogue entry.

(*b*) From librarians:

1. Publishers and printers change the book after cataloguing, resulting in inaccurate entries. In the LC experiment 48 per cent showed some change, however insignificant.

2. Some librarians prefer existing services, e.g. in U.S., LC and Wilson, and the many *ad hoc* regional schemes for small public libraries.

3. Professional decisions are still required to cater for local variations, possibly making the entry in the book inaccurate and misleading compared with the library's own records.

4. School librarians complained of too much detail in some entries.

5. Local reproduction of the entry is still required, this necessitating local plant.

6. Library of Congress cataloguers in particular complained of the unrewarding nature of the work because of changes after cataloguing, and LC as an institution estimated that the method if adopted on a full-scale level would cost more than publishers, libraries and LC itself would be willing to pay, including the need for regional representatives from LC.

The LC Report stated: 'The underlying purpose of the experiment was to ascertain whether a permanent, full-scale program of Cataloging-in-Source could be justified in terms of financing, technical considerations, and utility. As regards this, the answer must be a regretful negative.'

The report stressed that existing methods were more satisfactory including particularly its own card service, and various commercial services derived from its own cataloguing data, presumably as issued on its proofsheets. We cannot help feeling that Library of Congress itself was not the most impartial body to report on a system which, if adopted, would upset its own very complicated and painstaking organisation built up over half a century, and in which it stood to lose millions of dollars of income a year.

UNION CATALOGUE COMPILATION

Here we are concerned primarily with the principles and problems involved in compiling union catalogues which extend beyond one library system's holdings.

It should be confirmed at the outset that a union catalogue is a finding list for specific named works.

Throughout this section the 'agency' or 'centre' responsible for compiling or maintaining a union catalogue may be:

(a) a library, e.g. Birmingham Public Library as the centre for the West Midland Region in Britain; or

(b) an organisation whose primary function is its union catalogues, e.g. the National Central Library in London; or

(c) even certain individuals, e.g. Pollard and Redgrave, compilers of the *Short-title catalogue.*

Basic considerations

1. The type of material to be included. It is not enough merely to say e.g. 'periodicals', since different librarians may have different interpretations of the terms. Therefore, the compilers must ascertain first exactly what the need is, and then define their requirements in unambiguous terms.

2. The territorial or language coverage of type of material to be included. For example, the products of a country, or of a region of the world, or of all the world; or of English-language, or of Russian-language materials.

3. The territorial locations of libraries whose holdings are to be included. The contents of all of a nation's libraries may be decided upon, or the catalogue may be confined to a region, perhaps the London area. Perhaps even the whole world may be contemplated.

Another factor is that certain types of libraries within the chosen area may be excluded or included. This may be because:

(a) some are unlikely to have unique holdings, e.g. most school libraries; or possibly

(b) they may be private or very restricted libraries which are unlikely to allow use to be made of their holdings. However, certain 'private' libraries participate actively in a nation's library service, e.g. the older subscription libraries, such as the Birmingham Library, which built up runs of important journals contemporaneously with their publication from, say, the eighteenth century.

4. The physical form of the catalogue. In the past single copies on sheaf slips or cards have been common in Britain, as instanced by the Regional bureaux, and, embracing these, the National Central Library's *National union catalogue*. In these cases the type of material was monographic and included some element of ephemeral material; therefore there was, and still is, a considerable amount of insertion and withdrawal going on all the time. Such a form tends to the assumption that the centre maintaining the catalogue will act as a clearing house for requests: a considerable responsibility. The centre is run on subscriptions levied on libraries taking part. The value of the single-copy catalogue has increased with the introduction of the teleprinter as a rapid and accurate means of communication replacing postal communication.

However, the present custom is for multiple copies in printed form. These are sold to libraries, thus, we hope, making the catalogue economically feasible. Individual libraries are then usually responsible for requesting the material required from the holding library or libraries. (Libraries whose names, or symbols, come early in the alphabet have been known to think twice about where they should appear in future editions.) A problem to be settled in the case of printed catalogues is the method of up-dating, as discussed in Chapter 25.

5. The arrangement of the catalogue. Customarily, catalogues are arranged alphabetically by author and/or title. The choice of catalogue code, which decides headings, and the choice of filing rules, are relevant. One hopes, of course, for a degree of uniformity in heading practice between the cooperating libraries. The cost of editing entries, and even correctly identifying them, may be considerable. However, the British regional and national union catalogues of monographs were initiated at a time when the code then current, AA 1908, was diverged from, and even ignored, in many cooperating libraries. It is possible, as in the American *National union catalog*, to find the same work entered twice under different headings. One has to be realistic and reach a compromise

between cataloguing perfection and actually getting the catalogue published and into use.

Sub-arrangement at a heading has to be decided. If AACR's rules for uniform titles become accepted in practice, and if they themselves are applied uniformly, a great deal of editing could be avoided in the future. We assume here that the bibliographic unit for monographic works will be author-title, or uniform (collective) title in the case of works entered under title. A union catalogue is not primarily concerned with the range of works from one author. Therefore, some union catalogues employ a method of arrangement of

(a) author's surname only; then
(b) first word of title not an article.

This factor is also incorporated into Chapter 24, Filing.

Union catalogues of periodicals can cause problems, because cataloguing rules usually cater for two types of entry: some works go under titles, while others go under corporate authors responsible for their existence. Some catalogues may ignore such rules and have a rigid title entry principle. The bibliographic unit is the specific work and collocation under corporate authors, respecting intellectual responsibility, is irrelevant. So the only real difficulty may be differentiating between the many titles starting with such generic words as 'Proceedings' and 'Journal'.

Some suggestions have been made for, e.g. arranging by first noun, or first noun in the nominative case. It is doubtful whether this disinterment of the British Museum-type significant word principle is wholly satisfactory. Perhaps it would be preferable at a union catalogue centre to refuse to accept requests which do not conform to a rigid first-word form of citation. In the case of printed catalogues, it is obviously the responsibility of the subscribing libraries to learn to use the catalogue properly.

Further problems are generated by changes of names and titles. Since the bibliographic unit of union catalogues should be narrow, one would consider consecutive entry. However, there is a case for complete entry at one point, e.g. under 'best known' title. This is a very significant problem, and it is discussed at greater length in Section II on Catalogue codes.

6. Methods of compilation. Procedure may vary, depending on whether the catalogue is in one-copy unit record form, or printed form.

In the past, Britain's regional union catalogues of monographs have usually been compiled by sending boxes of slips round 'sub-circuits' within the region, these eventually being transcribed on to master slips in the union catalogue itself. Withdrawals have been notified direct by the library concerned, usually by sending in copies of catalogue cards representing the withdrawn items.

Another method is for all libraries to send slips direct to the catalogue centre, where all locations for each item are filled in. In some British regions there has been a practice of relying on the larger libraries in the regions for the most part.

Yet another is the circulation of lists of desiderata, these eventually going back to the centre where they are entered on to the master entry. This method has been used in Australia and New Zealand to some extent; it is known as LURB—*List of unlocated research books.*

Australia has also used microfilming: complete catalogues of libraries have been microfilmed on location in an effort to make up, retrospectively, a complete national union catalogue of monographs. The film is developed and stored; as staff time permits, full-size cards are xerographically printed and filed in. The agency compiling a catalogue may, then, send compilers to the contributing libraries to ensure that they get the information required, and in the way in which they require it. Sometimes libraries themselves do not know their own holdings: the compilers of the *British union-catalogue of early printed music,* during their visits to libraries, sometimes surprised the owners with material which they unearthed. When time is short, entries can be checked by telephone or teleprinter. Microfilming has also been used in North America for notifying additions to NUC by post.

Amalgamation of British public library authorities has sometimes cut across regional boundaries, causing a great deal of re-sorting and re-recording of locations: the *London union catalogue* has particularly been affected.

7. Details in entries. The basic requirements are:

(a) sufficient information to identify a document; and
(b) locations of each document.

(a) varies a great deal depending on what type of material is being dealt with. It is desirable for exact holdings of serials to be given, but a very irregularly taken run would cause too much complication and space consumption to be recorded in detail. Usually union catalogues of serials content themselves with start, and end if applicable, of holdings with a symbol indicating if incomplete. (*b*) locations are usually given in one of two ways:

(i) by arbitrary numbers, as in the British regional union catalogues; or, more usually,

(ii) by some form of abbreviations of libraries' names, perhaps prefixed by locations—the latter may be important when deciding which library to request from, or even to visit. Initials and acronyms are preferable to numbers, because they can incorporate literal mnemonic qualities.

Persuading contributors to send in information about the required types of material, in the required fullness, in the correct form, and by the required date can be an arduous task. Perhaps it is naïve to suppose that librarians should know what to cite and how to cite it.

8. Substitutes for union catalogues. In reference work it may be preferable to approach a library direct when it is well known for its subject coverage in a particular field, rather than go through the process of identifying likely documents in bibliographies and indexes and then locating them through union catalogues. In such cases, directories of libraries would be used.

9. The future. The time will undoubtedly come when a union catalogue is commonly in machine-readable form in the store of a computer. In this case, it can be tapped and 'conversed with'.

STANDARD BOOK NUMBERS

This item has been referred to from time to time, and librarians of the near future are more and more likely to come across, use, and even rely on standard book numbers. They are included here because they are a manifestation of cooperation between libraries, central cataloguing services, and the book trade. The topic is also very relevant to mechanisation in cataloguing.

The immediate object of SBN's is to produce a unique number for every work published. Ultimately, the number could be used whenever a specific work has to be cited. So, works can be cited uniquely, and also economically as compared with the present practice of having to name author, title, edition, etc. Since SBN's are in arabic numerals they can be easily quoted and are conveniently machine-readable. Part of the number is constant for any publisher and so serves to facilitate the citation of publishers also.

Possible applications include: Ordering and re-ordering of books—library to supplier, supplier to publisher; Ordering of catalogue cards or other records: SBN's will very likely replace BNB serial numbers; and Inter-library lending.

The SBN of a book is usually given on back of title page, back board of binding, and on dust wrapper. The intention is that every printed document shall have an SBN; that is, as far as Britain is concerned, that it should be possible in the future to identify every publication by its SBN. Some other countries have initiated, or put in hand, SBN programmes, notably U.S. and Australia. This will entail in the future, and in international control, the use of prefixes to represent countries. This could be done using letters, as with cars travelling abroad, e.g. GB for Britain. However, a more conveniently handled prefix might be an arabic number followed by a suitable, machine-readable, punctuation mark.

Precedents can be found for the use of, usually, arbitrary, identifying numbers for books. Some suppliers already use a numbering system for their stocks—W. H. Smith, for example, since computerising its records in 1965. BNB, LC and Wilson use numbers for card-ordering purposes. Whitakers have used a numbering system for many years. Also some libraries have given each physical copy of a work a unique number, usually consisting of a class number, author number, title number, possibly edition number, and a copy-number, comprising in combination a call number.

SBN's are administered in Britain by the Standard Book Numbering Agency, composed of Whitaker, BNB, and the Publishers' Association. In addition to coordination, it also handles the actual numbering for smaller publishers. Publishers assign numbers to works, about six weeks before publication date, and incorporating their own numbers. Basic records are kept by the Agency, including an SBN file, a publishers' number file, and an alphabetical publishers' index to the publishers' number file.

Each number consists of 9 digits, made up of 3 components:

(a) Publisher's number, from 2 to 6 digits;
(b) Title number, from 1 to 6 digits,
       such that (a) and (b) come to a total of 8 digits;

(*c*) A check digit. This number is recognised by computers in such a way as to ensure that clerical errors have not been made in (*a*) and (*b*): details of how this system operates are given in the Agency's publication *Standard book numbering*, page 6.

More prolific publishers receive the smaller numbers, and have available therefore more title numbers, and vice versa. An example of an actual number is Patrick Quigg's *Theory of cataloguing* 2nd edition—85157 061 5. In this, 85157 is the number of Bingley, the publisher; 061 is the title number on Bingley's list; and 5 is the check number. AACR British text is 85365 170 1. That is, LA 85365; title number 170; check digit 1.

Two possible faults in the scheme are self-evident:

(*a*) some publishers persist in not knowing of the existence of SBN's, or if they know, they may not bother to use them;
(*b*) numbers may be misquoted, as is always liable to happen with an arbitrary, non-expressive symbol.

However, it seems likely that inter-library computerisation will come sooner, if books can be cited by SBN's, because of the great economies in storage, handling, and transfer of information. In general, the introduction of SBN's will prompt libraries to ensure access to computers and so to hasten the day of full computerisation of information.

SECTION VI

MECHANISATION OF CATALOGUES AND CATALOGUING

Mechanisation of Catalogues and Cataloguing

Works cited in the text

BNB MARC Documentation service: Publications. No. 1: Marc record service proposals . . . presented by R. E. Coward. London: BNB, 1968. SBN 900220 08 2.

Also, No. 3 includes an account of the proposed use of PRECIS: BNB subject descriptors.

COUNCIL ON LIBRARY RESOURCES. Automation and the Library of Congress; Gilbert W. King, Chairman. Washington: Government Printing Office, 1963.   KING REPORT

FORD FOUNDATION. Scholars' work and works. The Foundation, 1963.

HOUGHTON, BERNARD. Computer-based information retrieval systems; edited by Bernard Houghton. London: Bingley, 1968. SBN 85157 059 3.

INTERNATIONAL BUSINESS MACHINES. Report of a pilot project for converting the pre-1952 National union catalog to a machine readable record: a study sponsored by the Council on Library Resources. Rockville, Maryland: I.B.M., 1965.

LIBRARY ASSOCIATION. *Cataloguing and Indexing Group.* Residential seminar on the United Kingdom MARC Project, University of Southampton, 28th to 31st March 1969. [Proceedings to be published.]

LIBRARY OF CONGRESS. *Information Systems Office.* The MARC pilot experience: an informal summary. Washington: L.C., 1968.

For the most part replacing the same department's Project MARC: an experiment in automating Library of Congress catalog data, 1967.

LOCAL GOVERNMENT COMPUTER COMMITTEE. Computer applications in the library service; First report on cataloguing: Report of a Working Party of the Local and Public Authorities' Computer Panel. London: The Computer Panel, 1967.

Other readings

ALLEN, PAUL. Exploring the computer. London: Addison-Wesley, 1967.

A straightforward programmed text for the beginner.

ANGLO-AMERICAN CONFERENCE ON THE MECHANIZATION OF LIBRARY

SERVICES, *Brasenose College, Oxford University, 1966*. Proceedings . . .; ed. by John Harrison and Peter Laslett. London: Mansell, 1967.

BATTY, C. D. Libraries and machines today . . .; ed. by C. D. Batty. [Scunthorpe, Lincs., England]: L. A. North Midland Branch, 1967.

BATTY, C. D. The library and the machine . . .; ed. by C. D. Batty. Scunthorpe, Lincs., England: L.A. North Midland Branch, 1966.

COATES, E. J. Computer assistance in the production of BTI, *in* Library Association record, vol. 70, no. 1, October 1968, p. 255-257.

COX, N. S. M. The computer and the library . . ., by N. S. M. Cox, J. D. Lewis and J. L. Dolby. Newcastle: University of Newcastle upon Tyne. Library, 1966.

COX, N. S. M. Organization and handling of bibliographic records by computer; ed. by N. S. M. Cox and M. W. Grose. Newcastle: Oriel Press, 1967.

KIMBER, R. T. The MARC II format, *in* Program, vol. 2, no. 1, April 1968, p. 34-37.

SHARP, JOHN R. Some fundamentals of information retrieval. (Details given in Section III.)

SWANSON, DON R. Dialogues with a catalog, *in* Strout, Ruth French. Library catalogs: changing dimensions . . . Chicago: University of Chicago Press, 1964, p. 113-125. Reprinted from Library quarterly, January 1964.

CHAPTER 30

The Background; Historical Evolution; Mechanisation other than the Computer

THE BACKGROUND

Definitions: Mechanisation; Automation

These terms receive varying interpretations.

(*a*) Some authorities regard them as differing in degree, i.e. 'mechanisation' applies if one operation previously performed by a human is then done by a machine but which itself is operated by a human, e.g. instead of copying information by hand a typewriter is used. Following this, a punched-tape typewriter may be used which can be programmed—or instructed—by a human before the operation is started. Theoretically, it can be set up, switched on, and left to operate itself. This would be automation, as no machine-minder would be necessary. In practice though, punched-tape typewriters usually have a supervisor to type in various headings and to feed in new punched tapes. This is where the difference is one of degree and not of nature.

(*b*) Other authorities may establish a clearer-cut difference, where 'mechanisation' means passing one specific job to a machine, while 'automation' means the whole operation is planned integrally, but an operator can step in to guide and select according to needs.

In this chapter, 'mechanisation' is used in a generic simple sense, embracing all forms of passing work over to machines.

Mechanisation is not a topic on its own: in cataloguer's terminology, it is a distributed relative. Whatever cataloguing topic is considered, there may be a mechanisation aspect to it: perhaps simple, perhaps complex. Cataloguing should not be considered in isolation from other library technical processes, but as one use of a common record of stock data, to be used for both catalogue and other purposes.

Why mechanise?

The important basic factors in mechanisation are speed, efficiency, and accuracy. A further one is economy, which may be overlooked under the influence of colleagues, other professions, and salesmen.

One machine may do two or more jobs effectively, such as a xerographic reproduction machine which can copy not only reference materials and administrative information to staff, but also catalogue entries.

The impact of these basic factors on the potential use of machines in relation to that of humans will now be examined.

There is an ever-growing quantity today of important library materials which cover an increasingly complex range of subject, language and authorship. Unless proper documentation is made, vital information may be overlooked, causing duplication of costly research. On the other hand, busy and highly paid research workers do not have time to scan large numbers of documents only to have to reject most of them as irrelevant. Many professional and clerical workers would have to be employed to do this job, and still they might not be able to work fast and accurately enough to keep up with demand. We reach the point when it becomes impossible to use humans in the traditional technical processing of documents, especially since these people require longer and more expensive education in both subject awareness and in library science.

Therefore, there is a need to investigate the potential of mechanisation in information retrieval of all sorts.

Part of such an investigation involves a systematic and detailed analysis of what is required from an information service and how these requirements are met. It may so happen that an investigation will result in a decision not to mechanise, but to streamline human processes. The important thing is to decide on a system which is most efficient, speedy and economic in the prevailing circumstances. In fact, there are not many sophisticated machines made especially for library purposes, and even those that are may not be suitable for every need. The principle involved is similar to library planning in that the librarian should know exactly what he wants, as, if a mistake is made, it is the library staff and the service which directly suffer. This does not mean that librarians should refrain from mechanising in case they make mistakes: it means that they must be aware of what can be put into machines and what can be got out of them. They have to differentiate between what is 'technologically feasible' and what is practicable and useful. In the early 1960's, for example, machine optical character recognition (optical scanning)—a machine which could 'read' print—and machine translating were being developed. It seemed that in a short time they would

"EXCUSE ME:

BUT YOUR

COMPUTER'S

SHOWING..."

There are actually two computer centres at District Bank.

We are quite proud of them, of course, and believe that their efficiency and speed of working can do much to maintain and improve the quality of our service.

At the same time, we are determined that the computers will never "take over." Our customers need never feel they are becoming merely names and numbers in our records. We still set great store by our tradition for friendly personal service which has been built up over many years. All our managers and staff like to know their customers personally.

Find out for yourself by walking into your nearest branch of District Bank. (You can look up the address in the phone book.)

DISTRICT BANK

 AN UNUSUALLY PERSONAL BANKING SERVICE
Head Office: Spring Gardens, Manchester 2
City Office: 75 Cornhill, London E.C.3.

20. Example of optical character recognition (machine optically 'readable') typography.

(But note that far more sophisticated forms have now been developed.)

be in common use. Yet, in retrospect, we can see that some of the assumptions made at the time were science fiction. Only in the past year or so has optical character recognition become more feasible, and machines can now 'read' numbers written by human beings. An example of the sort of alphabetical character which machines can conveniently handle optically at present is shown in the facsimile on page 377.

HISTORICAL EVOLUTION; MECHANISATION OTHER THAN THE COMPUTER

The first invention was printing from movable types 500 years ago—a recent event in the long history of human communications. This method is still the most common way of communicating the products of the computer to man's eyes. The computer's 'line-printer' is in effect a set of drums with the tops of types fixed to them.

Printing produced the first information explosion (if it is not the other way round). This created an unprecedented demand for inexpensive paper. Hence the mechanisation of papermaking. Again, were it not for very cheap paper, computers could not afford to be so prodigal in their consumption of it.

Next, we can consider the rising need for rapid but accurate calculating machines, stemming indirectly from the Renaissance and Enlightenment of the fifteenth to eighteenth centuries. Early in the seventeenth century, a man named Napier made a rudimentary multiplication and division machine known as 'Napier's bones', which now we would dub 'a breakthrough'. Various other calculating machines were devised over the next two hundred years, using increasingly sophisticated mechanisms, until 1822 saw the invention of Babbage's important but uncompleted 'calculating engine': nowadays we would say that his machine was technologically feasible. The rest of the nineteenth century saw the development of similar but more practical machines, usually worked by gears. The main application of such machines was in bookkeeping, i.e. the manipulation of figures—a heritage which librarians with their need for letter- and word-manipulation are still finding inconvenient. Towards the end of the nineteenth century, electricity was applied, with a resultant increase in speed and a decrease in size of machines.

The typewriter was invented and commercialised in the 1870's, though for several years it was rejected by some 'copper-plate' librarians.

In fact, there is at least one university library whose catalogue was in manuscript card form up till the 1950's.

During the last half of the nineteenth century came the invention and application of photography. Photocopying has been used in the British Museum for nearly a hundred years, although its potential for catalogue-copying seems, strangely, to have been overlooked. Microphotography has been used since the 1870's—the besieged Parisians in the Franco-Prussian war used a microphotographic pigeon post. Photographic and other forms of facsimile copying are important in catalogue reproduction, as was shown in Chapters 25 and 26.

During the 1890's, punched card sorting, by electrically operated machines, was introduced by Hollerith, originally to sort and collate data collected in a U.S. Census. 'Body-punched' cards can be sorted into order, interfiled (interpolated), and the results of calculations (matching) can be printed out (tabulated). The punched card method—essentially the manipulation of unit records (i.e. a physically separate unit for each document record) was a long-lasting precursor to the computer. The method is still used in systems where separate unit records are convenient, where occasional hand filing and human identification is useful, and where the system does not warrant the cost of a computer. It must be emphasised that the original punching of the holes into cards is a human job, and the operation must be checked (verified) before the card can be used. It must be remembered too that the items of information to be recorded must be coded, i.e. represented in numerical form, in order to be punched into the cards. Finally, a sort may take two or more operations. So, although the method is much faster and more accurate than hand-filing, it takes both time in itself and the time of a trained operator to set the required digits on the machine and to remove the packs of cards from their trays.

It may be salutary to bear in mind that although the electrical-mechanical sorting of punched cards was developed in the 1890's, it took several decades before it was used in librarianship at all commonly.

Punched cards can be used as computer input, and so here there is a connection between the established medium of punched card unit records and the more novel medium of electronic data processing.

Another well-established medium which took some time to become accepted in library usage is the teleprinter. Telegraphy (sending coded messages along wires as electrical impulses) developed gradually during the nineteenth century, and teleprinting is a further application of this. The important difference is that the operator types in the message at the transmitting end as though operating a normal typewriter, which makes a hard copy (normal human-readable copy on paper) simultaneously; while the receiver prints out a hard copy on paper tape automatically at the other end. There does not have to be a human operator:

(*a*) permanently waiting for messages, which
(*b*) he may possibly record inaccurately.

The teleprinter (trade-name Telex in Britain) was introduced into British inter-library communication in the late 1950's and early 1960's and it is now a fairly common method in some systems, e.g. for the speedy and accurate transmission of requests from branch libraries to headquarters; or between library systems; or between libraries and regional or national union catalogue centres.

The teleprinter is particularly relevant here because it is used in some libraries in combination with mechanical means of rapid access to the conventional card catalogue.

Trade-names of such types of card catalogue mechanisation are Kard-veyer and Lektriever. The machinery is simply a means of getting the required catalogue drawer to the member of staff who needs to use it. This type of apparatus is shown by the illustration facing page 300 in Chapter 25. The user presses buttons to have the appropriate tier of drawers or individual drawer brought before him. He then consults, and copies from, the catalogue manually.

Closed-circuit television has also been experimented with as a means of remote consultation of card catalogues, under the name 'telereference.' A rather cumbersome mechanical method of card turning would have to go with the system, and it does not seem to have been developed beyond the experimental stage.

Telefacsimile is still in its developmental phase in librarianship also. It means the transmission of a facsimile copy of an image along lines or wires, the original image being reproduced, say, on a xerographic machine at the other end. The principle involved is not new; pictures have been transmitted and received by radio (i.e. without lines) for newspaper use for many years. The potential value of telefacsimile (trade-name Telefax) in conjunction with teleprinting in library science is easily imagined, but it does not seem to have been used in the transmission of catalogue entries.

In general, cataloguing trends exhibit a form of dichotomy: either (*a*) multiple copies of printed union catalogues, a copy at each main service point; or (*b*) one copy of a grand union catalogue with quick and accurate access from each main service point. The principle of the latter seems more likely to become standard, while the former is likely to survive as a means of locating more specialised items, e.g. runs of periodicals or incunabula.

Another invention whose basic principle is of long standing, but whose application in librarianship is a fairly recent development, is that of punched tape. This has already been mentioned in Chapter 26 on the reproduction of catalogue entries. Here a reminder is needed that punched tape can be used as computer input. It has an advantage over punched cards in that it can be kept in the form of either unit records or of continuous records.

CHAPTER 31

The Computer

The type of computer with which librarians are usually concerned is the digital computer: it may cost £500,000 and it is capable of one single mathematical operation—it knows the difference between 0 and 1, or Yes and No. The main difference between it and humans is that it can make the distinction thousands of times a second and it does so accurately.

The computer's chief application at the moment is as a very rapid and accurate filing and printing device. Computers were originally designed for mathematical work, as the name means, i.e. handling numerals. Further, they were originally designed for printing out material—calculations—which would be used usually by a very few people and then discarded.

For this reason, computer printout up to the present has usually been unaesthetic, to say the least. Possible improvements are discussed later.

The method of operation of the computer is straightforward in principle.

(a) Data—in our case, catalogue entries—is fed into the computer in machine-readable form, e.g. as punched tape which may have been produced on a punched-tape typewriter, which at the same time produced 'hard copy' for visual checking and correction of mistakes.

(b) The store of the computer retains the information in the form of electromagnetic charges in binary patterns on, say, magnetic tape.

(c) An additional series of entries may then be fed in, as in (a), perhaps a supplement to be interfiled with the main sequence of entries.

(d) The two sequences are in effect interfiled or interpolated. For example, the contents of the two reels of magnetic tape might be merged, and the resulting single sequence is now represented by a single series of electromagnetic charges in binary form on a third magnetic tape.

(e) The final single sequence is printed out by the line-printer of the computer onto continuous zig-zag paper stock in natural language, i.e. hard copy or human readable form.

```
EDUCATION AND PSYCHOLOGY REVIEW (BARODA)
    1, NO. 1-, 1961-, LO.
    2-, 1962-, AB.

EDUCATION BOOK GUIDE
    2, 1957; 4-, 1959-, KE.

EDUCATION BULLETIN (BRITISH COLUMBIA)
    1-, 1957-, LO.
    1-2, MAR, 1957 - MAR, 1958, LD.

EDUCATION BULLETIN (L.C.C.)
    NO. 450-, 1958-, (INCOMPLETE), KE.

EDUCATION BULLETIN (TRANSVAAL)
    1-, 1956-, (INCOMPLETE), LO.
    1, NOS. 2-4, 1956; 2, NOS. 1, 2, 4, 1957; 3, NOS.
       1, 3, 1958; 4-7, 1959-62, BH.

EDUCATION CIRCULAR (W. AUSTRALIA)
    1954-, (INCOMPLETE), LO.

EDUCATION DIGEST
    13, NO. 5-, JAN, 1948-, (LACKS: 13, NO. 6; 14, NOS.
       2, 8; 16, NO. 9), BH.

EDUCATION ENFANTINE
    41, NO. 1, 15TH SEPT, 1947; 43, NO. 1 - 45, NO. 3,
       15TH SEPT, 1948 - NOV, 1950, LC.

EDUCATION EQUIPMENT
    6, NO. 5-, MAY, 1965-, DR.

EDUCATION ET BIBLIOTHEQUES
    NO. 1-, 1961-, LO: (INCOMPLETE), RE.

EDUCATION ET DEVELOPPEMENT
    1-, OCT, 1964-, SO.

EDUCATION FOR BUSINESS
    NO. 45-, 1963-, LO.

EDUCATION FOR TEACHING, FORMERLY BULLETIN OF EDUCATION
    2-, JUNE, 1943-, (LACKS: NOS. 3-5; 7-10; 15), NO.
       6, NOV, 1944; 11-, DEC, 1946-, (LACKS: 13, 15), BH.
    15-, MAR, 1948-, HL.
    15-, MAR, 1948-, (LACKS: 33-34, 37), BR.
    15-, MAR, 1948-, (LACKS: 17), RE.
    15, 17, MAR, DEC, 1948; 20-, NOV, 1949-, NW.
    16-, JUNE, 1948-, LD.
```

21. Paginated computer printout from: *Union list of periodicals held in Institute of Education Libraries. . .* 1966. (Produced at the University of Newcastle upon Tyne for Librarians of Institutes and Schools of Education.)
  A later edition (1968) is computer typeset in monophoto with upper and lower case and varied typefounts.

The next two operations are not directly connected with the computer.

(*f*) If this copy is the final version required, the printout is then photographically or xerographically facsimile-copied to produce the number of copies needed.

(*g*) These copies may then be bound, with the addition of title page, instructions for use, etc., produced by a probably more attractive conventional process, e.g. Varietyper/Multilith.

Book-form catalogues were produced in this way by some of the new London Boroughs when presented with the problem of rapid inter-filing of two or more catalogue sequences after authorities amalgamated in the 1960's. Good use was made of the computer facilities available at the time, though the resulting catalogues were not perfect. Nothing has been lost by these developments in computer-printed catalogues, and libraries in several countries have been passing through this development phase. Criticisms of these pioneer catalogues may be summarised as follows:

(*a*) The product is not aesthetically pleasing. Computer line-printers operate at a rapid rate and letters are often vertically out of line, or are indistinct, e.g. D may become confused with O, which can be important if these letters represent locations in a union catalogue.

(*b*) Early catalogues were in upper case only, although later efforts also include lower case; and the range of characters available was severely limited in other respects as well.

(*c*) The line-printer produces a very long line of print. These catalogues have often been 'title-a-liners'—an interesting hark back to some of the conventionally printed catalogues of the nineteenth century. The eye may find it trying to follow one entry taking perhaps a foot length of irregular type.

Further relevant experiments include:

(i) the photographic reduction of the printout to a more physically and usually manageable form, as in the University of Aston in Birmingham; and

(ii) the programming of the computer to make it paginate the print-out which can then be treated like a section of a book and folded to produce an octavo-size volume (a facsimile of such an example, from the University of Newcastle Computer Unit, is shown opposite);

(iii) the reduction of size seems to make the final print more readable, since gaps within individual letters are closed up, and of course the final volume is more convenient to handle, shelve, etc.: the facsimile illustrated is full size.

(d) Some complaints have been voiced about the brevity of entries. This can be important when short fixed fields are used, which restrict each part of the entry to a length which may often be shorter than needed for a full author heading or class mark. AACR often allows shorter author headings than previous codes, and so as it becomes adopted this problem may be alleviated to some extent. The real solution lies in variable fields, which allow each part of an entry to be as long as needed, as is used in MARC II (discussed in Chapter 32); this may extend an entry to more than one line of type, and so it is more expensive. It is doubtful if complaints about lack of imprint and collocation are well-founded, since the type of catalogue in question is intended mainly as a finding list or location guide.

In general, complaints about aesthetics will presumably be answered eventually, when computer photo-type-setting becomes more economic. It is already technologically feasible, and a few wide-circulation services use it, e.g. MEDLARS (MEDical Literature Analysis and Retrieval System, of the U.S. National Library of Medicine). It is not within the scope of this work to detail the process of photo-typesetting. It is enough to say that the process:

(a) obviates the use of normal type, and uses instead photographic images of symbols—letters, numerals, punctuation etc.;

(b) allows access to all the ranges of sizes and founts of type as in traditional printing; and

(c) is faster, and occupies less space, than conventional mechanised type-setting, e.g. Monotype or Linotype.

The ideal situation is when the photo-type-setting equipment can be used directly as a peripheral to the computer.

COMPUTER POTENTIAL AND INFORMATION RETRIEVAL

The filing and printing use of computers normally takes the form of batch jobs, i.e. the computer is hired for a certain time to print out a catalogue in reasonably conventional-seeming physical form and with entries under conventional headings, e.g. author, title, class numbers, and alphabetical subject index.

At this point we should go back to the beginning and revise:

(a) what a catalogue's ultimate purpose is;

(*b*) all of the processes as a whole, and their purposes, which take place in a library.

A catalogue serves as a means of access to the information in a library's stock. What is likely to be wanted ultimately is one or more of the following:

(*a*) The whole document, or certain parts of it. Conventionally this has been in the form of a normal printed full-size copy. More recently, we have come to accept the idea of a facsimile copy of the original, or at a further remove, a micro-copy of the original.

A more recent concept is that of having the micro-form of the document inserted in an aperture in a punched card. This method means that when the catalogue entry is found, so is the document itself. A more concentrated manifestation of the same principle is that all of the library's information is stored on strips of microfilm in 'storage banks' and the required parts are printed up full-size only when required. Access to this information, via a variety of approaches, could be through a computer. It has been claimed that 'a ten foot cube can house over three million volumes—about half the total of the world's largest public library' [New York Public Library]. (*Scholars' work and works*, p. 20-21).

Further, all the information itself could 'technologically feasibly' be stored electronically in a computer storage unit, then recalled, examined on a screen, and if wanted, printed out full-size direct from the computer.

(*b*) An abstract of the document may enable the enquirer to decide if he wants the whole document, in whatever physical form the library would retrieve it. The theorists who maintain that subject headings or descriptors should be coextensive with the subject of the document— if taken literally—would in fact probably finish up with something approaching an abstract. For an abstract indicates the 'kernel' subject, treatment, viewpoint, originality, method of presentation, and conclusion of a document: and this is a truly coextensive statement of the 'subject' of the document in its fullest sense. It is usually impossible to express fully the subject in this sense, in a subject heading or set of descriptors. The abstract may be in a printed or similar conventional form, even as a conventional entry, or in some form of computer storage or printout.

(*c*) The hitherto conventionally accepted approaches or headings may be used as a starting point, as when the document is recorded in a conventional card catalogue. These headings may be of three types.

(i) *Author* and similar, usually representing citation of a document known or suspected to exist, by author, editor, translator, etc.

(ii) *Title*, which is now assuming again an importance which we thought died out after Cutter's pronouncement that the subject heading for a work did not necessarily coincide with the document's title. A document may be cited by title or partial title for two purposes:

1. by its title pure and simple because it is known;
2. by subject words remembered from its title.

The latter title/subject approach is used in the KWIC (Key Word in Context) type of approach, in which the title receives very short multiple entry under each key word in its title, each entry being arranged in its appropriate place in the computer-printed, or otherwise produced, index.

This modern re-invention of the subject-catchword approach is often used with computers, since the chief human labour involved is only the clerical work of keyboarding the appropriate words copied from the title, i.e. not derived from professional subject analysis and subsequent consistent indexing of the document itself. There is admittedly a case for including KWIC in (iii) subject, below.

(iii) *Subject*, which may be:

1. conventional as in American-type dictionary catalogues and the H. W. Wilson indexes;
2. less conventional and possibly more specific, as in some modern indexes, e.g. BTI; or
3. in uniterm or uniconcept descriptors, as in coordinate indexing, described in Chapter 18.

The uniconcept type of descriptor is the more common in computer information retrieval. When information is required which fits all of a specified list of descriptors, the computer can be instructed to carry out its YES/NO routine on all of the descriptions of documents recorded in it. It will indicate the bibliographic details only of the documents which fit all of the descriptors simultaneously. This information will be supplied in a far shorter time than it would take to run packs of punched cards through a sorter. Post-coordinate indexing techniques are ideal for computer manipulation. It is usual for computer-printed, computer-controlled, or computer-compiled information systems to use lists of isolated descriptors, perhaps key subject words selected from abstracts of documents, as in R.I.L.M. [Music] *Abstracts*; see facsimile on page 387.

1970 WEBERN, Anton von. **Langsamer Satz; for string quartet**
rn   (New York: C. Fischer, 1965).
        WEBERN, Anton von. **String quartet (1905)** (New York:
        C. Fischer, 1965).
Review by Wallace C. McKENZIE, *Notes* XXIV/1 (Sept 1967) 148–
50.

1971 WHITE, Eric Walter. **Stravinsky; the composer and his works**
rb   (London: Faber, 1966).
Review by David C. BROWN, *Music Review* XXVIII/3 (Aug 1967)
254–55.

1972 WHITE, Eric Walter. **Stravinsky, The composer and his works**
rb   (Berkeley and Los Angeles: U. of Calif.,P., 1966).
Review by Lawrence MORTON, *Musical Quarterly* LIII/4 (Oct 1967)
589–95.

1973 rb ___
Review by Richard SWIFT, *JAMS* XX/3 (Fall 1967) 507–10.

1974 WHITTALL, Arnold. **After Webern, Wagner; reflections on**
ap   **the past and future of Pierre Boulez,** *Music Review* XXVIII/2
        (May 1967) 135–38.
A comparison of the influences of Webern, Schönberg, Debussy,
Berg, and Wagner on Pierre Boulez. *(Edna Libby Wilchinsky)*

1975 WHITTALL, Arnold. **A new starting-point?** *Opera* XVIII/4
ap   (April 1967) 285–288. *Port., illus.*
Changes in the form and style of 20th-century opera are discussed
with reference to the music and ideas of John Cage, Schönberg,
Strauss, Berg, Britten, Stravinsky, David Bedford, Menotti, Richard
Rodney Bennett, and Gordon Crosse. Crucial works, such as Schönberg's *Erwartung, Pierrot Lunaire,* and *Moses und Aron* and *Music
for Albion Moonlight* by David Bedford are also discussed. *(Frank
M. Catalano)*

1976 WHITTALL, Arnold. **Varèse and organic athematicism,**
ap   *Music Review* XXVIII/4 (Nov 1967) 311–15. *Music.*
A discussion of the sources of coherence in *Déserts. Additional key-
words:* atonality, Klangfarbenmelodie. *(Jeffrey Ingbar)*

22. Excerpt from computer produced abstracts: R.I.L.M. [Music] abstracts.

(*d*) Bibliographic coupling is a comparatively newly developed system, which assumes that the more a document is cited in other documents then the more useful and relevant it is to the subjects covered by the relevant documents. The chief manifestation of this principle is the *Science citation index*, itself computer-produced. Such a compilation is comparatively straightforward from the professional point of view. Operators cause the computer to record the full bibliographic details of each document covered by the service together with authors and titles, and relevant bibliographic data, for other documents cited in the document being indexed. There are complications in compiling such works, as for example mentioned by A. E. Cawkell in HOUGHTON, cited at the beginning of this Section. But there is no direct intellectual effort, e.g. subject analysis, in the author-citation element: recording is clerical copying and not professional interpretation. For this reason, the system responds readily to automation. *Science citation index* was launched amid great publicity, but there is still some doubt as to whether it is as vital as its publicists would have us believe.

(*e*) Other approaches may conceivably include any item normally represented in an entry for a document. One of the very positive advantages of mechanisation is that the range of approaches may be extended almost indefinitely, provided all likely approaches are 'tagged'. This will be expanded upon in Chapter 32. The only characteristic which does not seem to have been mentioned is whether or not a particular document is original in its content, and this may be the very first characteristic by which an enquirer may approach it.

PRINTOUT APPLICATIONS

So far, it has been assumed that the filing and printing use of computers has been for libraries' complete catalogues, or for union catalogues. The basic policy in such cases is frequent revision and cumulation for local use, and the products of such policies should not therefore be compared directly with more permanent bibliographic catalogues produced by major research libraries for national and international use. At present such catalogues are usually prepared by more conventional methods, but the time will come when they are computer processed and printed via computer-controlled photo-typesetting.

Other 'printout' uses include Selective Dissemination of Information (SDI) services. A 'profile' of each relevant user of the library is maintained showing his subject interests. These can be matched against the store of the computer, and so 'personalised' lists of relevant documents can be printed out. Such a service would be more effective if input included the analysis of serial and report material and even abstracts of documents where necessary. Also, input can be obtained ready-made from a central source in the form of magnetic tape.

Rather similarly to SDI, various types of 'limited catalogue' can be produced, basically either:

(a) certain types of entries may be omitted, or included; or
(b) certain parts of entries may be omitted, or included, according to needs.

In a public library, catalogues of works suitable for children, or of fiction, or of play collections, or reading lists on certain subjects could be produced quickly and accurately, usually for general distribution, but conceivably at the request of various individuals or groups—schools, societies, etc.

So far, we have assumed list-form, but catalogue cards may be printed selectively or fully. A disadvantage is that these would have to be filed manually. However, in cases where comparatively few are needed, as in SDI services, they may be more convenient because they are unit records.

In any case, it is true that manually operated systems are the most satisfactory for many information needs and these might as well be in card form, for the sake of flexibility, as in any other form.

Citation lists, already mentioned, could be produced by individual libraries, and at individual demand.

OTHER APPLICATIONS, INCLUDING THE FUTURE

So far, it has been assumed for the most part that the computer's end-product is 'hard copy', which users then take away and use as one would a conventionally produced list or catalogue, by selecting documents from it, and then locating them on the shelves or in files.

But efforts have been made for several years now to obviate the intermediate printout stage of computer usage. The basic principle is that the complete catalogue is kept only in machine readable form. A request is fed via a keyboard into the computer, which then produces a tentative answer, e.g. a list of potentially useful documents. The list is in the form of a projection on to a screen, like that in a television receiver: it is not permanent, and can be erased if it is not suitable. The enquirer may then decide he would like more information on certain documents, so the computer is then asked to 'project' abstracts of these documents. We are now almost into the realms of fantasy, but let us continue to the logical conclusion, even though it is impracticable at present. The enquirer may then decide, from the abstracts, that he wants to read a particular document in full, in which case the computer will then reproduce the document for him, in facsimile form and including diagrams and so on if these were in the original.

The most striking fact in the ultimate view of automation is that the library as a collection of physical objects called books, periodicals and so on, no longer exists. All the information previously contained in these exists (as far as this library is concerned) only in machine readable storage form—a series of electromagnetic charges on reels of tape, or on discs, or in 'memory cells'. The equivalent of one octavo sized book of about 400 pages of text could be stored on one magnetic disc of about the same size as a 12″ L.P. record (though in fact it is not likely that this form would be used here). Account must then be taken of access to the information in it. There are three main aspects of this:

(a) Reader access in a physical way. Is it worth machine recording a conventional text only to have to reproduce it again in hard form, perhaps frequently? Many readers use a library's stock at the same time, so a computer would have to cater for simultaneous multiple access all the time. In computer practice this means 'real time' 'on line' access, via keyboards for feeding in the questions, and screens for looking at and selecting from replies. This questioning and answering—called dialogues with computers—is as yet far slower than the usual 'reference interview' between an enquirer and a member of the staff. It can also be very frustrating because computers have no intuition or common sense.

(b) Computer physical access. A 'reading head' must be able to traverse, say, the disc to start to retrieve the information on it. This usually means having the discs in packs with sufficient space between them to allow a comb-like instrument to pass between them. Further, all the records must be more or less simultaneously available. In fact, a far more compact form of storage to facilitate this random access would be used in the type of case envisaged here, but the physical problem still exists. But all the information liable to be needed—a whole library's worth—must be on tap all the time.

(c) Computer 'technical' access. This means that the computer must be prepared for locating and retrieving any items of information in its store. The ability of a computer to recognise elements of information is achieved by 'tagging' the headings which lead into the information. Unless the computer is tagged it will not be able to get directly to the required information. The computer must be 'told' which words it must be prepared to recognise, in somewhat the same way that a conventional catalogue card for a document carries tracings of all other entries relating to that document. It must store these words in readiness for matching them against the data stored. This means that a high proportion—perhaps up to one-fifth—of the computer's store will consist of instructions; this space will not be available for data from the documents themselves. Thus, programming is particularly important.

The job of getting information into a computer's memory bank is probably more complicated and time-consuming than setting up the type for a book. It will remain so until either optical character recognition devices are made which can read the great varieties and founts of type in use, or until all documents are printed in a type which is automatically readable visually by machine. An example of one such type of print is shown in the facsimile on page 377. Once done, however, it could then be sold to all libraries as copies of a book are sold. This raises the vexed problem of compatibility—what is made as the input of one make of computer is not necessarily readily assimilable by another. Converting units are available for 'translating' machine readable data from one form into another; but even this can be quite time-consuming and complicated.

Relevant here is the dream of national, or even international, grids linking computers—or perhaps one massive computer and storage unit to a great number of service points. This could possibly replace present union catalogues and would possibly offer far more extensive services. International on-line systems are already used by certain organisations, e.g. I.B.M. and I.C.I., to transmit information from the organisation's plant in one country to the parent or branch in another. This is possible because each individual firm has planned it so. But to make direct links between all firms, or in our case all libraries, is another matter, because of lack of compatibility between their computers.

At the moment, a library using a computer either uses its parent organisation's machine, or it buys time on a computer owned by another authority or organisation. Certainly at present there is no likelihood of libraries having their own computers. In fact, it has been said that there is only one library in Britain which might conceivably need a computer of its own: the British Museum.

However, there is already some inter-authority computer cooperation, part of this being for library purposes. Authorities, government departments, and industrial organisations needing close liaison could well decide to choose economically compatible machines in the future, or to share machines, as is happening in the present (1969) group MARC experiments in Britain.

SYSTEMS ANALYSIS

Bearing in mind the difficulties mentioned already, we should nevertheless be aware of ways in which computers can be made more integral to the *whole* of a library service, and not merely an agent for its catalogue service.

It is true that catalogues of a library are its longest-lasting, and its most accurate, records. Therefore it is not surprising if they are more expensive than other records to produce and maintain. However, much of the data in a catalogue is the same as the data used in other records. It is possible that a library may generate ten or more records, not all identical, but including some common data: a selection record; an order record; an accession record; various catalogue records for the library itself plus at least one other to send to a regional or national union catalogue; a new books list or SDI record; a binding record; and even a withdrawal record. In addition, libraries with a lending service make an issue record of some sort each time a document is taken out, and if it is not returned on time, one or more overdue reminders may be sent. Records of documents reserved may also be needed. It is common still in many libraries for many of these records to be copied clerically, in manuscript or on a typewriter, taking time and necessitating checking for errors in copying. Some libraries use facsimile-copying of cards, thereby obviating clerical checking. But, even so, yet another physical record has so been generated, with attendant time and space consumption.

Most libraries keep other records as well, e.g. lists of registered members. These may need selective copying, for re-registration or for overdue or reservation purposes.

Further records are generated and maintained, usually derived from those already mentioned, e.g. statistics of stock, of members, and of issues in various categories.

The basic question is then: Is it possible to compile one complete record at the start, store it in a computer and draw upon it or alter it as needed? This possibility should be distinguished from the automatic reproduction of extra copies of records.

A technical possibility at least, exists for having a central computer data bank, controlled by various programmes, and with a number of access points on line to it. It would act as a combined ordering record, stock control, issuing system and catalogue, and it would be used for the generation of whatever records in printed form were needed from time to time.

Such a system sounds too neat to be true, and for some libraries it might be more expensive than their present methods. Components of such a system should be borne in mind by librarians so that it may be an ideal to aim at. This would be preferable to the piecemeal approach now accepted in many libraries. There may be records which are common to various parts of a local authority's services, e.g. health and education records of people. No doubt there would be difficulties to overcome before records, for health purposes say, could be used for book-issue purposes. There are also ethical and legal, as well as technical, problems. Such systems exist in embryo in some industrial organisations which use computers for a great variety of purposes. It is feasible that universities may well prove to be a useful experimentation ground, especially since the question of whether or not the system was economic at present would be less relevant, in the interests of research.

Detail has not been included in this chapter of even outstanding specific applications of computers and information retrieval systems. Accounts exist in book form at the moment and details of some are given in the reading list preceding this Section: others are briefly described, with readings, in the second edition of QUIGG. The next chapter, however, is devoted to the MARC project, which, as well as being the most ambitious project to date, will help to fit certain technical terms into their context.

CHAPTER 32

Marc: Machine Readable Catalogue

Many sophisticated computer applications so far have been in information storage and retrieval systems in the more limited but detailed meaning of the term, i.e. for 'depth' indexing, usually by subject. The present work concerns cataloguing as a whole and these types of information retrieval systems cannot be dealt with in detail here.

However, there has emerged since 1966 a project which falls squarely within the scope of this book, and, further, which should ultimately take in the 'depth' indexing approach. This is MARC: MAchine Readable Catalogue. The project is more ambitious than implied by its label, and as catered for especially in BNB's MARC II programme. More accurately the project concerns machine readable bibliographic data, it is not only a computerised version of BNB cards.

MARC I

The project was inaugurated in fact as a machine readable form of Library of Congress catalogue data.

The origin of MARC was conceived in the Library of Congress in 1964, following upon the KING REPORT of 1963. A grant was made by the Council on Library Resources in 1965, and the project was started at an experimental level in February 1966. With the advent of a more sophisticated format arising from the experiment, the original project has retrospectively been called MARC I.

MARC I set out to produce magnetic tapes of the type and fullness of information normally printed on LC cards, including tracings. Therefore, computers could be used to print out catalogue entries, with a variety of approaches. The basic purpose of the project was to find out if the computer format was satisfactory and if the type of data given was useful; also to ascertain the best way of distributing machine readable data. Sixteen libraries in North America were selected to experiment with the tapes, as being the ones most interested, with sufficient funds, and with suitable computer facilities. Weekly tapes were sent to them starting in November 1966. The documents catalogued were English-language monographic works: 50,000 items were catalogued during the trial year. Results of the experiments were collected by the Library of Congress, which established an office called LOCATE (Library of Congress Automation Technique Exchange): a central record of MARC and other experiments in automation. A noteworthy result—of reassurance to some British librarians, perhaps—was that organisations with small computers achieved as successful results as those with larger ones. An official generalised report is *The MARC pilot experience: an informal summary*, 1968.

At the British MARC Seminar held at Southampton in 1969, C. D. Batty presented a paper including examples of four American libraries' MARC I experiments. He emphasised that MARC I had limitations, such as fixed fields: i.e. each part of a catalogue entry could not exceed a certain length. Nevertheless, a surprising variety of experiments had emerged. For example, Toronto University used the tapes more or less as expected, to print out catalogue entries. However, Yale University included a Selective Dissemination of Information (SDI) service, and interpolated locally produced data, for foreign-language monographs, with MARC records. Indiana University also experimented with an SDI service, using $5'' \times 3''$ cards.

It might be claimed that these services could virtually have been run from LC cards and/or proofsheets. However, the fourth sample, at Rice University, Texas, attempted a 'systems analysis' or integrated service, using the data as raw material for a variety of processes, including selection, ordering, organisation, and cataloguing. Perhaps the most important finding was that unchecked requests could be matched against MARC data, with up to a 98 per cent success rate. The request data had to be treated so that only the consonants of the root stems of words were manipulated to prevent the rejection of, say, a participle when the form used in the MARC data was a noun. Mr Batty's general contention was that MARC I had not been a failure, as believed by some librarians, but a necessary basis from which to approach MARC II. Further, MARC II itself must be experimented with if ultimately it is to be fully exploited.

The U.S. revised format tapes are now being supplied by the Library of Congress at a subscription of about $600 a year. Each weekly tape is about 300 feet long, and contains LC bibliographic data for up to 1,500 items. It is intended that ultimately data obtained from Shared cataloguing will be included in MARC tapes. By this reckoning, the Library of Congress would probably become the largest computer catalogue centre in the world. Catalogue and classification decisions are as on LC cards, outlined in Chapter 28, e.g. LC's use of AACR North American text is confined mainly to 'superimposition'—at present (1969) at least. It seems likely, then, that many traditional author/title and subject headings will be perpetuated even though improved rules are now available. On the other hand, BNB's MARC II will use some different headings from LC's, e.g. AACR British text's author/title headings, and so data exchanged between the two centres will have to be edited. It remains to be seen which, if any, will become accepted internationally. (A reminder may be necessary here of the types of fundamental differences involved: (a) the North American text of AACR is far more conservative than the British text; and (b) BNB uses Britain's AACR fully, as compared with LC's use at present of North America's AACR for only new headings, with very few exceptions.)

U.K. MARC II

MARC II is so called because its format is derived from and built upon Library of Congress' original pilot project.

A typical MARC entry is arranged on the tape in the order of its standard book number, or failing this by BNB serial number. These two types of numbers are coded so that they cannot become confused with each other. A new, international, form of 10-digit SBN's was introduced by BNB after the U.K. experiment started, and there is now no fear of confusion between British and other SBN's, e.g. when LC MARC data is used by BNB.

Each weekly tape gives data for several hundred documents, the weekly BNB printed list serving as an index to it by author and title. Libraries wanting cumulations of several weeks' tapes into one sequence, for convenience in sequential scanning, will do this themselves.

Each entry consists of full standard data according to AACR interpreted by BNB, as outlined in Chapter 28.

A facsimile of a basic or 'raw' printout, from BNB, is given between pages 398-399. The appearance of the entry ultimately printed by a library—assuming a printed form is used—depends on local decisions and the computer used locally. Entries can be produced looking like a conventional catalogue entry in layout and wording. In fact, current BNB cards are now being produced from BNB's MARC data, although actually printed from masters made on an electric I.B.M. Executive typewriter from punched paper tape—an achievement made possible by experimental work conducted by the computer laboratory of the University of Newcastle upon Tyne.

The example of raw data given here happens not to include all the components potentially available. The full potential of British MARC can be appreciated from a study of BNB MARC *Documentation service publications*, the first of which is detailed in the reading list at the start of this Section. There follows a brief description of the sample of BNB MARC printout reproduced here.

Lines 1 and 2 are book identification numbers.

Line 3 is date of publication; country of publication (en = England); brief indication of types of illustration and form of work; and language of text (eng = English).

Line 4 gives BNB DC number.

Line 5 gives DC 17th edition number.

(There is also provision for LC class numbers, and even for UDC numbers when given in the document.)

Line 6 is main author heading.

Line 7 is title.

Line 8 is imprint.

Line 9 is collation.

Line 10 is price in sterling.

Line 11 is series statement.

Line 12 is a relevant note for this document.

(There is considerable provision for varieties of notes; also for contents list, for each part of which analytical entries can be made automatically.)

Line 13 is LC subject heading.

(It is intended also to give special BNB subject descriptors, at Tag 690. These are being developed especially for machine manipulation. An outline of their proposed form is given in Chapter 15.)

(Added entries and references, e.g. for authors, are also catered for where required.)

A most important aspect of MARC is that almost any element of the entry may be used as an approach. This degree of flexibility necessitates a complex programme, with a large number of 'tags', each ensuring that that element can be used as an approach term, in effect the equivalent of an added entry heading. In addition to the usual author, title and subject approaches, others might include place of publication, language of text, and even different types of work like conference proceedings. Any of these approaches may transpire to be the vital element through which a document might be traced. This aspect therefore represents one degree of flexibility.

Another degree of flexibility is that each element of an entry can be virtually of any length: i.e. variable fields are used, replacing the fixed fields of MARC I. So, catalogues generated from MARC data will not be liable to have any part of the entry suddenly truncated because it has used up the number of characters allowed for it in that part.

These two essential aspects of flexibility—variety of approaches, and unrationed lengths of components of the entry, cause considerable complications in programming. A tag is used to indicate the start of each field (part of entry) and a further signal is needed to indicate the end of it, before the next tag is brought in to indicate the start of the next field, and so on. e.g. for main entry headings there are available separate tags for personal names, conferences, and uniform title. Again, there are separate tags for title, edition statement and imprint. Each of these tags introduces a field, and each field may be divided into sub-fields. So, Tag 260 indicates Imprint, which in turn is divided into three sub-fields indicated as follows:

$a Place of publication
$b Publisher or agent
$c Date

To cater for two, or three, places of publication and publishers, sub-fields $a and $b can be repeated:

$a 1st place $b 1st publisher $a 2nd place $b 2nd publisher, etc.

The MARC programme caters for lower and upper cases, and for all punctuation used traditionally in cataloguing, i.e. as codified in AACR. However, many computers in use at present will not necessarily be able to reproduce all of them; in this case, local programmers must decide which symbols to use as substitutes.

MARC AND THE FUTURE

One can approach the need which MARC will help meet via a report (among others) produced in Britain: the Local Government Computer Committee's *Computer applications in the library service: First report on cataloguing*, 1967. This includes an account of the basic problems involved, summarised as follows:

1. Lack of uniformity existent, e.g. in catalogue codes and classification.
2. Lack of comprehensiveness in coverage by the central service.
3. Lack of a unique method of identifying each document.

These problems can be substantiated by reference to Section V, on Centralisation of cataloguing. Problems 1 and 2 are only too self-evident, despite the levelling (upwards in many cases) from nearly a generation of BNB usage. Problem 3 is now being answered, with Britain in the lead, by the institution of standard book numbers described in Chapter 29. Other countries are planning their own SBN projects, including U.S., and plans are being made for the international control of SBN's.

The above-mentioned report also gives an ambitious account of Britain's cataloguing needs:

1. There should be a central file of all current catalogue data which is likely to be needed.
2. This file must be economical to maintain, and so it needs subsidising.
3. There should be the possibility of selecting required data.
4. There should be maintained an efficient union catalogue.
5. There should be a centralised information service.
6. There should be full international cooperation.
7. There should be a retrospective service, especially for the period before 1950 (i.e. when BNB started publication). The possibility of computerising the British Museum's catalogues is relevant here. This, although obviously a gigantic task, is not out of the question: in the U.S. the Council on Library Resources sponsored in 1965 an I.B.M. *Report of a pilot project for converting the pre-1952 National union catalog to a machine readable record* which seems to regard the concept as feasible, at least.

One would stress particularly another factor, in relation to the provision of current data, and as proved during the U.S. MARC pilot scheme: that is, the supply of data must be up to date. Lack of promptness in supply of cards is one of the recurring criticisms of central cataloguing agencies. This criticism is not repeated idly: one appreciates only too well the practical difficulties involved. The only real and complete solution would seem to be an authoritarian government which would enforce deposit of a copy of each document—say in page-proof form—at least a month before publication: but one somehow cannot imagine a general election being fought on such an issue.

These then are some theoretical requirements. We shall now examine BNB's proposals for U.K. MARC, and it can be estimated how far the practice, even if only visualised at the moment, hopes to meet the requirements.

U.K. MARC sets itself and its subscribers a high standard from the start: 'There is no reason why we should be prepared to accept a lower standard of organisation in our book catalogues simply because they are machine produced' (BNB MARC *Doc. 1*, Section 3.8). And, 'The MARC record will be produced and used in fairly advanced computer systems and yet even these are scarcely able to meet more than the minimum demands made by a bibliographic record and a bibliographic file' (BNB MARC *Doc. 1*, Section 1.2).

The operating agency for MARC is of course BNB, which received a grant from the British Government's Office of Scientific and Technical Information (OSTI) to support a research, developmental and pilot project resulting from a proposal from BNB in 1967. It is noteworthy that BNB was already considering computerisation before the Library of Congress launched its first MARC pilot project, and that the two organisations quickly appreciated the value of collaboration. So far, Britain is learning from the U.S., but, conversely, one should remember that BNB was the first overseas agency to have its catalogue data incorporated into Library of Congress' Shared catalogue programme.

As has already been mentioned, MARC is not just a magnetic tape version of BNB cards. In one way, it is less in that its data is not ready for direct incorporation into a conventional catalogue; but—significantly —it is more in that the data may be manipulated and applied to a great variety of uses, as has already been mentioned in relation to MARC I.

An important fact then, mentioned above, but which should be emphasised, is that 'Unlike most automation projects its end result is not a system, but a product designed to be used in systems. The product is a bibliographic record sufficiently detailed to meet the requirements of virtually any system and yet so structured that local systems can extract just the data for elements required' (BNB MARC *Doc. 1*, Section 1.1). There is no doubt that this is an accurate statement, but it behoves a British-oriented library to accept BNB MARC decisions as much as possible without amendment, if the service is to be a really economic proposition. An examination of a typical printout and of the programming of MARC will show that it is easier to omit certain sections of a catalogue entry rather than change others, e.g. collation can be, so to speak, programmed out; but a change from a BNB AACR author heading to an AA 1908 heading could cause a great deal of professional, clerical, and computer labour. However, for example, MARC Tag 910 'Corporate author cross-reference' would probably cater for most alternative approaches, while the existing references in a manually compiled catalogue would probably cater for references in the other direction (see example in BNB MARC *Doc. 1*, Section 15.2: AERONAUTICAL RESEARCH COUNCIL/GREAT BRITAIN. *Aeronautical Research Council*). Basically, then, an economic use of MARC is based on selection, and perhaps, manipulation, rather than change of MARC data.

In the past in Britain, perhaps too much emphasis has been devoted to the conventional cataloguing of 'books', meaning monographic printed materials, and usually implying 'British' or even 'English-language'. Yet, more and more, certain information retrieval systems have become preoccupied with almost everything other than 'books'. However, in the first place, MARC is covering bibliographic data on monographic materials, and especially those deposited under British copyright law. But MARC could extend further: 'The format presented in this report is a medium for the exchange of bibliographic data of all types of material. It will be developed to include periodical and report literature, manuscripts, computer media and audio-visual material' (BNB MARC *Doc. 1*, Section 1.1).

It is not only the forms of material which is important, but also the ways in which the service can be used. BNB suggests the following 'Services to individual library systems which must be investigated' [but not by whom] (BNB MARC *Doc. 1*, Section 1.10-1.11):

1. Book ordering and accession information.
2. Tape of cataloguing information.
3. Printed cards.
4. Book catalogues.

And for large library groups:

1. Exchange of tapes with other national MARC agencies.
2. Re-organisation of these tapes for use in Britain.
3. Supply of MARC information to on-line systems, e.g. copyright and university libraries.
4. Supply of data to the National Union Catalogue.

Not content with this, BNB MARC also envisages the production of special subject lists, etc., e.g. for school and children's libraries: its format caters for designation of intellectual level of documents. And, of course, the national bibliography would continue, but now as a by-product of the whole system and not the basis of it as at present.

The success of MARC will depend inevitably on two related factors: (a) Whether or not the initiators can economically realise their ambitions; and (b) Whether or not the project receives the support and trust of the library profession. It might be worth emphasis that U.K. MARC is being introduced as part of the services of the Council of the British National Bibliography. BNB itself is young—it started publication in 1950. For several years it had a somewhat precarious financial existence. Also, it still occasionally offends some influential librarians in its cataloguing and—mainly—classification decisions. This symptomises at once the strength and weakness of its staff: they need to be single-minded to survive, yet their single-mindedness alienates a few of the profession all the time, and many of the profession some of the time. MARC, whatever form it takes, will not please everybody. Yet it is hoped that it can be made to please most of the people most of the time.

An attempt has been made in the discussion on mechanisation in this work to avoid computer jargon as much as possible, to the point of using many extra common words, and generalising possibly to the point of technical inaccuracy. Even the terms 'hardware' and 'software' (and the inevitable computer joke about 'underware') have been avoided. The reason of course is that this account is intended primarily for students with a limited knowledge and experience of both librarianship and computer technology. Yet, an international computerised record of bibliographic data suitable for most of the stock of most of the libraries in the English-speaking world is potentially available. In order to use this data economically and comprehensively, there needs to be bred a species of librarian combining an intimate and fundamental wisdom of library science needs with wisdom in computer lore. At the moment U.K. MARC II is being tested in, mainly, academic libraries. Yet the majority of subscribers to the present BNB lists and cards are public libraries.

Some people already appear to believe and act as though there are two disparate schools of thought in the organisation of knowledge in libraries: the traditional card-catalogue librarian; and the non-traditional push-button information retrievalist. It is to be hoped that MARC will demolish any difference in basic outlook between these two alleged breeds—if indeed they do exist—and that it will become a bridge between them.

SECTION VII

THE ADMINISTRATIVE BASIS OF CATALOGUING

The Administrative Basis of Cataloguing

Works cited in the text and diagrams

AMERICAN LIBRARY ASSOCIATION. Descriptive list of professional and non-professional duties in libraries. Chicago: A.L.A., 1948.

CATALOGUE AND INDEX, no. 12, October 1968, p. 4-5: Soundwell Technical College; and no. 13, January 1969, p. 7-10: Kent County Library.

    Both are parts of the Studies in central cataloguing series.

BRADFORD INSTITUTE OF TECHNOLOGY. *Library*. Know your library. [196-].

LIBRARY ASSOCIATION. Professional and non-professional duties in libraries. London: L.A., 1962.

LIBRARY OF CONGRESS. Regulations: . . . Organization and functions of the Processing Department. Washington: L.C., 1968.

NEEDHAM, C. D. Organizing knowledge in libraries. (Details in Section II.)

NEWMAN, WILLIAM H. Administrative action. . . . London: Pitman, 1951.

OLDING, R. K. Readings in library cataloguing. (Details in Section II.)

TAUBER, MAURICE F. Technical services in libraries . . ., by Maurice Tauber and associates. New York: Columbia University Press, 1954.

Other readings

AMERICAN LIBRARY ASSOCIATION. . . . Catalog use study. (Details in Section IV.)

    In 1969, the L.A.'s Cataloguing and Indexing Group also put in hand preparations for a British catalogue use study.

ASHMORE, W. S. H. Cataloguing, classification and book provision in the new London Boroughs, *in* Assistant librarian, vol. 59, no. 4, April 1966, p. 74-77.

BENNET, F. Mergers and catalogues, *in* Library Association record, vol. 70, no. 4, April 1968, p. 100-102.

DOWNING, J. C. A national cataloguing policy, *in* Catalogue and index, no. 13, January 1969, p. 1, 16.

FRIEDMAN, JOAN. Cataloguing and classification in British university libraries. . . . (Details in Section IV.)

GREAT BRITAIN. *Royal Commission on Local Government in England.* Local government reform: short version of the Report of the Royal Commission. . . . London: H.M.S.O., 1969 (Cmnd. 4039).

Gives an idea of the amalgamations which could take place between local government authorities, which would lead to repercussions on their libraries and of course cataloguing systems. (Maud Report.)

GROSE, M. W. On the construction and care of white elephants: some fundamental questions concerning the catalogue, by M. W. Grose and M. B. Line, *in* Library Association record, vol. 70, no. 1, January, 1968, p. 1-5.

Followed up by Line, M. B., White elephants revisited, *in* Catalogue and index, no. 13, January 1969, p. 4-5.

MANN, MARGARET. Introduction to cataloging and the classification of books. (Details in Section III.)

Chapters 13, 14, 17 and 18 are relevant.

PARGETER, PHILIP S. The organisation and running of the cataloguing department of Coventry City Libraries. Coventry: City Libraries, 1963. (Unfortunately now out of print.)

PHILIPS, W. HOWARD. A primer of book classification. 5th ed. London: A.A.L., 1961.

Pages 178-187 deal with 'Guides' and 'Display work.'

TAGG, E. J. Cooperation and interlending: the London union catalogue, *in* Assistant librarian, vol. 59, no. 4, April 1966, p. 81-83.

TOWER HAMLETS. *London Borough. Libraries Department.* Staff manual of cataloguing and classification. 2nd ed. 1967.

UNIVERSITY COLLEGE OF WALES, ABERYSTWYTH. Guide to the College libraries 1966/1967.

UNIVERSITY OF BIRMINGHAM. Introduction to the Library. 1965.

UNIVERSITY OF MALAWI. *Library.* Cataloguing practice. 1968.

UNIVERSITY OF WARWICK. *Library.* Notes for students. [196-].

The guides to libraries mentioned are representative examples of various kinds; they are not necessarily available permanently and to all applicants.

CHAPTER 33

Management

Administration; Organisation; Levels of Decision-making;
Organisation and Methods; Statistics; Budgeting

Cataloguing has to be administered even if—and perhaps especially if—there is no catalogue department. Whether or not there is a catalogue department, there must be a specific person ultimately responsible for supervision and coordination of all cataloguing and other technical processes. It will be assumed here that there is a catalogue department.

A further complication is that the work of the department is not necessarily restricted to cataloguing and classification. Some departments include, or are combined with, the acquisition (ordering, receipt and accessioning) of library materials. A link between acquisition and cataloguing is pre-cataloguing (dealt with in Chapter 27). The catalogue department may have a direct administrative connection with a bibliographic centre if the library has one: many of the reference works, bibliographies and catalogues required are common to both activities. The catalogue department may also have to do with stock administration, e.g. recording of allocation and transfers between departments and branches in a union catalogue. It may also be responsible for the physical processing (labelling, etc.) of stock, and possibly even for the supervision of the administration of binding. Again, the department may be responsible for the compilation and seeing through the press of some, or all, booklists, since data for these comes from the catalogues.

On the other hand, although we shall assume in general that cataloguing within a system is centralised, some special materials may be wholly or partly classified, catalogued and/or indexed in special departments. One example is that of a university library whose catalogue department does the basic author/title and descriptive cataloguing, also compiling an author/title union catalogue, but whose subject departments' specialists do the classification and subject cataloguing. A variation on this procedure, in some libraries, is that subject specialists come into the catalogue department regularly to catalogue, or advise on the cataloguing of, materials intended for their departments.

In such cases, it is particularly necessary for there to be liaison between the cataloguing and other departments to ensure a reasonable degree of uniformity—of entry at least, especially if a complete union catalogue is maintained. Division of labour and of responsibility must be clarified at the outset, and recorded in the staff manual.

THE LIBRARIAN AS 'TECHNICIAN'?

Sometimes there is the inference that a librarian will fall into one of three (or even more) categories, i.e. 'administration man', or 'techniques man', or 'bookman'. Undoubtedly, many librarians have predilections, which is why many become specialists. In Chapter 1 it was hoped that there is no firm dividing-line between the use of library materials and the technical processing of them. Here, we claim that all and any part of librarianship needs to be administered. This means administration in the real sense: ensuring that what has to be done is done, in the most efficient way, by the most suitable member of staff, and in an atmosphere of happiness—or at least contentment. It does not mean compiling statistics because they have always been compiled; not writing futile memoranda for the purpose of impressing colleagues; not expecting human beings to be unfeeling cogs in a machine run as a toy for the benefit of the so-called 'admin' man. The objective of real administration must surely apply in all departments whether they be labelled 'administrative', 'technical', or 'subject'.

ADMINISTRATION

The word has been defined as 'The guidance, leadership and control of the efforts of a group of individuals towards some common goal' (NEWMAN).

The components of administration as applied in librarianship are:

1. Planning: formulation of a programme based on the real objectives of the library.

2. Organisation: evolving of departments deriving from 1. 'Departments' is enlarged upon below.

3. Staffing: having the correct number and types of staff to achieve the objectives.

4. Coordination: ensuring liaison between and within departments, and with other related bodies.

5. Control: ensuring that tasks at all levels are done: that no jobs are duplicated, and that no jobs are omitted.

6. Budgeting: ensuring that funds are available to enable the objectives to be achieved in the most economical way.

We should accept that we live in an imperfect world peopled by fallible humans who forget things and get irritable. So the stark idealism implicit in these academic definitions will not be realised as neatly and completely as they imply.

ORGANISATION

Organisation, as defined above, is very relevant to technical processes in libraries, as departmentalisation may be planned according to a variety of characteristics, e.g. Cataloguing, classification, etc., are processes carried out on documents; while reference use of documents is associated partly with form and partly with method of use; and a subject department is associated with the subject content of its documents, whatever their form and whatever their method of use.

When setting up departments, as in designing a classification scheme, an order of precedence must be established. For our purpose, and to ensure that as many problems as possible are covered, we shall assume that process takes precedence. Generally, then, the technical processing of all materials will be assumed to take place in the catalogue department, and not in, say, subject departments.

Many libraries do not any longer have a catalogue department on a level with other traditional departments—in public library practice: reference, lending, children's departments, etc. Cataloguing is more likely to be part of, say, a technical services division, or a bibliographical services division, the purpose being efficient coordination of all activities associated with the handling of bibliographic data, not merely the production of catalogue entries. This type of 'conditions-based' organisation is likely to increase with the consolidation of sophisticated mechanisation, in which it is increasingly appreciated that information about library stocks may be used in almost any activity of the library from the receipt of requests to the sending of overdue cards. This attitude is expanded on further in Section VI, Mechanisation.

LEVELS OF DECISION-MAKING

The four 'levels' of decisions detailed here correspond to some extent with some of the components of 'administration' already described, and are in addition to levels of staff, which will occur again in Chapter 34.

The levels cannot help overlapping in parts, even in principles; in practice, it may be difficult to distinguish at all between some of them.

1. Broad policy decisions, possibly involving the library authority, and certainly involving inter-departmental discussion.

(a) Whether there will be a catalogue at all, e.g. if one can call the (British) National Lending Library for Science and Technology a trend, then there is a trend towards doing away with comprehensive library catalogues in the conventional sense. At a more modest level, a similar decision may have to be taken in relation to branches of a library system.

(b) The types of catalogues to be used: physical forms; internal arrangements; union catalogues.

(c) Following from (b), which classification scheme, cataloguing code, filing rules, subject headings or thesauri, etc., shall be used, and any radical modification of them.

(d) Degrees of centralisation, within the system, and in relation to other, e.g. central, agencies.

(e) Major recataloguing and reclassification decisions, e.g. change of scheme or code. This can affect all the other parts of this level. Recataloguing is dealt with in Chapter 23.

These are very high-level, highly professional, and highly influential decisions. They may apply in the setting up of a new library, the amalgamation of existing libraries, and in the radical reorganisation of an existing library, possibly associated with a change or extension of premises, or with a change of senior staff.

2. Technical administration, usually basic decisions within and between departments which decide 'running' policy.

(a) Detailed amendments to schemes, codes, etc.

(b) Details of catalogue entry layout, limited cataloguing, treatment of various categories of materials, e.g. fugitive materials. If relevant to department, rules for physical processing of materials.

(c) Allocation of duties to various levels of staff, including decisions as to which are professional, which are 'sub-professional' and which are clerical.

(d) Part played by department in inservice training.

(e) Allocation of basic bibliographies, etc., to the department.

(f) Which 'non-cataloguing' jobs shall be done in the catalogue department, e.g. preparation of book lists.

(*g*) What statistics are to be kept, and why.

(*h*) Budgeting.

(*i*) An element impinging on most others is the drawing up of organisation and flow charts and similar instructions, probably for inclusion in a staff instruction manual. Liaison between departments is particularly important, with other details of the responsibilities of various members of staff.

3. Day-to-day practising of mainly professional techniques; Sequential order, e.g. as in a flow chart:

(*a*) Checking in bibliographies, etc.

(*b*) Checking in library's master catalogue, and other files.

(*c*) Pre-cataloguing.

(*d*) Ordering, receipt, accessioning, allocation, etc.

(*e*) Author/title headings, including added and analytical entries.

(*f*) Compilation of unit entry, including notes.

(*g*) Classification ⎫ including added and analytical
(*h*) Subject cataloguing/indexing ⎭ subject entries.

(*i*) Checking.

(*j*) Usually clerical reproduction at this point.

(*k*) Filing including checking.

(*l*) Coordination of all tasks.

Also sorting of materials into categories takes place at some stage: it is rare for all documents to receive exactly the same treatment. One Obvious need is for (*a*) already in stock; (*b*) not already in stock.

Within these groups there may be differentiation between those whose author heading has already been decided, and those for which a decision has to be made. Similar categorisation may apply to subject work.

There may be variations in some processes depending on availability of staff, e.g. when subject specialists come into the catalogue department, and whether one member of staff catalogues and classifies one document from beginning to end, perhaps for a particular department, or whether there is specialisation within the catalogue department, say one person being engaged on subject work only, or music only.

There should be queries as to whether all the jobs listed are 'professional'. This in turn depends on the status and salary-level at which 'professional' starts in any library; also, on the size of the staff—the smaller it is the more 'generalising' and sharing of duties will there be.

Two documents which may help decide which duties are professional and which are not are: LIBRARY ASSOCIATION. *Professional and non-professional duties in libraries;* and AMERICAN LIBRARY ASSOCIATION. *Descriptive list of professional and non-professional duties in libraries.* However, local, accidental conditions tend to upset abstract principles, and pragmatic decisions often have to be taken, decided more or less by who is available at any given time.

The following is a possible descending order of 'professionalism'. It is open to comment and amendment depending on such factors as how seriously a particular activity is taken in any one library and how much other organisations' decisions are followed, e.g. central catalogue agencies and bibliographies. Also, it may happen that a particular document may be very simple to, say, classify, but it may present a very difficult collation problem.

(*a*) Deciding what is needed for each work, including sorting into categories for limited cataloguing.

(*b*) Checking professional decisions taken for the parts of each document's entries.

(*c*) Classification ⎫ all including added and analytical
(*d*) Subject cataloguing/indexing ⎬ entry decisions.
(*e*) Author/title headings ⎭

(*f*) Annotation (other than formal notes as exemplified in codes).

(*g*) Description.

(*h*) Pre-cataloguing.

(*i*) Checking catalogues, authority files and bibliographies.

(*j*) Filing.

(*k*) Clerical checking.

An overriding consideration in many cases is whether a precedent has already been established. Once a class number has been established for a subject, and provided the subject of a new document is correctly identified, classification can often be done direct from a well-compiled subject index or authority file, perhaps by a non-professional or at least by a 'pre-professional' trainee. All decisions should in any case be checked by a chartered librarian with a reasonable period of practice, and with a flair for the work involved if at all possible.

In general, perhaps too much mystery is built up around technical processing. It is not necessarily any more esoteric say, to 'subject-analyse' a book correctly and assign appropriate notation from a classification scheme in the required order, than it is to select it justifiably in the first place, or to recommend it with good reason to the appropriate reader afterwards. One fact which does seem incontrovertible is that wrong classification and cataloguing is there for all to see, while a dissatisfied reader does not wear a badge.

Nevertheless, the accurate application of a catalogue code under supervision could be acquired by suitable non-professional (i.e. unqualified) but intelligent people in a few weeks, provided they are given the correct inservice training. The method should give satisfactory results in perhaps 90 per cent of a library's intake. The real professionalism is required in:

(a) initial inservice training;

(b) checking work done and preserving a consistent standard;

(c) recognising the difficult problems; as well as

(d) actually cataloguing and classifying the more difficult works intelligently, sensibly, accurately and speedily.

An essential quality of the professional cataloguer is knowing when to stop, knowing the difference between essential bibliographic checking and pedantic time-wasting. We are all fallible humans, and examples of both stopping too soon and going on for too long can be found in most catalogues.

4. Clerical duties. Some of these may well overlap into item 3, as has been explained. A 'clerk' may be a near-moron, or an intelligent, practical, able and mature person capable of contributing more to a catalogue department than certain qualified librarians. A clerical worker may possibly be entrusted with many of the duties detailed in item 3 under the conditions already outlined. The non-controversial duties of clerical workers are given here:

(a) Checking existing entries and copying from or adding to them. This includes much of pre-cataloguing and of adding new copies of works to stock.

(b) Changing location records of documents in catalogues.

(c) Copy-typing entries, preferably from 'pro-formas'. This includes making added entries and references from tracings according to prescribed layouts.

(d) Operating duplicating machinery, e.g. for the mass production of entries, including masking or insertion of relevant headings, etc.

(e) Other forms of machine-operating, e.g. producing punched tape, punched cards, stencils, etc.

Many of these jobs require special training and qualifications: there are levels of 'clerical' workers just as there are of librarians.

There may be a great variety of other jobs, depending on basic departmental organisation, e.g. physical processing of documents.

ORGANISATION AND METHODS

Many librarians now accept that this phrase does not necessarily imply the intrusion of external 'admin. men' into the sacred mysteries of librarianship: it is something practised by the professional librarian as part of his normal duties. The librarian who bristles when organisation and flow charts are mentioned may well be the one with the most need for them. If he objects to the intrusion of other professionals, then this is all the more reason why he should be able to apply professional administrative methods himself. This applies to catalogue departments possibly more than to most other, if only because of the great quantity and variety of materials which pass through them, and because of the need for accurate and understandable records of stock, including while the technical processing is in progress and before permanent records appear in catalogues.

A staff instruction manual is needed for the efficient running of a catalogue department. Part of such a manual, and contributing to its purpose, is the use of organisation charts (called 'organograms' by the terminologically intoxicated), and of flow charts.

Organisation charts basically demonstrate the chain of command, or of responsibility, in an organisation. This factor is important in routine matters, such as who checks whose daily work. It can also be very important in fundamental or far-reaching affairs, such as when a serious difference of opinion arises between senior members of a staff: in fact it should obviate such a difficulty.

Flow charts are necessary to decide basically in what order processes shall be carried out on a document. These processes should be cumulative, e.g. the data recorded on a pre-cataloguing slip is fed to the cataloguer who then manipulates it into the form required. Flow charts should ensure that documents are processed in the most efficient way possible. In turn, then, flow charts are used to help decide the physical layout of the catalogue department itself, so that documents are not carried to and fro unnecessarily (see suggested plan on page 417).

Basically, two types of flow chart are needed for cataloguing:

(a) for new works, when all routines are involved; and

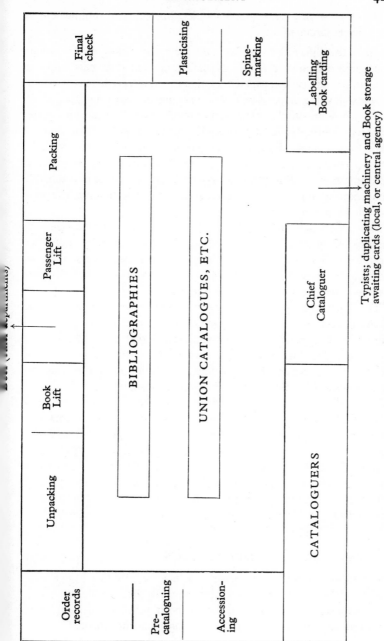

24. Layout of an acquisitions, cataloguing and physical processing department which would facilitate an economical flow of work.

(*b*) other works, e.g. duplicate copies, when certain routines can be short-circuited.

Further, there may be variations in the 'new works' flow, e.g. for certain documents which receive less detailed treatment than new works in general; perhaps certain paperbacks which are not regarded as of 'serious' or research value may not be fully catalogued or even catalogued at all.

To ensure smooth flow of work, the flow charts of the catalogue department may overlap, stem from, or lead into, those of other departments—all depending on the departmental organisation of the library as a whole.

In particular, minute and accurate flow charts are essential if mechanisation is being planned. Machines are incapable of intuitively compensating for oversight in organisation, such as even the least sensible human may do.

Flow charts indicate each decision, and the result of that decision, in the processing of documents, and so they are extremely useful for inservice training purposes, especially when it is not necessary for an assistant to know the overall sequence of operations—and in some instances the assistant may not be interested.

The illustration on page 419 is a generalised organisation chart of one of the largest technical processing systems in the world: that of the Library of Congress. It must be appreciated that each division, e.g. Descriptive Cataloging Division, would have a further organisation chart (or its equivalent in instructions) illustrating responsibilities and span of control for itself, within the overall organisation.

The illustration on page 420 demonstrates the value of a flow chart in clarifying each activity in the selection and cataloguing of stock in a small—in this case—technical college library (reproduced from *Catalogue and index* no. 12, October 1968, page 5). The flow chart of a larger library—Kent County Library—may be seen in *Catalogue and index* no. 13, January 1969, pages 8 and 9, reproduced between pages 420 and 421 of this book. Other examples of flow charts may be seen in NEEDHAM and TAUBER (detailed in reading list preceding this Section).

STATISTICS

The basic reason for keeping statistics is not 'because they have always been kept', but to use them as a means towards the quantitative assessment of achievement—and qualitative too if possible. In short, they constitute what is sometimes called 'management information'.

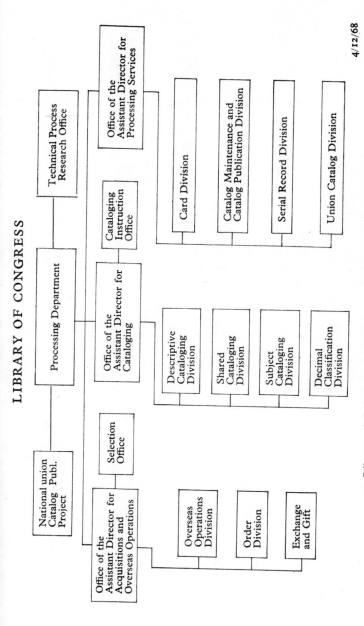

LIBRARY OF CONGRESS

4/12/68

25. Library of Congress: technical processing organisation chart. (1968)

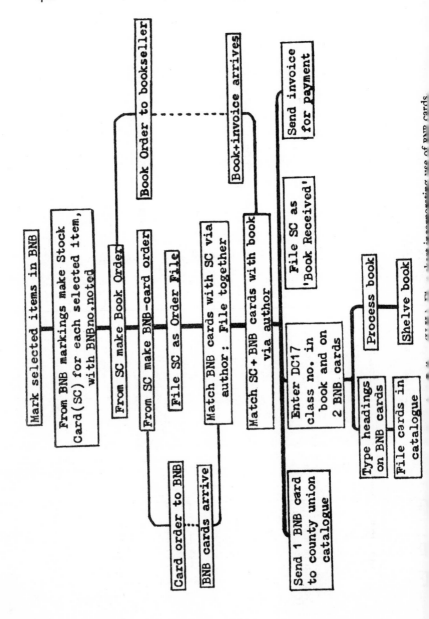

Mark selected items in BNB

From BNB markings make Stock Card(SC) for each selected item, with BNBno.noted

From SC make Book Order

Book Order to bookseller

From SC make BNB-card order

Card order to BNB

BNB cards arrive

File SC as Order File

Match BNB cards with SC via author : File together

Match SC + BNB cards with book via author

Book+invoice arrives

File SC as 'Book Received'

Send invoice for payment

Send 1 BNB card to county union catalogue

Enter DC17 class no. in book and on 2 BNB cards

Type headings on BNB cards

Process book

File cards in catalogue

Shelve book

They usually involve comparisons, and so it has to be ensured that standard and controlled methods are used for recording them. Comparisons may be made:

(a) With one's own library in previous periods.

(b) With other, comparable, libraries.

'Comparable' involves particularly: types of library; size of library; and quality of cataloguing done.

Ultimately, statistics are used for:

(a) Proof to the library's Authority that the library is doing its job: in this case, of professionally recording acquisitions to stock.

(b) Proof to the Chief Librarian, and to other departments of the library, that requests for increase in staff, equipment, space, etc., are justified.

A catalogue department may accumulate monthly or quarterly figures, these perhaps being incorporated into the Librarian's current reports to his Committee or Board. These may then be cumulated, probably generalised, and then included in the routine annual report of the library. This assumes, of course, that statistics are kept. Some libraries have decided that they are not used, and so have given up keeping statistics of works catalogued; however, almost all libraries keep records of total numbers of works acquired, and these may automatically correspond with numbers of works catalogued.

An alternative to routine recording of basic statistics is to make 'spot checks' over a short period for whatever purpose has arisen.

It is emphasised that our only concern with statistics is that of measuring the efficiency of a catalogue department: other uses of the same figures are not relevant here.

The following categories of works may take differing times and degrees of skill to catalogue, and so may conceivably qualify for statistical recording:

1. New stock: e.g.

(a) new copies;

(b) extra copies;

(c) replacements;

(d) special materials, as detailed in Chapter 20.

As an alternative, or possibly in addition, statistics may be kept according to which departments documents are allocated, e.g. in general a reference work may receive more cataloguing than a children's book.

2. Transferred items, if recording of locations is the responsibility of cataloguing staff.

3. Withdrawing items.

4. Recataloguing: the types of statistics needed can be worked out from Chapter 23 on Recataloguing, depending on the type of recataloguing concerned.

A particular application of statistics is to ascertain how many of a particular type of document a cataloguer can deal with in, say, a year, and how much it costs to catalogue particular types of document. Some notional figures are given in Chapter 34, on Staff. These are particularly important when budgeting, along with costs of expendable and capital-cost materials. Depressing as it may seem, it is probably unwise to try to absorb the considerable cost of cataloguing, say, gramophone records, if such an addition to the service is contemplated. A particularly noteworthy aspect of such a consideration is that if the new service is a great success initially, inadequate cataloguing could later lead to disillusion.

Entries, e.g. number of cards, per item: a summary

Factors to be taken into account:

1. Whether or not the catalogue department maintains records for all approaches for all items in stock, hence:

2. Numbers of added entries and reference of all types expected.

3. Additional inventory records maintained, particularly a stock or shelf list; but this may be made up from what was originally an order card, and which then became a draft catalogue entry.

4. Number of service points—the more service points, usually the more cards, as compared with many copies of a work at one service point.

A generous estimate would be about 5 cards per document per service point. It is doubtful if the choice of dictionary or classified catalogue would make any material difference.

BUDGETING: A summary

Items to be taken into account:

1. Salaries of all levels and types of staff, including catering for increments on salaries, and increases to keep pace with inflation and increased intake of stock. Regular, and once-only items, e.g. for a major recataloguing project, would probably have to be estimated separately.

2. Expendable materials, e.g. cards and all other forms of stationery. Replacement of reference works, bibliographies, cataloguing tools, etc.

3. Expansion of existing plant, e.g. card cabinets, desks.

4. Capital expenditure on purchase of new items of equipment, and possibly of certain major bibliographies and printed catalogues.

5. Recurring, as well as once-only, costs of hiring equipment, e.g. 'batch jobs' on computers.

6. Overheads, e.g. share of cost of maintenance of the whole building in all its aspects. If nobody in the library has yet hit upon this, it is likely that the Chief Cataloguer will allow himself to forget it too.

CHAPTER 34

Staff; Staff Manual;
Reference Works used in Cataloguing

STAFF

QUALIFICATIONS AND QUALITIES

Traditionally, staff are divided into two levels: (a) Professional; (b) Non-professional. It is becoming increasingly apparent, however, that a rather more sophisticated hierarchy is needed to take account of staff with the following characteristics (in Britain):

(a) Qualified librarian, with extensive experience and ability.

(b) Newly-qualified librarian, i.e. recently passed professional examinations but with little or no experience in a senior position.

Both (a) and (b) may be complicated by the addition of a university degree. In many countries outside Britain, librarianship is officially a graduate profession, so (a) and (b) would automatically be university graduates in addition to, or including, a recognised library science qualification. A degree can be particularly useful in specialised branches of cataloguing, e.g. in foreign languages or in music as well as in the numerous other traditional academic fields. Unfortunately, most British honours degrees are too specialised for direct application in librarianship, including cataloguing, which often calls for familiarity of the sciences or humanities in general.

(c) 'Pre-professional', i.e. the intending librarian or partly qualified librarian, is a category which may be dying out, but which is still common enough to be mentioned. A cataloguing assistant with a reasonable length of experience and some of his professional examinations can be very useful even if his appearance is transitory.

(d) 'Trainee' is a common category, being the new entrant to the profession who is gaining some experience before attending library school. He may be more transitory than group (c), but his enthusiasm can be put to (suitably controlled) use in cataloguing in common with other library activities.

(e) Clerical workers. As already stated, these may be responsible and even qualified people in their own right. Like qualified librarians, they vary in their interests and in their accuracy and speed. It is suggested that they can be of great value in the overall economy of catalogue production, and that they should be selected, retained—or passed on—with great care.

NUMBER OF CATALOGUING STAFF
REQUIRED IN DEPARTMENT

The cataloguing complement of a library may vary a great deal even between libraries of a similar size. Basic factors are:

1. Number of items added to stock. This is not conclusive, as it may include either:

(a) a great number of 'repeat' titles, as in county libraries with many service points; or

(b) many 'difficult' items, for various reasons—not necessarily confined to so-called research material, because a very minute subject may possibly be quite conveniently fitted into some classification schemes, and a very complicated-looking title page may very quickly resolve itself into simple title entry. Also, a very significant factor is that a precedent may already have been established, as mentioned in Chapter 4. On the other hand, a simple-looking music score or gramophone record may call for both considerable thought over its main entry, and a great deal of labour in making added entries and references. So, the proportion of non-book materials may be very relevant here, among other factors.

Hence, quantity, and quality and type of material may be important.

2. What proportion of stock is done by cataloguing department staff and what is done elsewhere, either:

(a) by a central catalogue agency, e.g. BNB; and

(b) by staff in other departments and in branches; e.g. special indexing, filing, general maintenance.

3. Relevant too is how much nominally professional cataloguing can satisfactorily be passed over to less highly-paid staff. The same number, and perhaps even more, may be employed, but the overall cost would be reduced.

4. Related to item 3 is the degree of limited cataloguing practised,

whether simplifying entries or reducing the number of them. Many public libraries practise simple title-page cataloguing for most fiction, the work being done by inservice-trained typists, or even by library suppliers. Title-page cataloguing usually obviates bibliographic checking and decision-making over forms of headings. The implications of unduly limiting cataloguing are discussed in the chapter on Limited cataloguing. It is worse than useless to save time in the catalogue department only to have to use more in making *ad hoc* decisions at the filing stage or even at use of the catalogue while an enquirer waits.

5. The degree of mechanisation can have a great influence—ranging from the use of card-duplicating machinery to computerisation. However, sophisticated mechanisation may entail the employment of specialised machine-operators whose work must be carefully, even rigidly, planned if their expertise is to be used efficiently for all the time they work: no more, no less.

6. Specialisation is more possible, hence more useful, when a department reaches a certain minimum size, and so the size of the department itself may be a deciding factor. In a technical job like cataloguing one senior can effectively check the work of only a comparatively small number of staff: the span of control may be as low as three. In turn, that senior becomes one of about three whose work is supervised by a yet more senior cataloguer. So, after a certain point is reached, the span of control and hierarchy may become unwieldy—we might call this the 'big fleas and little fleas' syndrome.

7. Any type of recataloguing takes extra staff, at least at the time—although the adoption of a new code may ultimately prove an economy. Apart from major projects, any library should regard day-to-day overhaul of the catalogue as normal, but such permanent revision still takes time; this time, however, as inferred above, should in turn be saved by others in their actual use of catalogues.

8. Activities other than technical processing, e.g. production of book lists, take extra time and expertise.

9. The keeping of statistics may take considerable time. This topic is discussed in Chapter 33.

10. Finally, and nebulously, the quality of the individual workers, from Chief, or Head, Cataloguer downwards, may make an appreciable difference to the average output per member of staff. At the risk of making a really brutal generalisation, let it be supposed that one cataloguer, with no other responsibilities, could deal with about 5,000

items per year, ranging from short-shrift treatment of current fiction to research monographs, and assuming standard cataloguing and classification according to, say, AACR and DC. Also, suppose a cataloguing assistant is paid about £1,250 sterling a year. So, cost per document is about 5s. sterling. This is a modest 'guesstimate'; others may go up to £2 per item. But surely a maximum of £1, even for difficult material, could be considered generous? To this must be added costs of material, plant, and clerical workers' time. This sort of costing must be taken into account when deciding whether to buy central catalogue agency cards. Taking BNB, and taking 5 to 6 cards per document, we have about 1s. per document, plus all overheads, additional administration, and adding headings to cards. Local amendments to central agency cards can be very relevant in costing. Further theoretical and practical details are given in TAUBER, pages 295, 403-405 and 409-411, under U.S. conditions. Some selective British information is given in FRIEDMAN.

STAFF MANUAL

The staff instruction manual may be a full-scale, detailed, comprehensive single work for the library as a whole, or it may be more sketchy, and in sections, one for each department. The former is preferable, since a basic reason for its existence is efficient coordination between all departments as well as within them.

It is not merely a lecturer's theory that even the smallest library needs a manual. However small the staff, and however well the members maintain contact with each other, there are occasions when people forget, leave, go sick, and have holidays. In fact, the occasion for starting a manual may be any of these factors.

The primary object of a manual is efficiency. This may be broken down into:

(a) Consistency.
(b) Completion of work required; but
(c) Prevention of duplication of work.
(d) Minimisation of direct supervision.
(e) Supplement to staff training.

Basically, a manual instructs staff at all levels in how to do their jobs. The type of contents of a manual, from the cataloguing point of view, are:

(*a*) Duties done in the catalogue department, or cataloguing duties to be done if there is no separate department.

(*b*) Sequence of cataloguing operations for new works, and for variations on this for other works.

(*c*) Other sequences of operations, e.g. for transferring of stock.

(*d*) Allocation of responsibilities.

(*e*) Methods in detail for all routines.

(*f*) Sample layouts to exemplify methods.

(*g*) Possibly, major departures from codes, schemes, etc. In addition, and more important, all working copies of the actual working tools will be annotated consistently to cater for local interpretations and variations.

(*h*) Possibly, decisions for expected problems not covered by tools. Again, in addition, and more important, these will be written into all relevant tools.

(*i*) Lists of works expected to be used in cataloguing: codes, etc.; bibliographies; other reference works.

(*j*) As part of the contents already outlined, the manual should include organisation charts and flow charts.

A pragmatic test of an effective manual is that it could be given to an intelligent, interested entrant to the job and that it would provide sufficient guidance to ensure that he did the day-to-day job without serious mistakes and without close supervision.

The process of compiling a manual is creative in itself. When staff are obliged to write down full details of jobs done and especially if flow charts, etc., are compiled, particularly for others to scrutinise, inconsistencies and examples of inefficiency are shown up, and these can be eradicated in the most satisfactory way possible. The first draft of a manual should be expected to stimulate changes in routines and responsibilities, both major and minor. Also, the compilation of a manual should be part of the detailed planning of a new or remodelled building or department. For example, flow charts should be submitted to the architect, for his comment, and for subsequent manifestation in the planning and equipment of the library. It may be necessary for the architect to refer back to the Chief Cataloguer his ideal requirements, perhaps because they conflict with the immutable location of lifts, or perhaps because floor space available will not allow for use of trolleys rather than fixed shelves for storage of works in process.

All of this sounds very rigid and formal. However, a manual should not fossilise the cataloguing practices of a library. Unfortunately, the more detailed and more directly useful the manual, the more inconvenient it is to change it. This is one reason why large institutions and their staff tend to get set in their ways: a change of detail in one routine may have wide repercussions. All we can say is that all staff should be prepared to give and receive suggestions for change. The moral is the same as with codes: just as codes are made for cataloguing and not vice versa, a manual is made for running a library and not vice versa.

REFERENCE WORKS USED IN CATALOGUING

This list is more comprehensive than would be found in most catalogue departments. Many works would be shared with other staff, and so might be in other departments. In some cases, older editions will usually suffice, current editions being in reference or subject departments. Many bibliographies and 'bibliographic catalogues' may be in a catalogue hall or bibliographic centre, possibly adjacent to the catalogue department. It should be remembered that the process of checking for requests may be dovetailed with pre-cataloguing, and so with final cataloguing. Detailed justifications are not given for the works listed here; it is up to the student to think about each item and to decide if it is needed in a particular context.

The list presupposes cataloguing in English-speaking countries.

1. Cataloguing tools

Fullest version of the library's own catalogue.

Subject and author authority files.

Staff manual. Excerpts available in multiple copies for personal use by relevant members of staff.

Catalogue code used.

Classification scheme used.

Subject headings list, if used.

These three will be available in multiple copies, one for each relevant cataloguer, annotated for local use.

Filing code, with alternatives indicated where they exist.

Other codes, etc., to supplement those used basically, e.g. Mary Piggott's *Notes on cataloguing foreign material*; Piette's *Guide to foreign languages* . . .; such products arising from the International Conference on Cataloguing Principles as Chaplin's *Names of persons*, and Suzanne

Honore's *International list of approved forms for catalogue entries for the names of states.*

2. Bibliographical tools

BNB; British catalogue of music.

Possibly English catalogue of books, especially for nineteenth century if relevant.

Cumulative book index; possibly also United States catalog.

Subject guide to books in print (U.S.).

Fiction index (British).

Fiction catalog (U.S.).

Sequels.

Possibly other relevant works, e.g. H. W. Wilson 'standard catalogs'.

Book review digest.

Various specialised items depending on slant in library concerned.

British Museum's printed catalogues; especially that of printed books.

Library of Congress' National union catalog, including relevant special materials, e.g. Phonorecords.

Various other printed catalogues, e.g. British Broadcasting Corporation's Music catalogue, London Library, Lewis' Medical Library. Choice of these will vary with need from library to library. Certain non-English language catalogues and bibliographies will also be needed, e.g. the catalogue of printed books of the Biblothèque nationale.

3. Quick-reference works

Access to Oxford English dictionary.

Shorter Oxford.

Concise Oxford: multiple copies.

Webster's International (American usage).

Penguin English dictionary (modern usage).

A usage dictionary, e.g. Gower's Complete plain words.

A dictionary of synonyms.

Roget's Thesaurus.

Multi-lingual dictionaries.

A technical dictionary, e.g. Chambers's.

One- or two-volumed encyclopaedia, e.g. Penguin.

Access to standard multi-volume general and some special encyclopaedias.

Who's who, and access to other national who's who's.

International who's who.

World of learning (corporate names).

Oxford atlas, and access to the Times Mid-century atlas.

Bartholomew's Gazetteer of the British Isles.

Columbia-Lippincott World gazetteer; probably just access to.

British Standards on bibliographical references and on proof corrections.

Others of almost any form or type may be required from time to time, e.g. the Kunitz and Haycraft series, especially Twentieth-century authors, is likely to be used frequently if conveniently available.

A final word of warning: too much bibliography and reference work checking by cataloguers can be worse than too little.

CHAPTER 35

Catalogue Maintenance and Use

Conclusion: Who uses the catalogue?

This topic could be the most important part of this book. It is pointless to use expert cataloguers and the best of codes if the results of their work do not get into the right places in the catalogue and if the catalogue itself is not used.

The staff manual should include instruction for the day-to-day maintenance of catalogues; but comparatively infrequent jobs, like the setting up of an adequate guiding system or the issue of a guide to the use of the catalogues, depend on imagination, conscientiousness and time available of the cataloguing staff. Probably the best method for cataloguers to find out if their work is wasted is for the cataloguers themselves to have turns of duty at the public catalogue for the specific purpose of aiding use of the catalogues and so of receiving feed-back—perhaps not only from the public, but also from other members of staff.

FILING

One of the best ways of introducing one's colleagues to the construction, hence efficient use, of catalogues is for public service staff to play a part in filing. This is also a way of ensuring that some of them at least know of new acquisitions to their department and where they are entered in their catalogue.

Whoever does the filing, the relevant staff must know the rules. This needs saying, if one's past experience of staff, even at fairly high levels, means much. Some rules in the first edition of the ALA *Rules for filing catalog cards* are extremely complicated. All staff should know which of the various alternatives are used—and stick to them.

Filing staff need not be professionally qualified, but they should have been through a rigorous inservice training in their specific craft. If, while at work on the catalogue, they can keep an eye open for apparent errors, need for extra guide cards, renewal of certain cards, and the need for 'moving round' when certain drawers become congested—so much the better for the resulting quality of the catalogue and for their own satisfaction and enjoyment of their job, i.e. filing is not a mechanical, unthinking job. Like many other allegedly menial jobs in libraries it can be made professional in the right hands, and one would like to think that the filers with 'nous' get a reward before they reach heaven.

The staff manual should include an interpretation of, and local examples illustrating, the rules used. Usually, filing is checked by a more senior person, if this is practicable. One way is 'filing over the rods': the checker can then glance along the protruding newly inserted cards, then withdraw the rod to allow the cards to drop, and then insert it again—and the cards are gone, probably for ever, right or wrong. There is no regular check of cards in catalogues like there is of books on shelves. After a card is in—it is well and truly in: mistakes will usually be found only by chance.

It is more economical to file a large consignment of cards at each go, but this economy leads to catalogues' being unnecessarily out of date. Usually, only the catalogue department's catalogue will have temporary entries in the form of 'in process' slips. Incidentally it may too have copies of order slips or cards filed into it to obviate double, or treble, checking. Staff using the catalogue must then ensure that they know exactly what these temporary entries mean. In many libraries filing is done weekly.

Occasionally cards have to be removed for legitimate reasons like compiling book lists or correcting. Whoever takes them out must leave a clear, preferably protruding, coloured note stating where they are, who has them, and when they will be returned.

GUIDING

This is essential especially in card—and, hopefully, sheaf—catalogues. It is needed particularly in the classified file of the classified catalogue where the user may have to rely on the logic of the classification scheme to work from general to specific. Unlike the seasoned classifier, he does not necessarily know by rote the contents and order of a class of a scheme.

Guiding is particularly important also in large catalogues, where there may be many entries at one heading. The handicap of lack of sequential visual scanning in a card catalogue is particularly apparen here. The British Museum's printed catalogue is an example of well-thought-out guiding, using type and punctuation to indicate sequence. A 'layout' is given at the start of each prolific heading.

However, the use of many guide cards has its disadvantages. They increase the size of the catalogue considerably and they may even reach the state of profusion—as theoretically in a chain-indexed classified file—where they obscure each other. In some cases it may be preferable to have a guide card explaining the sequence and contents of certain complex headings, as already mentioned in the British Museum's catalogue, especially in forms of filing where grouping is used. In classified file use, it needs emphasis that cards should give not only class numbers, but their meanings in natural language. Modern terminology should be used: some sets of guide cards, still on sale apparently, look as though they are reprinted from the nineteenth century.

Coloured cards, and cards with tabs in particular positions—left, centre or right—can be used for particular purposes. Kaiser in his system advocated: (*a*) left tab for Concrete; (*b*) centre tab for Place; and (*c*) right tab for Process (OLDING, p. 150); he also used colours for various purposes in combination with the tabbed guide cards. Whatever terminology and colours, etc., are used should be repeated at the appropriate parts of the shelves, to aid recognition, even if unconscious, on the part of the casual user.

It should be remembered always that many members of the public use library catalogues infrequently. If they are to be encouraged to use them meaningfully, the catalogues must be guided from their point of view. One has noticed that fresh criticisms of catalogue and other guiding tend to come from new members of staffs, before they become accustomed to local peculiarities which more experienced members of staff take for granted.

Catalogue guiding is necessarily an integral part of the guiding of a library as a whole, and it is proposed here to show it in its context. A complete 'chain' of guides could be as follows:

(*a*) Location of building.

(*b*) Locations and functions of departments, shown at entrance.

(*c*) Plan of each public department at its entrance, showing among other items, location of catalogues.

(*d*) On catalogues, clear and simple instructions on how to use for the various approaches, including examples, and emphasising the class number or other location at which the documents will be found.

(*e*) On drawers (assuming card catalogues), clear and up-to-date inclusive guides as to their contents.

(*f*) Within drawers, tabbed guides naming the main sections. Special tabbed cards should be made out for prolific headings.

(*g*) On guide cards, layouts of sequences at a main heading, whether numerical or in natural language.

(*h*) Entries themselves to be laid out clearly and unambiguously, the filing medium and the shelf location being particularly emphasised. In the classified file of a classified catalogue there should be feature headings which lead on from the tabbed guides and guide card 'layouts' used.

The conventionally accepted layout of the catalogue entry itself is subject to criticism; this is dealt with in Chapter 25, on Physical forms of catalogues.

PRINTED GUIDES AND PERSONAL INSTRUCTION

Use of the catalogue, with typical examples, is a necessary part of printed publicity on the use of the library. As with guides on the catalogue itself, the essence is simplicity and exemplification. Those readers who manifest a detailed interest can be further instructed by suitable members of staff. Relevant extracts from printed guides to libraries are shown in the facsimiles on pages 436-439.

Some libraries, especially those of educational institutions, run short courses on the effective use of the libraries' catalogues. The idea is good and necessary. But a difficulty is that catalogue entries are small, and classes tend to be large. One way of overcoming this difficulty is to ensure that each student has a copy of the library's 'guide to the use of the library' (or 'catalogue') pamphlet and the lecturer can use this as a basis. If small classes are possible, multiple copies of catalogue entries can be passed round and used as a stimulus for student-based discussion. At the other extreme, when large classes cannot be avoided, the use of a slide projector, or closed-circuit television, or moving films, can enable close-ups of entries to be shown accompanied by relevant instruction. Another method is a form of programmed 'self-guided tour' of the library. This consists of a 'handout' including brief instructions and short questions the answers to which are filled in by the student in the handout. The answers are marked, and if necessary remedial action can be taken by a student's personal tutor or a member of the library staff.

THE CATALOGUES

The card catalogues are designed to index from several angles (author, editor, series, subject) the main collection of books and pamphlets.

Author or name catalogue (first floor)

This is a single alphabetical list of authors, joint authors, editors and translators of books. Books issued in series by universities, societies and similar organisations are given additional entries, and biographies can be traced by the name of the subject as well as by author.

Anonymous works are entered by title, e.g. **A warning for fair women.** Periodicals are entered by title, but full details of holdings are given only in the periodicals list (see p 9.)   Societies, institutions and government departments are treated as authors, but British government publications are normally entered only if an extra copy is available (see p 11).

The filing is word by word, ignoring articles, e.g.

The OLD wives' tale
The OLD yellow book
OLDCASTLE, Sir John

8

28. University of Warwick Library: extract from *Notes for Students*—'The Catalogues'.

Classified catalogue

This catalogue lists the bookstock in the order of the classification scheme and thus in the order presented on the shelves. Secondary entries are given, on blue cards, for books relating to more than one subject. For convenience of use with the books this catalogue is divided into sections, each one placed with the subjects it covers.

A duplicate of the general science, mathematics, physics, and engineering sections of the catalogue (author and subject) is maintained in the Physics Library for the convenience of readers on the first site.

Subject indexes

The master subject index on the first floor gives the class number employed for every topic represented in the bookstock, e.g.

      Coal industry : Economics   HP 125
      Physical chemistry   QD 611-875

Sections of this index are repeated on the upper floor for use with the sections of the classified catalogue.

Series card (filed in the Name Catalogue)

NATIONAL BUREAU OF STANDARDS. MONOGRAPHS, 8

UNITED STATES. NATIONAL BUREAU OF STANDARDS

Mercury barometers and manometers, by
W.G. Brombacher, D.P. Johnson and J.L.
Cross. 1960.
Washington (D.C.), U.S. Govt. Print. Off.
59p. tables.
  (National Bureau of Standards. Monographs, 8)

M 531.787

Added subject card (filed in the Classified
Catalogue) The book is shelved at M531.787

[M 533.41]

UNITED STATES. NATIONAL BUREAU OF STANDARDS

Mercury barometers and manometers, by
W.G. Brombacher, D.P. Johnson and J.L.
Cross. 1960.
Washington (D.C.), U.S. Govt. Print. Off.
59p. tables.
(National Bureau of Standards. Monographs, 8)

M 531.787

---

29. Bradford Institute of Technology: extract from *Know your Library*—
'The Catalogue'.

Reference to help in finding the correct author
entry (filed in the Name Catalogue)

UNITED STATES. DEPARTMENT OF COMMERCE. National
Bureau of Standards

<u>See</u>

UNITED STATES. NATIONAL BUREAU OF STANDARDS

Subject index entries for this book would be made as
follows:

Manometers : Measurement : Mechanics : Physics		M531.787
Pressure : Measurement : Mechanics : Physics		M531.787
Measurement : Mechanics : Physics	M531.7
Mechanics : Physics	M531
Mercury barometers : Gas mechanics : Physics	M533.41
Liquid barometers : Gas mechanics : Physics	M533.41
Barometers : Gas mechanics : Physics	M533.4
Gases : Fluid mechanics : Physics	M533
Physics	M53

Fuller details of the contents of the catalogue and its

The examples mentioned here are usually thought of as being confined to students, but there is scope for—and some practice of—similar instructions for others, e.g. research workers. Perhaps the time is coming when formal classes should be run in public libraries with adults.

WHO USES THE CATALOGUE?

It has been assumed so far that the public expect to use the catalogue and so must be catered for. However, there is a point of view that a library catalogue is too complex and specialised a tool for the layman to understand, and that it should preferably be used only by staff on behalf of the public. This argument appears to assume that: (a) the staff—any staff on duty—know better than the user what the latter wants; (b) all staff are completely competent in the use of the catalogue; and (c) there are always enough staff available. Under these conditions, the catalogue could be less well guided than if intended for public use, since an assumption is that time need not be spent on making the catalogue 'layman-proof' if laymen never use it.

At the outset we must be reminded of the great variety of types and sizes of libraries and of library catalogues which exist. Also, the users of any one library themselves vary a great deal—whatever the type of library—from the infrequent, casual user to the regular, deeply interested, user, and levels of intelligence and library-awareness further cut indiscriminately across these modulations. If the users are not expected to use the catalogue, there must always be enough suitable staff available to cater for all their needs even at the busiest times. This, it is suggested for a start, rules out all libraries with a clientèle of any size, from county branches to research libraries like the British Museum. The only type which probably can meet these requirements is the small special library, which in any case may use special depth-indexing systems which the staff are usually required to operate.

A further point is that many users getting to know the catalogue is an essential part of their use of the library. This applies in children's public libraries to quite an extent—though views of librarians may vary; in all school libraries as part of the educational process; and—one hopes—in all tertiary level educational institutions. Together, these categories make up a large and growing proportion of the population who presumably expect to carry on using catalogues after successfully surviving their formal education.

Next is the simple fact that some people prefer to use catalogues themselves, either because they like to sort out their own problems, or because their needs are so specialised, detailed and time-consuming that it would inconvenience them to have a librarian coming between them and their work.

Finally, the dreadful truth exists that still there are library staffs who do not know enough about all types of catalogues to use them completely effectively. This even applies to some staff who are nominally qualified. It is not necessarily the direct fault of the staff themselves. It is possible for people to become qualified, in some choices of syllabuses and courses, with only a superficial awareness of catalogues—and this at a time when catalogues are inevitably becoming more complicated or varied to cater for the increasing complication and variety of library materials. A partial solution lies in thorough inservice training in all library systems. But a more permanent solution lies in an increasingly realistic and practical view of education for librarianship itself.

We close where we opened: it is not only cataloguers who need to know about catalogues: so, too, do all competent librarians.

Index

Introduction

Specific entries are used, usually in direct phrase form, e.g. PHYSICAL FORMS OF CATALOGUES, not CATALOGUES: PHYSICAL FORMS. *See also* references are made from broader headings to more specific headings stage by stage, and between other headings having something directly in common. They are given at the end of all the entries for the topic referred from, including compound headings for the topic. *See* references are made, where considered necessary, from unused, e.g. synonymous, forms to the form of heading used. In a very few instances, 'upwards' *see* references are made from specific to broader headings, i.e. when the parts of a general topic are dealt with together at one point in the text, e.g. Size (of books) as part of Collation.

Codes and other frequently-cited works are represented by initials or other shortened forms. A list of these abbreviations precedes the Index, and abbreviations are also given in the reading lists in the text, where full bibliographic details are given. The Index includes references to the latter pages in the text; these entries are given as *bib cit* followed by relevant page numbers. Titles of articles from periodicals and other parts of documents are given in quotation marks; those of monographic works are in italics.

Illustrations are cited in the Index where useful, and are indicated by *illus*.

Page numbers for readings on a topic precede *illus* and *bib cit*, and are given as *readings*. All these italicised divisions of a topic come at the end of the normal subject subheadings of the topic.

Sets of initials which are not acronyms (pronounceable as words) are filed at the beginning of each letter of the alphabet. Acronyms are filed in their appropriate places as pronounceable words.

The first page number or set of page numbers given for a topic represents the main, longest, treatment of that topic where relevant. Compound headings usually receive the citation order: (1) Problem, or Type of material; and (2) Code, or other Treatment. In a few instances, full double entry has been used.

This Index is itself an exercise in the use of direct phrase headings, as differentiated from structured headings. It is intended for use as a means of instruction and criticism like the text of the book.

Abbreviations used in the Index and the Text

AA 1908	LIBRARY ASSOCIATION. Cataloguing rules . . . 1908.
AACR	ANGLO-AMERICAN CATALOGUING RULES . . . 1967.
ALA 1941	AMERICAN LIBRARY ASSOCIATION . . . A.L.A. catalog rules, preliminary American ed. 1941.
ALA 1949	A.L.A. cataloging rules for author and title entries, 2nd ed. 1949.
BM	British Museum as a body; and, Rules for compiling the catalogue of printed books, maps and music.
BCM	British catalogue of music.
BNB	Council of the British National Bibliography, and the British national bibliography itself.
BTI	British technology index.
CCR	LUBETZKY, SEYMOUR. Code of cataloging rules . . . 1960.
COATFS	COATES, E. J. Subject catalogues . . .
CUTTER	CUTTER, C. A. Rules for a dictionary catalog, 4th ed. 1904.
DC	Decimal classification (Dewey).
HMSO	Her Majesty's Stationery Office.
ICCP	INTERNATIONAL CONFERENCE ON CATALOGUING PRINCIPLES, *Paris*, 1961.
LC	Library of Congress as a body; and, Library of Congress Subject headings list and subject cataloguing practice.
LCRDC	LIBRARY OF CONGRESS. Rules for descriptive cataloging, 1949.
LPRL	Long Playing Record Library.
LUBETZKY	LUBETZKY, SEYMOUR. Cataloging rules and principles . . . 1953.
MLA	MUSIC LIBRARY ASSOCIATION. Code for cataloging music and phonorecords . . .
MARC	Machine Readable Catalogue; MARC I: LC MARC 1966 Project; MARC II: BNB U.K. MARC Project.
METCALFE	METCALFE, JOHN. Subject classifying and indexing of libraries and literature.
NEEDHAM	NEEDHAM, C. D. Organizing knowledge in libraries . . .
OLDING	OLDING, R. K. Readings in library cataloguing . . .
PI	The PRUSSIAN instructions . . .
QUIGG	QUIGG, PATRICK. Theory of cataloguing . . .
SEARS	SEARS list of subject headings.
UDC	Universal decimal classification.

.